The Good Herb

OTHER BOOKS BY JUDITH BENN HURLEY

Garden-Fresh Cooking

Healthy Microwave Cooking

The Healing Foods (Patti Hausman, co-author)

The Healthy Gourmet (Patti Hausman, co-author)

The Surgeon General's Report on Nutrition and Health (Patti Hausman, co-author)

The Good Herb

recipes and remedies from nature

~~~~~

Judith Benn Hurley

William Morrow and Company, Inc.
NEW YORK

The information in this book is intended for educational purposes only
and is not a substitute for medical attention. If you think you have a health
problem, please see a health professional immediately.

Library of Congress Cataloging-in-Publication Data
Hurley, Judith Benn.
The good herb : recipes and remedies from nature / by Judith Benn Hurley.
p. cm.
Includes index.
ISBN 0-688-11324-9
1. Herbs—Therapeutic use. 2. Aromatherapy. 3. Cookery (Herbs)
I. Title.
RM666.H33H87 1994
615'.321—dc20   94-8381
                                  CIP

Printed in the United States of America

First Edition

1 2 3 4 5 6 7 8 9 10

BOOK DESIGN BY ALISON LEW

For my sweetheart,
Patrick Hurley

My unbounded thanks go to Maria Guarnaschelli and my literary agent, Helen Pratt, for trusting unfamiliar ground. My appreciation also goes to Elisa Petrini and Toni Sciarra for editorial support, and to Beatrice Tosti di Valminuta for moral support.

I am grateful to Richard Felber, Karen Capucili and Tom Eckerle for the luscious photographs that illustrate this book.

Many thanks to JoAnn Brader for culinary recipe testing, and to Nancy Zelko for research.

A special note of appreciation goes to these people for testing hair, skin, and gardening formulas, and for reviewing the products and companies listed in the resource section: Karl Erdlitz, Margelle Cascio, Allie Grace, Sharon Grace, Judy Lieberman, Teece Picher, Jane Runyeon, Andrea Smith, and Susan Stanton.

contents

PART TWO

An Everyday Herbal: using herbs to rejuvenate, heal, and beautify

introduction

During twenty years of writing about food, I have observed that people use herbs for more than just flavoring. Often, herbs are used to prevent minor health problems, as in India, for example, where such vegetables as cauliflower and cabbage are cooked with mustard seed to avert digestive distress. Vietnamese cooks add ginger to their steaming soups to ease the symptoms of the common cold. In Mexico, rosemary is a headache remedy.

In addition to their healing properties, common culinary herbs also serve as beauty aids. In Russia, dillseed is steeped in cooking oil, then massaged into the hands to strengthen nails and soften cuticles. Basil tea is a dandruff remedy in Zimbabwe.

And many gardeners use herbs, rather than chemicals, to keep pests away from their plants. English gardeners plant tansy to rebuff aphids. In Canada, sage is sometimes planted around roses to help keep the flowers insect-free.

The diversity of ways in which people around the world use and enjoy herbs is the rich and lively stew upon which *The Good Herb* is based. The book is divided into two main sections, the first of which is a guide to forty-five popular herbs, such as basil, tarragon, and thyme, with a separate chapter on each one. Each chapter includes specific herb lore, healing properties, ways to employ the herb to enhance your appearance, and growing particulars, along with cooking tips and recipes.

The Good Herb offers two hundred recipes based on the culinary wisdom of countries ranging from France and Italy, to Egypt to Thailand to the United States. If you're a new cook or a tired cook, or you simply want to adopt a more healthful eating pattern, you'll enjoy discovering herbs that create bold tastes with a minimum of fat, sugar, and salt. Each recipe lists calories and fat for each serving, and most of the recipes are well within the nutritional guidelines of the American Heart Association, the American Diabetes Association, and the National Cancer Institute.

The second section investigates traditional and modern ways of using herbs from around the world for preventing and treating dozens of health conditions, such as hay fever, asthma, prostate problems, menopause, fatigue, cancer, stress, and indigestion. Additionally, more general chapters cover body care, cooking with herbs, growing herbs, and aromatherapy.

Since much of the information in *The Good Herb* relates to the medicinal uses of herbs, it's important to know how to apply them wisely. Herbs can prevent and cure dozens of health conditions, but, wonderful as they are, you should not overlook other methods of health care when appropriate. For example, you can use the herbs evening primrose and dong quai to relieve some symptoms of menopause and still go to a gynecologist for regular check-ups. Or, as an herb-interested cardiologist put it, if you have full body sweats and crushing chest pains, don't go herbal—get to a hospital fast. Then, by all means, you can use herbs to help recovery.

Don't attempt to diagnose yourself for serious ailments. If you think you have a kidney, liver, heart, or other complex condition, please see an expert. If at first you can't find a health professional with the herb and other expertise you want, don't give up. A good herbalist, chiropractor, naturopath, physician, or whomever you need is probably only two phone calls away. Look in the phone book, ask friends, and check at herb shops and health food stores.

If it's a particular herb you're searching for, consult the resource section at the back of the book, which lists mail order purveyors for dried herbs, herb tinctures, Chinese herbs, Ayurvedic herbs, essential oils, and herb-based skin and hair care products, as well as herb publications and schools. Also listed are sources for herb plants and seeds and other gardening needs.

To guide beginning gardeners, as well as to enhance the skills of those who are more advanced, *The Good Herb* describes dozens of new growing techniques, tried out in six test gardens across the United States. If you don't have a garden, the book offers information on growing herbs inside on any windowsill.

As you peruse the pages of *The Good Herb*, you will discover a more wide-ranging group of herbs than fits the standard botanical definition. To me, an herb is an aromatic plant whose properties are indispensable in cooking, health, or body care. Ginger, for example, is not botanically considered an herb. But it is such an important ingredient in the herbal medicines of China and Japan that to omit it would be unthinkable. The same goes for lemon grass—not a standard "herb." But it so charmingly perfumes the cuisines and teas of Southeast Asia that it gains entry to the herbal pantry.

Recently, a joyful new gardener told me, "Everyone should grow an herb garden. You plant the herbs, then the next day you go outside and have thirty new friends!" As you explore this book, I hope you experience many similar delights.

Judith Benn Hurley

Life creates life,
Energy creates energy.
One must spend oneself in order to become rich.

—SARAH BERNHARDT

PART ONE

The Good Herbs

forty-five of the world's greatest

~~~~~~

anise hyssop

sweet talk

STEAM

AWAY

CONGESTION

~

REFRESH

OVERHEATED

SKIN

~

SWEETEN

FOODS

WITHOUT

SUGAR

~

Summer in Kansas can be a sweltering 120 degrees, as I discovered while driving through the state one July. The temperature was so intense that my car overheated and I was unable to use the air-conditioning. In contrast to the hammering yellow sun, all along the road were large mint-like plants with re-freshingly cool purple blossoms. The sweet anise aroma, and a photo identification from a regional wild plant book, told me the herb was anise hyssop. I picked a handful of flowers and leaves, rinsed them off, and added them to my water jug. Sipping water per-fumed with anise hyssop kept me cooler all the way to the Rocky Mountains.

Lore and Legend

Anise hyssop is a native of North America, growing wild particularly in the Prairie States. Because of its long-lasting flowers and sweet aroma, anise hyssop was gathered by the pioneers as a decorative wildflower.

Anise hyssop's name comes from two sources: "Anise" is from the anise seed–like smell and taste of the leaves, and "hyssop" is from the squarish stem, which is similar to that of the herb hyssop. The square stem is a common feature of members of the mint family and so anise hyssop is sometimes called "anise mint" or, because of the similarity of anise and licorice flavors, "licorice mint." Since the aroma of anise is like fennel, the herb is also called "fennel hyssop" or, because it can grow to almost three feet, "giant fennel hyssop." The herb's aroma has also inspired the name "fragrant giant hyssop," and its big lavender-blue flowers have earned the title "giant blue hyssop."

Healing

Cheyenne and Chippewa Indian tribes brewed anise hyssop flowers and leaves into a tea as a remedy for coughs. The Cheyenne used it in an herbal steam to ease congestion, and though its effectiveness has not been scientifically documented, it does seem to clear the nose and head. To try it, crush about half a cup of fresh anise hyssop leaves and flowers in a mortar. Then add the herb to a bowl filled with three cups of boiling water. Tent a towel over your head and inhale the steam for five to ten minutes.

Some Chippewa tribes used crushed anise hyssop leaves mixed with animal fats as a dressing for burns. Today we know that fats may make burns worse, but there's still a way to harness the healing powers of anise hyssop. To treat minor burns, crush fresh anise hyssop leaves in a mortar and swirl in an equal part of aloe jelly. Then apply to the skin and cover with a bandage. It will feel cool at first; when the burn begins to feel hot again, reapply the salve.

Looking Your Best

Anise hyssop can refresh overheated skin. To try it, make a tea by steeping a tablespoon of crushed fresh anise hyssop leaves and flowers in half a cup of boiling water, covered, until cool. Then strain and swirl in half a cup of liquid witch hazel, which acts as an astringent to help tighten pores. Splash your face with the mixture after washing and before applying moisturizer. Or pour the mixture into a spray bottle and spray your face from time to time throughout the day. If the mist from the spray bottle is very fine, you can spray right over your makeup without disturbing it. The mixture will keep, covered and refrigerated, for up to a week.

Growing

The fact that anise hyssop is an American original may be one reason it's so easy to raise. Buy small organically grown plants in the spring. Choose a location that gets at least six hours of full sun a day and prepare a standard herb soil of two parts garden or potting soil, two parts peat, one part sand, and one part compost or composted cow manure. Dig a hole twice the size of each herb's root ball, and throw in some extra sand or vermiculite—anise hyssop is a prairie herb and likes its soil well drained. Then set the herb in, scoop the soil back around it, and tamp it down. Water with warm water. Then, unless there is a drought, let nature do the watering. Anise hyssop can grow to a height of over two feet in two months and comes back stronger each year. Be aware that this prairie herb is not as happy indoors, so for the best results, keep it outside.

Anise hyssop's flowers, which bloom from June through September, stay fresh and lively on the plant for up to four weeks. They're a beautiful medium purple, shaped like baby ears of corn, and they're famous for attracting butterflies to the garden.

Cooking

Despite its name, anise hyssop neither tastes nor smells like the herb hyssop, but it does have the sweet licorice taste of anise seed. It is so sweet, in fact, that many cooks use its fragrant tea to sweeten foods without adding sugar. To make two cups of anise hyssop tea, add three tablespoons of bruised fresh leaves to two cups of boiling water and steep, covered, until the tea is light green and fragrant, about four minutes. Discard the leaves and use the refreshingly sweet tea to poach halved fresh peaches. Or make a dried fruit compote by simmering one cup of dried apricots in two cups of the tea until tender, about six minutes.

To add an interesting licorice accent, press a dozen or so fresh anise hyssop leaves into the crust of a cheesecake before filling and baking. Or try adding a quarter cup of fresh anise hyssop leaves to a green salad to serve four, then dress with lemon juice and olive oil. To sweeten fruit salad to serve four, add a quarter cup of minced fresh anise hyssop leaves just before serving.

Apple Tart with Anise Hyssop Crust

Fresh anise hyssop leaves in the crust add sweetness without sugar.

~~~~~~

FOR THE CRUST:

½ cup unbleached all-purpose flour

½ cup whole wheat pastry flour

2 tablespoons sweet (unsalted) butter, cut into small pieces, or canola oil

⅓ cup buttermilk or low-fat vanilla soy milk

About 20 fresh anise hyssop leaves

FOR THE FILLING AND GLAZE:

4 medium baking apples, peeled, cored, halved, and thinly sliced

1 large egg or ¼ cup Calendula Egg Substitute (page 47)

½ cup buttermilk or low-fat vanilla soy milk

3 tablespoons all-fruit apple butter

¼ cup unbleached all-purpose flour

2 tablespoons all-fruit red currant jelly

TO make the crust, toss the flours into a food processor. Add the butter or oil and whiz until the mixture is the texture of cornmeal. With the motor running, add the buttermilk and whiz just until a ball of dough forms. If the dough doesn't form a ball in about 6 seconds, add a splash of water and carry on. (If you don't have a processor, use a medium bowl and cut in the butter with a pastry blender or large-tined fork. Add the buttermilk and work it in vigorously.)

SPRAY an 11-inch tart pan with nonstick cooking spray. Press the dough evenly into the bottom and up the sides of the pan, then scatter the anise hyssop leaves over the dough and press them in. Refrigerate the crust for about an hour, or until firm.

MEANWHILE, preheat the oven to 375°F.

BAKE the crust until slightly dry, about 15 minutes.

ARRANGE the apple slices in the warm crust. Combine the egg, buttermilk, apple butter, and flour in the processor and whiz until smooth. (If you don't have a processor, combine the ingredients in a medium bowl and whisk well.) Pour over the apples and smooth with the back of a spoon.

BAKE until the filling is firm, about 30 minutes. Remove the tart from the oven and immediately brush on the currant jelly. (If the jelly is too thick to brush, heat it in a small saucepan until liquid.) Serve warm or slightly chilled. Store any leftover tart uncovered in the refrigerator.

MAKES 8 SERVINGS; 170 CALORIES PER SERVING, 4 GRAMS FAT, 22 PERCENT OF CALORIES FROM FAT.

Black Bean Salad with Anise Hyssop

Minced anise hyssop leaves emphasize the nutty flavor of black beans. Prepare this salad immediately before serving so the beans won't discolor the other ingredients.

~~~~~

2 cups cooked black beans, rinsed if canned	1 tablespoon minced fresh anise hyssop leaves
1/4 pound cooked green beans, cut into 1-inch pieces	1 teaspoon anise seed
1 medium red or yellow tomato, finely chopped	1 tablespoon balsamic vinegar
	1 tablespoon olive oil
1 shallot, minced	Curly red lettuce leaves for serving
1 tablespoon minced fresh chives or garlic chives	

IN a medium bowl, combine the black beans, green beans, tomato, shallot, chives, anise hyssop, and anise seed.

IN a small bowl, whisk together the vinegar and oil. Pour over the beans and toss well to combine. Serve on nests of curly red lettuce.

MAKES 4 SERVINGS; 175 CALORIES PER SERVING, 4 GRAMS FAT, 20 PERCENT OF CALORIES FROM FAT.

basil

~~~~~~~~~~~~~~~~~~~~~~~~~~~

good mood,
good food

*O*ffering an Arabic man food containing basil is very likely to offend him. In Arabic countries basil tea is often used to alleviate menstrual cramps, and many men consider it embarrassing to ingest the herb in any form. I found this out the hard way. While planning a party in honor of a diplomat from the Hashemite Kingdom of Jordan, I flavored some spinach and feta pastries with fresh basil. When the diplomat tasted a pastry, he threw his head back, clutched his heart, and raved that he hadn't tasted anything so wonderful since his dear departed mother cooked for him. Of course, I was delighted. But when I revealed that the secret ingredient was fresh basil from my garden, the diplomat was horrified and retreated to the powder room for at least twenty minutes. Meanwhile, another guest clued me in. Next time, I'll use oregano.

~

FRESHEN

BREATH

~

REVITALIZE

SKIN

AND HAIR

~

ADD

AROMA

TO FOODS

~

Lore and Legend

The Jordanian diplomat may not have been the first man to have a run-in with basil. In one seventeenth-century tale, a man in Siena, Italy, who used dried basil as snuff subsequently went insane and died. An autopsy revealed that his brain was crawling with scorpions. Some historians believe that basil got its name from the story, associating the herb with the mythical reptile the basilisk, whose mere glance could be deadly.

It's more likely, however, that basil was named by the early Greeks, perhaps even Aristotle. He was a great student of herbs and had a garden of over one hundred varieties. *Basileus* is the Greek word for "king," and basil came to Greece from India, where it was considered "the king of herbs." In fact, in India, basil was—and still is—offered in reverence to two important Hindu gods, Vishnu and Krishna.

Though India is considered basil's native country, a small-leafed, bushy variety can be found in Mexico, South America, and some Caribbean islands. In Haiti, fresh basil plants are used as an offering to Erzulie, voodoo goddess of love.

Healing

For all the fuss made about basil and menstrual cramps, you'd think it must really wipe them out. Unfortunately, both scientists and women who have tried the herb agree that it doesn't. However, basil is not without its healing properties.

People in Portugal use fresh basil plants to freshen their breath. They breeze by, snip off a sprig, and pop it into their mouths for a clean taste.

In India, basil plants are used for a kind of aromatherapy. Indians who rub a sprig to release and enjoy the uplifting aroma say that basil gives people *sattva,* enlightenment and harmony. This may be one reason that some health professionals recommend drinking basil tea to combat the nausea associated with chemotherapy and radiation treatments. To make a tea, steep one teaspoon of dried basil in one cup of boiling water, covered, for four minutes, then swirl in honey and lemon to taste.

Looking Your Best

Researchers report that basil contains antibacterial compounds. Consequently, essential oil of the herb is used by aromatherapists to treat skin conditions, including acne, as well as sluggish, congested complexions. A trained aromatherapist can prepare a skin lotion for you using essential oil of basil. But anyone can enjoy the skin benefits of basil by using a strong tea as a bracing toner. To try it, pack a handful of fresh basil, about three tablespoons' worth, into a sturdy mug and pound lightly with a pestle to bruise the leaves and release the oils. Pour in a cup of boiling water, cover the mug, and let the tea steep until it's a clear grass-green, at least twenty minutes. Strain and discard the leaves. For a soft yet nonoily feel, splash your face with the tea just before applying moisturizer. (Don't dry off.) Your face will appreciate it, especially if the air you live in is polluted. Just so you know, drinking a cup of this extra-strong tea will probably not harm you, but the taste is too intense to be enjoyable.

In remote parts of the African bush, basil tea is used as an after-shampoo hair rinse to help control dandruff and scalp psoriasis. Though this is not an officially documented remedy, at the very least, a basil tea rinse does leave the hair silky and the scalp feeling fresh.

If your skin and hair lose their luster when you travel, pack up some dried basil and take it with you. Pour about a cup of hot tap water over two teaspoons of dried basil, cover, and let sit overnight for use in the morning.

Growing

For the easiest cultivation, buy "six-packs" of small organically grown basil plants. Since the herb is sensitive to cold, be sure to wait until after the last frost to plant. Choosing a shady May day is also advisable, since small basil plants are easy targets for sunstroke. Usually, Mother's Day is an ideal planting time for basil.

Find a location that normally offers at least six hours of full sun a day, since adult basils need lots of summer sun. Prepare a soil that's two parts garden or potting soil, two parts peat, one part sand, and one part compost or composted cow manure. Dig a hole that's twice the size of the basil plant's root ball and set the basil in the hole. At this point, to give the herb extra nutrition, you can sprinkle in half a teaspoon of dried nettle herb. Fill the hole with the surrounding soil and tamp it down with your hands. Leave an inch or so of stem between the bottom leaves and the soil clear, to make room for mulch. As for spacing, plant basil plants about seven inches apart from each other and from other herbs.

Basil has a long taproot that doesn't like to be moved, so once the plants are in the ground, don't transplant them, or they may wilt and die.

Water newly planted basil with warm chamomile tea made by steeping one tablespoon of dried chamomile in one quart of boiling water, covered, for fifteen minutes. The tea will help ward off transplant shock and help prevent the young plants from harmful "damping off" (fatally soggy stems and leaves) to which they are prone.

Since basil plants are susceptible to Japanese beetles, you may want to hang Japanese beetle traps near the planting area. Alternatively, you can interplant the basil with jalapeño peppers. About three jalapeño plants per dozen basil plants will help keep the beetles away.

Basil also does well planted in pots and grown inside or out. For the best results inside, give basil a place near a window with at least six full hours of sun a day. If you need to augment the light, use a ninety-watt halogen flood, placed about three feet or more away from the top leaves. Check the soil for moisture daily, since the halogen light can dry it out. The halogen light can be left on for up to twelve hours a day.

Cooking

It's impossible to grow basil without imagining what it tastes like, since the herb has one of the most delicious aromas around. It's a scent echoing of mint, cloves, and a touch of thyme that is pleasantly sharp and uplifting. If seasonings formed a symphony, basil would be the clarinet. (Onion and garlic would be the deep horns.) And just as clarinets come in different keys, basil comes in several varieties, each with its own distinctive tone.

The easiest basil to use in cooking is sweet basil, sometimes called Italian basil. It's got the classic mint-clove-thyme taste that goes so well with ingredients like garlic, olive oil, and tomatoes. That classic quartet of flavors can be tossed with pasta or rice or made into a sauce for fish and chicken.

Take sweet basil's taste, make it a bit more subtle, add some lemon, and you have the taste of lemon basil. Since its flavor does not hold up well to intense heat, lemon basil is best used in salads. Or stir it into sautéed scallops during the last ten seconds of cooking. (Use about three tablespoons of minced lemon basil for a pound of scallops.)

Replace the lemon flavor with cinnamon and you get cinnamon basil. Toss a minced teaspoon of the sweetly flavored fresh leaves into a cup of warm fruit compote or a cup of savory tomato sauce to heighten the flavors without adding sugar.

Similar to the cinnamon variety is licorice basil, also called Thai basil, in which the mint-clove-thyme combo is joined by the sharp, sweet taste of licorice. Sprinkle two teaspoons of minced fresh licorice basil over two cups of a spicy Thai noodle salad or shrimp salad to add a cool dimension to a hot dish.

Basils also vary in leaf appearance. While the most common leaves are green ovals, one type has ruffled, fan-shaped leaves. Ruffled basil comes in two colors, purple and green, and though both taste like sweet basil, their ruffled texture makes them less likely to wilt when added whole to green salads. Ruffled basils are also great in place of lettuce on sandwiches—try some with smoked mozzarella and ripe tomato on a baguette.

There are several varieties of basil with oval-shaped, purple leaves, one of which is called opal basil. The purple leaves are beautiful in the garden, but their flavor is musty and dull compared to sweet basil's.

"Minestrone" Salad

Here's a delicious example of how sweet basil's mint-clove-thyme taste enhances fresh vegetables.

~~~~~

1/4 pound green beans	1 tablespoon minced fresh parsley
2 medium carrots, julienned	
1 small zucchini, julienned	2 tablespoons red wine vinegar
1/4 cup minced red onion	1 tablespoon fresh lemon juice
1 cup cooked tiny white beans, such as small Great Northern	2 teaspoons olive oil
	Freshly ground black pepper
2 medium tomatoes, chopped	Freshly grated Parmesan cheese or soy Parmesan
1/4 cup minced fresh basil (any type)	

TOP and tail the green beans, then cut them in half diagonally through the center. Toss them into a large serving bowl.

ADD the carrots, zucchini, onion, white beans, tomatoes, basil, and parsley.

TO make the dressing, whisk together the vinegar, lemon juice, olive oil, and black pepper to taste. Pour over the vegetables and toss well to combine. Sprinkle with Parmesan and serve.

MAKES 4 SERVINGS; 130 CALORIES PER SERVING, 2 GRAMS FAT, 14 PERCENT OF CALORIES FROM FAT.

Grilled Bell Peppers with Fresh Basil

You may already have a favorite recipe for roasted or grilled bell peppers, but this version incorporates a couple of interesting ways to use herbs. The first is to toss aromatic sprigs of herbs on hot coals to gently perfume what's being grilled. The other is to add a chiffonade (skinny ribbons) of fresh herbs to lift the flavor of the finished dish.

~~~~~~

16	sturdy red bell peppers, cored and seeded	2	tablespoons olive oil
2	handfuls of fresh thyme sprigs	1/3	cup fresh sweet (Italian) basil

PREPARE the grill. If you're using coals, they should be hot and completely white.

REMOVE the grill rack from the grill and arrange the peppers on it. Toss the thyme onto the hot coals and immediately set the grill rack into place, about 4 inches from the heat source. Let the peppers become completely charred, with black skins, turning them every 3 to 4 minutes. Remove the charred peppers to a large mixing bowl and cover it with a tea towel. Set aside until almost cool, at least 30 minutes.

WORKING over the sink, remove and discard the charred pepper skins. Then slice the peppers lengthwise into quarters and place them in a large serving bowl. Pour on the olive oil and basil and toss gently to combine. Serve as an appetizer with crusty bread. Or slice the peppers into thin strips and toss with ziti or other pasta.

MAKES 8 APPETIZER SERVINGS; 71 CALORIES PER SERVING, 3 GRAMS FAT, 37 PERCENT OF CALORIES FROM FAT.

Basil-Scented Rice with Porcini and Artichokes

The porcini-basil combination adds a rich flavor to the rice.

~~~~~

2	teaspoons olive oil	4	water-packed artichoke hearts, chopped
1	medium onion, minced		
1	clove garlic, minced	2	tablespoons minced fresh basil (any type)
	Pinch of saffron threads		
1 1/4	cups Arborio or other short-grain Italian rice	1/4	cup freshly grated Parmesan cheese or soy Parmesan
2 1/2	cups hot vegetable stock or defatted chicken stock	5	scallions, minced
1	bay leaf		Pinch of sea salt
2/3	cup fresh porcini mushrooms, chopped (see Note)		

HEAT a large (at least 10-inch) deep frying pan over medium-high heat and pour in the olive oil. When it's fragrant, add the onion and garlic, reduce the heat, and sauté for about a minute. Crush the saffron between your fingers, add it to the pan, and cook until the onion is fragrant and tender, about 5 minutes.

STIR in the rice, stock, bay leaf, and mushrooms and bring to a boil, uncovered. Reduce the heat to medium and cook, stirring frequently, until the rice is tender and has absorbed all the liquid, about 15 minutes. Swirl in the artichoke hearts, basil, cheese, scallions, and sea salt. Serve warm as a first course or entrée.

MAKES 4 ENTRÉE SERVINGS; 351 CALORIES PER SERVING, 6 GRAMS FAT, 16 PERCENT OF CALORIES FROM FAT.

NOTE: If you can't find fresh porcini, use 1/2 cup dried, and soak them in the hot stock (use a total of 2 3/4 cups) for 15 minutes to soften.

Angel Hair with Watercress, Basil, and Pecans

Enjoy this as a light spring dinner entrée.

~~~~~~

¹/₄ pound watercress, leaves only

¹/₃ cup fresh sweet (Italian) basil leaves

2 tablespoons olive oil

2 shallots, minced

4 cups hot cooked angel hair pasta (from ¹/₂ pound dried)

¹/₄ cup chopped pecans, toasted (see Note)

Freshly grated Romano cheese or soy Parmesan

WHIZ the cress and basil in a processor or blender until finely minced. (If you don't have a processor or blender, you can pound the greens in a large mortar, but they won't be as evenly minced.)

HEAT a large sauté pan over medium-high heat and pour in the oil. When it's warm and fragrant, add the cress mixture and shallots and sauté until the mixture is fragrant and the greens have brightened, about 2 minutes.

TOSS the greens with the pasta and pecans and sprinkle with cheese. Serve warm.

MAKES 4 SERVINGS; 280 CALORIES PER SERVING, 7 GRAMS FAT, 22 PERCENT OF CALORIES FROM FAT.

NOTE: To toast pecans, put them into a dry sauté pan on high heat, stirring constantly, until fragrant and toasted, about 2 minutes.

Pumpkin "Enchiladas" with Tomato-Basil Salsa

The combination of tomato and basil works together to develop the flavor of these enchiladas without the addition of fat.

~~~~~

1/2 teaspoon cumin seed

1/2 teaspoon coriander seed

1/2 teaspoon fennel seed

1 tablespoon olive oil, plus extra if necessary

1 medium onion, finely chopped

1 clove garlic, minced

1 red bell pepper, cored, seeded, and chopped

1 cup fresh or canned pumpkin puree

2 teaspoons minced fresh oregano or 1 teaspoon dried

Pinch of cayenne, or to taste

6 whole wheat pita breads

2 medium tomatoes, medium-chopped

1 tablespoon minced fresh basil (any type) or 1 1/2 teaspoons dried

Freshly ground black pepper

HEAT a large cast-iron skillet over high heat (if you don't have cast-iron, use the heaviest skillet you own). Add the cumin, coriander, and fennel seeds and toast until golden and fragrant, about 1 1/2 minutes. Grind the seeds in a mortar or spice grinder, and keep them handy.

PREHEAT the skillet over high heat, then add the olive oil and reduce the heat to medium-high. Add the onion, garlic, and bell pepper and sauté until wilted, about 4 minutes. Add the pumpkin puree along with the ground seeds, oregano, and cayenne, and cook for another 2 minutes. Remove from the heat.

DIVIDE the filling among the pitas, arranging it on one half of each. Fold each pita over to make a half-moon.

SCRAPE the skillet clean and reheat over high heat. If the skillet is well seasoned you won't need to add any oil; if it's not, use a pastry brush to apply a bit (about 1/2 teaspoon will do it). Set the folded enchiladas in the skillet and immediately reduce the heat to medium-high. (You'll probably only be able to cook 4 enchiladas at a time; just repeat the procedure with the remaining 2.) Heat the enchiladas until lightly browned, about 2 minutes on each side. When flipping them over, be careful not to press too hard, or the filling could ooze out.

MEANWHILE, to make the relish, combine the tomatoes, basil, and black pepper to taste in a small bowl.

SERVE the enchiladas warm, drizzled with the tomato relish.

MAKES 6 SERVINGS; 154 CALORIES PER SERVING, 3 GRAMS FAT, 17 PERCENT OF CALORIES FROM FAT.

Butterflies with Basil and Lemon Vinaigrette

Try this quick and easy pasta salad for a light and fragrant summer lunch or dinner.

~~~~~

2 1/2 cups cooked butterfly (bow tie) pasta (from a generous 1/2 pound dried)
1 cup spinach leaves, julienned
1 red bell pepper, cored, seeded, and julienned
1 scallion, minced
2 tablespoons fresh lemon juice
1 tablespoon olive oil
3/4 teaspoon Dijon mustard
1 clove garlic, minced
2 tablespoons minced fresh lemon basil or sweet (Italian) basil

IN a medium bowl, combine the pasta, spinach, bell pepper, and scallion.

IN a small bowl, whisk together the lemon juice, olive oil, mustard, garlic, and basil. Pour over the pasta and toss well to combine. Serve at room temperature.

MAKES 4 SERVINGS; 160 CALORIES PER SERVING, 4 GRAMS FAT, 22 PERCENT OF CALORIES FROM FAT.

Roti with Black Beans and Basil

These sandwiches are popular in Trinidad, where they are often filled with spiced meats and deep-fried. This is a vegetarian version that omits the deep-frying. Serve the roti for lunch or dinner with sides of steamed vegetables, or salad and soup. You can also slice the roti into small wedges and serve them as finger food with cocktails.

~~~~~

1 tablespoon plus 1 teaspoon olive oil

1 small onion, thinly sliced

1 clove garlic, mashed through a press

1 medium tomato, medium-chopped

2 teaspoons good-quality yellow curry powder

1 teaspoon dried hot red pepper flakes, or to taste

1/4 cup dry sherry or mirin

2 1/4 cups cooked rice

1/2 cup cooked black beans, rinsed if canned

1/4 cup minced fresh basil (any type)

4 pitas (whole wheat are tasty)

2 teaspoons Dijon mustard

HEAT a large sauté pan, then pour in 1 tablespoon of the oil. Add the onion, garlic, tomato, curry powder, and hot pepper and sauté over medium-high heat until the onion is just wilted, about 3 minutes. Add the sherry, rice, and beans and continue to sauté until the rice is warmed through, about 3 minutes. Remove from the heat and stir in the basil.

SPREAD each pita lightly with the mustard. Scoop equal portions of the rice mixture onto one-half of each pita. Fold each pita over into a half-moon shape.

WIPE out the sauté pan and heat the remaining 1 teaspoon oil until hot and fragrant. Set the roti in the pan and let them sizzle over medium-high heat until mottled with brown, about 2 to 3 minutes on each side. Serve hot.

MAKES 4 ENTRÉE SERVINGS; 395 CALORIES, 5 GRAMS FAT, 12 PERCENT OF CALORIES FROM FAT.

Spicy Thai Shrimp with Basil

The sweet, fragrant basil works with the hot pepper in this dish to create a satisfying flavor.

~~~~~

1¼ pounds jumbo shrimp, well rinsed but not peeled

1 large red bell pepper, cored, seeded, and julienned

¼ pound thin green beans, topped and tailed

1 tablespoon peanut oil

2 cloves garlic, mashed through a press

1 medium onion, very thinly sliced

½ teaspoon minced fresh ginger

1 teaspoon nam pla (Thai fish sauce)

1 teaspoon hot pepper sauce, or to taste

Juice of 1 lime (about ¼ cup)

2 tablespoons light cream or soy milk

¼ cup minced fresh licorice basil or sweet (Italian) basil

ARRANGE the shrimp in a single layer in a steamer rack, set it over boiling water, cover, and steam for about 2 minutes. Scatter the bell pepper and green beans over the shrimp and continue to steam until the shrimp are pink and just firm, about 3 to 4 minutes more. Remove the shrimp and vegetables from the steamer. When the shrimp are cool enough to handle, peel and devein them.

HEAT a large sauté pan over medium high, and pour in the oil. Add the garlic, onion, and ginger and sauté for 2 minutes. Add the nam pla, hot pepper sauce, lime juice, and cream and cook until fragrant, about 1 minute more. Tip in the shrimp and vegetables and toss well to combine. Remove from the heat and sprinkle on the basil, tossing again to combine. Serve at once. A vinegar-based cucumber salad and steamed rice would be tasty accompaniments.

MAKES 4 ENTRÉE SERVINGS; 210 CALORIES PER SERVING, 7 GRAMS FAT, 30 PERCENT OF CALORIES FROM FAT.

Grilled Red Snapper with Papaya and Basil

Papaya, basil, and lime give fish a festive twist.

~~~~~

1 pound red snapper fillets	1/3 cup fresh lime juice
1 tablespoon Dijon mustard	2 teaspoons honey
1 medium red onion, finely chopped	1 teaspoon hot pepper sauce, or to taste
1/4 cup vegetable stock or defatted chicken stock	2 tablespoons finely minced fresh basil (any type)
1 papaya, peeled, seeded, and finely chopped	Lemon and lime wedges for serving

PREPARE a grill or preheat a broiler.

RUB the snapper with the mustard. Grill or broil about 5 1/2 inches from the heat until cooked through, about 4 to 4 1/2 minutes on each side.

MEANWHILE, heat a medium sauté pan over medium-high heat. Add the onion and stock and cook, stirring, until the onion is lightly burnished and soft, about 6 minutes.

SLIDE the snapper onto a serving plate and cover with the onions and papaya. Keep warm.

POUR the lime juice, honey, and hot pepper sauce into the sauté pan and bring to a boil. Boil, stirring frequently, for about 3 minutes, or until reduced by half. Sprinkle in the basil, and drizzle the sauce over the fish. Serve with lemon and lime wedges.

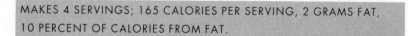

MAKES 4 SERVINGS; 165 CALORIES PER SERVING, 2 GRAMS FAT, 10 PERCENT OF CALORIES FROM FAT.

bay leaf

~~~~~~~~~~~~~~~~~~~~~~~~~~~~~~~~~~

the sodium slasher

*A*t the Saturday morning market in the town of Saint John, on the Caribbean island of Antigua, three beverages containing bay leaf are often sold. One, Guinness stout combined with seaweed and bay leaf, tastes like salty dark beer with a lemon twist. Hot chocolate with bay leaf is thick and milky with an allspice-like aroma. And peppermint leaf tea steeped with bay tastes like spicy mint. These beverages may not be your cup of tea, but many Antiguans believe that bay leaf brews offer protection from colds, flu, and bad omens.

Lore and Legend

Bay leaves have been used as safeguards since ancient times. When the early Greeks dedicated the temple at Delphi to the god Apollo, they covered the roof with bay leaves to ward off evil spirits. When an important message was to be delivered, the Greeks bound the scroll with bay to help ensure its arrival. The early Greeks also used bay leaves made into crowns to protect and honor their favorite poets and soldiers.

Similarly, the early Romans used bay wreaths as crowns to keep them safe from lightning and thunder. And to help guarantee a long and happy marriage, wedding cakes were baked on beds of bay.

Like the Greeks in their temples, some of the first Christians hung bay leaves in their churches, and bay leaves are still used ornamentally in churches, especially around Christmas, because their aroma is spicy and festive.

It is also reported that before a house is to be "exorcised" of evil spirits, three bay leaves are placed in the four corners of each room.

Healing

Bay is being tested at the Human Nutrition Research Center, in Beltsville, Maryland, for its potential in helping diabetics. Though the research is too new for home application, in a test tube, bay beats insulin's ability to break down blood sugar by three times.

Looking Your Best

One way to take advantage of bay at home is to make a soothing facial steam to calm stressed skin. Combine five dried bay leaves with two cups of water, cover, and bring to a boil. Remove the lid and continue to boil for about two minutes. Pour the brew into a large bowl, tent a large towel over your head, and lean over the bowl. Relax and let your face steam for ten minutes. Then follow with a facial mask, such as an oat and chamomile face mask (see page 347).

Growing

Bay is a stately, noble tree that thrives in tropical and subtropical areas. The leaves are pointed ovals, the color ranging from pea green in younger leaves to forest green in older ones.

To grow bay, buy an organically grown plant. Be sure it's *Laurus nobilis,* because some laurels can be poisonous. Bay plants won't make it outside in areas where it freezes, so the best thing to do in that case is to move the plant inside to a sunny window for the winter season. When it's time to plant outside again, just sink the pot right into the soil so that, come fall, you can pry it up without disturbing the roots.

Bugs at Bay

One of the most widely known herbal household tips is to tuck a bay leaf in a jar of grain or flour to keep the bugs away. But one hot summer, as an experiment in the test kitchens of *Prevention* and *Organic Gardening* magazines, brown rice, cracked wheat, amaranth, whole wheat flour, yellow millet, rice noodles, whole wheat spaghetti, and buckwheat were placed in individual tightly sealed quart glass jars with a bay leaf in each. After three weeks, all the jars were filled with bugs.

If you plan to repot a bay tree, use a typical herb mixture of two parts garden soil or potting soil, two parts peat, one part sand, and one part compost or composted cow manure. Personality-wise, bay is a slow grower that will remain robust-looking with ample water. Check the soil two or three times a week; if it is dry, soak with warm water.

If you want to cook with the leaves from your bay plant, you'll need to dry them first. Unlike other herbs, bay's flavor is more alluring dried than fresh. Start by snipping off leaves from the bottom of the plant, where they're larger and more flavorful. Arrange them in a single layer on a plate and leave them in a cool dry place, uncovered, for about a week, or up to two weeks if the weather's humid. The dried leaves will remain flavorful, tightly covered in a glass jar and kept out of direct sun, for up to six months.

Cooking

Bay is a familiar kitchen staple, prized for the allspice snap it brings to soups, stews, braised meats, roasted game, tomato sauce, crab boils, fish chowders, and any dish that needs a savory tang.

In Morocco, bay leaves are used to line the cooking vessels in which the tiny pasta couscous is steamed. Try tossing a leaf into a pot of boiling water to lightly flavor spaghetti or ziti as it cooks. Many cooks who are reducing salt in their dishes successfully substitute a bay leaf in the water when cooking pasta, rice, or beans.

It's possible that bugs or eggs could have been in the grains to begin with. For insurance, one insect expert suggests freezing all untreated whole grains for forty-eight hours after purchase. Then store the grains in tightly covered glass jars, with a bay leaf at the top and bottom of each jar, in a cool dry place. But if you really want to make sure that your flours and grains stay insect-free, it might be better to keep them tightly covered and refrigerated than to rely on the powers of bay.

In Brazil and parts of the West Indies and Africa, bay takes on a sweeter note, scenting the milk bases for delicate custards and puddings. For instance, the Brazilian flan-like desserts called *quindin* (keen-JEEN) and *quin-dao* (keen-JOW) are both flavored with bay and freshly grated nutmeg. Similarly, cooks in Zimbabwe use bay to spice up rice puddings and hot breakfast cereals.

Creamy Three-Grain Hot Cereal

Bay combined with cinnamon adds an invigorating aroma to this breakfast standby.

1	cup skim milk or low-fat soy milk	1/3	cup flaked rye (see Note)
2	bay leaves	1	teaspoon ground cinnamon
1/3	cup rolled oats	1/4	cup raisins
1/3	cup flaked wheat (see Note)	1/2	cup low-fat vanilla or strawberry yogurt or soy yogurt

continued

IN a small saucepan, combine the milk and bay and bring to a boil. Reduce the heat and simmer for 2 minutes.

DISCARD the bay leaves and add the oats, wheat, rye, cinnamon, and raisins. Simmer until all the liquid has been absorbed, about 5 minutes. Serve warm, with the yogurt swirled in.

MAKES 2 HUGE SERVINGS; 284 CALORIES PER SERVING, 4 GRAMS FAT, 13 PERCENT OF CALORIES FROM FAT.

Variation: For a quick breakfast, add half a bay leaf to each serving of regular oatmeal, wheat cereal, or rice cereal.

NOTE: Flaked wheat and rye are whole grains that have been flattened for quick cooking. They resemble rolled oats in shape and are available at health food stores and many supermarkets. Don't mistake cold cereal flakes for flaked wheat and rye.

Chick Peas and Rice with Bay
Hummos b'riz

In Syria, where this dish is popular, it is served as a side to lamb or roast poultry. But it can function equally well as a vegetarian entrée, perhaps accompanied by grilled eggplant.

~~~~~

1½ cups medium-grain brown rice	1 teaspoon cumin seed, ground in a mortar or spice grinder
½ cup dried chick peas	2 cloves garlic, mashed through a press
3 cups water	Juice of 1 lemon (about ¼ cup)
2 bay leaves	
3 tablespoons olive oil	2 tablespoons finely minced fresh parsley or coriander
2 large onions, very thinly sliced	

SOAK the rice and chick peas overnight in water to cover.

DRAIN the rice and chick peas and put them into a pressure cooker, along with the 3 cups of water and 1 bay leaf. Cook according to the manufacturer's instructions until tender, about 40 minutes. If you don't have a pressure cooker, use a large covered soup pot and bubble until tender, about 55 minutes.

MEANWHILE, heat 1 tablespoon of the olive oil in a large nonstick sauté pan. Add the onions and sizzle over medium to medium-high heat until browned and frizzled, about 7 to 8 minutes. Remove from the heat.

IN a small saucepan, combine the remaining 2 tablespoons oil along with the remaining bay leaf, the cumin seed, and garlic over medium heat and sauté until fragrant, about 3 minutes. Remove from the heat.

ADD the cumin mixture, along with the lemon juice and parsley, to the cooked chick peas and rice. Stir well to combine, taking care not to smash the rice. To serve, arrange the rice and peas on a platter and sprinkle the onions on top.

MAKES 6 ENTRÉE SERVINGS OR 12 SIDE SERVINGS; 265 CALORIES PER ENTRÉE SERVING, 7.8 GRAMS FAT, 27 PERCENT CALORIES FROM FAT.

Ayurvedic Beans

Ayurvedic East Indian herbalists recommend cumin seed, cayenne pepper, and ground turmeric to aid digestion. If you have trouble digesting beans, it makes sense to use these spices when cooking them. Here, the bay leaf adds a strong enough flavor to make salt unnecessary. Cutting back on salt may be good for your health, but it's good for the beans, too, since cooking them with salt can make their skins fly off.

~~~~

continued

1/2   pound pinto beans

2   quarts roasted barley tea
     or vegetable stock
     (see Note)

3   onions, chopped

2   cloves garlic, minced

2   roasted bell peppers,
     minced (see Note)

1   cup fresh or frozen corn
     kernels

1   carrot, grated

1/2 teaspoon cayenne, or to
     taste

1   teaspoon ground turmeric

1   teaspoon cumin seed

1   teaspoon lovage seed or
     celery seed

1   bay leaf

2   tablespoons brown rice syrup
     or honey

Minced chives for garnish

Minced coriander leaf for
     garnish

Spicy salsa for serving

SOAK the pintos overnight in water to cover; drain.

PLACE the drained pintos in a large stockpot. Add the tea or stock, onions, garlic, minced peppers, corn, carrot, cayenne, turmeric, cumin, lovage, bay leaf, and brown rice syrup and bring to a boil. Reduce the heat to low, cover loosely, and simmer until the pintos are tender, about 4 hours. (You can do this in a crock pot; simmer time will be about 4 1/2 hours on the low setting.)

TO serve, scoop the pintos into individual bowls and swirl in the chives, coriander, and salsa. Serve warm.

MAKES ABOUT 6 CUPS, OR 6 ROBUST ENTRÉE SERVINGS; 155 CALORIES PER SERVING, TRACE OF FAT.

NOTE: Roasted barley tea is available at health food stores, Asian markets, and some supermarkets. To make 2 quarts tea, simmer 1/2 cup of roasted barley in 2 quarts of water until deep brown, about 20 minutes; strain.

    To roast peppers, first core and seed them. Then broil, turning occasionally, until the skins are completely charred. Set the peppers in a bowl, cover with a tea towel, and let them cool completely before removing and discarding the skins.

Bay-Scented Bread Pudding

Bay added to dessert puddings improves their sweetness without the need for refined sugar.

~~~~~

3/4 pound not-quite-stale bread, muffins, or quick bread (such as banana or carrot)

1/2 cup chopped dried figs

1 1/2 cups whole milk, skim milk, or soy milk

2 bay leaves

1/2 cup pure maple syrup

2 large eggs or 4 large egg whites or 1/2 cup Calendula Egg Substitute (page 47)

PREHEAT the oven to 350°F. Lightly brush a 1 1/2-quart soufflé dish with oil.

CRUMBLE the bread into the soufflé dish, mixing in the figs as you go.

IN a small saucepan, heat the milk and bay leaves until hot and fragrant, but not boiling. (You can also do this in the microwave: put the milk and bay leaves in a 2-cup measure, cover with vented plastic wrap, and microwave on full power for about 4 minutes.) Take the bay leaves out of the milk but keep them handy.

IN a medium bowl, combine the milk, maple syrup, and eggs and beat with an electric hand mixer until well combined. Pour over the bread, patting down the top to level it out, then place the bay leaves on top. Bake in the center of the oven, uncovered, until firm and golden on top, about 20 minutes. Serve warm for dessert or brunch with maple syrup, yogurt, or sautéed bananas.

MAKES 6 SERVINGS; 304 CALORIES PER SERVING, 2.5 GRAMS FAT, 7 PERCENT CALORIES FROM FAT.

bee balm

kick a cold

BREATHE EASY

~

HELP CONTROL OILY SKIN

~

COOK WITH A TASTE OF NATIVE AMERICA

~

When our house was built, much of the natural landscaping—trees and ground cover—was left intact. Even so, for the first several years the area lacked its natural abundance of birds and butterflies. Then I planted bee balm. When the herb bloomed it enticed a flurry of butterflies and hummingbirds into the area. More than any other herb, bee balm can help bring a bit of nature back to suburbs and cities, and no garden should be without it.

Lore and Legend

Along with the birds and the butterflies, bee balm has a history of attracting tax evaders. In 1733, the American colonists, as we all know, tired of English tariffs, put their collective foot down and booted a load of English tea right into Boston's harbor. During the events that followed, bee balm became the trendy tea to drink.

Healing

The colonists got the idea to brew up bee balm from Native Americans settled around the Oswego River near Lake Ontario. That's why bee balm is sometimes called "Oswego tea." While it makes a pleasant enough beverage, the Chippewa, Cherokee, Fox, and Ojibwa Indians mainly used bee balm tea to alleviate the symptoms of head colds and coughs. And, indeed, we now know that bee balm contains antiseptic compounds that can help heal respiratory infections and clear nasal congestion. Try it by steeping two teaspoons of fresh (or one teaspoon dried) bee balm leaves in a cup of hot water, covered, for four minutes. Sip a cup three times a day.

Looking Your Best

Bee balm contains tannins, which can help control oily skin. To make a home potion, combine a quarter cup of bruised fresh bee balm leaves with one cup of boiling water, cover, and steep for about ten minutes. Then strain and stir in the juice of one lemon. Keep refrigerated for up to a week, and use, shaking well first, as a facial splash three times a day, especially in the summer, after cleansing.

Growing

Bee balm grows naturally around moist stream banks in North America, so in the garden bee balm needs lots of water as well as full sun. It likes the standard herb mixture of two parts garden soil or potting soil, two parts peat, one part sand, and one part compost or composted cow manure.

To grow bee balm, buy small organically grown plants. Dig a hole twice the size of each herb's root ball. Set the bee balm in the hole, push the soil back around it, then tamp it down. Soak with warm water. Bee balm can grow to be three feet tall, so plant it behind shorter herbs.

Bee balm leaves are long, pointed, medium- to bright-green ovals. They look like the leaves of the orange bergamot tree, and bee balm is sometimes called bergamot. Its flowers are shaped like little fireworks that have just exploded and can be blue, red, pink, fuchsia, or orange. They bloom in the spring—but here's a trick to coax them into a second bloom: Check the plants daily after spring blooming, and as soon as the first yellow leaf appears, snip the plants back to a three-inch height. They'll grow up all summer and bloom anew in the fall.

Bee balm spreads out like mad, but fortunately its runners are very shallow. To remove them, just grab a leaf cluster, zip it right along the soil toward the mother plant, and tug it out. You can plant the runners elsewhere or give them to friends to start their own bee balm patches.

Cooking

Bee balm is often called "Sonoran oregano," a name that reflects its leaf shape in early spring, its taste, and its presence in the cuisines of the Pueblo, Zuni, and other Indian tribes of the Sonoran desert and across the Southwest. These tribes add fresh bee balm leaves to salads in the spring and summer, and in the winter, they use the dried leaves to flavor beans, soups, and meaty stews. Try substituting bee balm for oregano in your recipes, using the same amount. It adds a sharp, peppery zing when sprinkled fresh or dried on pizza or simmered in spaghetti sauce.

Chili Chicken Salad with Bee Balm

For maximum flavor and wholesomeness, use free-range chicken in this dish.

~~~~~

1 orange, thinly sliced

1 lemon, thinly sliced

1 pound boneless skinless chicken breasts

1 teaspoon chili powder

1/4 teaspoon cumin seed, toasted and ground

Pinch of ground cloves

1 scallion, minced

1 shallot, minced

3 tablespoons minced fresh bee balm leaves

1 celery stalk, minced

1/4 cup plain nonfat yogurt or soy yogurt

1 teaspoon fresh lemon juice

Flour tortillas or lettuce leaves for serving

COMBINE the orange and lemon slices and enough water to cover the chicken in a shallow 10-inch frying pan. Set in the chicken, cover, and bring to a boil. Reduce the heat and simmer over low heat until the chicken is cooked through, about 20 minutes. Remove the chicken from the poaching liquid. When it's cool enough to handle, use your fingers to shred the chicken into bite-sized pieces.

IN a small dry skillet, heat the chili powder, cumin seed, and cloves over medium-high heat until fragrant, about 1½ minutes. Transfer to a large bowl and add the scallion, shallot, bee balm, celery, yogurt, and lemon juice. Mix well, add the chicken, and toss well to combine. Serve at room temperature or very slightly chilled, rolled up in tortillas or lettuce leaves.

MAKES 4 SERVINGS; 235 CALORIES PER SERVING, 3.5 GRAMS FAT, 14 PERCENT OF CALORIES FROM FAT.

Variation: To substitute tofu for the chicken, cut 1 pound of firm tofu into bite-sized chunks and poach for about 10 minutes, adding a splash of soy sauce to the poaching water. Drain and carry on with the recipe.

Whole Roasted Okra

Even if you think you hate okra more than any food in the world, try this recipe. Roasting leaves the okra with a surprisingly crispy texture, and it may soon become one of your favorite vegetables.

~~~~~

1 pound fresh okra (all pods about the same size)
1 tablespoon olive oil
heaping tablespoon minced fresh bee balm

1 tablespoon freshly grated Parmesan cheese or soy Parmesan

PREHEAT the oven to 500°F.

COMBINE the okra and olive oil in a 9- by 13-inch pan, making sure all the pods are lightly bathed in the oil. Bake in the center of the oven until the pods are roasted and just crisp, about 15 minutes for small pods and up to 25 minutes for large pods. Peek in the oven a couple of times and stir the pods.

REMOVE from the oven and immediately stir in the bee balm and cheese. Serve warm as an appetizer or as a side dish with spicy food. Or serve with a sandwich instead of French fries.

MAKES 4 SERVINGS; 80 CALORIES PER SERVING, 4 GRAMS FAT, 44 PERCENT OF CALORIES FROM FAT.

borage

~~~~~~~~~~~~~~~~~~~~~~~~~~~~~~~~~~~~~

the hero's herb

*T*he Pennsylvania Dutch, the Amish, and Mennonites practice a form of natural healing called "powwow," using verses from the New Testament and various herbs. Powwow customs originated in Germany and are passed down through families. Each powwow practitioner is a specialist, one powwowing for warts, another for menstrual cramps, still another for babies' bad coughs. Each expert employs a unique method, and one I met near Allentown, Pennsylvania, favored the use of borage. Her front yard held a huge patch of it, with blossoms that looked like giant pink and blue flowering African violets. She would steep the borage flowers and leaves in brandy that her clients would sip for relaxation before the healing ritual, the idea being that healing can begin if one's mind and body are calm.

~

HELP

HEAL

THE HEART

~

SQUELCH

STUBBORN

SKIN

INFLAMMATIONS

~

CREATE

STELLAR

SALADS

~

Lore and Legend

Borage has long been prized for inducing fortitude and calm, especially before long journeys. To ease their minds when facing the possible perils of plague, famine, and bandits, early travellers sipped wine steeped with borage at pre-travel send-offs given by friends and family. To enhance their bravery, soldiers drank the brew before marching off to battle. In fact, many of borage's ancient names, including Welsh and Celtic ones, make reference to courage.

Healing

Herbalists prescribe a tea made from dried borage to increase strength and energy and to help balance the functioning of the adrenal glands, especially after surgery. In the case of heart surgery, borage leaf is sometimes combined with hawthorne berries both to help post-surgery patients relax and to restore their spirits. Usually, a teaspoon each of dried borage leaf and hawthorne berry are steeped in one cup of boiling water, covered, for ten minutes. The tea is drunk three times a day. Borage tea has not been widely investigated scientifically, but according to researcher Daniel B. Mowrey, the hawthorne berry's positive effects on the heart have been verified in laboratory and clinical experiments in Europe and the United States. Nonetheless, do consult with a qualified health professional before taking the borage-hawthorne combination.

Looking Your Best

Recent scientific research shows that borage may be good for your skin. Borage seeds offer gamma linolenic acid (GLA), a compound that, according to studies at the University of California at Davis, can help improve inflammatory skin conditions, like eczema, when taken internally and applied topically. The GLA-rich oil is extracted from borage seeds, then made into capsules that are available commercially. Be sure to consult a qualified herbalist or other health professional on the proper dosage. Note that borage's healing powers may be squelched by extreme stress, alcohol abuse, and cigarette smoking.

Growing

Borage is native to the Mediterranean, where it is planted in gardens to attract honeybees. To start a patch, buy an organically grown plant. Borage likes the standard herb soil of two parts garden soil or potting soil, two parts peat, one part sand, and one part compost or composted cow manure. In the spring, after all danger of frost, find a place that gets at least six hours of sun a day. Dig a hole twice the size of the herb's root ball and set the borage in the hole. Fill in the hole, tamp down the soil, and water with warm water.

Borage can get to be two feet high and spread to three feet across, so if you don't plan on giving it a weekly snipping, allow it lots of space and plant it behind smaller herbs. Since borage sprouts beautiful pink and blue flowers (on the same plant!), it harmonizes well with other herbs in the cool palette, such as chives, lavender, and sage.

Borage dies off at the first cold snap, but it's what herbalists call a "self-seeder," meaning that in the fall it drops seeds that are sure to sprout into new plants the next spring.

Cooking

Young borage leaves taste like cucumber and can be added to spring salads along with dandelion greens and chives. Borage can also be used instead of lettuce in sandwiches. The older leaves are too fuzzy to eat raw, but when added to soup stocks, they impart a cool cucumber flavor. Add half a cup of fresh borage leaves to one quart of simmering stock, then use the stock to make a creamy cucumber soup.

Borage stems taste like cucumber too. Peel, chop, and add half a cup to an apple and pear salad to serve four. Or, to lighten the taste of a hearty soup or stew for four, add one cup of peeled and chopped borage stem.

Borage flowers make charming edible garnishes. Float the cucumber-scented pink and blue blossoms in lemonade, iced tea, or pale chilled soups such as summer squash. To bring a flash of color to a green salad, add to greens after tossing with a dilled vinaigrette.

Sangria with Borage

Here's a modern version of the borage brew that medieval travelers and soldiers drank before departing on their adventures. It may not, as once imagined, give you courage, but its unusual and refreshing taste will boost your rating as a host.

~~~~~~

Large handful of borage leaves
3 sprigs fresh rosemary
4 cups red wine (Chianti, burgundy, or cabernet)

2 cups pure apple juice
3 tangerines, sliced
Borage blossoms

PLACE the borage leaves and rosemary in a very large wide-mouthed jar and use a pestle to pound them lightly until bruised. This will release their fragrances so they can perfume the wine and juice. Pour on the wine and apple juice and add the tangerines, along with their juice. Cover and let steep, refrigerated, for at least a day. The sangria will keep, refrigerated, for 1 week. Strain and serve chilled with floating borage blossoms in balloon wineglasses, to accompany a light outdoor brunch or dinner.

MAKES 6 1-CUP SERVINGS; 140 CALORIES PER SERVING,
NO ADDED FAT.

Grilled Scallops with Cucumber Relish

In this recipe scallops are blanched beforehand, to set the protein, so they can be grilled fat-free without becoming leathery. This technique works for other fish too.

~~~~~

1	pound sea scallops	1	medium cucumber, seeded and julienned (if the skin is tough, peel it)
2	tablespoons chili sauce or tomato salsa		
2	teaspoons Worcestershire sauce	1	red bell pepper, cored, seeded, and julienned
1	teaspoon soy sauce (low-sodium is okay)	2	tablespoons minced small, tender borage leaves
2	cloves garlic, finely minced	Borage flowers for serving	
1/4	teaspoon finely grated fresh ginger		

TIP the scallops into a medium pan of boiling water and blanch them for about 45 seconds. Drain and pat dry.

IN a medium bowl, combine the chili sauce, Worcestershire, soy sauce, garlic, and ginger. Marinate the scallops in the mixture for about 15 minutes, while you prepare the grill or preheat the broiler.

THREAD the scallops onto skewers, piercing them through the sides so the full round surfaces will face the heat. To ensure even cooking, space the scallops evenly on the skewers without crowding them. Grill or broil about 5½ inches from the heat until just cooked through, about 1½ minutes on each side.

MEANWHILE, to make the cucumber relish, toss together the cucumber, bell pepper, and borage leaves in a small bowl.

SERVE the scallops hot, accompanied with the cucumber relish and garnished with borage flowers.

MAKES 4 SERVINGS; 130 CALORIES PER SERVING, 1 GRAM FAT, 8 PERCENT OF CALORIES FROM FAT.

Quick Salads with Borage Flowers

- Combine a pound of steamed and shelled shrimp with a sliced ripe avocado. Toss with olive oil and lime juice and garnish with a quarter cup of borage flowers. (Makes 4 servings.)

- Arrange about four ounces of sliced smoked trout on a nest of mustard greens. Sprinkle on a few whole borage flowers and a pinch of minced fresh dillweed. Drizzle with fresh lemon juice and olive oil. (Makes 1 serving.)

- Thinly slice a pound of purple onions into rounds, then grill or broil. Toss with balsamic vinegar and a splash of olive oil, and garnish with a quarter cup of borage flowers. (Serves 4.)

Spicy Thai Shrimp with Basil   -   Herbed Lemonade

Left to right: *Warm Herbed Cider - Easy Olives - Spicy Couscous Cake with Avocado Relish - Catnap Honey - Barley Dumplings with Parsley Sauce - Macedoine of Oranges and Plums*

Green Beans with Savory and Tomatoes   -   Grilled Mushroom Satay with Black Vinegar Dipping Sauce   -   Whole Roasted Shallots with Fresh Thyme   -   Roasted Onions with Jalapeño

Peri-Peri Hens   -   Black-Eyed Peas with Grilled Red Onion   -   Sangria with Borage

Clockwise, from right to left: *Fresh Thyme Mustard with Vermouth - Jalapeño and Mushroom Salsa - Sambal (Vietnamese Chili Paste with Garlic) - Meringue Baskets with Raspberries and Apricots - Apple Tart with Anise-Hyssop Crust*

Roasted Tomatoes and Sage with Rigatoni

burnet

~~~~~~~~~~~~~~~~~~~~~~~~~~~~~~~

cool as a cucumber

While helping a friend in St. Louis prepare his special recipe for chicken salad, I was sent to the garden to pick the secret herbal ingredient—burnet. He described it as a ferny herb about a foot high, with pale purple flowers about the size and shape of raspberries. I found the burnet easily and was immediately fascinated. Its leaves are twinned, set exactly across from each other on the stem so they looked like open-winged butterflies. Their taste is nutty and reminiscent of cucumbers, and indeed burnet is a delightful addition to a salad, chicken or otherwise. In fact, burnet leaves were a staple green in the presupermarket era; hence the herb's old-fashioned name, salad burnet.

Lore and Legend

Burnet's leaves and roots have been used throughout American history. The root was picked wild, dried,

~

HELP

HEAL

MOUTH

ULCERS

~

REVITALIZE

SUMMER

SKIN

~

ADD EXTRA

FLAVOR TO

SPICY FOODS

~

then ground and boiled with water to make a tea. Soldiers in the Revolutionary War drank it before battle to prevent extreme bleeding if they were wounded. In fact, burnet's second Latin name, *sanguisorba,* literally means "to absorb blood."

As for the leaves, Thomas Jefferson had burnet planted in some of his fields to feed his grazing cows. People of Jefferson's era enjoyed burnet, too, by dropping a few sprigs in a glass of red wine to lighten the mood and treat arthritis.

In England, the sixteenth-century philosopher Francis Bacon used burnet in his "stepping garden," along with mint and other aromatics. His idea was for people to walk through the garden and step on the herbs to release and enjoy their aromas.

Healing

Modern herbalists recommend burnet to help heal mouth ulcers. A teaspoon of fresh leaves is crushed in a mortar, packed into the mouth at the location of the sore, and left there for twenty minutes. The procedure is repeated two more times each day until the pain goes away.

Looking Your Best

Floral waters are alcohol- or water-based potions laced with flowers and herbs. They're used to refresh the skin of the face, neck, arms, and hands, especially in the summer or in places with stale air, like offices and airplanes. With its cucumber aroma, burnet makes a cooling floral water. To prepare it, steep three tablespoons of fresh burnet leaves and a sprig of mint in a cup of boiling water, covered, overnight. Then strain and pour the mixture into a spray bottle. Store it in the refrigerator for up to a week, and use to cool and restore your skin. If the spray is fine enough, you can use it right over makeup without streaking. Be sure to spray the back of your neck too.

Growing

Burnet comes from central and northern Europe and grows wild as far north as Norway. In the United States it was a favorite of Shaker herbalists, and one thing they discovered about growing burnet is that it likes dry soil. Burnet is happy in a sandy variation of the standard herb soil, combining two parts garden or potting soil, two parts peat, two parts sand, and one part compost or composted cow manure.

To plant burnet, buy small organically grown plants. Find a place that gets at least six hours of sun a day. Then dig a hole twice the size of each plant's root ball. Sprinkle a handful of sand or vermiculite into the hole, set the plant in, pile the soil back up around it, and tamp it down. Water with warm water. Then, unless you have a drought, let nature do the watering.

Indoors, burnet grows well in a wide clay pot. Clay keeps the soil drier than plastic and the shape gives the burnet room to stretch out. Indoors, burnet needs six hours of sun a day. To augment the sunlight, use a ninety-watt halogen flood placed about three feet away from the plant. The halogen can stay on for up to twelve hours a day.

Cooking

Burnet's ferny leaves taste like cucumber, so adding some to a recipe gives a cool cucumber flavor without watering down the dish as cucumber can. Take raita, for example, the East Indian condiment made of thickened yogurt, dill, and chopped cucumbers. It's normally served along with spicy stews to offer a cool contrast to their heat. Normally, raita must be made just before serving because the cucumbers release liquid that causes the yogurt to separate as the mixture sits. But replace the cucumbers with burnet (three tablespoons of fresh, chopped leaves equal a half cup chopped cucumber), and the raita remains thick and luscious for hours.

Fiery foods, including Thai curries and Mexican salsas, benefit from burnet's cooling taste. Sprinkle some chopped leaves on top as an edible garnish, in the same way you'd use fresh coriander leaf. Use about two tablespoons for each cup of salsa or curry.

A less exotic but no less tasty idea is to pack burnet in sandwiches instead of lettuce. Try it on a sandwich of grilled feta cheese on whole wheat sesame bread, or an avocado and sprout sandwich drizzled with salsa on multigrain toast.

For the best flavor, burnet must be used fresh. Fortunately, the herb remains green even in the wildest of winters. It retains its taste and sometimes actually becomes slightly sweeter. If the leaves become tough from a sudden blast of cold, harvest the more tender ones at the middle, or crown, of the plant, and mince them before eating.

Fresh Tuna Salad on a Nest of Greens

Here, burnet is a cool, nutty salad green, emphasizing the flavor of the mustard-coated fish.

~~~~~

8 ounces fresh tuna, about 1½ inches thick

1 tablespoon coarse mustard

1 red bell pepper, cored, seeded, and julienned

3 cups loosely packed pungent greens, such as mustard greens

1 cup fresh burnet leaves

¼ pound cooked green beans, cut into 1-inch pieces

2 scallions, julienned

2 teaspoons olive oil

1 tablespoon red wine vinegar

1 tablespoon vegetable stock or defatted chicken stock

1 teaspoon minced fresh oregano

1 clove garlic, very finely minced

PREPARE a grill or preheat the broiler. Rub the tuna with the mustard. Grill or broil until just cooked through, about 5½ minutes on each side. Let relax for about 4 minutes.

MEANWHILE, in a large salad bowl, combine the bell pepper, greens, burnet, green beans, and scallions.

IN a small bowl, whisk together the olive oil, vinegar, stock, oregano, and garlic. Pour most of the dressing over the greens and toss until well coated.

TO serve, slice the tuna thinly against the grain. Arrange the greens in nests on individual plates, top with the tuna, and drizzle with the remaining dressing.

MAKES 4 SERVINGS; 250 CALORIES PER SERVING, 3 GRAMS FAT, 11 PERCENT OF CALORIES FROM FAT.

Spicy Steamed Trout with Burnet

Cool burnet offsets hot and spicy fish.

~~~~~~

1 pound trout fillets

4 bay leaves

2 teaspoons olive oil

2 cloves garlic, mashed through a press

1 leek, topped, tailed, rinsed, and minced

2 tomatoes, chopped, with their juices

1 green bell pepper, cored, seeded, and minced

2 tablespoons minced fresh parsley

2 scallions, minced

1 teaspoon hot pepper sauce, or to taste

2 tablespoons minced fresh burnet

ARRANGE the trout fillets in a steamer, tucking the bay leaves under them. Steam, covered, over boiling water until cooked through, about 7 minutes.

MEANWHILE, heat a sauté pan over medium-high heat and add the oil. Sauté the garlic, leek, tomato, green pepper, parsley, scallions, and hot pepper sauce until fragrant and slightly thickened, about 4 to 5 minutes.

ARRANGE the trout on a serving plate and spoon on the sauce. Sprinkle with the burnet and serve warm.

MAKES 4 SERVINGS; 135 CALORIES PER SERVING, 2.5 GRAMS FAT, 17 PERCENT OF CALORIES FROM FAT.

calendula

super skin soother

HEAL
BURNS AND
BLEMISHES

~

PREVENT
CATARACTS

~

PREPARE A
FAT-FREE
EGG
SUBSTITUTE

~

The stress of travel, as well as the dry air in planes and hotels, always makes my skin seem lined and dull. But once, when I arrived in Houston on a multicity media tour, dreading having to face the unforgiving television cameras, an herbalist friend gave me some invaluable advice. She told me to buy calendula cream from a health food store or herb shop, choosing the kind based on a nut or seed oil, such as sesame or grapeseed (petroleum-based creams can exacerbate dry skin). I slathered myself with the cream from head to toe after my shower, since moist skin absorbs oils better than dry. By the next morning, just in time for an early television spot, my skin was virtually back to normal.

Lore and Legend

Calendula got its name from the early Romans, celebrating the fact that it is almost always in bloom. The name acknowledges that the herb's flowers are likely to be present on *calends,* or the first day of every month. In the Middle Ages, the Anglo-Saxons gave calendula its more familiar moniker, "marigold." When a rash of people claimed to have seen the Virgin Mary adorned with golden blossoms, monks of the time changed calendula's name to "Mary Golde" in her honor.

Healing

Herbalists all over the world recommend calendula's orange-gold blossoms to soothe the skin. Modern science supports these traditional uses, for it's been shown that calendula contains essential oil compounds that soothe inflammation and help new tissue form. To treat minor cuts and burns, make a poultice to apply to the skin. Steep about half a cup of fresh or dried calendula petals (no green parts) in half a cup of boiling water until soft, about two minutes. Then squeeze the petals together and press the wad on the afflicted area. Tie on the poultice with cotton gauze and leave it on for about thirty minutes, repeating three times a day until the pain is gone and the skin has begun to return to normal.

If you're not the poultice type, commercial calendula preparations are widely available. Creams are recommended by many German herbalists for chapped or cracked winter hands and lips. In China, calendula ointment is a popular topical treatment for hemorrhoids. And homeopathic practitioners prescribe such preparations to heal minor wounds and skin ulcers, as well as to relieve soreness after tooth extraction. Since the herb is so gentle, it's often recommended for people with sensitive skin.

New research also hints that calendula might offer some protection against cancer since it contains beta carotene (the plant form of vitamin A) and other carotenoids. Another study done by the USDA links carotenoids and vitamin C with helping prevent cataracts. Since calendula blossoms contain both carotenoids and vitamin C, you may want to add them to your diet as a regular ingredient in green salads.

Looking Your Best

Calendula's gentle healing, which restored my travel-weary skin, is also effective on blemished and sensitive skin. To make a soothing toner, steep the petals from two blossoms, minus the green flower heads (about one tablespoon), in a cup of hot water for four minutes. Strain and splash on sensitive skin. The toner is especially helpful for men who have irritated skin from shaving. To have it at your fingertips, store the splash, covered, in the refrigerator for up to a week.

Growing

Calendula is such a light-sensitive plant that it can help you predict the weather. Peek outside around 7 A.M.: If the flowers are still closed, it's going to rain. If the calendula blossoms are open, the day will be sunny.

Be sure to plant this light-lover in a spot that gets at least six hours of sun a day. Then mix the standard herbal mixture of two parts garden or potting soil, two parts peat, one part sand, and one part compost or composted cow manure. Buy small organically grown calendula plants and dig a hole for each one that's twice the size of the root ball. Set the plants in, fill in with soil, and tamp it down. Then soak with warm water. For extra blossoms, spray the plants with a fish emulsion solution once a week, or according to the manufacturer's instructions. Fish emulsion is a natural fertilizer made from fish and water that can be found at garden centers.

Cooking

Almost forty years of research have shown that a low-fat diet may result in a healthier heart, improved digestion, normal blood pressure, reduced risk of cancer, and a longer life. Calendula can help promote a low-fat diet as a chief ingredient in an egg substitute (page 47). Calendula's sunny yellow flowers make the vegetarian substitute look as if it contains a rich yolk.

To use calendula flowers in recipes, remove the petals from the blossoms, discarding the green parts. Add about a tablespoon of the vibrant petals to each serving of green salad or such pale foods as rice, creamy soups, cheese spreads, sandwich spreads, and dips. The petals taste slightly peppery and, with garlic and dill, make a good herb mix for tossing with steamed carrots, broccoli, cauliflower, or Brussels sprouts or hot pasta.

Calendula Egg Substitute

Use one-quarter cup of this no-fat-added, salt- and preservative-free mixture to replace each egg in a recipe. You can't scramble it, but it's great in batters for muffins, quick breads, pancakes, waffles, and scones or as a glaze for French toast. Oddly enough, the egg substitute also makes a good hair styling gel, especially for blondes!

~~~~~

1 cup boiling water
Petals from 1 fresh or dried
    calendula blossom
    (about 1 tablespoon)

1 tablespoon flaxseed
    (see Note)

POUR the water over the calendula petals and cover. Let steep until the color is a rich yellow, about 5 minutes. Strain and discard the petals.

POUR the calendula tea into a small saucepan and toss in the flaxseed. Bring to a boil and boil for about 3 minutes, until the tea is reduced to about 3/4 cup. Transfer the mixture to a food processor or blender and whiz for about 30 seconds to coarsely crush the seeds. Then strain to remove most of the seeds (it's OK if some seeds remain). The substitute will smell slightly sweet and spicy. Refrigerate until cool, at least 15 minutes before using, or cover and refrigerate for up to 2 weeks.

MAKES ABOUT 2/3 CUP; NO ADDED FAT.

NOTE: Flaxseed is available at health food stores and some supermarkets.

Apricot-Banana Pancakes with Sunflower Seeds

These delicious pancakes satisfy without fat-laden eggs, and refined sugar is replaced by all-fruit preserves.

~~~~~~

1/2 cup whole wheat pastry flour	2 tablespoons all-fruit apricot preserves
1/2 cup unbleached all-purpose flour	1/4 cup Calendula Egg Substitute (page 47)
1 1/2 teaspoons baking powder	3/4 cup skim milk or low-fat vanilla soy milk
2 tablespoons rolled oats	1 ripe banana, mashed
Pinch of sea salt	About 1 teaspoon canola oil
1 tablespoon unsalted sunflower seeds	

IN a medium bowl, combine the flours, baking powder, oats, sea salt, and sunflower seeds.

IN another medium bowl, combine the preserves, egg substitute, milk, and banana and beat well with an electric hand mixer. Pour over the flour mixture and use a large rubber spatula to combine. Don't overmix; about 15 strokes should do it.

HEAT a well-seasoned cast-iron skillet over high heat. (If you don't have cast-iron, use any large heavy skillet, but don't preheat.) Paint on 1 teaspoon canola oil with a pastry brush; if your skillet's not well seasoned, you may need more oil. Reduce the heat to medium and add the batter, using about 2 tablespoons for each pancake. Let the pancakes sizzle until cooked through, about 2 1/2 minutes on each side. This is delicious with a drizzle of pure maple syrup.

MAKES 12 PANCAKES, OR 4 SERVINGS; 190 CALORIES PER SERVING, 3 GRAMS FAT, 14 PERCENT OF CALORIES FROM FAT.

catnip

~~~~~~

calm after
a storm

O ne of my herbal teachers was an old German woman who drank catnip tea nearly every day, claiming that it relaxed her and helped her to think clearly. Her job was to help me identify herbs in the wild, so we spent much of our time together in the woods. Walking ahead, she used a wooden stick to keep her balance in the shadows. When she found something, the walking stick waved up and down furiously, my cue to come meet a new herb. At the end of each session, we left the woods through the edge of a farm field, where we always found catnip.

Lore and Legend

It's an old farm custom to plant catnip at the perimeter of a field of grain to keep the rats away. The procedure may indeed work, because cats love catnip, and if cats are around, rats are likely to stay clear of the area.

~
TAKE THE
STING
OUT OF
STRESS
~
MAKE A
CAT
HAPPY
~
ENJOY A
ROMAN
SALAD
~

Famous for feline fun, catnip is one herb that lives up to its legend. Cats love to eat it, smell it, roll in it, and rub every part of their bodies in it. An easy way to treat a cat to some nip is to buy organically grown dried catnip and sprinkle it in any open-topped corrugated carton, the kind you get from the supermarket. Cut little peek-out holes in the sides of the carton, and the cat will leap in to play and enjoy some nip without making a total mess of the room. To choose the best dried catnip, smell it first. If it has no aroma, the cat won't be attracted to it.

Healing

Catnip is especially effective with sick and elderly cats who refuse to eat. Many such cats have at last been enticed to dine when fresh or dried catnip leaves are stirred into wet cat food or meat-based baby food.

What attracts cats to catnip is a volatile oil that contains compounds similar to those that make the herb valerian a sedative. This may be why some people find drinking catnip tea to be soothing and relaxing. To make a cup, steep one teaspoon of dried catnip in one cup of boiling water, covered, for four minutes. Strain, then sip.

Growing

Plant catnip well away from your other herbs in its own designated kitty garden. Otherwise, your cats will roll and play in your other herbs too, some of which are too delicate to take all that cat commotion.

Catnip, which is a native European plant, has medium-green heart-shaped leaves. Some catnip varieties are low creepers, and others grow to three feet tall, so choose plants according to your space and needs.

Catnip likes full sun, so find a place to plant it that gets at least six hours a day. The herb also likes dry soil, so use a variation of the standard herb mix, combining two parts garden or potting soil, two parts peat, two parts sand, and one part compost or composted cow manure. To plant catnip, dig a hole twice the size of the root ball. Sprinkle in some extra sand or vermiculite, then set in the catnip, push the soil back around it, and tamp it down. Douse with warm water. Then, unless you have a drought, let nature do the watering.

Indoors, grow catnip in a shallow pot, placed on the floor where the sun will hit it. Whatever you do, don't grow the catnip on the windowsill, because your cats will fling it to the floor.

Cooking

Catnip seeds look like poppy seeds and can be substituted for them by using the same amount in recipes. Their slightly minty flavor adds a nice accent to quick breads, pastry fillings, and muffins.

Fresh catnip leaves, which taste like very strong mint, can add robustness to green salads. The early Romans used them more generously, but start out with a tablespoon of fresh leaves for each serving of greens, then dress with olive oil and lemon juice.

Biscotti with Turmeric and Catnip Seed

In these biscuits, the minty taste of catnip seed enlivens the earthy turmeric.

~~~~~

1/2 cup toasted unsalted sunflower seeds	4 tablespoons sweet (unsalted) butter, softened
3/4 cup whole wheat pastry flour	1/4 cup canola oil or rice bran oil
3/4 cup unbleached all-purpose flour	1/3 cup medium-packed brown sugar
2 teaspoons baking powder	2 large eggs (see Note)
3/4 teaspoon ground turmeric	
1/4 cup catnip seed	

PREHEAT the oven to 375°F.

WHIZ the sunflower seeds in a processor or blender for about 25 seconds, until evenly ground. In a large bowl, stir the sunflower seeds, flours, baking powder, turmeric, and catnip seed together.

IN a medium bowl, combine the butter, oil, and sugar. Use an electric mixer to beat until smooth. Add the eggs and beat until well mixed.

continued

FOLD the egg mixture into the flour mixture and combine well. Don't overmix; about 15 strokes should do it.

LINE a large baking sheet (or two medium ones) with parchment paper. Divide the dough into two balls and set the balls on the parchment. Shape the balls into rectangles about 12 inches by 2 inches, leaving at least 4 inches between them. Smooth out the tops of the rectangles, eliminating any cracks. Bake in the middle of the oven until very lightly brown and the tops feel firm, about 12 to 15 minutes.

REMOVE the pan(s) from the oven and, using a sharp knife, gently cut each rectangle into $\frac{1}{2}$-inch slices. (You can do this right on the pan; don't remove the rectangles.) Turn each little slice on its side, then return the pan to the oven and continue to bake until the slices are dry to the touch and gently browned, about 5 to 7 minutes. (In case you're wondering, a *biscotti* means "twice baked.")

ENJOY the biscotti for breakfast, dessert, or snacks, with coffee, lemonade, or catnip tea. Store the biscotti in a paper bag for up to 3 days.

MAKES ABOUT 2 DOZEN COOKIES; 115 CALORIES PER COOKIE, 7 GRAMS FAT, 50 PERCENT OF CALORIES FROM FAT.

NOTE: If you'd like to reduce the fat a bit, use 4 large egg whites in place of the 2 whole eggs.

Catnap Honey

Some people find this honey to be gently relaxing, so try it swirled into chamomile tea before bed. The idea of infusing herbs in honey comes from ancient Egyptian herbalists, who used their potions as general body tonics and digestive aids. The technique spread to Europe, where it is sometimes still used with such bitter herbs as dandelion leaves.

~~~~~

$1/4$ cup fresh lemon balm leaves (about 24 large leaves)

$1/4$ cup fresh lemon verbena leaves (about 14 large leaves)

1 cup fresh catnip leaves and flowers

1 pound dark wildflower honey or brown rice syrup

COMBINE the lemon balm, lemon verbena, and catnip in a food processor, spice grinder, or blender and whiz until very finely ground but not quite a paste. Don't skimp on this step, or the texture won't be smooth and silky.

HEAT the honey in a small saucepan over medium heat until liquid, then stir in the herbs. Let the mixture cool slightly, then pour into a jar and cover. Drizzle it onto scones or muffins to enjoy with afternoon tea, swirl it into iced coffee, thin it with lemon juice to make a dressing for fruit salads, or use it as a condiment for roast lamb.

MAKES ABOUT $1^3/4$ CUPS; OR 70 CALORIES PER 1-TABLESPOON SERVING, NO ADDED FAT.

chamomile

~~~~~~

better than counting sheep

BEAT

ANXIETY AND

INSOMNIA

~

RELIEVE

INDIGESTION

~

SOOTHE

IRRITATED

SKIN

~

*A*s some people hold a fondness for their first sweetheart, I have a place in my heart for my first herb, chamomile. As a child, when I became unruly, I was given chamomile tea to calm me down. For smoother skin as a teenager, I rinsed my face with chamomile tea—a practice that I've continued. As a remedy for college exam anxieties, I drank chamomile tea before tests, which allowed me to focus my mind and think clearly. And I do the same today when stress begins to build up. I even take the herb along when traveling. I may barely remember my first boyfriend, but I never forget to keep chamomile on hand.

Lore and Legend

Herbalists throughout history have recommended chamomile tea to soothe nerves and irritability. Among the first to use chamomile were the early Egyptians, who dedicated the herb to the sun because it warmed and relaxed people suffering from malarial chills. Dioscorides, the Greek military doctor who served in Nero's army, advised his jittery patients to add chamomile to their bathwater.

Healing

Science supports chamomile's traditional role as a stress antidote. According to recent research, chamomile contains volatile oil compounds that act as a mild sedative, helping to relieve anxious feelings. East Indian Ayurvedic herbalists hold that chamomile tea relieves anxiety by harmonizing emotions. They recommend it to treat restlessness in children or throbbing on one side of the head. To make a cup, steep one or two teaspoons of dried chamomile flowers in a cup of hot (not boiling) water for four minutes. Cover the cup during steeping so the fragrance doesn't escape. Since chamomile has a soothing effect on digestion, after the evening meal is an ideal time to enjoy the apple-scented herb. As a variation, aromatherapists often mix half chamomile and half lavender flowers as a calming combination.

Though it's been observed that chamomile tea seems to have little or no calming effect on active alcoholics and drug abusers, the tea is soothing for many people who have given up the habits.

Chamomile tea also helps relieve inflammation and can be used to soothe sore gums. Use it as you would mouthwash, swishing it around in your mouth for at least thirty seconds before spitting it out. For convenience, you can brew up some chamomile tea and keep it in the refrigerator for up to a week.

Looking Your Best

The same chamomile tea can be used for a once-a-week face rinse to help keep your skin smooth, especially in harsh weather. It's mild enough to use on babies' skin, and even your dogs and cats can benefit from a gentle fur-deruffling with an occasional chamomile rinse.

Another use for chamomile tea is to perk up the tired, puffy undereye area. Dip cotton pads in cool chamomile tea and set them over your eyes. Lie back and relax for about fifteen minutes, redipping the pads midway. Remove the pads from your eyes and see the difference.

Growing

Since chamomile is very difficult to domesticate and grow, do not thwart any chance of relaxation by attempting to do so. For the best quality and most reliable chamomile, buy organically grown dried herb flowers that are whole and fragrant.

However, chamomile does have a place in the garden as comfort to herbs suffering from transplant shock or a bout of bad weather. These stressed-out herbs can often be revived with a chamomile mulch. Sprinkle a light dusting of fresh or dried chamomile flowers at the base of the stressed herb plant, then water with hot water.

chervil

~~~~~~~~~~~~~~~~~

insight for
irritated eyes

~

TRY AN

EASY

DIGESTIVE

TONIC

~

ENJOY A

TASTY

SPRING

PICK-ME-UP

~

SNAP UP

SPRING

FOODS

~

Anya, a Norwegian herbalist and old friend, says that spring is the time of the year to "clean the blood." French, Austrian, German, and Norwegian herbalists believe the body becomes deficient in nutrients during the winter months, and in early spring they prescribe eating greens for rejuvenation. Among the popular spring-cure greens are dandelion, watercress, and chervil. In many parts of Europe, especially Norway and France, bowls of minced fresh chervil leaves often accompany meals and are liberally sprinkled on salads, soups, and stews.

Anya made me a spring-cure soup from the herb nettle, on which we sprinkled chervil. The soup was accompanied by a five-grain bread spread with a soft white cheese and sprinkled with more chervil. With this meal, we drank aquavit, a strong, clear, caraway-scented liquor. I'm not sure if my blood was actually cleaner after the lunch, but I've since made chervil my antidote to winter.

Lore and Legend

Chervil has been used as a spring tonic since the time of the ancient Greeks. In the Middle Ages, chervil was eaten raw in salads to renew the blood. It was also part of the preparations for Easter, and chervil soup is still eaten on Holy Thursday in parts of Europe. The herb's association with resurrection may be due in part to its parsley-licorice flavor, reminiscent of the aroma of myrrh, one of the gifts the Three Wise Men gave to the baby Jesus. The fact that chervil sprouts around Eastertime with a similar scent is a symbol of the renewal of Christ.

Healing

Many modern herbalists recommend chervil as an aid to sluggish digestion, particularly for elderly people. To try it, sprinkle a tablespoon of fresh chervil leaves on a serving of green salad, and eat with a meal.

As for other parts of the body, chervil in tea form is a soothing wash for the eyes. For minor eye irritations or fatigue, make a chervil tea by steeping one tablespoon of the fresh herb in a cup of medium-to-hot water until cool, about twenty minutes. Cover the cup during steeping so the fragrance doesn't escape. Strain the tea, then close your eyes and use a soft cotton pad to soak them with the tea for about ten minutes. To be prepared for out-of-season irritations, freeze the chervil tea in an ice cube tray. When the cubes are frozen, transfer them to a plastic bag. Defrost a cube whenever you need it.

Growing

Chervil is an easy herb to grow if you know its idiosyncrasies. For one, because of a long taproot, chervil hates to be transplanted, so tuck it in where you're sure you want it. If you want to grow chervil indoors, make sure to find a pot deep enough to accommodate the taproot.

Another quirk is that, unlike most other herbs, chervil likes the shade. Make a place for it in your herb garden under a bush, where it can hide from the full sun. By day, chervil is not a gorgeous herb anyway. It looks like pale, dainty parsley. At night, however, when its silvery-white flowers reflect the moonlight, chervil becomes a bouquet of dancing glitter.

To plant chervil, buy a small organically grown plant. Find a shady spot and dig a hole twice the size of the root ball. Use the standard herb mixture of two parts garden or potting soil, two parts peat, one part sand, and one part compost or composted cow manure. Set the chervil in the hole and pile the soil back up around it, tamping it down. Soak with warm water. Don't water again until the soil feels bone-dry when you insert your finger. In most climates, chervil is a spring-only herb, lasting for about six weeks.

Cooking

Chervil is the classic herb for flavoring such spring foods as salmon, trout, new potatoes, spinach, asparagus, and tender green beans. Its gentle parsley-licorice flavor neither overwhelms nor is overpowered by other delicate spring flavors. Chervil also goes well in salads with other spring herbs, like dandelion, chives, and sorrel.

When cooking with chervil, never expose it to heat for very long, or its flavor will be lost. Swirl it into warm potato-leek soup at the very last minute or sprinkle it on sautéed soft-shelled crabs just before serving, using about a tablespoon of whole or minced leaf for each portion.

Chervil's licorice snap also enhances such cold main dishes as lightly dressed crab salad, egg salad, wild rice, and tofu or chicken salads. Try adding a loosely packed quarter cup of fresh chervil leaves to a green salad that serves four.

Fresh Chervil Relish

Chervil relish gives food enough life that salt isn't required. Swirl a teaspoon of this condiment into a cup of salt-free soup and see for yourself. Also try it in combination with mustard as a sandwich spread, or serve it with warm or chilled trout or salmon.

~~~~~

1 cup packed fresh chervil leaves

2 tablespoons minced red onion

2 tablespoons fresh lemon juice

1 teaspoon olive oil

COMBINE all the ingredients in a food processor or blender and whiz until finely minced but not a paste. The relish will keep, covered and refrigerated, for about a week.

MAKES $1/2$ CUP; 3 CALORIES PER 1-TEASPOON SERVING, TRACE OF FAT.

Wontons with Mushrooms, Ricotta, and Chervil

1 teaspoon olive oil

1 tablespoon minced onion

2 scallions, minced

2 ounces fresh cremini or shiitake mushrooms, trimmed and minced

1 shallot, minced

2 tablespoons nonfat ricotta cheese

20 wonton skins

Pinch of sea salt

3 tablespoons minced fresh chervil leaves

2 teaspoons sweet (unsalted) butter or olive oil

Freshly ground black pepper

TO make the wonton filling, heat a sauté pan over medium-high heat and pour in the oil. Add the onion, scallions, mushrooms, and shallot and sauté until fragrant and barely wilted, about 2 1/2 minutes. Scoop the vegetable mixture into a bowl and stir in the ricotta.

TO assemble the wontons, lay out a skin on the counter and drop a rounded teaspoon of filling, slightly off-center onto it. Wet the edges of the skin, and fold it into a triangle, pressing the seams tightly so the filling won't escape. Repeat the process with the remaining wonton skins.

TO cook the wontons, place them in a skillet of bubbling water, to which you've added the sea salt, and let them poach for about 3 1/2 minutes, until they are heated through and float to the surface. Immediately remove the wontons with a slotted spoon and drain them briefly on a towel. While the wontons are still warm, toss them with the chervil, butter, and pepper to taste, and serve.

MAKES 2 ENTRÉE SERVINGS OR 4 SIDE OR APPETIZER SERVINGS; 330 CALORIES PER ENTRÉE SERVING, 7 GRAMS FAT, 19 PERCENT OF CALORIES FROM FAT.

Variation: If you're off dairy, substitute crumbled blanched firm tofu for the ricotta and use the olive oil instead of the butter.

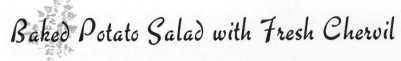

Baked Potato Salad with Fresh Chervil

Chervil and mustard combine to give baked potatoes a rich flavor without adding any fat.

~~~~~

3 pounds baking potatoes (about 3 large ones)	1/4 cup plus 2 tablespoons plain nonfat yogurt
3 scallions, minced	2 teaspoons coarse mustard
2 tablespoons very finely minced red onion	2 tablespoons minced fresh chervil

PREHEAT the oven to 500°F.

RINSE the potatoes and poke each in about five places with a knife. Bake, right on the oven rack, until just tender, 45 to 60 minutes, depending on the variety of potato.

MEANWHILE, in a large bowl, combine the scallions, onion, yogurt, mustard, and chervil.

LET the potatoes cool on a wire cake rack, to keep them from getting soggy, until they're cool enough to handle. Cut them into slices and add to the yogurt mixture. Combine gently with a rubber spatula, so the slices don't crumble; it's okay if a few break. Serve warm or very slightly chilled.

MAKES 6 SIDE SERVINGS; 140 CALORIES PER SERVING, NO ADDED FAT.

chives

~~~~~~~~~~~~~~~~~~~~~~~~~~~~~~~~~~~~

onion benefits
without tears

*T*he Tennessee Smoky Mountains are the place to find wild chives, which are also called ramps. One spring, to search them out, I set off on a mule named Bill along the steep mountain paths that overhang the Big River, famous for its trout. After riding for two hours I found a clearing where ramps were growing. Their leaves were a medium green, wider and flatter than regular garden chives. I dug them out with a pocket knife, then rinsed them off in a cold stream.

I ate my ramps raw and without accompaniment. But the proper way to eat ramps in eastern Tennessee is on cornbread with a type of bacon that's so fatty it's called "streak o' lean." With or without bacon, ramps are guaranteed to wake up taste buds that have been dulled by a long winter. And though I can't always make it to eastern Tennessee for a ramp spring cure, the spring chives from my garden provide a tasty memory.

Lore and Legend

Ancient Chinese herbalists recommended eating raw chives to control internal bleeding. But when Marco Polo brought them to Europe, herbalists claimed that eating raw chives would cause "evil vapors" in the brain. Still, chives found a niche in European households, where it became the practice to hang bunches around the house to ward off evil spirits.

Healing

Chives, like garlic, scallions, and leeks, belong to the allium family. All contain sulfur, which accounts for the penetrating flavor. They also contain alliin and an enzyme, allinase, which combine to form the chemical allicin. Recent research suggests that allicin may be the factor that makes chives and the rest of the family beneficial to health. They've been linked to reducing blood cholesterol levels, lowering blood pressure, and helping to prevent certain types of cancer. Though chives contain the least amount of allicin in the family, don't overlook them. Since the best-tasting chives are not cooked, they may preserve more of their heat-sensitive health-giving properties.

Growing

Chives are such effortless growers that they boost any gardener's confidence. Just give them some sun, water them once a week, and watch them grow. Snip them back, and in a week they grow again.

To plant chives, find a spot that gets at least six hours of sun a day. Chives like the standard herb mixture of two parts garden soil or potting soil, two parts peat, one part sand, and one part compost or composted cow manure. Buy tiny organically grown plants with several chives in each pot. Dig a hole for each pot that's twice the size of the root ball. Sprinkle a bit of extra sand in the hole, then set in the chives, pile the soil back up around them, and tamp it down. Water with warm water, and then water about once a week thereafter.

Chives grow especially well indoors, as long as they're placed in a wide shallow pot that lets them spread out. Give them at least six hours of sun a day, which can be augmented with a ninety-watt halogen flood placed about three feet from the chives. The halogen can be left on for up to twelve hours a day.

Most chives bloom in the spring, with beautiful purple blossoms that look particularly nice planted near purple-blooming sage. Chinese chives, also called garlic chives, bloom in the fall, with white blossoms. Planting both types gives you flowers to enjoy at both seasons, and the tasty leaves last all summer.

Cooking

With their delicate onion flavor, chives enhance almost every food except sweets. Even canned soup benefits from a tablespoon of minced fresh chives sprinkled on just before serving. Garlic chives, with flatter leaves than regular chives, can be found tied in bunches at Chinese and other markets. They can be minced and used in any recipe that requires a hint of garlic.

The big secret to cooking with chives is never to cook them. Try them sprinkled on broccoli, new potatoes, poached salmon, brown rice, grilled chicken, or even corn on the cob, using a tablespoon of minced fresh chives per serving. Here's an added benefit: Cooks who sprinkle chives onto food often find the flavor so vibrant they omit salt completely.

Chive blossoms, both regular and garlic, are tasty too. Pick the petals off one by one and toss them into potato salads, green salads, chilled vegetable soups, or marinated vegetables. The taste is strong and oniony, so use just two tablespoons (not packed) of blossoms for four servings. Whole blossoms can be cooked tempura-style and dipped in a gingery soy sauce before enjoying.

Scrambled Tofu with Mustard Sauce and Chives

Tofu has little flavor of its own but readily absorbs the flavors around it. Here, chives, tahini, and mustard combine to jazz it up.

~~~~~

1/4 cup (not packed) dried shredded daikon radish (see Note)

1 large dried shiitake mushroom cap

1 10 1/2-ounce package firm, reduced-fat tofu

Splash of olive oil

1 small onion, sliced

1 teaspoon tahini or sesame butter

1 teaspoon Dijon mustard

1 teaspoon white miso

2 teaspoons kudzu or arrowroot

Splash of soy sauce

2 tablespoons minced fresh chives (any kind)

IN a small bowl, combine the daikon, mushroom, and boiling water to cover, and let soak for about 15 minutes. Drain the vegetables but save the soaking water. Mince the mushroom.

MEANWHILE, blanch the tofu in boiling water for about 2 1/2 minutes to make it easier to digest. Drain and pat dry. When it's cool enough to handle, crumble it coarsely.

PREHEAT a large well-seasoned cast-iron skillet over medium-high heat. (If you don't have one, use a nonstick sauté pan but don't preheat.) Use a pastry brush to paint on the olive oil. Add the onion, daikon, and mushroom and sauté for about 2 minutes, until the onion is lightly brown and fragrant. Toss in the tofu and sauté for another 3 minutes.

MEANWHILE, in a small bowl, combine the tahini, mustard, miso, kudzu, and daikon-mushroom soaking water. Whisk well to combine.

POUR the mustard sauce over the tofu, add the soy sauce, and stir to coat. Serve warm for breakfast or brunch, sprinkled with the chives. Or pack into a whole wheat pita half and serve for lunch or dinner.

MAKES 2 LARGE SERVINGS; 145 CALORIES PER SERVING, 3.5 GRAMS
FAT, 19 PERCENT OF CALORIES FROM FAT.

NOTE: You can pick up such ingredients as dried daikon, shiitake mushrooms, miso, tahini,
kudzu, and tofu in Oriental markets, health food stores, and many supermarkets. While
you're there, buy a good-quality soy sauce that's free of artificial coloring and preservatives.

Fresh Peas and Smoked Trout with Linguine

Chives add zip that highlights the smoky flavor of the fish.

~~~~~

1/4 cup dry white wine	1/2 cup nonfat ricotta cheese
1/4 cup vegetable stock or	or blanched, soft tofu
defatted chicken stock	2 teaspoons olive oil
3/4 cup shelled fresh peas	3 cups hot cooked linguine
3 ounces skinned and boned	(from a generous 1/3 pound
smoked trout or smoked	dried)
salmon	1/4 cup minced fresh chives
	(any kind)

COMBINE the wine and stock in a small saucepan and bring to a boil. Add the
peas and boil until the peas are bright green and just tender, about 1 minute.

MEANWHILE, place the trout and ricotta in a medium bowl and mash well with
a fork, adding the oil as you go.

WHEN the peas are cooked, tip them, with their liquid, into the trout and cheese
mixture and combine well. Toss with the linguine and chives and serve warm
or very slightly chilled. A salad of watercress and sorrel makes a tasty accompaniment.

MAKES 4 SERVINGS; 270 CALORIES PER SERVING, 2.5 GRAMS FAT,
9 PERCENT OF CALORIES FROM FAT.

Steamed Chinese Dumplings with Fresh Chives

Minced chives are classic in Chinese dumplings, adding flavor to the otherwise bland steamed dough.

~~~~~

FOR THE DOUGH:

2¹/₂ cups unbleached all-purpose flour

¹/₂ cup whole wheat pastry flour

¹/₃ cup minced fresh chives (any kind)

1 cup boiling Chinese tea

FOR THE FILLING:

1 teaspoon peanut oil

1 small onion, minced

4 cloves garlic, mashed through a press

1 large carrot, grated

1 cup grated white cabbage

1¹/₂ cups chopped greens, such as rapini or kale (see Note)

1 teaspoon nam pla or nam nuoc (Thai or Vietnamese fish sauce)

1 teaspoon mirin or dry sherry

FOR THE SAUCE:

¹/₄ cup defatted chicken stock or vegetable stock

1 teaspoon nam pla or nam nuoc (Thai or Vietnamese fish sauce)

1 teaspoon toasted (dark) sesame oil

TO make the dough, combine the flours and chives in a medium bowl. Pour in the tea and use a rubber spatula to combine well. When the dough begins to stick to the spatula, continue mixing with your hands. Knead the dough on a lightly floured board for about 3 minutes, then put it back in the bowl, cover with a tea towel, and let relax for 30 minutes.

MEANWHILE, to make the filling, heat a large sauté pan over medium-high heat and pour in the oil. Add the onion, garlic, carrot, cabbage, and greens and sauté for about 3 minutes. Add the nam pla and mirin and cook until the vegetables are soft and the filling is thickened, about 2 minutes more.

TO make the dumplings, pinch off a well-rounded tablespoon of dough for each dumpling and roll it out into a 3¹/₂- to 4-inch circle. If it's a humid day, flour your rolling surface to prevent sticking. Set a rounded tablespoon of filling on each circle and fold the circle in half, then wet the edges with water and pinch them tightly so the filling won't escape during steaming.

TO make the sauce, combine the stock, nam pla, and sesame oil in a small bowl.

STEAM the dumplings on a lightly oiled rack over boiling water until the dough is cooked, about 10 minutes. (Arrange the dumplings so they're not touching, or they will stick together.) Serve hot, with the sauce for dipping.

MAKES 20 DUMPLINGS; 82 CALORIES PER DUMPLING, 1 GRAM FAT, 11 PERCENT OF CALORIES FROM FAT.

NOTE: Rapini, also called broccoli rabe, is a mustardy-tasting green with large bright green serrated leaves and tiny yellow flower buds that resemble broccoli. Rapini is similar to what the Chinese call "flowering broccoli."

Variation: Instead of using the vegetable filling, try stuffing a shelled and deveined large, uncooked shrimp into each dumpling. For extra flavor, marinate the shrimp in a mixture of fresh garlic, ginger, and sesame oil for 30 minutes before stuffing. Steam as for the vegetable dumplings.

Homemade Low-fat Creamy Cheese with Chives

Minced fresh chives give this low-fat cheese a robust flavor. This satisfying spread is great on baked potatoes, as a garnish for spicy soups, tossed with hot pasta and fresh basil, or as a filling for low-fat canapés.

~~~~~

1 cup buttermilk	1 tablespoon finely minced
1 cup skim milk	fresh chives (any kind)

COMBINE the buttermilk and skim milk in a small saucepan. Heat over medium-high heat until the whey (the thin, pearly liquid) separates out and the curds form a solid mass. At this point, little bubbles will appear around the edge of the pan. Let the cheese bubble gently for about 4 minutes, but don't boil it, or the cheese will end up rubbery. And don't stir, or you'll disrupt the curd.

REMOVE from the heat and let the cheese sit in the pan for a full 3 hours. Don't rush this step, or the cheese will be too runny.

GENTLY dump the cheese into a strainer or colander lined with two layers of cheesecloth. Set it in the sink so the whey can go right down the drain, and let the cheese drain until it's like fluffy cream cheese, ideally overnight. Stir in the chives and use as you would cream cheese. It will keep, covered and refrigerated, for about a week.

MAKES ABOUT ⅔ CUP; 15 CALORIES PER 1-TABLESPOON SERVING, TRACE OF FAT.

Jalapeño Bullets

To make these tasty low-fat snacks, core and seed fresh jalapeños. Use gloves to protect your hands from the hot pepper juice, which can burn the skin. Then use a baby spoon to fill each jalapeño with Homemade Low-fat Creamy Cheese with Chives (page 70), using about a tablespoon of cheese per medium jalapeño.

~~~~~

Snap Peas with Sesame and Chives

In this simple side dish, chives combine with sesame to create a full flavor without excessive fat or salt.

~~~~~~~

1 pound sugar snap peas
1 teaspoon toasted (dark) sesame oil
1 tablespoon rice vinegar or other mild white vinegar

1 tablespoon finely minced fresh chives (any kind)
1 teaspoon sesame seeds

BLANCH the peas in boiling water until bright green and just tender, about 2 minutes. Pat them dry.

TIP the peas into a large bowl. Add the oil, vinegar, and chives, and toss well to combine.

SPRINKLE the sesame seeds into a dry nonstick sauté pan and heat over medium-high heat. Stir constantly until toasted, about 1 1/2 minutes, keeping a close eye on the pan to avoid burning the seeds.

TOSS the peas with the seeds and serve warm as a side dish, or cover and refrigerate to enjoy later as a salad.

MAKES 4 SERVINGS; 47 CALORIES PER SERVING, 1.5 GRAMS FAT, 26 PERCENT OF CALORIES FROM FAT.

Roasted Vegetable Salad

Here's an example of how chives can bring lightness to foods with a deep, roasted flavor.

~~~~

- 1 eggplant (about 1 pound), cut into 1-inch cubes
- 1 whole garlic bulb, separated into cloves and peeled
- 2 medium onions, thinly sliced
- 2 small zucchini, cut into chunks
- 4 small beets, quartered
- 1 tablespoon olive oil
- 3 tablespoons vegetable stock or defatted chicken stock
- 1/4 cup chopped fresh thyme
- 4 slices whole wheat bread
- 2 teaspoons Dijon mustard
- 1 tablespoon balsamic vinegar
- 3 tablespoons minced fresh chives (any kind)
- About 2 cups mustard greens or chicory

PREHEAT the oven to 450°F.

BLANCH the eggplant in boiling water until just tender, about 4 minutes. Drain and pat dry.

PLACE the eggplant in a 9- by 13-inch baking dish along with the garlic, onions, zucchini, beets, olive oil, stock, and thyme and stir to coat the vegetables. Roast uncovered until the vegetables are fragrant and cooked through, about 25 minutes, stirring once midway.

MEANWHILE, spread the bread with the mustard and cut each piece into crouton-sized chunks. Heat a well-seasoned cast-iron skillet over medium-high heat and add the croutons. Toast, stirring constantly, until lightly browned and crisp, about 3 minutes.

WHEN the vegetables are ready, toss them with the vinegar and chives. Serve on a nest of greens, sprinkled with the croutons.

MAKES 4 SERVINGS; 170 CALORIES PER SERVING, 3.5 GRAMS FAT, 19 PERCENT OF CALORIES FROM FAT.

coriander

tame a hot tummy

*A*fter two weeks in Kuala Lumpur, Malaysia, we retreated to a country house about an hour away. The house was built where the jungle and beach met, on the Strait of Malacca, the famous spice route on which ancient ships carried precious cargoes of aromatics.

The house cook was Mr. Lem, whose background and cooking style were "noyno," a combination of Chinese and Southeast Asian. For lunch he prepared a large, bass-like fish caught that morning. It was covered with a smooth, thick sauce made of tomato, carrot, onion, garlic, and hot peppers, and sprinkled with fresh coriander leaf. As the ocean breeze cooled the clear hot day, I was reminded of how the cool taste of coriander does the same for a spicy dish.

~

HELP

STIMULATE

DIGESTION

~

EASE

ITCHY

RASHES

~

BE A

"COOL"

COOK

~

Lore and Legend

Though coriander leaf is cool in the kitchen, the seeds were used to heat up love lives in the Han Dynasty (207 B.C. to A.D. 220) in China. Herbalists of the era advised drinking liquor laced with coriander as an aphrodisiac. What's more, a similar potion, used for the same purpose, is mentioned in *The Thousand and One Arabian Nights*.

Whether coriander is an effective love potion or not is a matter of personal taste. But the herb does possess a certain "staying power," since seeds found buried in ancient Egyptian tombs are still able to germinate.

Healing

East Indian Ayurvedic herbalists claim coriander "cools" a hot stomach, banishes intestinal gas, and generally aids digestion. They recommend eating two tablespoons of fresh coriander leaf, which they call *dhanyaka*, as soon as indigestion hits. For prevention, the same amount can be sprinkled atop a plate of food.

Ayurvedics also say that "overeating destroys intellect." To protect your reasoning powers (and to prevent the bloat of overeating), they advise taking coriander and fennel after a big meal. Combine a teaspoon each of coriander seed and fennel seed in a dry pan. Heat over high heat, stirring constantly, until the seeds are fragrant and toasted, about two minutes. Then combine with a pinch of sea salt and eat, chewing well.

Ayurvedics also use coriander topically to relieve hot, itchy rashes. They mash the fresh leaves and apply them as an anti-fire, or anti-*pitta,* poultice, then have the patient sip a cup of coriander tea. To make it, steep two teaspoons of coriander seed in one cup of boiling water, covered, for seven minutes. For mild rashes, the coriander cure is safe to try at home.

Growing

Coriander's cool nature will show up in its behavior in your garden. Tuck a plant into the soil early in the season and watch it carefully when the weather starts to get hot. Coriander is famous for bolting in the heat, which means you may wake up one morning and find your plant has sprung out wildly in all directions. But though it looks strange, heat-shocked coriander is healthy and fine to eat.

Coriander, which looks like ferny, medium-green parsley, likes a dry variation of the standard herb soil, of two parts garden soil or potting soil, two parts peat, two parts sand, and one part compost or composted cow manure. Buy small organically grown plants and find a place for them that gets at least six hours of sun a day. Dig a hole for each plant that is twice the size of the root ball. Sprinkle a little sand in the hole, since coriander likes dry soil. Then set the plant in the hole, fill in with the surrounding soil, and tamp it down. Soak with warm water, then let nature do the watering. Coriander is happier growing outside than in. If you don't have a garden you can buy fresh coriander for cooking at Oriental markets, Latin markets, and many supermarkets.

Cooking

Many cuisines use coriander to balance the flavor of hot and spicy dishes. In Thailand, for instance, steak salad fired up with red curry paste is garnished with fresh coriander leaf. In Morocco, coriander offsets harissa, the spicy red sauce used on couscous stews. And it plays a similar role in the spicy cuisines of regions of Mexico (where it's called cilantro or culantro), Central America, South America, India, Vietnam, China, Tibet, Indonesia, Malaysia, Spain, and Africa. Cooks in these countries use coriander leaf as Americans use parsley, adding one or two teaspoons of the fresh leaf for each serving.

Though coriander looks like flat-leafed parsley, it tastes completely different. The herb's flavor is a strong combination of lemon, pine, and sage. If you're a newcomer to cilantro, chop up about a quarter cup of leaves and swirl it into two cups of spicy tomato salsa. Then drizzle the mixture over poached red snapper or grilled chicken. As for the taste, there's no in-between: You'll either love it or hate it.

Even if you don't like the leaves, you'll want to try dried coriander seed, which has a milder taste with less pine and more lemon. For a cool yet slightly spicy taste, grind a tablespoon of the seeds in a mortar or spice grinder and add to a spicy stew and curry to serve four. To make a livelier pepper, try grinding the seeds along with whole black peppercorns in a pepper mill and use as a table condiment on green salads, rice, soups, or stews. In India, ground coriander seed is combined with ground cumin seed and ground turmeric and added to spicy rice and lentil dishes.

Fresh coriander root tastes similar to the seeds, but slightly nuttier. In Thailand it's finely grated and added to spicy chicken, fish, and vegetable salads. A little mound of grated coriander root is also a tasty garnish for gumbos and jambalayas.

 Coriander Chutney

Versions of this flavorful condiment are served in parts of India, minus the pumpkin seeds but with the addition of green chilies and sugar. In parts of Africa, where it often accompanies spicy tomato-based stews, coriander chutney is made with yellow rather than green onion and topped with chopped peanuts. This chutney is great with Curried Corn Samosas (below).

~~~~~~

1 cup packed fresh coriander leaves	2 tablespoons rice vinegar or other mild white vinegar
4 scallions, chopped	3 tablespoons unsalted, raw pumpkin seeds
1 clove garlic, mashed through a press	

COMBINE all the ingredients in a processor or blender and whiz until you have a coarse paste. Serve at once (don't make ahead, or it will separate) as a condiment for spicy curries, stews, or grilled fish and poultry. You can also swirl a spoonful into a bland soup to snap up the flavor.

MAKES ¹/₂ CUP; 28 CALORIES PER 1-TABLESPOON SERVING, 1.5 GRAMS FAT, 45 PERCENT OF CALORIES FROM FAT.

 Curried Corn Samosas

These little pockets get a boost of sophistication from the combination of coriander seed and fresh coriander leaf. But since the dough is very easy to handle, this is a good recipe for nonbakers. Don't attempt to reheat samosas, as there's not enough fat in the dough to keep it from becoming tough.

~~~~~~

½ cup whole wheat pastry flour

1½ cups unbleached all-purpose flour, plus extra for kneading and rolling

2 teaspoons coriander seed, finely ground

Pinch of sea salt

About ⅔ cup water

1 cup corn kernels (cut from 2 large ears)

¼ cup fresh coriander leaves, minced

2 scallions, minced

1 clove garlic, mashed through a press

½ teaspoon cumin seed, finely ground

1 teaspoon ground turmeric

Pinch of cayenne, or to taste

3 tablespoons freshly grated low-fat mozzarella or soy mozzarella

About 2 teaspoons olive oil

TO make the dough, combine the flours, coriander seed, and salt in a medium bowl and mix well. Pour in ⅔ cup water and work it with a large rubber spatula until you have a dough, adding a bit more water if necessary. Transfer the dough to a lightly floured counter and knead for about 3 minutes. Then return the dough to the bowl, cover, and let it relax at room temperature for about 15 minutes.

MEANWHILE, make the filling: Combine the corn, coriander leaves, scallions, garlic, cumin, turmeric, cayenne, and mozzarella in a small bowl.

PLACE the dough on a lightly floured counter and slice it into 8 pieces. To make the samosas, roll each ball out to a 4-inch circle, place a tablespoon of the filling in the center, fold the circle in half, and pinch the edges closed.

TO cook the samosas, heat a well-seasoned cast-iron skillet over high heat. Use a pastry brush to paint the oil into the skillet. Set the samosas in the pan and let them sizzle until lightly browned, about 2 to 3 minutes on each side. Serve warm, as part of an appetizer assortment with Coriander Chutney (page 76), or as a main course with soup or salad.

MAKES 8 SAMOSAS; 148 CALORIES PER SAMOSA, 1 GRAM FAT, 7 PERCENT OF CALORIES FROM FAT.

NOTE: To make a quick dip for the samosas, combine equal parts of spicy salsa and plain nonfat yogurt.

Spicy Coriander Pickles

Coriander seed and leaf give an unusual zing to these pickles.

~~~~~~

1 teaspoon coriander seed, crushed	Scant 1/2 cup mild red wine vinegar
1 dried hot chili pepper (about 2 inches in length)	Pinch of sea salt
2 cloves garlic, minced	1 pound cucumbers (2 medium)
Splash of hot pepper sauce, or to taste	1 heaping tablespoon minced fresh coriander leaves
1 teaspoon toasted (dark) sesame oil	5 nasturtium blossoms

IN a small saucepan, combine the coriander seed, hot pepper, garlic, hot pepper sauce, sesame oil, vinegar, and sea salt.

CUT the cucumbers into 1-inch-thick slices (if the skins are tough, peel them). Add them to the saucepan and bring the mixture to a boil. Reduce the heat and simmer until the cucumbers are fragrant, about 3 minutes.

MIX in the minced coriander and nasturtium blossoms and let cool. Chill before serving. The pickles will keep, covered and refrigerated, for up to a week.

MAKES 2 CUPS; 17 CALORIES PER 1/4-CUP SERVING, TRACE OF FAT.

Roast Duck with Daikon Pickle and Fresh Coriander

This is a popular way to cook duck in Vietnam. The cool coriander balances the spiciness of the duck, and the daikon pickle, eaten at the end of the meal, is said to aid digestion. Daikon is a large white radish, widely used in Southeast Asian and Japanese cooking. If you can't find it, substitute sliced red radishes.

~~~~~~

1   4 -to 5- pound Muscovy or wild duck

1/2 cup hoisin sauce (Chinese red bean sauce)

2   cloves garlic, mashed through a press

2   tablespoons dry sherry

1   teaspoon coriander seed, finely ground

2   tablespoons hot pepper sauce

8   thin slices daikon radish

3   tablespoons rice vinegar or other mild white vinegar

1/2 cup fresh coriander leaves

USE poultry shears to quarter the duck. Trim away and discard the excess neck fat. Lightly scrape the skin with the tines of a dinner fork about every 2 inches or so to allow the fat to run out during cooking. Don't scrape all the way to the flesh, however, or the cooked duck may be dry.

ARRANGE the duck quarters skin side down in a steamer basket, cover, and steam over boiling water for 20 minutes. (This step gets rid of a lot of fat.) Meanwhile, preheat the oven to 425°F.

IN a small bowl, combine the hoisin sauce, garlic, sherry, ground coriander, and hot pepper sauce.

WHEN the duck has finished steaming, pat it dry and rub it all over with the hoisin mixture. Set the quarters skin side up on a roasting rack set over a drip pan filled with about 1/2 inch of water. Roast in the middle of the oven until cooked through, about 45 minutes. The leg quarters need less cooking, so peek in the oven after about 30 minutes: If they're done, remove them. (The best way to tell if the duck is done is to slice in and take a look. Note that wild duck requires less cooking time since it contains less fat.)

WHILE the duck is roasting, arrange the daikon slices on a dinner plate and sprinkle on the vinegar. Weight the slices down with something heavy, such as a stockpot, and let the slices pickle until the duck is cooked.

TO serve, arrange the duck quarters on a pretty platter, with the coriander strewn atop. Surround with the diakon pickle.

MAKES 4 SERVINGS; 275 CALORIES PER SERVING (WITHOUT THE SKIN), 7 GRAMS FAT, 23 PERCENT OF CALORIES FROM FAT.

Scallop Satay with Green Curry Sauce

Smooth-textured scallops are receptive to the flavor of coriander.

~~~~~

1 pound sea scallops (all about the same size)

2 tablespoons fresh lime juice

1 teaspoon olive oil

3 cloves garlic, minced

1/2 teaspoon finely grated fresh ginger

1 teaspoon hot pepper sauce, or to taste

3 tablespoons vegetable stock or defatted chicken stock, plus extra if necessary

1 tablespoon nam pla (Thai fish sauce) or reduced-sodium soy sauce

2 tablespoons minced fresh coriander leaves

2 tablespoons minced fresh basil

2 tablespoons unsweetened coconut milk (see Note)

IN a medium bowl, toss the scallops with the lime juice, olive oil, garlic, and ginger. Let marinate, refrigerated, for about 30 minutes.

PREPARE the grill or preheat the broiler.

THREAD the scallops on bamboo skewers (through the sides, not through the center of the rounds). Grill or broil the scallops 4 inches from the heat until just cooked through and very lightly browned, about 2 to 3 minutes on each side.

MEANWHILE, combine the hot pepper sauce, stock, nam pla, coriander, basil, and coconut milk in a processor or blender and whiz until smooth. If necessary, splash in a bit more stock.

SERVE the scallops warm, drizzled with the sauce.

MAKES 4 SERVINGS; 135 CALORIES PER SERVING, 3 GRAMS FAT, 21 PERCENT OF CALORIES FROM FAT.

NOTE: Unsweetened coconut milk is available at specialty food stores, Asian markets, and some supermarkets.

Spicy Eggplant Salad

In the cuisines of India, coriander seed is often paired with cumin seed and hot pepper.

~~~~~

1½ pounds eggplant, cut into chunks

3 bay leaves

2 teaspoons olive oil

2 cloves garlic, mashed through a press

1 leek, topped, tailed, rinsed, and minced

1 teaspoon finely grated fresh ginger

1 teaspoon cumin seed, crushed

1 teaspoon coriander seed, crushed

1 dried hot chili pepper (about 1 inch long), crushed, or 1 teaspoon dried hot red pepper flakes

2 medium tomatoes, chopped

1 red bell pepper, cored, seeded, and chopped

2 scallions, minced

2 tablespoons minced coriander leaves

PLACE the eggplant on a steamer rack and steam over boiling water, to which you've added the bay leaves, until very tender, about 10 to 12 minutes.

MEANWHILE, heat a medium sauté pan over medium-high heat. Pour in the oil, then add the garlic, leek, ginger, cumin seed, coriander seed, hot pepper, to-matoes, and bell pepper and sauté until fragrant and saucy, about 4 minutes.

COMBINE the steamed eggplant with the tomato mixture in a shallow bowl, taking care not to squash the eggplant. Sprinkle with the scallions and cori-ander leaves and serve warm or slightly chilled. The salad makes a great ac-companiment to poached fish.

MAKES 4 SERVINGS; 110 CALORIES PER SERVING, 3 GRAMS FAT, 27 PERCENT OF CALORIES FROM FAT.

Alu Gobi (Spicy Potatoes and Cauliflower)

Potatoes and cauliflower take on an East Indian flavor when combined with coriander seed and other typical spices.

~~~~~

1 tablespoon olive oil

1 teaspoon fennel seed, finely ground

1 teaspoon cumin seed, finely ground

1 teaspoon coriander seed, finely ground

1 teaspoon ground turmeric

1 large onion, chopped

2 cloves garlic, minced

1 pound potatoes, cubed

1 large head cauliflower (about 1 3/4 pounds), cut into bite-sized florets

1/2 lemon, thinly sliced (including the skin)

3 bay leaves

1 1/2 cups vegetable stock or defatted chicken stock

1/4 cup dry white wine

2 tablespoons tomato paste

Pinch of cayenne, or to taste

Minced fresh coriander leaves for garnish

HEAT a large frying pan over medium-high heat, and pour in the oil. Add the fennel, cumin, coriander seed, turmeric, onion, and garlic and sauté until the onions are fragrant and wilted, about 5 minutes.

ADD the potatoes, cauliflower, lemon, bay leaves, stock, wine, tomato paste, and cayenne. Bring to a boil, then reduce the heat to a gentle simmer. Cover loosely and simmer until the potatoes and cauliflower are very tender, about 25 to 30 minutes. Serve warm, sprinkled with the coriander leaves, as an entrée with rice or an interesting bread.

MAKES 4 LARGE SERVINGS; 223 CALORIES PER SERVING, 3.5 GRAMS FAT, 16 PERCENT OF CALORIES FROM FAT.

Green Beans with Tiny Potatoes and Coriander Vinaigrette

Fresh coriander gives an elegant spin to ordinary beans and potatoes.

~~~~~~~

1/2 pound slender green beans, steamed until tender

1/2 pound tiny new potatoes, halved or quartered (to 1-inch pieces) and steamed until tender

1 shallot, thinly sliced and separated into rings

1 tablespoon cider vinegar

2 teaspoons olive oil

Pinch of dry mustard

Pinch of cayenne

2 tablespoons minced fresh coriander leaves

Freshly ground black pepper

COMBINE the beans, potatoes, and shallot in a medium bowl.

IN a small bowl, whisk together the vinegar, oil, mustard, cayenne, coriander, and black pepper to taste. Pour over the beans and potatoes and toss well to combine. Serve warm or at room temperature as a light lunch, appetizer, or salad.

MAKES 4 SERVINGS; 115 CALORIES PER SERVING, 2.3 GRAMS FAT, 16 PERCENT OF CALORIES FROM FAT.

dill

bone up on calcium

~

HELP

PREVENT

OSTEOPOROSIS

~

BEAUTIFY

HANDS

AND NAILS

~

COOK

WITH A

VERSATILE

HERB

~

I was ten when I first felt the urge to grow things, but since I lived in a high-rise apartment, I had to wait nearly twenty years to start my first real garden. I began with sprigs of herbs that were the gift of an elderly neighbor—mint, tarragon, and dill. Within two months the dill fulfilled my agricultural dreams by bursting forth with its parasol-shaped blooms. Not long afterward, new dill plants began to sprout up all over.

By the following June my dill had filled a fifty-foot bed, hopped across the yard to colonize my hostas, and had even begun to peek through the spaces between the bricks on the patio. But I couldn't cut it back: It was the fruit of my first garden, after all. I just sat back and admired its wild, weedy tenacity.

Lore and Legend

The early Greeks and Romans liked to grow dill too. They hung bunches of the herb in their homes to freshen stale air and burned the seeds as incense. In the Middle Ages, witches used dill in magical spells to stave off storms. Astrological herbalists of the seventeenth century claimed that dill was ruled by the planet Mercury, imparting strong intellectual powers to anyone who consumed it.

The early colonists of the United States called dill "meetin' seed," because it was chewed for refreshment during long church meetings. But the name comes from a Norse word meaning "to lull," since a tea of dillseed was used to induce sleep.

Healing

Tea made from dillseed is recommended by modern herbalists to relax and settle cranky stomachs. In India this brew, which is a popular children's colic remedy, is bottled and called "gripe water." Russians call it plain old dill water and dole it out to relieve the pangs of overeating. Both gripe water and dill water are available at health food stores, herb shops, and some pharmacies.

Dillseeds also contribute calcium to the diet. One tablespoon contains 100 milligrams of calcium. For comparison, that's more than the amount of calcium available in a third of a cup of skim milk. Health professionals typically recommend calcium to help prevent endometrial cancer, colon cancer, loss of bone mass, muscle stress, and high blood pressure. Since most Americans don't get nearly enough calcium, and much of what they do get comes from high-fat dairy sources, adding dillseed to the diet can be a health plus. For people who have difficulty digesting dairy, dillseed is a must. The best way to make high-calcium dill tea is to steep a tablespoon of dillseed in a cup of boiling water, covered, for four minutes. Drink the tea, then chew and swallow the seeds. The tea's taste is an aromatic combination of caraway and fennel, and it can be used as a tasty and quick vegetarian stock for soups.

High-Calcium Herbs at a Glance

HERB	MG./TBS.
Allspice	40
Anise seed	43
Basil	95
Caraway seed	46
Celery seed	115
Cinnamon	84
Cloves	43
Cumin seed	56
Dillseed	100
Dill weed	55
Fennel seed	69
Mustard seed	58
Poppy seed	127
Rosemary	42
Savory	94
Tarragon	55
Thyme	81

The Recommended Daily Allowance of Calcium for both sexes over the age of 24 is 800 mg. For both sexes ages 11 to 24, as well as pregnant and nursing women, the RDA is 1200 milligrams. These recommendations are set by the National Research Council's Food and Nutrition Board. The information in this chart is from the U.S. Department of Agriculture, *Agricultural Handbook* No. 8–2, January 1977. All amounts are for dried herbs.

Looking Your Best

Dillseed oil is an old-fashioned preventive and cure for chapped hands and split nails. To make the oil, heat half a cup of olive oil, grapeseed oil, or canola oil in a small saucepan over medium heat until just warm. Then pour into a bottle to which you've added two tablespoons of dillseed. Also add a teaspoon of wheat germ oil, which is a natural preservative. Cover and let the oil steep in a cool, dark place for one week; then strain. To use the oil, rub into your hands, cuticles, and nails while they are still damp from washing. Use the oil on your feet too.

Growing

Yellow-green ferny-looking dill is a native of the Mediterranean and southern Russia but it can make itself at home anywhere. Some varieties can grow to be two feet tall, which makes them a good backdrop to shorter herbs such as parsley. Alternatively, you can pick up one of the "featherleaf" varieties, which grow no more than a foot tall. As the name implies, their leaves are more feathery than those of their taller cousins.

Once you've decided which dill to grow, find a space in the garden that gets at least six hours of sun a day. Dill grows happily in the standard herb mixture of two parts garden soil or potting soil, two parts peat, one part sand, and one part composted cow manure or compost. Dig a hole for the dill that's twice the size of the herb's root ball, then set the herb in the hole. Fill in with the surrounding soil, and tamp it down. Soak with warm water; then, unless you have a drought, let nature do the watering. Dill spreads out, so plant it about two feet away from other plants. If you don't want dill to take over your garden, cut it back before the flowers drop their seeds.

Dill is just as happy to grow indoors as out, as long as it gets at least six hours of sun a day. You can augment the sunlight with ninety-watt halogen floods, which can be left on up to twelve hours a day. About every five days stick your finger in the soil, and if it's dry, water the dill. The best dill for cooking is fresh, so if you like to cook with it, make a point to grow it.

Cooking

Dill leaves combine well with many foods because they contain just two volatile flavor oils. (By contrast, other herbs, such as rosemary, may contain five or more.) These two oils have the familiar tastes of celery and lemon, which are light enough to harmonize with, rather than overwhelm, delicate foods. Dill is a natural with fish and chicken, as well as in creamy sauces, soups, and salad dressings. Start out by using two teaspoons of fresh dill in a dish to serve four. For the finest flavor, snip dill with sharp kitchen shears, because mincing with a knife rips and smashes the leaves, wasting those flavorful volatile oils.

Chapati Perfumed with Dill

Chapati is a popular flatbread in India, where it's enjoyed as a snack with tea or used as an edible scoop for various curries. It's great with soups, stews, and chilies.

1 cup unbleached all-purpose flour

1/2 cup whole wheat bread flour, plus extra for rolling

1/2 cup yellow cornmeal

2 teaspoons dillseed, lightly crushed in a mortar

3/4 to 1 cup room-temperature water

1 tablespoon sweet (unsalted) butter, melted

1/2 teaspoon minced fresh dill

IN a medium bowl, combine the flours, cornmeal, and dillseed. Use a rubber spatula to mix well. Slowly add the water, mixing as you go, until you have a ball of dough. Depending on the temperature, age of the flour, and humidity of the day, you may need from 3/4 cup to 1 cup. (If you discover you've added too much water, toss in some extra flour to compensate.)

WITH floured hands, divide the dough into pieces the size of a golf ball. Flour a counter and roll each ball out to a 5-inch round.

HEAT a well-seasoned cast-iron skillet over medium-high heat. (If you don't have a cast-iron skillet, use a nonstick sauté pan and increase the cooking time slightly.) Set each round into the hot skillet to bake, shaking the pan to be sure the chapati doesn't stick. If it does, nudge it loose with a spatula. Let each chapati bake until just firm and very lightly dotted with brown, about 1 minute on each side. The bread is ready to flip over when its edges become slightly raised and gentle whiffs of steam sneak out. Continue the routine until all the chapatis are baked.

TO serve, line a basket with a cotton or linen napkin and arrange the chapatis inside. In a small bowl, combine the butter and dill, then drizzle over the warm chapati. They're best served at once but will keep, napkin-wrapped, for about 8 hours.

MAKES 8 CHAPATI; 120 CALORIES PER CHAPATI, 1 GRAM FAT, 8 PERCENT OF CALORIES FROM FAT.

Four-Grain Bread with Garlic and Dill

Garlic, dill, and olive oil give the whole grains in this bread a rich taste.

~~~~~~

2½ cups tepid water (110° to 115°F)

2 tablespoons barley malt or honey

2 tablespoons active dry yeast

2 tablespoons olive oil

1 cup flaked rye (see Note)

1 cup flaked wheat (see Note)

¾ cup oat bran

¼ cup yellow cornmeal

2 teaspoons minced dried dill

1 tablespoon minced garlic

2 to 2½ cups unbleached all-purpose flour

2 cups whole wheat bread flour

POUR the water into a large bowl and stir in the barley malt and yeast. When the yeast has dissolved, stir in the oil. Add the rye and wheat flakes, oat bran, cornmeal, dill, and garlic and stir until blended. Gradually add the flours, ½ cup at a time, until the dough comes together into a ball and can be kneaded. It will feel a bit sticky; that's okay.

TIP the dough onto a floured counter and knead until smooth and elastic, about 8 minutes. Spray a large bowl with nonstick cooking spray and set in the dough. Turn the dough to coat it. Cover with plastic wrap and let rise in a warm place until doubled in size, about 45 minutes.

PUNCH the dough down and cut it in half. Set the dough into two 9- by 5-inch loaf pans sprayed with nonstick cooking spray. Cover the pans with plastic wrap and let the dough rise again for about 30 minutes.

PREHEAT the oven to 375°F.

SPRAY each loaf with water from a plant mister to ensure a crisp crust. Bake in the middle of the oven until cooked through, about 45 minutes, spraying again midway through baking. Remove the loaves from the pans and let them cool on wire racks before slicing and serving.

MAKES 2 LOAVES, 8 SLICES EACH; 160 CALORIES PER SLICE, 2.5 GRAMS FAT, 15 PERCENT OF CALORIES FROM FAT.

NOTE: Flaked rye and wheat are whole grains that have been flattened for quick cooking. They're available at health food stores and some supermarkets. Don't confuse them with cold cereal flakes.

Dill and Smoked Salmon Cheese

This is the perfect spread to prepare and stash in the refrigerator to use on weekends and holidays. Try it on crusty bread, topped with watercress, or piped onto zucchini or yellow squash rounds and garnished with dill sprigs, tossed with cooked pasta (about a quarter cup to one cup of pasta), or plopped onto split baked potatoes.

~~~~~

1/2 cup part-skim ricotta cheese

4 ounces low-fat cream cheese

2 tablespoons finely minced smoked salmon

2 tablespoons minced fresh dill

1 small tomato, cored and chopped (about 1/4 cup)

2 tablespoons finely minced red onion

1 teaspoon Dijon mustard

Splash of Worcestershire sauce

COMBINE all the ingredients in a food processor or blender and whiz until smooth. Covered and refrigerated, this keeps for up to 3 days, but bring to room temperature before serving for tastiest results.

MAKES 1 1/4 CUPS; 175 CALORIES PER 1/4-CUP SERVING, 4.6 GRAMS FAT, 24 PERCENT OF CALORIES FROM FAT.

Variation: For a non-dairy "cheese," substitute 3/4 cup blanched tofu for the ricotta and cream cheese.

Dill Crisps

Dill and Locatelli cheese make these crisps an elegant addition to your hors d'oeuvres tray. Serve with smoked mussels or salmon or as an accompaniment to roasted peppers.

~~~~~

2 whole wheat pitas
2 tablespoons olive oil
2 teaspoons minced fresh dill

1 tablespoon freshly grated Locatelli cheese or soy Parmesan

PREHEAT the oven to 400°F.

USE kitchen shears to slice each pita into 8 triangular wedges. Separate each triangle into two at the seam. Set the triangles, crumbly side up, on a slotted broiler rack.

IN a small dish, combine the olive oil, dill, and Locatelli. Use a pastry brush to paint the mixture lightly onto the triangles. Bake in the center of the oven until just brown at the edges and slightly curled, about 5 to 7 minutes. Serve warm or at room temperature.

MAKES 32 TOASTS; 12 CALORIES PER TOAST, TRACE OF FAT.

White Bean Salad with Lemon and Dill

Dill is a natural with lemon and garlic.

~~~~~

2   cups cooked white beans (if using canned beans, rinse, drain, and pat dry)

1   cup cooked tiny pasta, such as orzo, elbow macaroni, or ditalini (from about 2 ounces dried)

1/3 cup finely minced celery

1/3 cup finely minced red bell pepper

3   scallions, finely minced

Juice of 1/2 lemon

1   teaspoon olive oil

1   clove garlic, very finely minced

1   teaspoon minced fresh dill

Curly red lettuce or purple perilla for serving

COMBINE the beans, pasta, celery, bell pepper, and scallions in a large bowl.

IN a small bowl, whisk together the lemon juice, olive oil, garlic, and dill. Pour over the bean mixture and toss well to combine. Serve at room temperature or very slightly chilled on a nest of red lettuce for lunch or a light dinner.

MAKES 4 SERVINGS; 175 CALORIES PER SERVING, 2 GRAMS FAT, 11 PERCENT OF CALORIES FROM FAT.

Curried Cracked Wheat with Dill and Toasted Pistachios

Dill lightens and enlivens the flavor of whole wheat.

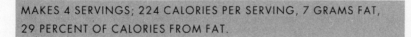

1	cup cracked wheat	1	teaspoon curry powder
1½	cups vegetable stock or defatted chicken stock	2	tablespoons pistachios, chopped
1	clove garlic, mashed through a press	1	teaspoon minced fresh dill or ½ teaspoon dried
2	teaspoons olive oil		

COMBINE the cracked wheat, stock, garlic, oil, and curry powder in a small saucepan and bring to a boil. Cover loosely, reduce the heat to medium, and simmer until the wheat is tender, about 5 minutes. If there's any liquid remaining, drain it away.

MEANWHILE, in a small dry sauté pan, toast the chopped pistachios over medium-high heat until fragrant and golden-brown, about 2 minutes. Stir constantly to prevent burning.

WHEN the cracked wheat is ready, swirl in the nuts and dill. Serve warm as a side dish or on a nest of greens for lunch. Blanched sugar snap peas or snow peas make nice garnishes.

MAKES 4 SERVINGS; 224 CALORIES PER SERVING, 7 GRAMS FAT, 29 PERCENT OF CALORIES FROM FAT.

Broccoli and Potatoes with Dill

Dill, scallions, capers, and lemon can give ordinary vegetables a lift.

~~~~~~

2	medium red potatoes (about 1 pound), cut into 1-inch chunks	2	teaspoons capers, minced
	Handful of fresh dill sprigs	3	tablespoons fresh lemon juice
1/2	pound broccoli florets (about 1 1/4 cups)	1	tablespoon olive oil
3	scallions, minced	1	teaspoon minced fresh dill or 1/2 teaspoon dried
			Freshly ground black pepper

STEAM the potatoes, covered, over boiling water to which you've added the handful of dill for about 5 minutes. Add the broccoli and continue steaming until the vegetables are tender, about 5 minutes more.

TIP the potatoes and broccoli into a large serving bowl and add the scallions, capers, lemon juice, olive oil, dill, and pepper to taste. Toss well. Serve warm as a side dish or very slightly chilled as a salad. Or use as a filling for crêpes or omelettes.

MAKES 4 SERVINGS; 187 CALORIES PER SERVING, 3.5 GRAMS FAT, 17 PERCENT OF CALORIES FROM FAT.

echinacea

~~~~~~~~~~~~~~~~~~~~~~~~~~~~~~

the bodyguard herb

~

FIGHT OFF

COLDS

AND FLU

~

HEAL

MINOR CUTS

AND

SCRATCHES

~

GIVE YOUR

IMMUNE

SYSTEM

A SHOT IN

THE ARM

~

I first came across echinacea at a small herb shop in London near the British Museum. I was jet-lagged, the weather was cold and wet, and there was a nasty flu going around that I wanted to avoid. To boost my immune system, the shop's herbalist recommended echinacea tincture taken in water twice a day. Jet lag aside, I felt great for the entire week's stay and never did come down with the flu.

Lore and Legend

Though echinacea is a popular cure in Europe, the plant is a native of North America, growing wild in the Plains States and the South. The Plains Indians boiled echinacea root in water, then used it as a foot bath to enable them to walk across hot coals during spiritual and purification ceremonies.

Echinacea root was also used in Indian sweat lodge ceremonies. To make a sweat lodge, animal skins and wood planks were fashioned into a tent, with a fire pit dug in the middle. When the firewood in the pit burned to embers, people entered to sweat out both physical and mental impurities. Water was poured on the coals to make steam, and frequently echinacea root was added to the water for extra purification.

Healing

Echinacea's healing properties are so valued in Germany that it has been approved by Kommission E, the equivalent of our FDA, and the costs of prescriptions are reimbursed by insurance companies. It's used to stimulate the immune system, to treat infections, and to help purify the lymphatic system. In the United States, herbal treatments are less conventional, but current scientific research is confirming echinacea's effectiveness. One of its compounds, echinsin, has been shown to be an antiviral agent that behaves in a similar way to the body's own interferon. Another compound, echinacoside, has antibiotic properties, as such North American tribes as the Winnebago, Teton Sioux, and Choctow knew centuries ago. They used echinacea topically for wound healing, a practice that American settlers picked up and used until the invention of sulfur drugs in the 1920s.

To treat minor cuts and scratches, simply mix echinacea tincture drop for drop with pure castor oil and apply to the wound. The mixture can be used on adults and children, and even dogs and cats. The straight tincture can be applied directly to insect bites to soothe itching and dotted on facial blemishes to help them heal. Many herbalists also recommend taking echinacea tincture internally to help banish skin eruptions. The normal dosage for adults is twenty-five drops in water or tea twice a day for one to two weeks. Other herbs, such as burdock, red clover, and yellow dock, are often added to suit each individual's condition, so be sure to check in with a health professional about the treatment that's right for you.

The form of echinacea easiest to use is its tincture, which can be purchased in health food stores and herb shops. But before you buy, ask how the tincture was obtained. Some companies sell false echinacea that comes from a type of chrysanthemum and lacks the true herb's healing properties. To test it, put a drop of the tincture right on your tongue. If it tingles and feels very slightly numb, it's probably echinacea tincture. Another reason to be careful about what you buy is that wild echinacea is an endangered plant. What you want is a tincture made from cultivated echinacea, grown without chemicals.

Of course, another option is to make your own tincture. It was long thought that the only part of the plant worth extracting was the root, but Michael Moore, a New Mexican herbalist, holds that echinacea's flower heads also contain health-giving compounds. Begin by gathering enough flower tops to fill a widemouthed jar. (You can save flowers, covered and refrigerated, for up to two weeks, until you have enough.) Use kitchen shears to quarter the flower heads, then pack them into the jar. Pour on cider vinegar to cover, seal the jar, and leave it on a sunny windowsill for two weeks, shaking the jar daily. Then strain and discard the flower tops, bottle the tincture, and store it in the refrigerator.

To fight off colds and flu, some scientists suggest taking echinacea as soon as an outbreak hits your area. About twenty-five to thirty drops of extract taken in water or tea twice a day is the normal dose for adults, but consult with a health professional to be sure about your personal dosage. If a cold or the flu has already set in, echinacea will help alleviate symptoms, but will not be as effective as if you had taken it earlier. Roy Upton, an herbalist, lecturer, and executive with the American Herbalists Guild, suggests augmenting the echinacea with hot lemon tea to help sweat out the symptoms. To try it, simply squeeze the juice of a whole lemon right into a cup, pour on one cup of hot water, and add about twenty-five drops of echinacea tincture. Drink a cup three times a day.

Growing

Another name for echinacea is "purple cone flower," because most varieties have pale purple petals. In fact, they look like huge, slightly droopy purple daisies. The plants can grow to two feet tall, so plant them behind shorter herbs—purple sage, for instance.

Buy small echinacea plants and find a place for them in the garden that gets at least six hours of sun a day. Echinacea is happy with the standard herb mixture of two parts garden or potting soil, two parts peat, one part sand, and one part compost or composted cow manure. Dig a hole that's twice the size of each plant's root ball and set it in. Fill the hole in with the surrounding soil and tamp it down. Soak with warm water. Then, unless you have a drought, let nature do the watering.

Two challenges face an echinacea gardener. First, echinacea hates being moved, so you must plant it where you really want it. Second, chipmunks and other garden visitors love to dig up echinacea roots, particularly around the time of a full moon when the weather is hotter than normal. To discourage diggers, strew fresh branches of the herb southernwood all around the base of your echinacea plants. Stamp the southernwood into the ground with your foot as hard as you can to release its aromas, and the chipmunks should stay away. If by chance they don't, at least you'll know the neighborhood rodents are cold- and flu-free.

evening primrose

recipe for beautiful skin

SOOTHE

PMS AND

MENOPAUSE

SYMPTOMS

~

HELP

PREVENT

HIGH BLOOD

PRESSURE

~

SMOOTH

AND SOFTEN

DRY SKIN

~

At the first tinge of menopause, I decided to take an herbal approach to help prevent the symptoms that come with "the change." To fend off hot flashes, dry skin, irritability, hormone-induced headaches, digestive distress, heart disease from high blood cholesterol levels, stress, fatigue, and irregular hormone production, I chose evening primrose, occasionally in combination with such herbs as black cohosh, dong quai, and ginseng. And despite a sometimes stressful life, my hormones seem to have remained on an even keel. A diet free from caffeine, refined sugar, saturated fats, and dairy products, as well as regular exercise, also contributes to an almost symptom-free menopause, but I think it's my evening primrose that really makes a difference.

Lore and Legend

Evening primrose is a traditional North American Indian medicine. Too-chubby Cherokee drank a tea of the herb to help them lose weight. Iroquois and Ojibwa tribes used mashed evening primrose, applied topically, to heal skin irritations. These same applications for evening primrose are just two of the incredible array being investigated by scientists today.

Healing

Evening primrose has recently been the subject of dozens of health-related studies that indicate it may be helpful in preventing a huge range of health troubles, including high blood cholesterol levels, high blood pressure, stroke, rheumatoid arthritis, obesity, dry skin, allergies, symptoms associated with premenstrual syndrome, symptoms associated with menopause, and even cancer. Scientists think that the compound that confers all the benefits is gamma-linolenic acid (GLA). GLA is an essential fatty acid, similar to the beneficial one found in fish oil (Omega-3), which the human body needs but does not produce. GLA is found in evening primrose oil, made from the seeds of the herb, and capsules containing the oil are available in health food stores and pharmacies.

Medicinal doses of evening primrose range from 500 to 1500 milligrams a day. But since many of the conditions that evening primrose can help are serious, consult a health professional to find out what dosage is right for you and if, in fact, you can take evening primrose. Women with breast cancer, for example, should not take evening primrose because of the phyto-estrols it contains.

Even if the exciting health promises of evening primrose are fulfilled, it is not a substitute for wholesome habits. Research has shown that alcohol consumption or a diet high in saturated fat will prevent GLA from doing its job.

Looking Your Best

Some people report great success in preventing dry skin, especially the kind that comes with middle age, by taking evening primrose capsules. An average dose is 250 milligrams up to three times a day, but check with a health professional for your personal dosage. One skin expert says that, along with evening primrose, avoiding prolonged sun exposure, alcohol, caffeine, and refined sugar helps keep the skin soft.

Growing

As its name suggests, evening primrose is a magical creature of the night. While other herbs are fast asleep, evening primrose comes alive to literally glow in the dark. The reason is that its yellow flower petals store sunlight while they're closed during the daytime. Then, at night, the petals burst open and glisten with the stored light.

Since evening primrose flowers all summer long, you can enjoy repeat performances of this glimmering herb. Plant it along garden paths to light the way, or use it in a moon garden with silvery-leafed herbs that reflect the lights of night.

Evening primrose is a native American herb, so it's quite easy to grow in the United States. It likes the standard herb mix of two parts garden or potting soil, two parts peat, one part sand, and one part compost or composted cow manure. To keep it glowing, give it a place with a full six hours of daytime sun. Buy organically grown small plants. Dig holes for them that are twice the size of the root balls, set the plants in the holes, fill in with the surrounding soil, and tamp it down. Soak with warm water; then, unless you have a drought, let nature do the watering.

fennel

~~~~~~

the gas guzzler

*T*he Middle East is home to *Unani,* a type of herbalism based on an ancient Greek medical system. Unani herbalists believe that liquids in the body, such as blood and bile, are directly related to such elements in nature as earth and air and so can be unbalanced by heat, dryness, or other kinds of weather. When there is an imbalance, headaches, colds and flu, or gastric distress may ensue. Unani herbalists, usually family elders, prescribe various herbs to treat these conditions, and also to get rid of *djinn,* or evil spirits, which are a metaphor for health-impairing negative emotions.

For instance, when a patient is nervous, an Unani herbalist may call it a "cold, windy" condition. The remedy, then, would be a tea made from "warming" fennel, an herb no Unani household is without.

~

CALM

THE

INTESTINES

~

CLEAR A

STUFFY

NOSE

~

MAKE

MORE

MOTHER'S

MILK

~

Lore and Legend

Some historians believe that fennel's warming properties won the herb the Greek name of *marathron*, meaning "to be thin." The seeds were believed to "warm up" the metabolism, thus acting as a weight-loss aid.

Other historians contend that the Greeks named fennel *marathon*, after a village twenty-five miles from Athens where the herb grew abundantly. In 490 B.C., when the Greeks defeated the Persian army, a runner from Marathon brought the news to Athens. To celebrate his feat, his hometown's name has become the label for a twenty-six-mile endurance race.

Healing

Digestive-soothing fennel seed can be a real boon for those trying to add fiber to their diets. Whole grains, dried beans, and fresh vegetables will enhance your health, but they can produce intestinal gas. There are three steps to take to ensure socially acceptable intestines: First, increase your fiber consumption slowly; the worst thing you can do is make a pot of lentil chili and eat it for four days in a row. Next, drink eight to ten eight-ounce glasses of non-iced water a day. And finally, keep a supply of fennel seed on hand.

Fennel seed is unparalleled at relieving intestinal gas. Try making a tea using two teaspoons of lightly crushed fennel seed steeped, covered, in one cup of hot water for ten minutes, then strained. (Though the brew is effective, it's gentle enough for children.) In a pinch, you can toss a teaspoon of fennel seeds right into your mouth, chew them until completely pulverized, and swallow them. This habit is popular in India, where fennel seed is called *mukhwas* and is served after meals to soothe digestion and freshen the breath.

In Jamaica, herbalists harness fennel seed's clean, warming aroma to soothe symptoms of head colds. Sipped hot, fennel seed tea temporarily relieves respiratory congestion.

European herbalists rely on fennel seed tea as a galactagogue, a substance containing volatile oils that help nursing mothers produce milk. Normally, one cup of tea is taken three times a day.

Growing

The best way to get a quantity of fennel seeds is simply to buy organically grown ones. The plant itself is easy to cultivate but doesn't produce enough seeds for frequent use. Fennel is worth growing for its handsome feathery leaves, which may be either green or purple-bronze. Growing up to three feet tall, it's an attractive backdrop for shorter yellow-flowering herbs such as feverfew and santolina.

To raise fennel, buy small organically grown plants. Since fennel is a Mediterranean native, it likes full sun, so find a place in the garden that gets at least six hours a day. Fennel likes a rich soil, so use a variation of the standard herb mix combining two parts garden or potting soil, two parts peat, two parts compost or composted cow manure, and one part sand. Dig a hole that's twice the size of each herb's root ball and set the fennel in the hole. Fill in the hole with the surrounding soil and tamp it down. Soak with warm water. Then, once a week, stick your finger in the soil; if it's dry, water the fennel.

As a bonus, fennel plants often attract a huge black and chartreuse-striped caterpillar, which eventually grows up to be the gorgeous anise swallowtail butterfly. Its three- to four-inch wing spread patterned in lemon, orange, blue, black, and white makes it a welcome guest in any garden.

Indoors, plant fennel in a pot that's about eight inches deep and wide and give it at least six hours of sun a day. To augment the light, use a ninety-watt halogen flood, placed about three feet away from the fennel. Though fennel tends to grow spindly and tall, keeping it clipped to one foot will produce thick, robust leaves.

Cooking

Fennel seed has a pleasant, earthy taste, combining the flavors of licorice, lemon, and pine, that makes it a classic complement to fish (especially fatty ones) and duck. A staple in Indian curry blends, it can also animate such bland foods as potatoes and breads. For a change of pace, substitute fennel seed for dill seed or caraway seed in recipes for potato soups and salads, rye bread, or Irish soda bread. A good rule of thumb is to add a tablespoon of seeds for every four servings of soup or salad or for the dough for one loaf of bread.

Fennel leaves, which taste like a slightly bitter version of the seeds, can be minced and added to a creamy dressing for fish salads or to creamy fish soups. Use a teaspoon of very finely minced leaf to a quantity that serves four.

If you like the taste of fennel seed, you might want to try finocchio (also called sweet fennel or simply "fennel"), a variety of the herb that produces a large edible bulb. It has the texture of celery with the taste of fennel seed and can be minced and added raw to fish sautés and salads. Or, it can be served on its own as a side dish, sliced and sautéed with garlic in olive oil. A large bulb serves four.

Granola with Fennel and Pecans

Here's an unusual, healthy breakfast cereal with a hint of the sweetness of licorice.

~~~~~

3 cups rolled oats	2 tablespoons fennel seed, crushed in a mortar or spice grinder
3/4 cup sunflower seeds	
3/4 cup pumpkin seeds	
3/4 cup wheat bran	1/4 cup canola oil
3/4 cup oat bran	1/2 cup brown rice syrup
1 1/2 cups chopped pecans	1 cup dried cherries or blueberries

PREHEAT the oven to 300°F.

IN a large bowl, combine the oats, sunflower seeds, pumpkin seeds, wheat bran, oat bran, pecans, and fennel seed.

COMBINE the oil and syrup in a small saucepan and heat over medium heat until the mixture is warm and thin, about 2 1/2 minutes. Pour the syrup onto the oat mixture. Use a metal spoon to mix well (the granola will stick to wood), making sure all the ingredients are lightly coated with the syrup.

SCOOP the granola onto two large baking sheets with sides. Set the trays in the oven and bake until golden brown, about 25 to 30 minutes, stirring every 10 minutes or so. (The granola in the bottom pan will probably bake faster, so switch locations if it looks as if it might burn.) The pumpkin seeds may pop, but that's okay.

LET the granola cool, then stir in the cherries. Store the cereal in tightly covered glass jars. Serve it for breakfast with milk or add it to muffin and pancake batters.

MAKES 8 CUPS, OR 16 SERVINGS; 270 CALORIES PER SERVING, 5 GRAMS FAT, 17 PERCENT OF CALORIES FROM FAT.

"Bouillabaisse" Salad

Aromatic fennel, combined with saffron, celery seed, and hot pepper, makes this fish salad satisfying and filling with minimal fat.

~~~~~

1 pound large shrimp, shelled and deveined	1/2 teaspoon saffron threads
1/2 pound sea scallops	1/2 teaspoon fennel seed
1/2 pound firm-fleshed fish, such as shark or swordfish, cut into chunks	1/2 teaspoon celery seed
	1/2 teaspoon dried hot red pepper flakes, or to taste
1 orange, cut into slices	1 tablespoon tomato sauce
2 teaspoons olive oil	1/4 cup dry white wine
2 cloves garlic, minced	1 tablespoon fresh lemon juice
1 onion, peeled and chopped	1/4 cup minced fresh parsley
1 leek, topped, tailed, rinsed, and chopped	Freshly ground black pepper

STEAM the shrimp, scallops, and fish over boiling water to which you've added the orange until cooked through, about 8 to 10 minutes.

MEANWHILE, heat a large sauté pan over medium-high heat and pour in the oil. Sauté the garlic, onion, and leek for about 1 minute. Add the saffron, fennel seed, celery seed, red pepper flakes, tomato sauce, wine, and lemon juice and cook until the mixture is fragrant and the vegetables are limp, about 3 minutes.

SCOOP the onion mixture into a medium bowl. Add the fish, parsley, and black pepper to taste, and toss well. Serve warm with crusty bread or tossed with hot linguine.

MAKES 4 LARGE SERVINGS; 305 CALORIES PER SERVING, 6 GRAMS FAT, 18 PERCENT OF CALORIES FROM FAT.

Shrimp Salad with Fennel, Hot Pepper, and Mango-Lime Dressing

Fennel and hot pepper enrich the tropical flavors of mango and lime.

~~~~~

1 pound large shrimp, peeled and deveined

1 tablespoon vegetable stock or defatted chicken stock

1 teaspoon chili powder

1 teaspoon fennel seed

Splash of hot pepper sauce, or to taste

1 medium tomato, finely chopped

1 cup finely chopped fresh pineapple

1 small red onion, thinly sliced and separated into rings

1 ripe mango

Juice of 1 lime (about ¼ cup)

Curly red lettuce leaves for serving

HEAT a large nonstick sauté pan over medium-high heat. Add the shrimp, stock, chili powder, fennel seed, and hot pepper sauce and cook, stirring, until the shrimp are cooked through and fragrant, about 3 minutes. Remove the pan from the heat and fold in the tomato, pineapple, and onion.

TO make the dressing, peel the mango, working directly over a processor or blender so you don't lose the juices. Then slice the flesh away from the stone into the processor, saving a few good-looking slices for a garnish. Use your hands to wring the juice out of the flesh around the stone. Pour in the lime juice and whiz until smooth.

LINE a pretty platter with lettuce leaves and arrange the shrimp salad on it. Garnish with the reserved mango slices and drizzle the mango dressing over all.

MAKES 4 SERVINGS; 196 CALORIES PER SERVING, 2.5 GRAMS FAT, 12 PERCENT OF CALORIES FROM FAT.

Swordfish with Fennel

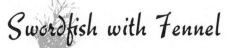

Olive oil, wine, garlic, and fennel are all classic flavorings for fish.

~~~~~~

1 teaspoon olive oil
2 tablespoons dry white wine
1 to 2 cloves garlic, chopped

1 teaspoon fennel seed
1 pound swordfish steak, about 1/2 inch thick

COMBINE the olive oil, wine, garlic, and fennel in a mortar or spice grinder and crush to a coarse paste. Rub the paste all over the fish.

PREHEAT the broiler or prepare the grill.

BROIL or grill the fish until just cooked through, about 3 to 4 minutes on each side. Serve warm with a salad of mustard greens.

MAKES 4 SERVINGS; 170 CALORIES PER SERVING, 4.5 GRAMS FAT, 30 PERCENT OF CALORIES FROM FAT.

Coconut and Fennel Mukhwas

In India, this tasty mixture is munched after spicy meals to refresh the palate and calm the intestines.

~~~~~~

1/4 cup fennel seed

1 tablespoon very finely grated fresh coconut

PREHEAT a cast-iron skillet over medium-high heat. Toss in the fennel seeds and swirl them constantly until lightly toasted, about 2 minutes. Remove the toasted seeds to a little dish, then add the coconut to the skillet and swirl until toasted, about 1 minute. Add the coconut to the fennel. Pass the mukhwas around after a spicy meal so each diner can munch a refreshing spoonful.

MAKES ABOUT 1/4 CUP, OR 12 SERVINGS; ABOUT 9 CALORIES PER SERVING, TRACE OF FAT.

feverfew

~~~~~~

roar and peace

SOOTHE A

MIGRAINE

~

REPEL

INSECTS

IN THE

GARDEN

~

KEEP

BEES

AT BAY

~

"*I* was driving home from work when suddenly my head began to hurt so badly I wanted to bang it on the steering wheel. I had to pull over because of the pain."

"Migraine headaches ruin your life. You can't plan a trip or do anything without worrying about getting one."

That's how two of the twenty-five million migraine sufferers in the United States have described to me what it's like to be a migraine captive. Headache experts say that about one quarter of migraine sufferers gain some relief by modifying their diets, eliminating coffee, aged cheeses, red wines, and foods that contain preservatives. Research also shows that synthetic drugs help lessen the pain and frequency of migraines. One drug's literature claims a 50 percent cure rate, and that's pretty good. But the herb feverfew looks even better.

Lore and Legend

Centuries before scientists began to examine feverfew, herbalists used it to treat headaches. Astrological herbalists in the 1700s dedicated feverfew to the feminine planet Venus, and they used wine steeped with feverfew and ground nutmeg to treat women with tension-induced headaches.

Healing

In the 1980s, after hearing about a coal miner who had cured his migraines with feverfew, a physician at a migraine clinic in England gave ten of his patients the herb. Seven out of the ten sufferers subsequently reported less frequent migraines and less intense pain, as well as reduced nausea and vomiting. Intrigued, the doctor then set up a study for more than two hundred and fifty patients. Half were given feverfew and half were given a placebo. Again, a whopping 70 percent of the feverfew group reported an improvement in relief of their migraines.

Not everyone accepts the results of this study, but most researchers would agree that feverfew bears investigation. At this point, scientists are not even quite sure how feverfew works. One theory is that the herb contains a compound that stops blood vessel spasms from occurring. Since migraines first contract the blood vessels in the head, then wham-bam dilate them, the theory may pan out. Many researchers also agree that feverfew is particularly effective on the type of migraines that can be soothed by heat.

Health professionals usually advise eating one fresh feverfew leaf one to three times daily to help prevent migraines. Some migraine patients report mouth irritations from chewing the leaves, so the equivalent amount of feverfew in capsules is often prescribed. If you're a migraine sufferer and want to try feverfew, consult with a health professional about your personal dosage.

Growing

Whether or not you suffer from migraines, feverfew can be a welcome addition to your garden. For one thing, it contains a compound called pyrethrin that is a natural insect repellent and so can protect culinary herbs such as basil that are susceptible to insect infestation. But keep feverfew away from plants that need pollination, such as fruits, since bees hate the herb and won't come near when it's blooming. If you're a gardener who's allergic to bee stings, plant feverfew all around and you'll have one less headache to worry about.

Feverfew is easy to raise. It grows wild in rocky places, such as cracks in walls, in North and South America and Europe. Find a place in the garden that gets at least six hours of sun a day. Then prepare the standard herb mix of two parts garden or potting soil, two parts peat, one part sand, and one part compost or composted cow manure. Buy small organically grown feverfew plants. To plant, dig a hole twice the size of each root ball and set the herb in. Fill in with the surrounding soil and tamp it down. Soak with warm water; then, unless you have a drought, let nature do the watering. For the best results, grow feverfew outside, not indoors.

garlic

~~~~~~~~~~~~~~~~~~~~~~~~~~~~~~

the health heavyweight

O ne time, when I arrived in San Francisco with a dry, scratchy cough, my Asian taxi driver offered an old family remedy. I followed his instructions, peeling and mincing an entire bulb of garlic into a shallow bowl. I poured on enough honey to cover the garlic, covered the bowl with plastic wrap, and let the mixture marinate overnight. During the night, the garlic released its juices into the honey, making a penetrating syrup. I swallowed a tablespoonful in the morning, then another at noon, and that was the end of my cough.

Lore and Legend

Garlic is celebrated around the world for its strength-giving properties. Ancient Chinese herbalists prescribed it, chewed raw, to ward off colds and coughs. Today, centuries later, it's been reported that Chinese prisoners are required to eat raw garlic every morning to keep

~

PREVENT

AND CURE

INFECTION

~

HELP

PREVENT

CANCER AND

HEART

DISEASE

~

MAKE

LEAN FOODS

TASTE

ROBUST

~

them healthy, energized, and able to work. Vietnamese herbalists, too, believe that raw garlic prevents sickness and fatigue.

Egyptian slaves were fed garlic and onions to give them the vitality needed to build the Pyramids. In fact, in ancient Egypt, garlic was so highly revered that citizens of the time swore their vows not on a holy book but on a bulb of garlic.

In folklore, garlic is thought to ward off vampires and, even more important, the plague. During one period of pestilence, four condemned thieves in Marseilles, France, were assigned to collect infectious dead bodies. They supposedly kept themselves healthy by drinking mashed garlic steeped in vinegar. "Four Thieves Vinegar" remains a popular folk tonic in France today.

Healing

Current research reveals that fresh garlic indeed does contain compounds that can help prevent and cure infection. An average clove of garlic (about the size of an almond) contains substances equivalent to one hundred thousand units of penicillin—about one fifth the average dose—minus penicillin's side effects. If you want to try the garlic treatment to help fend off or treat such infections as cold and flu, check with a health professional about the dosage that's right for you.

Garlic can also help prevent certain types of cancer, including stomach, skin, breast, esophageal, oral, and colon. According to reports from the National Cancer Institute and *The Journal of Interferon Research,* compounds in garlic help to stimulate the immune system, increase the body's ability to produce cancer-fighting interferon, and reduce the body's stress from pollution. Garlic also contains germanium, a mineral that can help prevent cancer cells from reproducing. Though ingesting garlic is not an ironclad guarantee that you'll never get cancer, it can't hurt.

Heart health is another area in which garlic gets high marks. Garlic can help lower high blood pressure as well as help reduce high levels of blood cholesterol. Experts caution that you must eat one to three fresh cloves of garlic a day for at least three months before any positive effects show up. If you're interested, consult with a health professional, who should also advise you to adopt a heart-healthy diet and an exercise routine along with the garlic treatment.

Garlic even holds good news for diabetics: It can help regulate blood sugar levels. Though not a substitute for insulin, a clove or two of garlic each day can be a good supplement to standard therapy—with a health professional's approval, of course.

There's one drawback to this amazing bulb: You have to eat it raw for its health benefits, since it's suspected that heat may destroy some of the health-giving compounds. But raw garlic may be hard to swallow if you're not used to it. To lessen its assault on your taste buds, try to keep your tongue out of the way while you're chewing, or chase the garlic with peppermint tea, a slice of whole wheat bread, or a spoonful of fennel seeds (chew them well). If you find the garlic gives you gastric distress, eat raw garlic just before a meal and never let it sit on an empty stomach.

Some people experience a slight lack of concentration or spaced-out feeling after eating raw garlic. That may be why Ayurvedic East Indian herbalists feel that eating raw garlic can be *rajas,* or limiting to spiritual growth. If you're a yogi or Buddhist monk, or are studying for a calculus exam, be forewarned.

As for the inevitable "garlic breath," you can chew a sprig of fresh tarragon to temporarily relieve it, but the scent will be present in your sweat for hours. Some people with sensitive noses prefer to get the health benefits by taking what's called "odorless garlic" in capsules, available in health food stores, pharmacies, and many supermarkets.

Growing

Though fresh garlic is available at every corner market, you may want to grow your own for the fun of it. Wait until fall, then grab a whole bulb of organically grown garlic and break it into separate cloves. Find a place in the garden that gets at least six hours of sun a day. Prepare the standard herb mixture of two parts garden or potting soil, two parts peat, one part sand, and one part composted cow manure or compost. Plant the garlic cloves four inches apart and about two inches deep. Sprinkle some sand and a pinch of dried kelp in with each clove before covering with soil and tamping it down. Soak with warm water; then, unless you have a drought, let nature do the watering.

The following summer, cut off the stalks so all the plant's energy will go into making the tasty bulbs. (You can mince the stalks and use them like chives.) When fall comes, dig out the garlic bulbs, let them relax in the shade for a couple of days, then enjoy. Fall to fall may sound like a long time to wait, but the delicious homegrown garlic will reward your patience.

Garlic is also useful in the garden, as an intensely aromatic spray that keeps predator bugs from eating other herbs. To make it, soak one-quarter cup minced or mashed garlic in a quart of water overnight, and strain. This spray is particularly effective against whitefly, so use it to protect such vulnerable herbs as bay and lemon verbena. Spray the herbs two days in a row, wait two weeks, and then spray two days in a row again.

Cooking

Although it's true that cooked garlic is somewhat less curative than fresh, once garlic moves from medicine chest to kitchen, new doors open. Its mellow-rich onion taste can uplift virtually any main dish, providing a satisfying robustness that can obviate the need for saturated fats. Try it in soups, casseroles, stir-fries, sauces, and savory breads. If you're a novice, use one or two cloves for a recipe that feeds four people. Devotees will want to add much more.

There are two secrets to success in cooking with garlic. First, don't burn it, or it will taste strong and acrid. Let your nose be your guide: The minute you begin to smell a change in aroma, lower the heat or remove the pan from the heat. Second, for the best flavor, always use fresh garlic, staying away from garlic powders and salts. They are pale shadows of the real thing.

To keep garlic fresh and flavorful, keep whole bulbs in a cool, dry, airy place, perhaps in an open basket on a counter. Never store it in the refrigerator. Discard any smashed or bruised cloves or bulbs, because they'll encourage the others to rot.

Sambal
Vietnamese Chili Paste with Garlic

Swirl this fiery condiment into vegetable soups, fish soups, or bean stews. Use it to spice up homemade mayonnaise or creamy dips and spreads. This is hot stuff, so start out with one-eighth teaspoon of sambal for each one and a half cups of soup, and squeeze in the juice from a wedge of lime for balance.

~~~~~

1/2 cup fresh hot red chilies (scant 2 ounces)	1/4 cup defatted chicken stock or vegetable stock
5 cloves garlic, mashed through a press	3 tablespoons rice vinegar
	2 tablespoons peanut oil

COMBINE the chilies, garlic, and stock in a small saucepan and bring to a boil. Be careful not to put your face right over the pan, as the fumes will make your eyes burn. Reduce the heat to low, cover loosely, and let simmer until the chilies are tender, about 10 minutes. Remove the pan from the heat and let the mixture sit for 10 minutes.

POUR the mixture into a processor or blender, and add the vinegar and oil. Whiz until smooth. This can be stored for up to a year, covered and refrigerated.

MAKES ⅔ CUP; ABOUT 2 CALORIES PER ⅛-TEASPOON SERVING, TRACE OF FAT.

Frizzled Brussels Sprouts

In this dish sautéed garlic enlivens a cabbage cousin. These sprouts are especially nice with duck.

~~~~~~~

1 pound medium Brussels sprouts	2 teaspoons olive oil
4 large fresh shiitake mushrooms	2 cloves garlic, mashed through a press

USE a sharp paring knife to slice the stem ends off the sprouts. Remove and discard the shiitake stems. Put the sprouts and mushrooms into a steamer basket over boiling water, cover, and steam until the sprouts are just tender, about 12 minutes. Remove from the heat. Use tongs to remove the shiitakes from the steamer basket, and slice them into ribbons.

HEAT a large sauté pan over medium-high heat. Add the oil and swirl it around so it covers the bottom of the pan. Add the garlic and sauté for about a minute, until it is fragrant and softened. Add the sprouts and sliced shiitakes and sizzle until fragrant and the sprouts are just barely tinged with lightly browned garlic, about 2 minutes. Serve warm.

MAKES 4 SERVINGS; 70 CALORIES PER SERVING, 3 GRAMS FAT, 25 PERCENT OF CALORIES FROM FAT.

Talas
Turkish Vegetable-Stuffed Pastry

Talas (pronounced tuh-LAASH) is a savory Turkish pastry filled with vegetables, garlic, and cheese. It's quite appropriate to eat a talas while learning about garlic, since the Turks were responsible for bringing the plant to Europe. In 1683, Turkish troops were camped outside of Vienna, Austria, planning to storm the town. When forced by another army to head for the hills, they left both coffee and garlic behind. That's how the charming Viennese coffee shops came to be, and that's why garlic plays a big part in Viennese cooking.

~~~~

FOR THE PASTRY:

3/4 cup whole wheat pastry flour

2 cups unbleached all-purpose flour, plus extra for rolling

1/4 cup olive oil

1/4 cup plain nonfat yogurt or soy yogurt

5 to 7 tablespoons ice water

FOR THE FILLING:

1 tablespoon dry white wine, vegetable stock, or defatted chicken stock

1 medium carrot, grated

1 cup finely chopped broccoli florets and stalks (about 4 ounces)

3/4 cup finely chopped onion

4 cloves garlic, mashed through a press

1/4 cup crumbled Greek feta cheese or firm tofu

1 tablespoon minced fresh thyme

1/4 cup minced fresh parsley

IN a large bowl, combine the flours. Whisk together the oil and yogurt (right in your measuring cup), and pour the mixture into the flours. Use a large rubber spatula to combine well. When a dough begins to form, pour in a tablespoon of the water. Continue to mix, adding more water as you need it, until the dough forms a ball. Divide the dough in two, wrap each half in waxed paper, and refrigerate while you prepare the filling.

PREHEAT the oven to 425°F.

HEAT a large cast-iron skillet or nonstick pan over medium-high heat and pour in the wine. Add the carrot, broccoli, onion, and garlic and simmer the vegetables until they are fragrant and crisp-tender, about 3 minutes. Remove from the heat and swirl in the feta, thyme, and parsley.

LIGHTLY flour a counter. Roll out half of the dough to an 8- by 12-inch rectangle. Cut the dough into 6 squares. Arrange about 2 tablespoons of the filling in the middle of each square. Lightly wet the edges of each square and fold in half on the diagonal to make a triangle. Seal the edges shut. Crimp the edges with the tines of a fork. Repeat the process with the remaining dough and filling. Use a toothpick to poke a couple of steam holes into each talas.

ARRANGE the talas on a large baking stone or on a parchment-lined cookie sheet. Bake until dry to the touch and gently browned, about 12 minutes. Serve warm or at room temperature as a snack, appetizer or, with soup, as a light entrée.

MAKES 12 TALAS; 150 CALORIES PER TALAS, 5.6 GRAMS FAT, 33 PERCENT OF CALORIES FROM FAT.

Shell Beans with Garlic

Shell beans are beans in midlife. Green beans exemplify the young stage, with small immature seeds that are hardly noticeable, in pods tender enough to eat; and dried beans, pods long shed, their essence concentrated, represent old age. In midlife, it is the fresh vital seeds (cranberry beans and limas) that become the object of our sustenance. Try this in the spring, when shell beans reach their peak, as a side dish or tossed with hot pasta and chopped ripe tomatoes as a light entrée.

~~~~~

2 cups shell beans, such as favas (from about 2 pounds whole pods)

About 2 cups defatted chicken stock, vegetable stock, or water, or enough to cover

1 bay leaf

1 tablespoon olive oil

2 cloves garlic, mashed through a press

1 to 2 tablespoons freshly grated Romano cheese or soy Parmesan

continued

COMBINE the beans, stock, and bay leaf in a medium saucepan and bring to a boil. Reduce the heat to low, cover loosely, and let simmer until the beans are tender, about 20 minutes for average-sized beans. Drain.

HEAT a large sauté pan over medium-high heat. Add the oil, then add the garlic. Tip in the beans and sauté until the garlic is cooked through and fragrant, about 2 to 3 minutes. Toss with the Romano and serve warm as an appetizer, as part of an antipasto tray, or as a side dish.

MAKES 4 SIDE SERVINGS; 135 CALORIES PER SERVING, 4 GRAMS FAT, 25 PERCENT OF CALORIES FROM FAT.

Rigatoni with Brokenhearted Sauce

Garlic, olive oil, and flavorful olives are the classic seasonings for pasta with artichokes. The name does not refer to star-crossed lovers, but to the hearts of the artichokes, which are smashed to make the sauce.

3 cloves garlic, finely minced
2 tablespoons dry white wine
3 tablespoons olive oil
8 water-packed artichoke hearts

12 Kalamata (dark Greek) olives, pitted
4 cups cooked rigatoni (from about 1/2 pound dried)
Freshly grated Parmesan cheese or soy Parmesan

COMBINE the garlic and wine in a small saucepan and bring to a boil. Reduce the heat to medium and let the mixture bubble until the garlic is soft and fragrant, about 1 to 1½ minutes.

POUR the garlic and wine into a food processor or blender and add the olive oil, artichoke hearts, and olives. Whiz for about 7 to 10 seconds, until the olives are finely chopped and the artichokes are broken up but not puréed. Toss with the rigatoni and Parmesan and serve warm or at room temperature.

MAKES 4 SERVINGS; 309 CALORIES PER SERVING, 10 GRAMS FAT, 30 PERCENT OF CALORIES FROM FAT.

Peri-Peri Hens

This dish is from Zimbabwe, where peri peri is the national barbecue sauce, featuring garlic, lime juice, and hot peppers. In Zimbabwe, the hens are cooked on a braii (pronounced BRA-ee), a grill made of the metal disk of a farm plow suspended over a fire. Jacaranda wood is often used for grilling, which makes the hens taste rich and slightly sweet, but the recipe adapts beautifully to any type of grill or broiler. Plan ahead, since the hens must marinate for a whole day.

~~~~~~

1/4 cup cider vinegar	Dash of hot pepper sauce, or to taste
2 tablespoons fresh lime juice	1 dried hot red chili pepper
1 tablespoon Worcestershire sauce	1 fresh jalapeño pepper
1/2 teaspoon paprika	3 cloves garlic, minced
	2 Cornish hens, split in half

IN a large glass baking dish, combine the vinegar, lime juice, Worcestershire, paprika, and hot pepper sauce.

USING rubber gloves, split the dried chili and the jalapeño in half, remove the seeds, and mince. Toss the minced peppers into a mortar and mash with the garlic into a paste. Alternatively, you can use an electric spice grinder. Add the paste to the vinegar mixture and stir to combine.

PLACE the hens in the marinade, turning them a couple of times so they're well bathed. Cover and let marinate, refrigerated, for 24 hours.

PREHEAT the broiler or prepare the grill. Broil or grill the hens 4 inches from the heat source until cooked through, about 10 to 15 minutes on each side. Watch them during cooking; if they are beginning to burn, move them farther away from the heat.

MAKES 4 SERVINGS; 190 CALORIES PER SERVING (WITHOUT THE SKIN), 4.5 GRAMS FAT, 23 PERCENT OF CALORIES FROM FAT.

germander

evergreen grower

~

EASE

MIDWINTER

BLUES

~

RAISE AN

HERBAL

GROUND

COVER

~

GROW A

FOUR-

SEASONS

FOOD

GARNISH

~

a friend who lives in Oregon developed a condition known as seasonal affective disorder (SAD). The northern winters, reduced daylight hours, bleak skies, and generally grim weather caused her to become depressed and restless. She finally solved the problem with a two-pronged approach, by installing full-spectrum lights and planting germander in window boxes. Unlike most other herbs, germander remains a lively, shiny green regardless of snow, ice, or cold, bringing a cheery note of sunny warmth throughout the winter.

Lore and Legend

Availability at all seasons may be the reason why germander was long considered a popular folk cure for dozens of illnesses. During the Middle Ages, germander tea was used to heal wounds and relieve rheumatism, coughs, respiratory problems, stomachaches, gout, water retention, fevers, depression, snake bite, epilepsy, and gum disease. But scientific research has never backed up any of these claims, and herbalists throughout the ages have replaced germander cures with more effective treatments. In fact, it is rare to find major mention of germander in an herb book or ship's medicine-chest log dating from later than 1750.

Growing

However, germander found a niche in the famous knot gardens of Elizabethan England. Since the herb looks like a tiny evergreen hedge, it was planted as borders in swooping rows; from a hilltop, the swoops looked like knotted ribbons. Knot gardens are still grown for their visual drama and bright winter greenery.

Not too many people have the space to grow a proper knot garden, especially since it must be viewed from above to be fully appreciated. But if you'd like to see an example, visit the National Herb Garden at the National Arboretum in Washington, D.C.

In a regular garden, germander's shiny green leaves lend elegance to beds containing ferny-leafed herbs such as tansy, yarrow, and feverfew. A native of Central and Southern Europe, the herb likes full sun, but will take partial shade. To plant it, prepare a standard herb mixture of two parts garden or potting soil, two parts peat, one part sand, and one part compost or composted cow manure. Buy small organically grown plants, choosing the "creeping" variety if you need a ground cover, the "upright" varieties if you want a hedge. To plant, dig a hole twice the size of each herb's root ball and set it in. Fill in with the surrounding soil, then tamp it down. Soak with warm water. Stick your finger in the soil about once a week thereafter; if the soil feels dry, water.

Even if you don't garden, you can plant germander in a pot inside near a sunny window. The herb needs about six hours of sun a day, which you can augment with ninety-watt halogen floods, placed about three feet away. If you *really* don't garden, you can keep germander sprigs in an opaque vase or glass filled with water, where they'll stay green for up to five months. Change the water once a week, and, to avoid rotting, be sure that no leaves go below the water line. A vase of fresh germander is a welcome sight at the winter dining table, and though not particularly tasty, the tiny sprigs make attractive garnishes for food.

ginger

~~~~~~

the motion potion

~

DE-STRESS

DIGESTION

~

NEGATE

NAUSEA

~

SPICE UP

RECIPES

~

*A*t a hotel in Taipei, I sampled yam cha, a Taiwanese version of Chinese dim sum dumplings. Filled with minced carrot and cabbage, they were accompanied by mao tai, a Chinese rice wine that smells like old socks and is usually served with flavor-masking condiments. First the waiter offered me goat blood to improve the mao tai, but I passed. He then brought snake bile, a Chinese tonic for maintaining strength during the winter months. Not for me. Finally, he arrived smiling, with a plate of sliced tiny lemons and grated fresh ginger. The lemons are okay, he said, but ginger makes everything good.

Lore and Legend

Ancient yogis made ginger the predominant flavoring in their foods, especially before religious retreats. In India, where garlic and onion were seasonings of choice, the yogis chose ginger because it left the breath sweet and inoffensive to the gods. Yogis still favor ginger, claiming it promotes mental clarity.

In early China, cooks discovered that adding ginger to fish dishes could sometimes mask the flavor of a less-than-fresh catch, but its popularity grew because it simply tastes good. In northern China, especially, it became the classic complement to lamb because ginger cuts the meat's fatty taste.

In the sixth century, ginger sailed from China to Japan, along with Buddhism and soy foods. Ginger was adopted there immediately and remains Japan's favorite culinary herb, especially popular in sauces and soups and, in its pickled form, with raw fish (sashimi). The Japanese also found medicinal uses for ginger, prescribing a ginger tea for cranky digestion and topical compresses to relieve aches and pains.

Before long, the Moors discovered ginger and brought it to Spain. The Spanish in turn introduced it to the West Indies. There, the Jamaicans used it to make the refreshing digestive aid that we know as ginger ale. Many people still drink ginger ale to help banish digestive problems, especially nausea. If you buy ginger ale for that purpose, be sure it contains real ginger, not artificial flavors, or it won't work.

Healing

Science has finally put its stamp of approval on what people have known for centuries—that ginger can be an effective remedy for indigestion and nausea. In one study, ginger was found to be more effective in staving off nausea than a leading motion sickness drug. Ninety percent of the people who used ginger experienced no motion sickness when they took two to four capsules of the dried herb before traveling in a car, boat, plane, or train. Ginger capsules are available at health food stores, herb shops, pharmacies, and many supermarkets.

Research also shows that ginger can reduce morning sickness. It seems to work best when pregnant women take it at the first sign of nausea, before getting out of bed in the morning, and remain in bed (or at least relax) until every trace of nausea is gone. Just how much ginger will do the trick varies with the individual; one study suggests starting with three capsules of dried ginger for morning sickness. As with any medication taken during pregnancy, be sure to check with a health professional about safety and about the dosage right for you. So you know, four capsules of dried ginger equal 125 milligrams, about the equivalent of one teaspoonful of fresh grated ginger.

In larger doses, ginger seems to be helpful in preventing some of the symptoms of stomach flu. Again, to be effective, the ginger should be taken at the very first sign of a queasy stomach. Four to six capsules are often recommended, but doses will vary with the individual. If you're prone to catching the flu, get your personal ginger dose set up by a health professional before the season starts.

Scientists are also investigating ginger for soothing the nausea associated with chemotherapy. Before trying it, of course, check with a health professional, who can also advise your dosage and the best way to ingest it.

Ginger's soothing powers don't stop at the stomach. In parts of Africa, ginger tea is a folk remedy for headaches, and in Asia, a ginger bath is said to relieve tension, as well as minor aches and pains. Aficionados of the ginger bath claim it helps remove toxins from the body, and it's certainly helpful in opening a stuffed nose due to allergies, sinus trouble, or colds. To try it, finely grate about five ounces of fresh ginger, then squeeze the gratings to release the juice right into the bath water, which should be as hot as you can stand it. (Compost or discard the gratings.) Soak yourself in the bath for about fifteen minutes, then wrap up in something warm and slip into bed. (It's especially important that your feet be covered and warm.)

A ginger footbath can be almost as soothing. Add about a quarter cup of ginger juice (made by grating and squeezing about half a cup of fresh ginger) to a basin of hot water. If the skin on your feet is dry, swirl in a couple of drops of castor oil or olive oil. Put your feet into the basin, and drape a large bath towel over the basin to keep the water warm. Soak for about fifteen minutes, then wrap your feet in something warm and relax.

Grating and squeezing ginger to make juice is also the preferred method for making ginger tea. Use about one teaspoon of juice to one cup of hot water. Herbalists recommend ginger tea for cranky digestion, clearing the head from cold symptoms, and dispelling feelings of nausea.

Growing

The part of the ginger plant normally used is the root, which looks like a smooth-skinned, gnarly potato with several protruding fingers. That's why it's sometimes called a "hand" of ginger.

To grow ginger, set a piece of an organically grown "hand" on a sunny counter and wait about a week for it to begin to sprout. (Unless you live in a warm climate, you should plant your ginger indoors.) Put the sprouted "hand" in a large pot filled with a sandy version of the standard herb mixture, combining two parts garden or potting soil, two parts peat, two parts sand, and one part compost or composted cow manure. Soak with warm water, and from then on, be sure that the soil never dries out. Give it as much sun as you can, at least six hours a day, which can be augmented with ninety-watt hal-ogen floods, placed about three feet from the top of the plant. In about ten days you should be rewarded by the appearance of bamboo-like stems and leaves. The leaves are quite aromatic and can be minced and used as a garnish for spicy soups and salads.

You can, of course, wait six to nine months and then dig up the roots and eat them too. But many herb lovers prefer to buy ginger for consumption, and keep their plants to enjoy the attractive tropical appearance.

Cooking

Ginger's flavor is fresh, spicy, and lemony with a floral touch, so it can really zip up a dish. Beginners can add it to their favorite chili recipe, starting with a teaspoon of fresh grated ginger (or ginger juice) for four servings. After tasting the chili, you'll find it easy to imagine how ginger can enhance other dishes—stir-fries, Asian noodle dishes, fried rice, spicy sauces, and curries. Ginger's flavor brings out the perfume of fresh fruit so that it tastes vivid and sweet without adding refined sugar. Stir a quarter teaspoon of finely grated fresh ginger into two cups fresh fruit such as sliced peaches, apricots, straw-berries, or plums. Fruit compotes and sauces are also excellent jazzed up with fresh ginger, using about a half teaspoon of finely grated ginger to a recipe to serve four.

Ginger juice is better for marinades and soups, when you want to maintain a smooth texture. Use a teaspoon of juice per half a cup of marinade, or in a soup to serve four. Coarsely grate fresh ginger, then squeeze the grat-ings to extract the juice. You can make this easy by bundling up the gratings in a double thickness of cheesecloth, then squeezing the bundle.

Ginger is widely available fresh or dried. Use fresh organically grown roots if you can, since they're livelier and tastier, and save the dried version for cake, cookie, and pudding recipes that call for it specifically. But one kind of dried ginger you might want to try is galangal, an exotic relative of the familiar root that can be found in Asian markets (it might be labeled "laos" or "ka," its Thai name). Don't buy the powdered kind, because its aroma will be weak. Go for dried slices and grate them yourself with a nutmeg grater. Popular in soups, salad dressings, and sauces, galangal has the flavor of ginger, but it's softer and more flowery. Use half a teaspoon of it in a marinade for red snapper or other fish, along with fresh lime juice, hot peppers, garlic, and soy sauce. Or use galangal anytime you would use ginger.

Pear and Ginger Breakfast Muffins

Some herbalists say that ginger stimulates digestion, making it a healthful addition to a morning muffin.

~~~~~

1 1/2 cups bran nugget cereal	1/4 cup pure maple syrup
1/2 cup pure pear or apple juice	2 large egg whites or 1/4 cup Calendula Egg Substitute (page 47)
1 pear, coarsely grated	
2 teaspoons finely grated fresh ginger	1 tablespoon canola oil
	1 1/4 cups unbleached all-purpose flour
1/2 cup plain nonfat yogurt or soy yogurt	2 teaspoons baking soda
1/4 cup all-fruit pear or apple butter	1 teaspoon ground cinnamon

PREHEAT the oven to 400°F.

IN a medium bowl, combine the cereal, juice, pear, and ginger. Let the mixture soak for 10 minutes. Then stir in the yogurt, pear butter, maple syrup, egg whites, and oil.

IN another medium bowl, combine the flour, baking soda, and cinnamon. Pour the liquid ingredients into the flour mixture and use a large rubber spatula to combine. Don't overmix; about 15 strokes should do.

LIGHTLY oil 12 muffin tins and divide the batter among them. Bake until cooked through, 18 to 20 minutes.

MAKES 12 MUFFINS; 136 CALORIES PER MUFFIN, 2 GRAMS FAT, 13 PERCENT OF CALORIES FROM FAT.

Barley Pilaf with Ginger-Grilled Apples

For convenience, you can make this tasty breakfast the night before, store it in the fridge, and reheat it when you're ready. If the pilaf appears to have dried out a bit in the night, swirl in a bit of apple juice while reheating.

~~~~~

1 teaspoon olive oil or canola oil	1½ cups pure apple juice, plus extra for glazing
1 cup barley	1½ cups water
1 teaspoon finely grated fresh ginger	2 tart apples, such as Granny Smith
1 vanilla bean, split	Apple juice and ginger juice for glazing

HEAT a medium saucepan over medium-high heat and add the oil. When it's hot, toss in the barley, ginger, and vanilla bean and sauté until fragrant, about 2 minutes. Pour in the juice and water and bring to a boil. Reduce the heat, cover, and simmer until the barley is tender, 45 to 60 minutes. Peek into the pot at 45 minutes to see if all the liquid has been absorbed; if not, continue simmering and checking.

MEANWHILE, prepare the apples by coring and cutting them into thin rounds. Arrange them on a broiler pan, and use a pastry brush to paint on a bit of apple and ginger juice. Broil until burnished, about 3 minutes, then flip and broil for about 2 minutes more.

SERVE the hot apple slices atop the pilaf.

MAKES 6 SERVINGS; 180 CALORIES PER SERVING, 1 GRAM FAT, 7 PERCENT OF CALORIES FROM FAT.

Variation: Substitute pears for the apples. Or, in season, use fresh peaches, but grill for only half the recommended time.

Morning Wheat with Cider and Cranberries

Ginger brings a snap to hot whole wheat cereal sweetened with apple cider and dried fruit, for a hearty breakfast that satisfies without saturated fat or refined sugar.

~~~~

1	cup bulgur	1/2	teaspoon very finely grated
1 3/4	cups apple cider		fresh ginger
1/4	cup dried cranberries or	1	cinnamon stick
	raisins	1/4	cup chopped almonds

COMBINE the bulgur, cider, cranberries, ginger, and cinnamon in a 2-quart saucepan and bring to a boil. Reduce the heat slightly, cover, and simmer until all the liquid has been absorbed and the bulgur is just tender, about 6 to 8 minutes.

MEANWHILE, toast the almonds in a dry sauté pan over medium-high heat, 2 to 3 minutes, stirring constantly.

SERVE the bulgur warm, sprinkled with the almonds.

MAKES 3 HUGE SERVINGS; 349 CALORIES PER SERVING, 7 GRAMS FAT, 18 PERCENT OF CALORIES FROM FAT.

Maple-Ginger Waffles

These waffles feature two fat- and cholesterol-slashing strategies: First, yeast makes them light and fluffy, without the addition of egg yolks, and second, toasted oats added to the batter give them a rich, nutty flavor, without high-fat nuts.

~~~~~

1/3 cup rolled oats	1 teaspoon minced fresh ginger
3/4 cup unbleached all-purpose flour	2 tablespoons pure maple syrup
1/3 cup oat bran	1 tablespoon active dry yeast
1/2 cup buttermilk or soy milk	2 large egg whites or 1/4 cup Calendula Egg Substitute (page 47)
1/2 cup pure apple juice	

TOAST the oats for 4 to 5 minutes in a dry cast-iron or nonstick sauté pan over medium-high heat, stirring constantly to prevent burning. Tip into a large bowl, and stir in the flour and bran.

IN a small saucepan, heat the buttermilk and apple juice until just warm, about 110° to 115°F. Remove the pan from the heat and whisk in the ginger, maple syrup, yeast, and egg whites.

POUR the liquid ingredients into the dry and combine well. Cover the bowl with plastic wrap and set in a cozy, draft-free place to rise for about 20 minutes. (You'll have about 3 cups of batter.)

USE a pastry brush to lightly paint canola oil onto a waffle iron, and preheat according to the manufacturer's instructions. Pour enough batter onto the iron so it's about two-thirds full. Bake the waffles until set, about 4½ minutes. They're great served with sliced fresh fruit.

MAKES 4 LARGE OR 8 SMALL WAFFLES, OR 4 SERVINGS; 240 CALORIES PER SERVING, 2 GRAMS FAT, 7 PERCENT OF CALORIES FROM FAT.

Warm Barley Salad with Lemon-Ginger Dressing

A pinch of fresh ginger makes salt-free salad dressings sparkle.

~~~~~~

1/2 cup pearled barley

1/4 cup wild rice

1 1/3 cups vegetable stock or defatted chicken stock

2 cloves garlic, mashed through a press

1 bay leaf

1 1/2 cups medium-chopped broccoli florets and stalks (about 4 ounces)

1 large carrot, sliced

2 teaspoons olive oil

Juice of 1/2 lemon

1/2 teaspoon ginger juice (squeezed from about 1 teaspoon grated fresh ginger)

1 tablespoon minced fresh chives

1 teaspoon toasted sesame seeds (see Note)

2 tablespoons raisins

2 tablespoons chopped toasted almonds

HEAT a heavy-bottomed skillet over medium-high heat. When the pan is hot, add the barley and wild rice and toast, stirring constantly, until the barley is golden brown, about 3 to 4 minutes. Add the stock, garlic, and bay leaf. Bring to a boil, then reduce the heat, cover, and simmer until the barley and rice are tender, about 30 minutes. If there's any liquid remaining, drain it off.

MEANWHILE, steam the broccoli and carrot over boiling water until they're tender and bright in color, about 5 minutes. Remove from the steamer and pat dry.

IN a large bowl, combine the oil, lemon juice, ginger juice, chives, and sesame seeds, whisking to combine. Add the broccoli, carrot, barley and rice, raisins, and almonds and toss well. Serve warm.

MAKES 4 SIDE SERVINGS OR 2 ENTRÉE SERVINGS; 195 CALORIES PER SIDE SERVING, 2.5 GRAMS FAT, 17 PERCENT OF CALORIES FROM FAT.

NOTE: To toast sesame seeds, heat on medium high in a dry nonstick sauté pan, stirring constantly for about 2 minutes.

Grilled Mushroom Satay with Black Vinegar Dipping Sauce

Woodsy, earthy mushrooms gain a vibrancy from fresh ginger that only increases with the length of time you marinate them. Serve these as part of an Asian buffet, as a side dish or appetizer with a stir-fry, or as a light meal on a mound of steamed rice, with a side of soup.

~~~~~

1	pound button mushrooms	1 1/2	teaspoons grated fresh ginger
1/3	cup rice vinegar	1/4	cup Vietnamese black vinegar or robust red wine vinegar
1/2	teaspoon toasted (dark) sesame oil		
	Splash of hot pepper sauce, or to taste		Splash of soy sauce
2	cloves garlic, mashed through a press		

BLANCH the mushrooms in boiling water for 2 minutes; drain. Blanching not only makes the mushrooms more receptive to the marinade, but it also helps them grill evenly without the need for much oil.

IN a medium glass bowl, combine the rice vinegar, sesame oil, hot pepper sauce, garlic, and 1 teaspoonful of the grated ginger. Add the mushrooms and toss well to combine. Cover and let marinate in the refrigerator overnight or up to 5 days.

PREPARE the grill or preheat the broiler.

THREAD the mushrooms onto bamboo skewers. Grill or broil them about 5 inches from the heat source, turning them frequently to prevent burning, until mottled with brown on all sides, about 4 to 5 minutes.

MEANWHILE, to make the dipping sauce, combine the black vinegar, soy sauce, and the remaining 1/2 teaspoon ginger.

SERVE the mushrooms warm or at room temperature.

MAKES 4 SERVINGS; 40 CALORIES PER SERVING, 2 GRAMS FAT, 45 PERCENT OF CALORIES FROM FAT.

Pear and Ginger Strudel

Ginger and lemon are classic flavorings for pears.

~~~~~

1/2 cup dried apricots, chopped	1/3 cup pure maple syrup
1 1/2 cups sliced peeled pears	8 sheets phyllo dough
1 teaspoon finely grated fresh ginger	3 tablespoons sweet (unsalted) butter, melted, or 3 tablespoons canola oil
1 tablespoon fresh lemon juice	1/4 cup walnuts, finely ground

PREHEAT the oven to 350°F.

IN a medium bowl, combine the apricots, pears, ginger, lemon juice, and maple syrup and mix well.

LAY the phyllo sheets out flat and cover the stack with a damp towel to keep them from drying out. Lay one sheet on the counter with a long side facing you and brush very lightly with butter or oil. Cover with another sheet and brush lightly again with butter or oil. Continue with the remaining sheets.

SPRINKLE on the walnuts. Spread the pear mixture over the lower half of the sheets, leaving a 1-inch border along the bottom and a 1/2-inch border on each side. Fold the sides over and brush lightly with butter or oil. Fold the bottom edge up over the filling and then roll the strudel up jelly-roll fashion. Brush the roll with butter and set seam side down on a cookie sheet lined with parchment paper. Bake until fragrant and golden, about 35 minutes. Cut into slices and serve warm.

MAKES 8 SERVINGS; 190 CALORIES PER SERVING, 6 GRAMS FAT, 28 PERCENT OF CALORIES FROM FAT.

Frozen Plum Custard

The velvety-sweet richness of fresh plums gets a spicy counterpoint from fresh ginger juice.

~~~~~

1 cup evaporated skim milk or low-fat vanilla soy milk

2 teaspoons cornstarch

1 pound ripe red plums, halved and pitted

2 tablespoons white grape juice

2 large egg whites or 1/4 cup Calendula Egg Substitute (page 47)

1/2 teaspoon ginger juice (from about 1 teaspoon grated fresh ginger)

1 teaspoon pure vanilla extract

1/3 cup pure maple syrup or honey

IN a small saucepan, whisk together the milk and cornstarch. Bring just to a simmer over high heat; do not boil. Transfer to a food processor or blender.

COMBINE the plums and grape juice in another small saucepan and cook over high heat until the plums are fragrant and just beginning to soften, about 3 minutes.

ADD the plum mixture to the milk mixture and whiz to combine. Add the egg whites, ginger juice, vanilla, and maple syrup and whiz until smooth. Pour the mixture into a saucepan and cook over medium heat, whisking constantly, until the mixture begins to thicken and coats a spoon, 5 to 6 minutes. Let cool completely.

FREEZE the cooled custard in an ice cream maker (see Note) according to the manufacturer's instructions. Serve.

MAKES 4 SERVINGS; 194 CALORIES PER SERVING, LESS THAN 1 GRAM FAT.

NOTE: If you don't have an ice cream maker, you can freeze the mixture in a stainless steel or glass bowl, stirring every 20 minutes or so to break up the large ice crystals. It will take about 2 1/2 hours to freeze.

Blueberry Sauce with Fresh Ginger

In this zesty dessert sauce, ginger accentuates the flowery taste of blueberries.

~~~~~

2   cups (1 pint) blueberries
1/2 teaspoon finely grated fresh
    ginger

3   tablespoons white grape
    juice (see Note)
1   tablespoon fresh lime juice

COMBINE all the ingredients in a small saucepan and bring to a boil over high heat. Reduce the heat to medium and let the sauce bubble until fragrant and slightly thickened, about 4 minutes. Serve warm or chilled over frozen yogurt—peach, banana, and strawberry are especially good—or with lime or pineapple sherbet. The sauce keeps, covered, in the refrigerator for up to a week.

MAKES ABOUT 1 3/4 CUPS; 44 CALORIES PER 1/4-CUP SERVING, NO ADDED FAT.

NOTE: If the blueberries are particularly tart, add a splash or two more of grape juice.

Gingered Carrot Squares with Apricot Glaze

Low-fat baked goods made without refined sugar can taste bland and pasty, but ginger lends flavor excitement. Serve these squares for breakfast with chilled orange sections or as a snack with tea.

~~~~~~

1/3 cup rolled oats	1/4 cup water
1/2 cup fresh orange juice	1 tablespoon arrowroot
3/4 cup unbleached all-purpose flour	1 teaspoon pure vanilla extract
1/2 cup whole wheat pastry flour	2 teaspoons finely minced peeled fresh ginger
1 teaspoon nonaluminum baking powder	1 carrot, grated
Pinch of sea salt	1 tablespoon canola oil
1/3 cup pure maple syrup	1/4 cup all-fruit apricot jam

PREHEAT the oven to 375°F.

IN a medium bowl, combine the oats and juice and let soak for 10 minutes.

IN another medium bowl, stir together the flours, baking powder, and salt.

ADD the maple syrup, water, arrowroot, vanilla, ginger, carrot, and oil to the oat mixture, whisking well. Add the flour mixture and combine well; don't overmix.

LIGHTLY oil and flour an 8-inch square baking pan. Pour in the batter, and bake in the center of the oven until a thin knife comes out clean, about 18 minutes. Remove from the oven and immediately spoon on the jam, using the back of a spoon to spread it evenly. Let cool, then cut into 2-inch squares. The squares keep well in a cookie tin for up to 3 days.

MAKES 16 SERVINGS; 66 CALORIES PER SERVING, 1 GRAM FAT, 14 PERCENT OF CALORIES FROM FAT.

Maple-Candied Ginger

If you suffer from motion sickness, take this crunchy ginger along on your travels to munch at the first sign of queasiness.

〰〰〰

1/2 cup pure apple juice

1/4 cup pure maple syrup

1/2 cup thinly sliced peeled fresh ginger

COMBINE the apple juice and syrup in a small saucepan and bring to a boil. Add the ginger slices, and reduce the heat to a gentle simmer, and cook until all the liquid has evaporated, about 20 minutes. Stir frequently to prevent burning, especially toward the end of the cooking time when most of the liquid is gone.

MEANWHILE, preheat the oven to 200°F.

ARRANGE the hot ginger pieces on a cookie sheet lined with parchment paper. Bake until all the pieces are dry and snap when broken, about 1 hour and 30 minutes.

MAKES ABOUT 1/2 CUP; ABOUT 10 CALORIES PER 1-TABLESPOON SERVING, NO ADDED FAT.

hot peppers

~~~~~~~~~~~~~~~~~~~~~~~~~~~~

warm up to good health

~

TONE UP

YOUR

TUMMY

~

RUB

AWAY

ARTHRITIS

~

SPICE UP

LEAN

FOODS

~

*I*n the cuisines of Africa, hot peppers play two roles that weave together as one. The spicy pods are used both for flavor and to invoke skin-cooling sweat in the sweltering climate. I discovered this for myself at a lodge in the African bush along the Zambia-Zimbabwe border, where I had a meal under the stars at which each course was perfumed with hot peppers. First came an appetizer of chick peas, boiled and then roasted with hot pepper and garlic, to be eaten with my hands. Then came a small roasted bird that had been marinated in hot pepper, garlic, and lime juice. The bird was accompanied by sweet and white potatoes tossed with hot pepper and toasted peanuts. The still evening air was close to ninety degrees, but I was comfortable and satisfied.

Lore and Legend

Historians speculate that varieties of hot peppers have been cultivated for thousands of years in Africa, India, and the tropical Americas, where they were dried and used to flavor soups and stews, as well as to relieve head colds and digestive distress. But the first documented mention of them in Europe didn't appear until after Christopher Columbus brought them back from the New World. At first—and against doctor's orders—a popular use for dried hot peppers was as an alarmingly sharp additive to snuff.

It took more than two hundred years before English gardeners began to grow hot peppers. Astrological herbalists of the seventeenth century classified fiery hot peppers under the red planet Mars, and some believed they emitted "dangerous vapours." This theory was undoubtedly born when an herbalist's nose and eyes were assaulted by the strong spicy fumes from a hot pepper.

Healing

African and Mexican herbalists have recommended hot peppers for digestion for centuries. And, indeed, modern science has determined that the smell and taste of hot peppers come from a compound called capsaicin, which stimulates the flow of saliva and related stomach juices. Ayurvedic East Indian herbalists also recommend hot peppers in small amounts as a digestive and circulation tonic and say the herb has *agni,* meaning it stimulates the stomach and related organs. To sample its effects, add a teaspoon of dried crushed hot pepper to a soup, stew, or stir-fry to serve four. Studies show that ingesting hot peppers with meals does not cause gastric discomfort in people with normal digestion. But if you experience discomfort or an internal burning sensation, stop eating hot peppers, and consult a health professional.

In Zaire and Zambia, since ancient times, hot peppers have been made into a salve and rubbed on the skin to soothe the pain of arthritis. Modern science has given this cure a "thumbs-up," and there are currently several capsaicin-based salves available in stores. Officially, they're known as rubefacients, or compounds that redden the skin and encourage circulation in the area. Health professionals favor these topical salves because, unlike painkillers, they don't interfere with other medications the patient may be taking.

Research has also shown that hot peppers may be an effective treatment for cluster headaches. A capsaicin compound sprayed into the nostril on the same side as the headache seems to bring relief. Researchers feel the capsaicin works by diminishing feeling in the nerve endings that induce pain. Of course, consult a health professional before trying such sprays.

Growing

Hot pepper plants are shrubby with stiff branches. Attractive additions to any herb garden, most hot pepper plants are one to two feet tall, though some varieties can reach five or six feet. Hot peppers need all the sun you can give them and, though easy to grow, produce more abundantly in hot climates. Find a place in the garden with a southern exposure. Then prepare a standard herb mixture of two parts garden or potting soil, two parts peat, one part sand, and one part compost or composted cow manure. Buy small organically grown hot pepper plants. Dig a hole for each plant that's twice the size of the root ball, set the plant in the hole, and fill in with the surrounding soil. Tamp the soil down and water with warm water. Stick your finger in the soil every five days; if it's dry, water. Don't let the soil dry out completely, or the hot peppers will have difficulty flowering and developing pepper pods.

Indoors, hot peppers need to be near a window with a southern or western exposure. Augment the light with a ninety-watt halogen flood placed about three feet from the plants.

Hot pepper plants, especially jalapeños, can help protect your other herbs from predators. For example, Japanese beetles love to munch on basil and can strip a plant down to a skeleton overnight. But when jalapeño plants (about three for a dozen basil plants) stand guard, the beetles stay away.

Cooking

Hot peppers add interest to otherwise bland foods, especially when they're combined with herbs that add aroma and contrast to their fire. In India, for instance, minced fresh hot peppers are combined with cool mint, then swirled into yogurt to make a condiment for flat breads and roasted vegetables. Thai cooks mix hot pepper sauce with cool coriander leaf, fresh lime juice, and nam pla (fish sauce) to make a marinade for fish fillets and prawns. Italian cooks like to toss in a whole dried hot pepper when sautéing broccoli and garlic in olive oil to make a light but lusty sauté for hot pasta.

The amount of capsaicin, and therefore heat, that a pepper packs is measured in Scoville units. The standard bell pepper, the mildest member of the family, has zero Scoville units, while the habanero, the hottest pepper in the world, has about 250,000 Scoville units. For comparison, the average jalapeño has only about 5500 Scoville units. The amount of capsaicin in any individual hot pepper also depends on specific growing conditions like sun, rain, and soil.

To add hot peppers to a recipe, start with one minced fresh pepper in a dish to serve four. As a rule of thumb, the smaller the pepper, the hotter it tastes. The seeds and inside ribs of the pepper contain the most fire, so including them will make the dish hotter. If you prefer, you can mince one dried hot pepper into a dish to serve four people. Or to disperse heat evenly throughout a dish, you can soak a dried hot pepper in hot stock until soft, then puree it in a spice grinder or mortar before adding to soups, stews, sauces, or dips.

Dried hot pepper flakes are commonly available at markets. Use a half teaspoon to a teaspoon of flakes in a recipe to serve four. Start with the smaller amount, taste, and add more if you need it. If you're using ground hot pepper, try a smaller amount first—about a quarter teaspoon to a recipe for four.

Hot Peppers at a Glance

Here are five of the most common fresh hot peppers, or chilies, you'll run across:

ANAHEIM looks like a thin, dark green bell pepper. It has a moist texture and sweet-hot flavor. Add a whole minced Anaheim to a gazpacho or a pot of warm vegetable soup that serves four.

BANANA peppers are pale yellow to light green, about four inches long, and an inch or so wide. They're moist-textured and hot. For a classic preparation, sauté minced banana peppers with garlic in olive oil, then toss with hot pasta.

HABANERO peppers are bonnet-shaped, slightly smaller than a golf ball, and range from light green to red, when ripe. The habanero, and its close

Just so you know, if you eat something that is too spicy, gulping water is likely to spread the fire. Try eating a piece of bread instead or a mouthful of plain rice, or the best antidote of all, rinse your mouth with vinegar.

Use your head when handling anything that contains capsaicin: Wear gloves, or be extra careful where you put your fingers after you've handled a hot pepper or salve, avoiding your eyes and other delicate areas. To help remove the capsaicin from your fingers, rinse them in cider vinegar, rub with toothpaste, and then rinse the toothpaste away with vinegar.

relative, the Scotch bonnet, are the hottest peppers in the world, famous for spicing up red chili sauce. Add one minced habanero to a pot of chili to serve eight. The longer the habanero cooks, the hotter the chili will be, so beginners may want to add the pepper toward the end of cooking. Commercially prepared bottled habanero sauces are available at specialty stores and many supermarkets. Add a splash or two to salsa or fish chowder.

JALAPEÑO peppers are two-inch-long blimp-shaped bullets that range from bright green to red, when ripe. They have a moist texture and a hot, tangy flavor. Mince one jalapeño and add it to one cup of dip or sandwich spread.

SERRANO peppers are thinner than jalapeños and about one inch long, ranging from dark green to red, when ripe. They are dry-textured, hot, and spicy. Add one minced serrano to a garlicky stir-fry with tofu or beef.

Fava Beans with Tiny Pasta

Balsamic vinegar and fresh basil balance the heat of the hot pepper sauce and garlic in this dish.

~~~~~

3	medium carrots, thinly sliced	1	clove garlic, very finely minced
1½	cups cooked fava beans	1	tablespoon fresh lemon juice
1½	cups cooked orzo, acini di pepe, or other tiny pasta (from a scant ¼ pound dried)	½	teaspoon hot pepper sauce, or to taste
¼	cup minced fresh basil	1	tablespoon balsamic vinegar
2	tablespoons minced fresh chives	2	teaspoons olive oil
			Pinch of dry mustard

BLANCH the carrots in boiling water until just tender, 1 to 2 minutes. Drain, pat dry, and place in a medium bowl. Add the beans, pasta, basil, chives, and garlic.

IN a small bowl, combine the lemon juice, hot pepper sauce, vinegar, oil, and mustard, whisking well. Pour the dressing over the beans and pasta and toss well to combine. Let marinate for at least a couple of hours before serving. Serve at room temperature or very slightly chilled, as a salad on Romaine petals, as a side dish with grilled fish, or as a vegetarian entrée.

MAKES 4 SERVINGS; 175 CALORIES PER SERVING, 3 GRAMS FAT, 16 PERCENT OF CALORIES FROM FAT.

Sizzling Beans with Peanuts

Green beans sautéed with dried hot peppers and spices are a mainstay in the Sichuan Province of China.

~~~~~~~

3/4 pound green beans, topped and tailed

1 teaspoon olive oil

1 tablespoon reduced-sodium tamari

1/2 teaspoon ginger juice (squeezed from 1 tablespoon grated fresh ginger)

2 cloves garlic, very finely minced

3 small dried hot chili peppers

1 tablespoon chopped unsalted peanuts

STEAM the beans over boiling water until bright green and just tender, about 3 minutes for medium-sized ones. Drain and pat dry.

MEANWHILE, heat a well-seasoned cast-iron skillet over medium heat for about 5 minutes. (If you don't have cast-iron, use a nonstick skillet but don't preheat it.)

USE a pastry brush to paint the olive oil onto the bottom of the hot skillet. Add the beans, tamari, ginger juice, garlic, and hot peppers and sauté until sizzling hot, about 2 minutes. Use a wooden spatula to scrap the tasty bits off the bottom of the pan as you cook. Remove from the heat and keep warm.

PLACE the peanuts in a small dry sauté pan and heat over medium-high heat, swirling the peanuts around until fragrant and toasted, about 2 minutes. Sprinkle over the beans and serve hot with rice or as a side dish to poached fish.

MAKES 4 SERVINGS; 50 CALORIES PER SERVING, 1.5 GRAMS FAT, 27 PERCENT OF CALORIES FROM FAT.

Roasted Onions with Jalapeño

Velvety-smooth balsamic vinegar and fresh lemon juice combine with hot peppers to enhance a roasty onion flavor.

~~~~~

2 bunches scallions
1 large red onion, thinly sliced and separated into rings
2 fresh jalapeños, cored, seeded, and sliced into rings
1 teaspoon olive oil

1 bay leaf, finely crushed
1 shallot, minced
1 tablespoon fresh lemon juice
2 teaspoons balsamic vinegar
2 tablespoons freshly grated Locatelli cheese or soy Parmesan

TIDY up the scallions by trimming off the roots and ragged tops.

BLANCH the scallions and onion rings in boiling water until wilted but not limp, 3 to 4 minutes. Drain and pat dry.

PREHEAT the broiler. On a large baking sheet with sides, combine the scallions, onion, jalapeños, and oil and toss well to coat. Spread into a single layer and broil until browned and tender, about 7 minutes, flipping the vegetables midway. Watch carefully to make sure they don't burn.

WHEN cool enough to handle, slice the scallions into 1-inch pieces and place them in a medium bowl along with the onion and jalapeños. Add the bay leaf, shallot, lemon juice, vinegar, and cheese and toss to combine. Serve warm or at room temperature, piled on crusty bread or as a side dish to grilled tuna or swordfish.

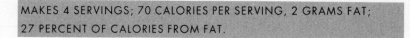

MAKES 4 SERVINGS; 70 CALORIES PER SERVING, 2 GRAMS FAT; 27 PERCENT OF CALORIES FROM FAT.

Shrimp and Chilies with Rice

Whole dried hot pepper, ground chili powder, and zesty tomato salsa spice up nutty short-grained rice.

~~~~~

1²/₃ cups hot vegetable stock or defatted chicken stock	1 teaspoon chili powder, or to taste
1¹/₄ cups Arborio or other short-grain Italian rice	¹/₄ cup grated part-skim mozzarella or soy mozzarella
¹/₂ cup dry white wine	2 tablespoons spicy tomato-based salsa
1 dried hot chili pepper	
2 teaspoons olive oil	3 scallions, minced
2 cloves garlic, minced	2 tablespoons minced fresh coriander or parsley
1 pound jumbo shrimp, peeled and deveined	

BRING the stock to a simmer in a medium saucepan. Add the rice, wine, and chili pepper and bring to a boil. Reduce the heat, cover, and simmer, stirring frequently, until the rice is tender and all of the liquid has been absorbed, about 15 minutes.

MEANWHILE, heat the olive oil in a large sauté pan over medium-high heat. Add the garlic, shrimp, and chili powder and sauté until the shrimp are pink and beginning to curl, about 3 minutes. Remove from the heat.

WHEN the rice is done, stir in the shrimp mixture, the cheese, salsa, and scallions. Cover and let sit for about 5 minutes. Serve warm, sprinkled with the coriander.

MAKES 4 SERVINGS; 414 CALORIES PER SERVING, 7 GRAMS FAT, 15 PERCENT OF CALORIES FROM FAT.

Spicy Turkey Dumplings

Hot pepper sauce, chili powder, and shallots give lean turkey a rich taste.

~~~~~~

1	pound turkey cutlets	1	shallot, very finely minced
3/4	teaspoon chili powder		
1/2	teaspoon hot pepper sauce, or to taste	1 1/2	teaspoons balsamic vinegar
3	cloves garlic, very finely minced		Splash of olive oil

CUT the turkey into 1-inch chunks. Put them in a processor along with the chili powder, hot pepper sauce, garlic, shallot, and vinegar. Whiz until finely chopped, about 15 seconds. If you don't have a food processor, mince the turkey fine with a sharp knife, then mix in the seasonings. Form the mixture into little balls or patties. (If you wet your hands first, the mixture won't stick to them.)

HEAT a well-seasoned cast-iron skillet over medium-high heat. (If you don't have cast-iron, use a nonstick skillet, but don't preheat it.) Use a pastry brush to paint a bit of olive oil on the bottom of the skillet. Add the turkey patties and sizzle until lightly browned and cooked through, about 4 minutes on each side. Serve warm as an appetizer.

MAKES 6 SERVINGS; 85 CALORIES PER SERVING, 1 GRAM FAT, 10 PERCENT OF CALORIES FROM FAT.

NOTE: For a quick dipping sauce, try coriander chutney, salsa, or honey mustard sauce.

hyssop

~~~~~~~~~~~~~~~~~~~~~~~~~~~~~~~~~~~~

calm a cough

E A S E

C O L D

S Y M P T O M S

~

H E L P

C O N T R O L

O I L Y

S K I N

~

GROW A

LOW

MAINTENANCE

HERB

~

One hot summer in Los Angeles, I had a facial that left my skin so oily that powder practically ran off my face. In a panic, I brewed a strong pot of hyssop tea—a quarter cup of dried herb to one cup of boiling water. I let the tea steep for twenty minutes, then strained it and cooled it. I threw a handful of rolled oats in a blender and, with the motor running, poured in enough of the hyssop tea to make a thick paste, which I slathered on my face and let dry. It took two more hyssop-oat treatments, at four-hour intervals, but after that my skin was normal once again.

Lore and Legend

Hyssop got its name from the Greek *hussopos*, meaning "holy," and the Hebrew *esob,* meaning "herb." It was used ritually to purify sacred places and to cleanse lepers, perhaps because of its medicinal aroma, which resembles the smell of sharp catnip. In the pre-Christian era, it was also used as a "strewing herb," literally strewn about the floors of a house so that as people stepped on it, its clean aroma was released to purify the air.

Healing

A more direct medicinal application was employed by the Cherokee Indians, who made hyssop into a syrup to relieve congestion, asthma, and other respiratory complaints. Current scientific research reveals that the volatile oils in hyssop do make it a good remedy for mild respiratory problems, especially those associated with colds. Hyssop also contains a bitter compound, marrubin, which acts as an expectorant. The best way to take hyssop is in tea form, made by steeping one teaspoon of fresh hyssop (or one-half teaspoon of dried) in three quarters of a cup of hot water for four minutes. "Herbal" Ed Smith, co-founder of the Pacific College of Naturopathic Medicine, advises drinking hyssop tea cool to bring out its best expectorant capabilities, and hot to relieve the congestion of a cold. Some herbalists recommend steeping hyssop with an equal amount of sage to boost its decongestant properties, then swirling honey into the tea before drinking.

For clearing the sinuses, many herbalists prescribe a hyssop-sage oil that you can make yourself. Fill a widemouthed jar with slightly less than half a cup each of fresh hyssop and sage leaves and flowers. Use a pestle to bruise the herbs, thus releasing their aromas. Heat half a cup of olive oil, grapeseed oil, or canola oil in a small saucepan, but don't boil. Pour the hot oil over the herbs, cover the mixture, and leave it in a sunny window for two weeks, shaking the jar once a day. Then strain and discard the herbs. To use the oil, dip your fingers into it and rub them over the clogged sinus area. Press hard for fifteen seconds, then lightly for fifteen seconds, or until the pain subsides.

In Japan, hyssop, along with other tannin-rich plants, is being investigated for antitumor and anti-HIV activities. Though the research is far from complete, it holds promise.

Looking Your Best

The tannin in hyssop makes it helpful in controlling oily skin. Try mixing about a tablespoon of bruised fresh flowers and leaves with half a cup of whatever commercial facial toner you're using. Splash the toner on your face after washing and before moisturizing. If you prefer, you can use strong hyssop tea as your toner. Steep one tablespoon of fresh hyssop flowers and leaves, covered, in one cup of boiling water for ten minutes. Strain, then cover and refrigerate until use. It will keep up to a week.

Growing

Since hyssop is native to Europe, the Middle East, and eastern Asia, it grows easily almost anywhere, even in a coffee can on your windowsill. It tolerates lack of water, too much sun or too little, and crowding by its neighbors. It's the perfect herb for beginner gardens, kids' gardens, and weekend gardens. Hyssop's foliage has an elegant rosemary-lavender look, and come early summer it sends up delicate sprays of pink or white flowers that butterflies and bees can't resist.

To grow hyssop, buy small organically grown plants and find a place for them that gets at least six hours of sun a day. Prepare a sandy version of the standard herb mixture that includes two parts garden or potting soil, two parts peat, two parts sand, and one part compost or composted cow manure. Dig a hole for each plant that's twice the size of its root ball. Set in the plant and fill in with the surrounding soil. Tamp the soil down and soak with warm water. Then, unless you have a drought, let nature do the watering.

lavender

climb out of depression

~

CREATE

AN HERBAL

ANTISEPTIC

~

RELAX AND

REJUVENATE

MIND

AND BODY

~

HELP

NORMALIZE

OILY

SKIN

~

One autumn I spent a week at a six-hundred-year-old inn in Haslemere, England, which had a courtyard filled with blooming lavender. Each day three elderly women, residents of the town, came there for tea. On the third day of my trip, one of them accurately observed that I looked as if I hadn't been sleeping well. I explained that the stress of travel and the howling night wind were keeping me awake.

One of her companions excused herself to chat with the waitress, who soon began snipping away at the lavender bushes. They then presented me with an envelope filled with lavender flowers. "For a good night's sleep," my elderly friend counseled, "sprinkle them between your pillow and pillow case before you go to bed, dear." And, indeed, that night lavender's soothing scent lulled me into a sound sleep.

Lore and Legend

If you washed clothes for a living a couple of centuries ago in England, you would have been called a "lavender," from the Latin meaning "to wash," and so it is its fresh, clean aroma that gives the herb lavender its name. Even in appearance—cool purple blossoms atop silvery-green leaves—lavender is fresh and clean. It may well have been these features that first tempted ancient herbalists to use lavender as a disinfectant and antiseptic.

Greek, Roman, and Arab herbalists recommended lavender soaps and bath oils to help prevent and cure skin infections. But the popularity of these potions led to some questionable business dealings. To drive up the price of lavender and lavender-based cosmetics, some ancient Egyptian herbalists launched a rumor that deadly asps lurked under lavender bushes, making harvesting perilous. The rumor succeeded in making lavender an expensive cosmetic herb, but the asp association undermined its popularity in headpieces and hair ornaments. What the harvesters gained from cosmetic sales, they lost in ornamental use.

By the sixteenth century, however, English herbalists were using lavender in healing headpieces. They prescribed wearing a skullcap stuffed with lavender flowers to cure headaches or "swimming of the brain." They also used essential oil of lavender to keep wounds from becoming infected.

Glove makers in France used the herb to scent the leather with which they crafted gloves. Since glove makers had a reputation for remaining healthy during plagues, lavender potions became a popular preventive aid. Some herbalists recommended steeping lavender flowers in vinegar, then rubbing the scented vinegar on the body to remain disease-free. Others fashioned huge beak-shaped masks filled with smoking lavender for their customers to wear in the germ-ridden streets.

Healing

Scientific research on lavender flowers verifies the intuition of our ancestors. The herb actually does possess antiseptic and other healing properties. Herbalists recommend dotting pure essential oil of lavender (the plant's concentrated essence) on cuts, scratches, insect bites, burns, and blemishes. Herbalists and aromatherapists also prescribe it to banish mild cases of anxiety and depression and to create calm and tranquility. (For serious mental distress, of course, you should consult a health professional.) To try it, sprinkle three drops of essential lavender oil into a basin of steaming water and inhale the vapors, or add about ten drops to half a cup of grapeseed oil for a massage.

You can also add eight to ten drops of lavender oil to half a cup of your favorite body lotion, shower gel, or bath oil. A few drops may sound like a light dose, but essential oils are incredibly potent.

Before buying essential oil of lavender, make sure that it comes from the right variety. In one experiment, essential oil of lavender was diffused into the air at several health spas, to create a calming effect. But instead, patrons complained about the smell and a couple of them even became slightly nauseated. The problem was that French lavender (*L. spica*) was used instead of the more expensive English lavender (*L. officinalis* or *L. vera*). In short, buy essential oil of lavender from a reputable purveyor. If you don't know one, check the resource section on page 389.

Looking Your Best

Lavender flowers contain tannins, which have an astringent action on the skin. That explains why adding several fresh or dried lavender flowers to half a cup of facial toner or aftershave lotion can help regulate an oily complexion. Use your lavender toner after washing and before moisturizing, or pour the mixture into a spray bottle and mist your face throughout the day.

Growing

The easiest lavender to grow in the northern United States, with its searing summers and cold winters, is *L. Munsted*. Its flowers are a clear medium purple and wildly fragrant. *L. Hidcote*'s blossoms are a more dramatic purple, but the variety only grows well in perfectly balmy areas. There's also a pink variety of lavender, *L. Jean Davis,* which is less striking than its purple cousins but seems to attract more butterflies than the other strains.

Lavender can be a little temperamental. It won't thrive indoors, but you can plant it in a clay pot on a terrace if you don't have a garden. It also hates having wet feet, so when planting, use a sandy version of the standard herb mixture, combining two parts garden or potting soil, two parts peat, two parts sand, and one part compost or composted cow manure. Find a place in the garden for lavender that gets at least six hours of sun a day. Dig a hole for each plant that's twice the size of the root ball. Then, to keep the roots dry, sprinkle in a handful of extra sand and two tablespoons of garden lime before you set the plant in the hole. If your area is rainy, don't mulch your lavender—the last thing you want to do is hold water around the base of the plant. If you need to mulch to keep the weeds down, try using gravel or small rocks.

Lavender can bring romance to your garden. Its silvery leaves shine in the moonlight, so plant it along walks to illuminate the way at night. The blooming plants will perfume your legs as you walk by and brush against them.

Cooking

To use those beautiful blooms in cooking, snip off the flowers when they're open and looking lively. Lavender tastes flowery, clean, and sharp and combines well with rosemary. Try using half a tablespoon of each per loaf in bread doughs for a soft piny taste. You might want to make an herb butter to complement grilled fish or corn on the cob by creaming four tablespoons of butter with two teaspoons each of minced fresh lavender and rosemary. Or take a standard mint jelly recipe and substitute equal parts of lavender and rosemary for the mint. A tablespoon of lavender and rosemary added to a garlicky marinade for lamb or chicken will give the dish a bright, lightly floral flavor.

Lavender vinegar can lend a velvety perfume to dressings for summer salads and to marinades for such hearty winter vegetables as parsnips, turnips, and beets. To make it, fill a ten-ounce jar with equal amounts of lavender flowers and rosemary sprigs. Pack the herbs fairly loosely. Cover with a cup of warmed white vinegar and let steep, covered, at room temperature for two weeks. Strain and use in vinaigrettes, marinades, and to deglaze sauté pans.

Using Lavender in the Kitchen

Tuck several fresh lavender flowers into the sugar jar to perfume it.

When your hands smell oniony, rub two fresh lavender flowers between them for about thirty seconds. Your hands will then smell fresh.

Zip the lavender petals off the stem right into a fresh fruit salad. Use one whole flower for each cup of fruit.

Use the flowers as a garnish for pale soups, such as chilled creamy cucumber.

lemon balm

mind and body tune-up

~

HELP RELIEVE

HIGH

BLOOD

PRESSURE

~

MAKE A

COOL

SKIN

SPRITZER

~

ADD A

LEMON

LIFT

TO FOODS

~

a skin-care specialist I know employs the principles of Kahuna, an ancient Hawaiian method of healing. Kahuna holds that every disease is caused by stress and can be treated with anxiety-reducing meditation, massage, prayer, exercise, foods, and herbs. One area where stress shows up is the face, in the form of dark undereye circles, dull skin, wrinkles, and blemishes. To relieve these symptoms, Kahuna advises regular facial massage, daily exercise, drinking at least eight eight-ounce glasses of water a day, and eating lots of dark, leafy greens, as well as avoiding caffeine and alcohol and foods that contain refined sugar. But before any treatment, it is important to relax the mind and body so that they will be receptive to healing. For that purpose, my specialist offers her clients lemon balm tea.

Lore and Legend

Early Greek and Roman herbalists prescribed lemon balm leaves steeped in wine for relaxation and "against the bitings of venomous beasts." Arab herbalists used the same brew to strengthen the heart. Shakespeare knew about the healing properties of lemon balm. In his *Merry Wives of Windsor,* lemon balm appears as a strewing herb, tossed on floors before parties so that its aroma would make the guests merrier.

Lemon balm also features in the medieval method of treating illness with herbs called the Doctrine of Signatures. The doctrine held that a plant's appearance revealed its healing qualities. For example, the round, wrinkled walnut shell was thought to resemble a tiny brain, and consequently walnuts were used to cure madness. While that treatment never panned out, other recommendations of the doctrine did, including its assessment of lemon balm.

Healing

In keeping with the doctrine, lemon balm, because of its heart-shaped leaves, was thought to aid heart health. Amazingly enough, current research proves this to be true, as drinking lemon balm tea can cause slight dilation of the blood vessels, helping to lower blood pressure. If you have high blood pressure, be sure to get a health professional's approval before trying this ancient nostrum (which is by no means a substitute for proper diet or prescribed medications). To make lemon balm tea, steep a tablespoon of bruised fresh lemon balm leaves in a cup of warm, not hot, water. Cover and let steep for twenty minutes, then strain and sip up to three times a day.

Lemon balm tea is also a digestive aid. It contains a volatile oil called eugenol, which is an antispasmodic, meaning that it calms the gastrointestinal tract. Lemon balm may also relax the rest of the body, since another of its volatile oils, citronellal, has shown a sedative effect on the nervous systems of rodents. Aromatherapists have used essential oil of lemon balm for centuries to heal the mind and body of the stresses of the outside world. While the results are not scientifically documented, fans of lemon balm massage rave about its relaxation abilities and its calming effect on the heart, nerves, and digestion. For an at-home lemon balm massage, combine five to seven drops of essential oil of lemon balm with a quarter cup of grapeseed or canola oil. Before bed, massage your hands, feet, and ears with the oil. Or encourage a friend to give you a lemon balm back massage.

Looking Your Best

Extra-strong lemon balm tea makes a refreshing skin mist, especially in summer heat. To make it, add a quarter cup of fresh lemon balm leaves to half a cup of warm, not boiling, water, then cover and steep for about twenty minutes. Strain and add a tablespoon of liquid witch hazel or commercial facial toner. Pour into a small spray bottle and mist your face after cleansing and before moisturizing. Carry the bottle with you and spray your face throughout the day.

Growing

Lemon balm grows wild in southern Europe, but it fares well in most North American gardens. It is a bush about two feet tall, with bright green heart-shaped leaves that may remind you of mint. To grow lemon balm, buy small organically grown plants. Find a place in the garden that gets at least four hours of sun a day. Lemon balm is susceptible to powdery mildew, but planting it near sage will help keep the mildew away. Prepare a standard herb mixture of two parts garden or potting soil, two parts peat, one part sand, and one part compost or composted cow manure. Dig a hole for each plant that's twice the size of the root ball, and set the plant in. Fill in with the surrounding soil and tamp it down. Soak with warm water; then, unless there is a drought, let nature do the watering.

With lemon balm in the garden, expect to attract lots of bees. The herb's botanical name is *melissa,* which means "honeybee," and beekeepers in Europe and the Middle East sometimes plant lemon balm around hives to attract bees to the area.

Lemon balm can get tall and leggy around midsummer. Since it looks best when it's bushy, keep it trimmed. A good use for the trimmings is as a furniture polish. Grab a handful of fresh leaves and rub on wood furniture, just as you would with an oiled cloth. The result is a beautiful patina. The leaves will become dark after you rub for a few minutes, so discard and replace them occasionally.

Cooking

Lemon balm has the flavor of a delicate, flowery lemon. Float fresh sprigs in iced tea or water for a tasty garnish, or make lemon balm tea and freeze it as ice cubes to cool juices and summer spritzers. For visual appeal, freeze tiny sprigs of lemon balm in each cube.

Lemon balm tea can be used as a poaching liquid for fruit, such as peaches and nectarines. Or toss lemon balm leaves right into fruit salads for a tangy lift, using two teaspoons of minced fresh leaves for each cup of fruit. You can also add it to sauces for a lemony zing, using one tablespoon of minced leaves for each half cup of sauce. For example, a homemade mayonnaise to accompany chilled salmon will be tastier with a sprinkle of lemon balm. If it's true that good food feeds the heart, the Doctrine of Signatures was right again.

 Herbed Lemonade

The sweetness level of this refreshing beverage is about that of unsweetened grapefruit juice, minus the sour aftertaste. If you like your lemonade sweeter, simply add more honey.

3 cups loosely packed lemon balm leaves	Juice of 4 lemons (about 1 cup)
6 cups hot water	3 tablespoons light honey or brown rice syrup

PACK the leaves into a 2-quart wide-mouthed jar or pitcher, using a wooden spoon to bruise them lightly to release their aroma. Pour the water over the leaves and let them stand for about an hour.

STRAIN and discard the leaves, then add the lemon juice and honey. (To keep the honey from sticking to the spoon, rinse it with water before using.) Stir or shake before serving hot or chilled, with sprigs of lemon balm for garnish.

MAKES 6 CUPS, OR 6 SERVINGS; 36 CALORIES PER CUP.

Jalapeño and Mushroom Salsa

The combination of hot peppers and mushrooms is popular in southeastern Pennsylvania, the mushroom-growing capital of the United States. When Mexican immigrants came to work in the mushroom houses, they brought their hot peppers along, and a new salsa was born.

~~~~~

3   medium-large fresh jalapeños

2   teaspoons olive oil

12 ounces fresh button mushrooms, sliced

2   cloves garlic, mashed through a press

2   Italian plum tomatoes, cored and chopped

Juice of 1 lime

3   tablespoons very finely minced fresh lemon balm

ROAST the jalapeños over a gas flame or under a broiler until charred, about 5 minutes. The easiest way is to use a gas burner and tongs, but the jalapeños will "pop," so be careful. Set the charred jalapeños in a bowl, cover with a tea towel, and set aside.

HEAT a large sauté pan over medium-high heat. Pour in the oil, then add the mushrooms, garlic, tomatoes, and lime juice. Sauté for about 5 minutes.

MEANWHILE, use a paring knife to remove and discard the charred jalapeño skins. Mince the jalapeños.

ADD the jalapeños to the mushrooms. Sauté for 5 minutes more, or until the salsa is thickened. Swirl in the lemon balm and remove from the heat. Serve warm or at room temperature with corn chips, over cornbread, or on an antipasto tray. Or use as a filling for enchiladas.

MAKES 2 CUPS, OR 8 SERVINGS; 40 CALORIES PER SERVING, 1 GRAM FAT, 23 PERCENT OF CALORIES FROM FAT.

Lemony Oatmeal Cookies

No eggs are needed in these cookies, because the lemon balm and arrowroot combine to hold the dough together.

~~~~~

$1/3$ cup canola oil

$1/2$ cup pure maple syrup

$1/4$ cup lemon balm tea or water

2 tablespoons arrowroot or kudzu

1 tablespoon fresh lemon juice

1 teaspoon pure vanilla extract

$1'1/4$ cups whole wheat pastry flour

$1/4$ teaspoon baking soda

1 teaspoon baking powder

$1/4$ cup very finely minced fresh lemon balm leaves

1 cup rolled oats

$1/2$ cup raisins

PREHEAT the oven to 350°F.

IN a medium bowl, combine the oil, maple syrup, tea, arrowroot, lemon juice, and vanilla. Use an electric hand mixer to mix well.

IN a large bowl, combine the pastry flour, baking soda, baking powder, minced lemon balm, oats, and raisins. Mix well. Beat in the wet ingredients, using a large rubber spatula. Don't overmix; about 15 strokes should do.

LINE a cookie sheet with parchment paper, then drop the batter onto it in scant tablespoon-sized mounds. (You'll probably need to bake the cookies in two batches.) Bake in the middle of the oven until lightly browned around the edges, about 12 minutes. Let cool on a wire rack before serving.

MAKES $2^1/2$ DOZEN COOKIES; 62 CALORIES PER COOKIE, 2.8 GRAMS FAT; 35 PERCENT OF CALORIES FROM FAT.

Variation: If you'd like to glaze the cookies, use a pastry brush to spread a bit of all-fruit apricot jam on each one while they are still hot.

lemongrass

~~~~~~

"a" for attitude

~

HELP

BALANCE

DEPRESSION

AND

JET LAG

~

TREAT

OILY

SKIN

~

GIVE

FOODS A

FLORAL

ZEST

~

*A*n herbalist created a personal jet lag formula for me, made from essential oil of lemongrass, with other supporting herbs. After a fourteen-hour flight to Hong Kong I gave it a try by shaking a few drops out on a hanky and inhaling. I repeated the lemongrass inhalation once an hour and was able to remain alert until about 10 P.M. Hong Kong time. Surprisingly, I did not awaken at 3 A.M. as I usually do after extensive travel, but slept through to morning. That day, when I became sleepy at 3 P.M., I repeated the hourly lemongrass inhalation and felt refreshed and revived.

Lore and Legend

In Jamu, the ancient herbalism practiced in Indonesia and parts of Malaysia, lemongrass tea is used to combat depression and bad moods. In Indonesia, lemongrass is called *sereh,* and even though nowadays modern medicine is favored over Jamu, it's not unusual to smell the flowery citrus aroma of the herb in your lunchtime soup in Jakarta.

Healing

Western aromatherapists use essential oil of lemongrass to create a cheerful and elevated mood. It's sometimes combined with lavender and rose geranium, also in essential oil form, and mixed with grapeseed oil or olive oil for a rejuvenating massage. To try it, combine three drops of essential oil of lemongrass, three drops of essential oil of rose geranium, and five drops of essential oil of lavender (all available at herb shops and health food stores) in a quarter cup of grapeseed oil or canola oil. Then massage your arms, hands, feet, and ears.

East Indian Ayurvedic herbalists recommend lemongrass tea for colitis. To make a cup, combine one teaspoon of dried lemongrass leaves (available at health food stores and herb shops) in one cup of boiling water and steep, covered, for ten minutes. Then strain and sip. Additionally, aromatherapists advise dropping two drops of essential oil of lemongrass on a tissue and inhaling the aroma.

For diarrhea, East Indian Ayurvedic herbalists advise combining half a teaspoon each of dried lemongrass and ground ginger in a cup of boiling black coffee. Steep, covered for eight minutes, then strain before drinking.

Looking Your Best

If your skin is oily, try treating it with a lemongrass splash. Jamu herbalists recommend steeping one teaspoon of the dried herb in one cup of boiling black tea, covered, for five minutes. Strain the tea, let it cool, and then splash it on your face after cleansing. Repeat the splash at least three times a day. Or you can pour the splash into a spray bottle and mist yourself throughout the day to keep oiliness in check.

Aromatherapists advise adding essential oil of lemongrass to commercial facial cleansers, toners, and moisturizers to help control oily skin. For each half cup of the product, add three drops of essential oil of lemongrass. Shake well the before using.

Growing

Lemongrass grows wild in India, Sri Lanka, and parts of Africa as well as Indonesia, but with some care it can be cultivated in North America. Its leaves seem to pop right out of the ground, making a mature plant look like a three-foot herbal fountain.

To grow lemongrass, buy several whole fresh lemon grass spears at an Asian or Indian market. Each spear will produce a few others. Cut the leaves back to two inches. Plant the spears in a deep pot in a sandy version of the standard herb mixture, combining two parts garden or potting soil, two parts peat, two parts sand, and one part compost or composted cow manure. Leave the two inches of leaves sticking out. If it's warm, keep the pot outdoors, but bring it inside when the weather grows colder.

Lemongrass likes at least six hours of sun a day and constantly moist soil. When the fountain of leaves starts to droop and water won't perk it up, it's time to harvest the scallion-like bulbs from the soil to use in teas and such dishes as soups and curries. To keep the crop going, always replant one or two bulbs in the same manner in which you started. (Curing the bulbs first is not necessary.)

Cooking

When chefs get together to eat, they like to identify the individual flavors in the dishes they're served. Lemongrass is one ingredient that can stump even the most expert tasters. It tastes lemony, but what throws people off is that lemongrass is not the least bit acidic. In fact, it's quite floral.

Lemongrass is rarely used alone and is instead combined with other herbs and flavors of its native countries. In India that means turmeric-based curries. In Southeast Asia, particularly in Thailand, lemongrass is often mixed with garlic, ginger, coriander leaf, hot chilies, and Thai fish sauce (nam pla). These complex combinations make the presence of lemongrass even harder to detect, but provides the accent that keeps the stronger flavors in balance.

Fresh lemongrass looks somewhat like a large scallion, with slightly more gray in the green. Zip off the tough, dryish outer leaves and use them to give a citrus zest to clear soups. Remove them before serving, as you would a bay leaf.

Underneath are the tender leaves and the white bulb, the parts most prized by chefs. Mince and add to stuffings for sole or game hen. Sprinkle them into marinated vegetable salads, the batter for tea bread, or anywhere you want an uplifting soft lemon flavor—using about a teaspoon per serving.

Lemongrass is also available in little dried curls of leaf and sliced bulb. Smell it before you buy it. It should have a flowery lemon-lime aroma. If it doesn't, buy your lemongrass elsewhere. Dried lemongrass lends a floral snap to soups, stews, and casseroles. Grind one teaspoon of dried curls in a mortar or electric spice grinder and add to a curried vegetable recipe to serve four.

Corn Fritters with Lemongrass

Minced lemongrass brings subtle citrus tones to fresh corn.

~~~~~~

1 cup chopped kale (cut into ½-inch-wide strips)

1 cup fresh corn kernels (from 2 ears)

2 tablespoons minced fresh lemongrass

2 scallions, minced

3 tablespoons grated low-fat mozzarella cheese or soy mozzarella

2 large egg whites or ¼ cup Calendula Egg Substitute (page 47)

1 tablespoon cornstarch

2 teaspoons olive oil

PLACE the kale in a strainer in the sink and pour boiling water over it for about 10 seconds. Drain and pat dry.

TRANSFER the kale to a medium bowl and add the corn, lemongrass, scallions, cheese, egg whites, and cornstarch. Combine well.

HEAT a large well-seasoned cast-iron skillet over medium-high heat. Pour in the oil and swirl the pan to coat the bottom. (If you don't have cast-iron, use a nonstick sauté pan but don't preheat.)

TO make the fritters, scoop out well-rounded tablespoons of the batter and form them into balls. The batter will be slightly loose. Set the balls into the hot skillet, flattening each one gently with a spatula. Let the fritters sizzle until gently browned, about 3 minutes on each side. Serve warm as a first course, a snack, or a side dish with poached salmon or trout.

MAKES 4 SERVINGS; 89 CALORIES PER SERVING, 3 GRAMS FAT, 30 PERCENT OF CALORIES FROM FAT.

Potato Soup with Lemongrass

Lemongrass is the grace note in this classic spring favorite. For the best texture, be sure to use waxy-textured new, red or white potatoes, not baking potatoes.

～～～

2 teaspoons olive oil

1 tablespoon plus 1 teaspoon minced fresh lemongrass

1 leek, topped, tailed, rinsed, and minced

1 clove garlic, mashed through a press

4 cups vegetable stock or defatted chicken stock

1 pound new potatoes, cut into small chunks (about 3 cups)

1/4 cup minced fresh coriander

2 tablespoons minced fresh garlic chives or regular chives

Cayenne (optional)

HEAT a large soup pot over medium-high heat and pour in the oil. When it's warm, add the lemongrass, leek, and garlic and sauté until fragrant and slightly tender, about 2 minutes. Take care not to let the garlic burn.

ADD the stock and potatoes and bring to a boil. Reduce the heat to a simmer, cover loosely, and let the soup bubble gently until the potatoes are tender, about 10 to 12 minutes. Remove from the heat and immediately sprinkle in the coriander. To serve, pour the soup into a tureen or individual soup bowls, and swirl in the chives and cayenne (if you're in a spicy mood).

MAKES 4 SERVINGS; 145 CALORIES PER SERVING, 4 GRAMS FAT, 25 PERCENT OF CALORIES FROM FAT.

Mussels with Lemongrass

The herbs and lemongrass in this easy-to-prepare recipe give the mussels an exotic perfume.

~~~~~~

2 teaspoons peanut oil

1 leek, topped, tailed, rinsed, and minced

4 stalks lemongrass, well trimmed (no green or tough parts) and minced

2 cloves garlic, mashed through a press

1 dried hot chili pepper, or to taste

1 teaspoon minced fresh ginger

½ cup dry white wine

½ cup vegetable stock or defatted chicken stock

4 dozen mussels, cleaned and beards removed

1 tablespoon plus 1 teaspoon nam pla (Thai fish sauce)

¼ cup fresh coriander leaves

HEAT the oil in a large stockpot over medium-high heat. When it's warm, toss in the leek, lemongrass, garlic, chili, and ginger and sauté until fragrant and just wilted, about 3 minutes.

POUR in the wine and stock, then add the mussels. Increase the heat to high, cover loosely, and let the mixture bubble until all the mussels have opened, about 3 to 5 minutes. As the mussels open, remove them with tongs so they don't overcook, putting them right into individual soup bowls. If any mussels have not opened after 5 minutes, discard them.

SWIRL the nam pla into the broth in the pot, then pour over the mussels. Garnish with the coriander and serve warm, along with crusty bread for dunking.

MAKES 4 ENTREE SERVINGS; 135 CALORIES PER SERVING, 2 GRAMS FAT, 14 PERCENT OF CALORIES FROM FAT.

Blueberry Breakfast Cake with Lemongrass

The spiciness of blueberries and sweetness of orange are enhanced by lemongrass. This cake is especially tasty with a cup of hot peppermint tea.

~~~~~~

1 cup whole wheat pastry flour

1 cup unbleached all-purpose flour

1 tablespoon ground dried lemongrass

1 teaspoon baking powder

1 teaspoon baking soda

1 cup blueberries

2/3 cup skim milk or low-fat vanilla soy milk

1/4 cup frozen orange juice concentrate, thawed

2 tablespoons canola oil

2 tablespoons all-fruit apricot jam

PREHEAT the oven to 375°F.

IN a medium bowl, combine the flours, lemongrass, baking powder, baking soda, and blueberries.

IN a small bowl, combine the milk, orange juice concentrate, and oil, and use an electric hand mixer to beat until well combined. Pour the liquid ingredients into the flour bowl, mixing with a rubber spatula to combine well. Don't overmix; about 15 strokes should do.

LIGHTLY oil and flour a deep 9-inch pie dish. Add the batter. Lightly wet one hand and use it to even out the top. Bake in the center of the oven until a thin knife comes out clean, about 20 to 25 minutes. While the cake is still warm, spread on the jam with the back of a spoon. Let cool completely before slicing.

MAKES 8 SERVINGS; 183 CALORIES PER SERVING, 3.5 GRAMS FAT, 16 PERCENT OF CALORIES FROM FAT.

Lemony Quinoa with Maple-Sautéed Apples

Lemongrass and cinnamon enliven a bracing breakfast dish.

~~~~~

2 cups pure apple or pear juice

2 teaspoons dried lemongrass

1 cup quinoa (see Note)

3 slices lemon (including the peel)

1 tablespoon canola oil

3 medium cooking apples, cored and sliced

1/2 teaspoon ground cinnamon

2 tablespoons pure maple syrup

Pinch of sea salt

COMBINE the juice and lemongrass in a small saucepan and bring to a boil. Reduce the heat and simmer, loosely covered, for about 4 minutes. Strain and discard the lemongrass. Return the juice to the saucepan.

ADD the quinoa to the juice, along with the lemon slices, and bring to a boil. Reduce the heat to a simmer, cover loosely, and simmer until the quinoa is tender, about 15 minutes. When cooked, the quinoa grains will have doubled in size and each will have a tiny, white curly tail (the germ of the grain). Discard the lemon slices.

MEANWHILE, heat a large sauté pan over medium-high heat and pour in the oil. Add the apples and cinnamon and sauté until the apples just become soft around the edges, about 2 minutes. Pour in the maple syrup and continue to cook for another 30 seconds. Sprinkle on the sea salt.

SCOOP the apples over the quinoa. Serve warm for breakfast.

MAKES 3 HUGE SERVINGS; 397 CALORIES PER SERVING, 8 GRAMS FAT, 18 PERCENT OF CALORIES FROM FAT.

NOTE: Quinoa is a whole grain from South America that is available at specialty stores, health food shops, and many supermarkets.

Coffee Cake with Pears and Lemongrass

Though lemongrass is traditionally used with savory foods, it gives a floral undertone to sweets that is especially welcome in those with no refined sugar. In this case, lemongrass brightens a whole wheat cake with a fruit filling.

~~~~~

FOR THE FILLING:

1 pound ripe pears, peeled, cored, and chopped (about 3 1/2 cups)

1 tablespoon minced fresh lemongrass

2 teaspoons ground cinnamon

FOR THE BATTER AND GLAZE:

1 3/4 cups whole wheat pastry flour

1 3/4 cups unbleached all-purpose flour

1 tablespoon baking powder

1/2 teaspoon baking soda

1 cup nonfat ricotta cheese or crumbled tofu

1 cup rice syrup or barley malt

1/3 cup water

3 tablespoons kudzu or arrowroot

1/3 cup canola oil

Pinch of sea salt

2 teaspoons pure vanilla extract

1/4 cup all-fruit apricot preserves

PREHEAT the oven to 375°F.

TO make the filling, combine the pears, lemongrass, and cinnamon in a medium bowl. Set aside.

IN a large bowl, combine the flours, baking powder, and baking soda. Mix well. In another bowl, combine the ricotta, rice syrup, water, kudzu, canola oil, salt, and vanilla, beating well with an electric hand mixer. Use a large spatula to fold the ricotta mixture into the flour mixture and combine well.

LIGHTLY oil and flour a 10-inch Bundt pan. Spread one-third of the batter evenly over the bottom of the pan. It will be sticky, so use damp hands to handle it. Scoop in half of the filling and spread it evenly over the batter. Top with half the remaining batter and then the remaining filling. Spread the remaining batter over the filling and smooth the top.

BAKE in the center of the oven until a knife comes out clean, about 40 minutes. Start checking at 30 minutes; if the top begins to brown too quickly, cover loosely with foil. Let the cake cool for about 10 minutes, then carefully remove from the pan by setting a cake plate upside down on top of the cake and flipping the whole thing over. Remove the pan and spread on the preserves. Let cool completely before slicing.

MAKES 16 SERVINGS; 220 CALORIES PER SERVING, 4 GRAMS FAT, 16 PERCENT OF CALORIES FROM FAT.

Mango Ice with Lemongrass

The subtle citrus of lemongrass enhances the velvety sweetness of mango.

~~~~~

1 1/2   cups chopped ripe mango
         (2 whole mangoes)
3/4   cup brewed lemongrass tea
2   tablespoons brown rice
         syrup or light honey

1   tablespoon fresh lemon juice
Fresh lemon balm or lemon
     verbena sprigs for garnish

COMBINE the mango, tea, brown rice syrup, and lemon juice in a processor or blender and whiz until smooth. Scoop the mixture into an ice cream maker and process according to the manufacturer's instructions (see Note). Serve garnished with the fresh leaves.

MAKES 4 SERVINGS; 50 CALORIES PER SERVING, NO ADDED FAT.

NOTE: If you don't have an ice cream maker, you can freeze the mixture in a stainless steel or glass bowl, stirring every 20 minutes or so to break up the large ice crystals. It will take about 2½ hours to freeze.

Warm Herbed Cider

Lemongrass lightens a spicy cider.

~~~~~~

4 cups apple cider
3 bay leaves
3 cinnamon sticks

3 star anise
2 teaspoons dried lemongrass

COMBINE all the ingredients in a large soup pot and bring to a boil. Lower the heat, cover loosely, and simmer for about 20 minutes. Strain and serve warm.

MAKES 4 CUPS, OR 4 SERVINGS; 120 CALORIES PER SERVING, NO ADDED FAT.

lemon verbena

~~~~~~

stomach de-stressor

*O*ur packed 737 airliner was just crossing the Honduras-Guatemala border when it began to lurch and jerk. Smoke pouring out of one of the engines on the left obscured the jungle. A flight attendant told us to put our heads between our knees and to prepare for an emergency landing. Her tone masked anxiety, and the passengers were silent.

It seemed like only seconds, however, before the plane touched ground, and fire trucks with screaming sirens raced to the scene. We were led, shaking, from the aircraft as the firemen smothered the engine with jets of white foam. We were driven to the terminal in a military vehicle complete with mounted machine guns. There, a kind local woman soothed me with a drink made from lemon verbena. She promised that it would help me relax, and it did.

~

RELIEVE

INTESTINAL

GAS

~

CREATE

INSTANT

AROMATHERAPY

~

ADD

SWEET

LEMON

FLAVOR

TO FOODS

AND TEAS

~

Lore and Legend

While most herbs traveled from the Old World to the New, lemon verbena sailed in the opposite direction. Seventeenth-century Spanish explorers brought the herb from Central and South America to Europe, where it was immediately adopted by herbalists. They prescribed a tea of lemon verbena to relieve nervous stomachs, depression, headaches, and heart palpitations. Lemon verbena's fresh, citrus aroma also made it a popular ingredient in perfumes and liquors. Additionally, it was, and still is, a favorite garden ornamental, grown for use in sachets and potpourri.

Healing

Called *herba Luisa* in Central and South America, lemon verbena tea is prized for its ability to relax overtaxed stomachs and to relieve intestinal gas. To try it, steep one tablespoon of fresh leaf, or one teaspoon dried, in a cup of hot water for four minutes. Be sure to cover the cup while the tea is steeping so the delicious aroma doesn't escape. Sometimes, especially in Ecuador, hibiscus is added to lemon verbena, and the combination is very refreshing.

Whether fresh or dried, a leaf or two of lemon verbena tucked in your pocket can serve as instant aromatherapy. Rub the leaves from time to time throughout the day, then smell the aroma on your fingers. The scent will lift your spirits.

Growing

In its native Chile and Peru, lemon verbena is a ten-foot-tall tree with long medium-green oval leaves. It will reach that height in one season elsewhere, too, especially if it has at least six hours of sun a day. If you don't want your lemon verbena to grow that tall, trim it weekly. Lemon verbena likes a rich version of the standard herb mixture, combining two parts garden or potting soil, two parts peat, two parts compost or composted cow manure, and one part sand. Buy a small organically grown plant and dig a hole for it that's twice the size of the root ball. Set the plant in, fill in with the surrounding soil, and tamp it down. Soak with warm water, then continue to water about once a week. For indoor growing, give lemon verbena a big pot—it's a tree, after all—and place it where it will get six hours of sun a day, which can be augmented with ninety-watt halogen floods, placed about three feet away from the plant. The halogen can be left on for up to twelve hours a day.

Lemon verbena, unfortunately, is a magnet for whitefly. It's not uncommon to see entire plants completely covered with the tiny white pests. Not only that, but once they've gotten hold of your lemon verbena, they'll go on to make mincemeat of the rosemary, bay, and scented geraniums in your garden. To combat whitefly, soak a handful—about half a cup—of fresh feverfew leaves in a quart of boiling water for one hour, then strain and use as a garden spray. If you're squeamish about the possibility of attracting whitefly to your garden, buy organically grown lemon verbena dried for use in teas and food.

Cooking

Lemon verbena has the intense citrus taste of lemon zest without being at all bitter. In fact, lemon verbena is the most lemony of all herbs, which makes it a favorite in the kitchen. Rub a fresh leaf on a slice of cantaloupe to bring out the fruit's flavor, or add several leaves to a cup of fresh strawberries or blueberries for sweetness without added sugar.

Since prolonged heat destroys the flavor of fresh lemon verbena, use only the dried herb in cooking. Try adding two teaspoonfuls to rice pilaf to serve four or to the batter for a dozen carrot muffins.

To dry your own lemon verbena, just lay a branch on a plate and store it in a cool dry place for a week to ten days, depending on the humidity. Store the dried leaves in a tightly covered glass jar away from sun and heat. To use, rub the dried leaves between your hands to release their aroma before adding to recipes.

Apple Crisp with Lemon Verbena

Lemon verbena brings out the sweetness of fruit, so you don't have to add refined sugar.

~~~~~

1 cup rolled oats	2 tablespoons unbleached all-purpose flour
2 pounds cooking apples, peeled, cored, and thinly sliced	1/3 cup (not packed) dried lemon verbena leaves
Juice of 1 lemon (about 1/4 cup)	2 tablespoons pure maple syrup or rice syrup
1/2 cup all-fruit apple butter	

PREHEAT the oven to 375°F.

TOAST the oats in a dry sauté pan over high heat, stirring frequently with a spatula; after about 3 minutes, start watching them carefully, making sure they don't burn. When they're light brown, tip them out of the pan into a bowl. Set aside.

COMBINE the apples, lemon juice, apple butter, and flour in a deep 9-inch glass pie dish. (If you use a dark metal pie dish, reduce the oven temperature to 325°F.) Crumble the lemon verbena between your hands and mix it in.

POUR the maple syrup into the oats, stirring so that all the oats are very lightly coated. (It's easiest when the oats are still a bit warm.) Scoop the oats over the apple mixture and even out the top. Cover the dish with foil and bake in the center of the oven for about 20 to 25 minutes, or until the apple mixture has begun to bubble and the apples are tender. Remove the foil and continue to bake just until the oats are crisp, about 5 minutes. Serve warm or slightly chilled for breakfast, brunch, or dessert.

MAKES 6 SERVINGS; 170 CALORIES PER SERVING, TRACE OF FAT.

Couscous Cake with Orange-Caramel Pears

To add flavor without fat or sugar, replace the water in dessert recipes with lemon verbena tea.

~~~~~

2 cups couscous	1 tablespoon all-fruit raspberry jam
2 cups lemon verbena tea	Juice of 1 orange
1 teaspoon sweet (unsalted) butter or canola oil	Pinch of sea salt
3 pears, peeled, cored, and sliced	2 tablespoons toasted slivered almonds
½ teaspoon ground cinnamon	

COMBINE the couscous and tea in a small saucepan and bring to a boil. Reduce the heat to low and simmer, loosely covered, until all the liquid has been absorbed, about 5 minutes. Transfer the couscous to a 9-inch glass pie dish and spread out with a spatula.

MELT the butter in a large sauté pan over medium-high heat. Add the pears, cinnamon, jam, orange juice, and salt, and cook, stirring, until the cooking juices are caramel-like and thick, about 5 to 7 minutes. Scoop the pears onto the couscous and spread them out evenly. Sprinkle the almonds over the cake. Chill the cake for at least 30 minutes. Then slice into wedges and serve.

MAKES 8 SERVINGS; 155 CALORIES PER SERVING, LESS THAN 1 GRAM FAT, 5 PERCENT OF CALORIES FROM FAT.

Meringue Baskets with Raspberries and Apricots

Fresh lemon verbena leaves brighten the flavor of fresh raspberries and apricots, without adding sugar.

~~~~~

2 large egg whites, at room temperature	1/8 teaspoon cream of tartar
1/2 teaspoon fresh lemon juice	3 cups fresh raspberries
2 tablespoons pure maple syrup	3 cups sliced fresh apricots
	3 tablespoons small fresh lemon verbena leaves

PREHEAT the oven to 275°F. Line a cookie sheet with parchment paper and lightly trace four 3-inch circles on it.

IN a medium bowl, beat the egg whites with an electric hand mixer until bubbly. Add the lemon juice, maple syrup, and cream of tartar and beat on high until the whites are stiff and glossy, but not dry, about 4 minutes.

SCOOP the meringue into a pastry bag fitted with a star tip. To make the baskets, drop stars onto the parchment, following the traced circles. (Don't fill in the middle of the circles.)

BAKE the meringue baskets in the center of the oven until just lightly browned, about 9 minutes. Turn off the oven and leave the baskets in the turned-off oven with the door closed for about an hour, or until dried and crisp.

MEANWHILE, combine the berries, apricots, and lemon verbena.

TO serve, set each basket on a pretty dessert plate and spoon in the raspberry mixture.

MAKES 4 SERVINGS; 115 CALORIES PER SERVING, TRACE OF FAT.

lovage

~~~~~~~~~~~~~~~~~~~~~~~~~~~~~~~~

healthy
heartthrob

*F*eng shui (pronounced "fung shway") is the Chinese art of placement, of orienting buildings and the furnishings within them to bring serenity and good fortune. Conceived in sixth-century China, feng shui literally means "wind" and "water." Emperors believed that proper placement of temples and palaces would prevent wind and water from destroying them, thus preserving the peace and harmony of their kingdoms and ensuring their own prosperity.

Fourteen centuries later, feng shui is still practiced by ordinary people, who rely on it to help bring peace and harmony to their homes, office buildings, and even gardens. It is an amazingly complex art, so I felt lucky that a problem in my own garden had a very simple solution. A protruding brick wall made the garden feel harsh and inhospitable, so I was directed by a

~

DRINK AN

HERBAL

DIURETIC

~

SOOTHE A

SORE

THROAT

~

TRY A

FLAVORFUL

SALT

SUBSTITUTE

~

feng shui expert to obscure the wall with large and leafy lovage. Now my garden is the sanctuary I planned it to be.

Lore and Legend

Lovage was a staple in the Middle Ages, when its leaves were tucked into traveler's boots to help keep feet fresh, or floated in bathwater to give it a garden scent. The leaves were also combined with yarrow leaves and sugar, then steeped in brandy to make a popular love potion. Hence, since its leaves look like oversized parsley, lovage was also known as "love parsley."

Medieval herbalists recommended drinking lovage tea for colic, jaundice, and intestinal gas. They also prescribed the tea as a wash for irritated eyes. Fried in lard, lovage leaves were used as a poultice to treat boils.

Healing

Present-day herbalists sometimes recommend a tea of ground dried lovage root as a diuretic, especially for women who retain water before menstruation. Be sure to check with a health professional before you try it, since lovage root may irritate certain kidney conditions. It may also encourage menstruation to begin, so pregnant women (or those who suspect they are pregnant) must avoid it.

Osha, a species related to common lovage, tastes like strong celery seed. The dried root was used by the Paiute Indians as a cough remedy and is still popular among Rocky Mountain herbalists for treating sore throats and colds. A small piece of dried root, about the size of a pea, can be sucked on for about ten minutes to relieve the symptoms of respiratory infections.

The dried root of another cousin, Chinese lovage, is one of the ingredients in the famous Four Things Soup, a Chinese tonic for women made of four herbs. It's recommended by Chinese herbalists to help balance the minds and bodies of women who are premenstrual, going through menopause, or suffering from fatigue and stress.

Growing

Lovage is a great choice for a child's garden because it grows fast, becomes huge, and usually readily reveals what it needs. When the leaves begin to turn pale, lovage needs some nutrients from a spray of fish emulsion. If the stems begin to lean over, the plant needs to be cut back. The hollow stems (minus leaves) can be fun to use as drinking straws for refreshing summer beverages. Or you can arrange the cut stems and leaves in a vase to perfume the house with a refreshing celery aroma.

Lovage is a Mediterranean native and likes a rich version of the standard herb mixture, combining two parts garden or potting soil, two parts peat, two parts compost or composted cow manure, and one part sand. Buy a small organically grown plant and dig a hole for it that's twice the size of the root ball. Remember that lovage can grow to over six feet tall, so plant it behind other herbs. Lovage likes at least six hours of sun a day, but will take part shade if that's all you've got. Set the plant in the hole, fill in with the surrounding soil, and tamp it down. Soak with warm water, then water about once a week thereafter. Since lovage is so large, it's best to keep it outdoors. It will, however, grow well in a big pot on a terrace or patio.

Cooking

Lovage is worth its height in taste, especially for people who are reducing salt in their diets. It has the flavor of robust celery, and young, tender leaves and stems can be substituted for celery. Try adding a teaspoon of minced fresh lovage leaf to a pot of soup or vinaigrette for four to heighten the taste without using salt. One teaspoon may sound like a small amount, but lovage is strong and can overwhelm other flavors in a recipe.

Spicy Soba with Lovage

Lovage blends and enhances the garlic and chives in this dish.

~~~~~

4 cups cooked soba (Japanese buckwheat noodles) (from ¹/₂ pound dried)

1 medium carrot, julienned

1 clove garlic, mashed through a press

¹/₂ teaspoon sambal (Vietnamese hot chili paste, or see page 114)

1 teaspoon nam nuoc (Vietnamese fish sauce)

Juice of 1 lime

2 teaspoons toasted (dark) sesame oil

1 teaspoon minced fresh lovage leaves

1 tablespoon minced fresh regular chives or garlic chives

COMBINE the soba and carrots in a serving bowl.

IN a small bowl, stir together all the remaining ingredients. Pour over the soba and toss well before serving.

MAKES 4 ENTRÉE SERVINGS; 240 CALORIES PER SERVING, 2 GRAMS FAT, 8 PERCENT OF CALORIES FROM FAT.

Cracked Wheat with Olives, Feta, and Spinach Ribbons

Lovage, when combined with chives, garlic, and lemon, arouses the nuttiness of whole wheat.

~~~~~~

2 cups cooked cracked wheat (or bulgur)

5 Greek olives, pitted and chopped

2 scallions, coarsely chopped

2 tablespoons minced fresh chives

1 clove garlic, very finely minced

2 teaspoons minced fresh lovage

Juice of 1/2 lemon

2 teaspoons olive oil

1/2 cup packed stemmed fresh spinach leaves

2 tablespoons crumbled Greek feta cheese or soy Parmesan

COMBINE the cracked wheat, olives, scallions, chives, garlic, and lovage in a medium bowl.

IN a small bowl, combine the lemon juice and olive oil. Pour over the cracked wheat, and mix well.

TO chiffonade the spinach leaves, stack them and roll them up like a cigar. Starting at one end of the roll, slice the spinach into thin ribbons with a sharp knife. Arrange the spinach ribbons on a plate and pile the cracked wheat on top. Sprinkle with the feta and serve.

MAKES 4 SIDE SERVINGS; 135 CALORIES PER SERVING, 4 GRAMS FAT, 26 PERCENT OF CALORIES FROM FAT.

mustard

the heart specialist

~

BEST BET

FOR THE

MINERAL

MAGNESIUM

~

DEFEND

AGAINST

CANCER

~

ENJOY A

NATURAL

SOURCE OF

VITAMIN C

~

About a quarter mile from our house is a field that, each May, is filled with wild mustard. I keep watch, and when the plants are about four inches high I begin picking the leaves. I eat mustard leaf salads with lemon vinaigrette, and mustard leaves sautéed in garlic and olive oil. I pack mustard leaves into sandwiches, enchiladas, sushi rolls, and egg rolls and I mince them to swirl into soft polenta. I enjoy every spicy, tangy bite throughout the month, for the harvest is over in June, and then I must wait patiently for another spring.

Don't harvest wild herbs unless you're sure of what you're picking. Your county extension office may be able to help you learn to identify herbs in all stages of growth. Then you too will be rewarded every spring.

Lore and Legend

When prehistoric families squatted down for a meal, they often chewed whole mustard seeds along with their meats, creating an instant condiment when they crushed the seeds between their teeth. In ancient Chinese, Greek, and Roman kitchens, mustard seed was mixed with wine and mashed to a paste in a crock. Since the mustard kept well and masked rancidity in pre–refrigeration-era meats, its use was soon ingrained around the globe. Today, in the remotest areas of the Bolivian Andes, people carry spice pouches, called *ajo,* around their waists as they travel the mountains. The pouches are filled with mustard seed and dried hot peppers, which are added to a pot filled with potatoes and mountain water to make a tasty stew.

Healing

Mustard is not only tasty, it's good for you. Mustard seeds contain magnesium, a mineral that can help regulate blood cholesterol levels and help regulate blood sugar levels in insulin-dependent diabetics. It has given energy to people with chronic fatigue syndrome and may help regulate an irregular heartbeat. One tablespoon of ground seed contains thirty-three milligrams of magnesium. That's about one tenth of the daily recommendation. For comparison, cooked oatmeal, which is considered a good source of magnesium, contains only twenty-eight milligrams per half cup. So adding mustard to marinades, vinaigrettes, and sandwich spreads can be a smart, as well as savory, idea.

Herbalists recommend using ground mustard seed in a foot bath to help relieve respiratory congestion. To try it, add one tablespoon of ground mustard seed to two quarts of hot water in a basin, and soak your feet, covering the basin with a towel. After five minutes, rub your feet with a soothing lotion or oil (for example, Soothing Lavender Skin Oil, page 344), put on socks, and go to bed.

Mustard greens are also potent herbs. In India, where mustard and other greens are called *saag,* they're sautéed with spices such as ginger, fennel, and chilies. East Indian Ayurvedic herbalists say that *saag,* especially when cooked with spices, helps stimulate digestion.

Mustard greens are an excellent source of beta carotene, the plant form of vitamin A. Beta carotene in the diet is associated with lowered risk for certain types of cancer. You might want to eat mustard greens if you're taking medication to lower your blood cholesterol, since those drugs, when taken over extended periods of time, may deplete beta carotene levels.

Mustard greens also offer vitamin C, a nutrient that can help fight infection and may help prevent heart disease. To get the maximum benefit, eat the greens raw, not cooked, as vitamin C is diminished by heat.

High-Magnesium Herbs and Spices

HERB	MG./TBS.
Anise seed	11
Basil (dried leaf)	19
Caraway seed	17
Cardamom (ground)	13
Celery seed	29
Chili powder	13
Cloves (ground)	17
Coriander seed (ground)	17
Cumin seed	22
Dillseed	17
Dill weed	14
Fennel seed	28
Fenugreek	21
Mustard seed	33
Poppy seed	29
Sesame seed	28
Turmeric (ground)	13

Figures are from the U.S. Department of Agriculture, *Agricultural Handbook* No. 8–2, 1977. Note that many of these herbs and spices are used in large amounts to make Indian curry blends. It's not hard to imagine how a curry meal could be a good source of magnesium.

Growing

Mustard grows wild almost all over the world, and so it's easy to cultivate. It likes at least six hours of sun a day and a rich version of the standard herb mixture, combining two parts potting or garden soil, two parts peat, two parts compost or composted cow manure and one part sand.

Buy small organically grown mustard plants. You might want to try a red-leafed Japanese or Indian variety, or a thin-leafed green variety called *mi-*

zuna. Dig a hole that's twice the size of each plant's root ball and set in the plant. Fill in with the surrounding soil, and tamp it down. Soak with warm water, and continue to water about once a week thereafter. Plant mustard in the spring and the fall, since harsh summer heat can make it bitter-tasting.

After the first frost, harvest all but a few tiny leaves from each plant, then cover the plants with pine needles. They'll stay alive all winter, and in milder climates you can even continue to pick the leaves, though the crop will be small. When spring arrives, remove the pine needles and the mustard will grow quickly, thanks to its mature root system.

Mustard plants can be grown indoors near a window that gets at least six hours of sun a day. To augment the light, use ninety-watt halogen floods placed about three feet away from the herbs. Harvest the leaves at any size. Since a reasonable crop of mustard plants won't produce enough seed to use in cooking or for healing, buy organically grown seed.

Cooking

Mustard greens taste sharp and spicy and can be mixed half-and-half in salads with milder greens. Or sauté them in olive oil and garlic and toss with hot pasta, using about a cup of raw greens for each serving.

Mustard seeds have a pointed robustness that can eliminate the need for salt in recipes. Add them to marinades for grilled foods, such as vegetables and fish, using half a teaspoon of ground seed in a marinade for food to serve four. Or try adding some seeds to your pepper mill for full-bodied flavor: Use two parts peppercorns, one part mustard seed, and one part allspice berry, and grind as usual.

You might also want to try mustard oil, which is available at East Indian stores and some specialty food stores. It can be used alone or mixed half-and-half with olive oil for dressing salads, making marinades, or sautéing vegetables.

Fresh Thyme Mustard with Vermouth

The perfume of fresh thyme smoothes the spice of the mustard seed. Enjoy as a dip for herbed breads, serve with grilled chicken, or use in a vinaigrette or marinade.

~~~~~~~

1/4 cup ground mustard seed (one 0.85-ounce tin)	2 tablespoons honey or brown rice syrup
1/4 cup white vermouth	1 tablespoon olive oil
1/4 cup packed fresh thyme leaves	

COMBINE the mustard and vermouth in a small saucepan and stir well. Heat over high heat until just bubbly, about 1 1/2 to 2 minutes. Remove from the heat.

MEANWHILE, in a mortar or electric spice grinder, grind the thyme until very finely minced.

STIR the thyme into the hot mustard, along with the honey and oil. Cover and let sit in the fridge overnight to blend the flavors. The mustard will keep, covered and refrigerated, for up to a month.

MAKES ABOUT 1/3 CUP; 24 CALORIES PER 1-TABLESPOON SERVING, LESS THAN 1 GRAM FAT.

Hot Pepper Mustard with Beer

Mustard seed, hot pepper sauce, and chili oil team up to make a very spicy beer-based sauce for sandwiches and marinades. Or brush on fish before grilling, swirl into gazpacho or other chilled soups just before serving, or mix half-and-half with plain yogurt as a dipping sauce for chilled shrimp.

~~~~~~~

$^1/_4$ cup ground mustard seed
(one 0.85-ounce tin)

$^1/_4$ cup beer

1 teaspoon hot pepper sauce,
or to taste

1 tablespoon hot chili oil

2 tablespoons honey or brown
rice syrup

COMBINE the mustard and beer in a small saucepan, stirring well. Heat over high heat until just bubbly, about $1^1/_2$ to 2 minutes. Remove from the heat and stir in the hot pepper sauce, oil, and honey. Cover and store in the refrigerator overnight to let the flavors mellow. The sauce will keep, refrigerated, for up to a month.

MAKES A SCANT $^1/_3$ CUP; 24 CALORIES PER 1-TABLESPOON SERVING, LESS THAN 1 GRAM FAT.

Toasted Sesame Mustard with Sake

The rich flavor of toasted sesame oil gives a velvety taste to this mustard. This sauce is great on skinny Chinese noodles or used as a condiment with egg rolls, samosas, pakoras, and other finger foods.

$^1/_4$ cup ground mustard seed
(one 0.85-ounce tin)

$^1/_4$ cup sake or dry white wine

1 tablespoon soy sauce
(reduced-sodium is okay)

1 tablespoon toasted (dark)
sesame oil

2 tablespoons honey or brown
rice syrup

COMBINE the mustard and sake in a small saucepan and stir well. Heat over high heat until just bubbly, about $1^1/_2$ to 2 minutes. Remove from the heat and stir in the soy sauce, sesame oil, and honey. Cover and refrigerate overnight to unify the flavors. Store refrigerated for up to a month.

MAKES A SCANT $^1/_3$ CUP; 24 CALORIES PER 1-TABLESPOON SERVING, LESS THAN 1 GRAM FAT.

Chick Pea Salad with Red Onion and Mustard Greens

Garlic and oregano are classic flavorings for tangy mustard greens.

~~~~~~

1	tablespoon fresh lemon juice	1½	cups cooked chick peas (canned are okay, but rinse before using)
1	tablespoon red wine vinegar	1½	cups thinly sliced mustard greens
2	teaspoons olive oil		
½	teaspoon Dijon mustard	1	small red onion, thinly sliced and separated into rings
1	clove garlic, mashed through a press		
1	teaspoon minced fresh oregano or ½ teaspoon dried	2	tablespoons crumbled blue cheese or soy Parmesan

IN a small bowl, whisk together the lemon juice, vinegar, oil, and mustard. Stir in the garlic and oregano.

PUT the chick peas, mustard greens and onion into a medium bowl. Add the dressing, and toss well to coat. Serve at room temperature or very slightly chilled as a side dish or appetizer.

MAKES 4 SERVINGS; 210 CALORIES PER SERVING, 6.5 GRAMS FAT, 30 PERCENT OF CALORIES FROM FAT.

nasturtium

~~~~~~~~~~~~~~~~~~~~~~~~~~~~~~~~~~~

clobber a cold

An herbalist I met who trained in India with Ayurvedic experts holds that Indians have healthier teeth and gums than Americans. Though this may be partially due to diet, he explained that Indians also massage their teeth and gums with peppery-flavored herb leaves such as nasturtium, which both stimulate and cleanse. I followed his instructions and rolled a nasturtium leaf around my index finger, holding it in place with my third finger. I then massaged my gums and teeth using small, circular motions. Afterward my teeth felt sparkling clean and smooth, and my gums were gently tingly. When the leaves are in season, I make a point to practice the nasturtium teeth and gum massage every day.

Lore and Legend

Nasturtium has been used for centuries by Peruvian Indians as a remedy for coughs, colds, and the flu. The

~

BEAT

BRONCHITIS

~

TONE UP

YOUR

SKIN

~

GROW

FLOWERS

FOR THE

GARDEN

~

traditional cure is a tea made from two teaspoons of bruised fresh leaves steeped in a cup of hot water for ten minutes. In the late sixteenth century, nasturtium reached Europe when English pirates brought it home from Peru. English herbalists called it "Indian cress," in honor of its origin, and used it to treat scurvy, digestive problems, menstrual problems, influenza, and even baldness, as well as respiratory complaints.

Healing

Modern research supports the Peruvians' use of nasturtium as a cold and flu cure. We now know that fresh nasturtium leaves contain a natural antibiotic that is effective against respiratory conditions. To treat respiratory congestion, herbalists recommend eating three fresh nasturtium leaves three times a day. If you prefer, you can take nasturtium as a tea by bruising three fresh leaves, then steeping them, covered, in boiling water for about ten minutes. Strain before sipping, and take three times a day.

Herbalists also use nasturtium topically as a poultice for minor cuts and scratches. To try it, first wash the injured area well. Then, using the back of a spoon, lightly bruise three or four fresh nasturtium leaves. Pack the leaves around the cut or scratch and tie on with gauze. Leave the poultice on for about an hour, then repeat two or three times a day, until healing begins.

Looking Your Best

What you put in your body shows up on your skin. For a radiant glow, Chinese and other herbalists recommend eating one to two cups a day of fresh leafy herbs and greens, such as nasturtium. So try nasturtium leaves in salads or chopped and sprinkled on soups, sautés, or stir-fries before serving. If you tire of the taste of nasturtium, incorporate other greens such as dandelion, sorrel, parsley, mustard, and kale. In about two weeks, your skin should look healthy and clear with an attractive glow. (Note that alcohol, caffeine, refined sugar, and cigarette smoking will diminish the benefits of nasturtium.)

Growing

Nasturtium leaves are a lively green and look like open parasols. The gorgeous flowers flourish all summer and come in shades of flaming coral, pink, peach, orange, yellow, and magenta. To raise nasturtiums, find a place in the garden, a spot on your terrace, or even a windowsill that gets at least six hours of sun a day. Nasturtium likes the standard herb soil mix of two parts garden or potting soil, two parts peat, one part sand, and one part compost or composted cow manure. Buy small organically grown plants and dig a hole for each that's twice the size of the root ball. Set the plant in the hole and fill in with the surrounding soil. Tamp it down and soak with warm water. Check the soil twice a week thereafter by sticking in your finger; if the soil is dry, water.

Nasturtium plants attract aphids, which give plants a virus that turns their leaves yellow. To combat aphids, plant the herb tansy near nasturtiums, or make a tansy spray by adding a cup of bruised fresh tansy leaves to one quart of boiling water and steeping for one hour before straining. You can also use bruised fresh tansy leaves as a mulch for nasturtium.

Cooking

Nasturtium has the peppery-mustard taste of watercress but with larger leaves and no tough stems. You can use it like watercress in sandwich spreads as English cooks do, or in soups, minced in vinaigrettes, and chopped in mayonnaise as a sauce for chilled fish. For sauces and salad dressings, use one to two tablespoons of minced fresh leaf in a recipe to serve four. Try making salads using half nasturtium and half milder greens. Or do as the French do, serving a handful of fresh nasturtium leaves as a snappy accompaniment to roast chicken.

The vivid nasturtium blossoms are also edible. They have the same peppery taste as the leaves, and they look dramatic in green salads or floated on pale soups. You can also make a beautifully colored herb vinegar by placing five nasturtium flowers in a one-cup jar and covering with hot (not boiling) white vinegar. Add a sprig or two of fresh dill to the mixture if you like. Either way, cover the jar and let it steep at room temperature for a couple of weeks. Then use, unstrained, in salad dressings and in marinades for fish, or to add a peppery bite to sauces.

Even the closed green nasturtium buds have a place in the kitchen, for many cooks pickle them to use instead of capers. To try it, put a quarter cup of buds into a jar and add one-third cup of hot (not boiling) cider vinegar, a peeled clove of garlic, and a pinch of sea salt. Cover and let steep in the refrigerator for a couple of weeks before enjoying. Serve the buds, drained, as an accent on smoked trout or salmon.

Crab Salad with Nasturtium

Chili powder and hot pepper sauce combine to boost nasturtium's peppery flavor.

~~~

2   teaspoons olive oil
1   small onion, minced
1   clove garlic, very finely minced
1   small carrot, coarsely grated
1   large Italian plum tomato, finely chopped, with its juices

1   teaspoon good-quality chili powder
    Splash of hot pepper sauce, or to taste
    About 10 large nasturtium leaves and/or flowers, minced
½ cup lump crabmeat, picked over for shells and cartilage

IN a small bowl, combine the oil, onion, garlic, carrot, tomato, chili powder, hot pepper sauce, and nasturtium. Add the crab and toss well. Serve as a main-dish salad on lettuce leaves, or on crusty whole wheat rolls for a sandwich. If you have extra nasturtium flowers, use them for garnish.

MAKES 2 SERVINGS; 85 CALORIES PER SERVING, 2.7 GRAMS FAT, 28 PERCENT OF CALORIES FROM FAT.

Smoky Tomato Soup with Nasturtium

Tangy nasturtium lightens the roasted flavor of the tomatoes in this soup.

~~~~~

2¹/₄	pounds ripe Italian plum tomatoes	1	small onion, minced
1	tablespoon olive oil	1	cup loosely packed nasturtium leaves, plus 4 nasturtium flowers
1	teaspoon cumin seed		
1	clove garlic, very finely minced		

PREPARE the grill or preheat the broiler.

IN a large bowl, toss the whole tomatoes with the olive oil to prevent them from singeing on the grill. Grill about 5 inches from the heat source, turning frequently, until the tomatoes are roasted and tender, about 5 minutes. They'll pop and spit while grilling, so be careful. As the tomatoes are done, return them to the bowl.

TOAST the cumin seed in a dry nonstick sauté pan over high heat until lightly browned, about 2 minutes. The seeds pop and jump around while toasting, so pay attention.

TIP the roasted tomatoes into a processor or blender along with the toasted cumin, garlic, onion, and nasturtium leaves. Whiz until smooth. Serve warm, at room temperature, or very slightly chilled, garnished with the nasturtium flowers.

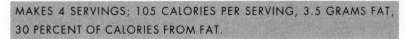

MAKES 4 SERVINGS; 105 CALORIES PER SERVING, 3.5 GRAMS FAT, 30 PERCENT OF CALORIES FROM FAT.

NOTE: For an accompaniment, grill bread alongside the tomatoes: Paint a split baguette lightly with olive oil and rub with fresh garlic, then grill cut side down.

oregano

~~~~~~~~~~~~~~~~~~~~~~~~~~~~~~~~

digestion
suggestion

~

IMPROVE

DYSPEPSIA

~

GROW A

FRAGRANT

BUSH

~

COOK

WITH

EASE

~

*T*wo Jamaican herbalists showed me how they make sticks of incense from herb and flower essences. In one particular batch, the key essence was oregano. As I watched, the herbalists dipped thin sticks in the moist and powdery oregano essence, allowing it to dry before dipping them again. As they worked, they explained that according to their teachings, burning spicy oregano incense helps prevent and soothe coughs and other respiratory complaints. Although scientific research does not verify the delightfully fragrant oregano cure, Jamaican devotees swear by it.

Lore and Legend

Oregano has brought pleasure to people for centuries. Its name comes from the Greek for "joy of the mountain"—*oros* for mountain and *ganos* for joy. Early Greeks liked to let their livestock graze on wild oregano so the meat would be tastier, and ancient herbal-

ists prescribed oregano tea to treat poisonous insect bites, coughs, and digestive problems.

Healing

The strong volatile oils that give oregano its flavor also act as a digestive aid.
So sprinkling oregano on pizza, tossing it with pasta, or adding it to a marinade for roasted poultry may improve your dyspepsia as well as enhance your
dinner.

Growing

Oregano mingles well with other herbs in the garden. A staunch little bush, it
makes a nice visual contrast to such viney herbs as hops and the tall, leafy
lovages and angelicas.

A Mediterranean native, oregano likes at least six hours of sun a day.
Prepare a standard herb mixture of two parts potting or garden soil, two parts
peat, one part sand, and one part compost or composted cow manure. Dig a
hole for each oregano plant that's twice the size of the root ball. Set a plant
in each hole, fill in with the surrounding soil, and tamp it down. Soak with
warm water. Then, unless there is a drought, let nature do the watering.

For indoor growing, plant oregano in a wide pot so it has room to
spread out. Place it in a window that gets full sun and use ninety-watt halogen
floods, placed about three feet from the herb, to give it more light. Since indoor
climates are drier that outdoors, check the soil once a week by sticking in your
finger; if it's dry, water.

There are some fifty types of oregano, but the best to plant are small
specimens of the organically grown Greek variety (*Origanum vulgare hirtum*
or *O. vulgare heracleoticum*). Finding Greek oregano can be difficult, but
rather than wandering around clutching notes with six-syllable botanical
names, let your nose be your guide. Go to a nursery and approach an oregano
plant. Rub its leaves to release the aroma. If it smells like peppery thyme,
you've got the good stuff. Even simpler, if the plant smells like something
you'd like to eat and cook with, buy it.

Cooking

Oregano is easy to cook with because its peppery thyme flavor blends well
with foods. It neither loses its own flavor nor overpowers others. Try mari-

nating a swordfish steak for about thirty minutes in a couple of tablespoons of olive oil mixed with a minced clove or two of garlic and some oregano. (Use a tablespoon of minced fresh oregano or a teaspoon of dried per pound of fish.) Then grill or broil. You'll discover a seamless blending of flavors.

Oregano deepens the flavor of sauces and soups. Mince a tablespoon of fresh leaves and add to a quarter cup of tomato salsa or vinaigrette or a serving of vegetable soup. If you don't have fresh oregano, use one and a half teaspoons dried.

You might also want to experiment with Cuban oregano. This low-growing herb with fuzzy, disk-shaped leaves that look like little green teddy bear ears isn't actually an oregano at all, but a coleus. It does, however, have a great oregano flavor. Add one minced leaf per serving to simmering black bean soup. Or, for a Cuban bouquet garni, use kitchen string to tie together split Cuban oregano leaves, bay, and celery, and add to a spicy tomato-based soup.

Onion Kulcha with Cumin and Oregano

This flatbread is popular in India, where it's eaten as a snack or appetizer with mango chutney or served as a side dish with a spicy lentil soup. For an exotic touch, add a few oregano seeds with the leaves. The seeds are called *ajwain* in India, where they are used in a tea to restore strength to new mothers.

~~~~~~

1/2 cup unbleached all-purpose flour

1/2 cup whole wheat pastry flour, plus extra if necessary

1 teaspoon baking powder

1/2 cup nonfat plain yogurt or soy yogurt

2 tablespoons minced fresh oregano or 1 tablespoon dried

Freshly ground black pepper

Splash of olive oil

1 medium onion, finely chopped

1 tablespoon cumin seed

IN a medium bowl, combine the flours, baking powder, yogurt, oregano, and black pepper to taste and mix well. When the dough starts to come together, begin to knead with your hands. Continue kneading for about 3 minutes, adding more pastry flour if the dough is too sticky to handle. Form the dough into a disk.

HEAT a 9-inch cast-iron skillet over high heat. Use a pastry brush to paint on a small amount of olive oil. Add the onion and cumin seed and sauté until the onion is just soft and fragrant, about 2 minutes. Then place the dough disk in the skillet and use your hands or a lightly oiled spatula to press it out into a circle 8 to 9 inches in diameter. Bake, pressing down with a spatula, until browned and crisp, about 3 to 3 1/2 minutes on each side. Serve warm, letting diners break off pieces with their hands.

MAKES 4 SERVINGS; 150 CALORIES PER SERVING, TRACE OF FAT.

Grape Leaves with Brie and Toasted Almonds

The filling shows how oregano unites the flavors of other foods.

~~~~~~

2 ounces unblanched almonds ($^1/_2$ cup)	$^1/_4$ cup minced fresh oregano
10 ounces Brie, rind removed, or soy cream cheese	12 fresh or canned grape leaves (all about the same size)
2 slices whole wheat bread, torn into pieces	2 lemons

PREHEAT the oven to 400°F.

TOAST the almonds in a dry skillet over medium-high heat, stirring frequently until golden, about 2 to 3 minutes. The almonds may make popping sounds but that's okay.

COMBINE the toasted almonds, Brie, bread, and oregano in a processor or blender and whiz until the mixture is crumbly but not pureed.

IF the grape leaves are fresh, blanch them in boiling water until bright green, about 1$^1/_2$ minutes. If they're jarred, unroll the leaves and rinse them under hot tap water.

SET the leaves out on the counter, shiny side down. If the stems are tough, snip them off. Form about a tablespoon of the Brie mixture into a ball and set it near the stem end of a leaf. Fold over the sides, then roll up like a jelly roll into a little bundle. Repeat until all the leaves are stuffed.

ARRANGE the bundles seam side down in a small glass baking dish. Squeeze the juice of 1 of the lemons right onto the bundles. Slice the second lemon and arrange the slices over the bundles to cover and protect them during baking. Cover the dish with foil and bake until warmed through, about 15 minutes. Serve warm or very slightly chilled. For an unusual presentation, you can arrange the stuffed leaves on a tray along with feta cheese that's been drizzled with olive oil and sprinkled with minced fresh oregano.

MAKES 12 BUNDLES; 75 CALORIES PER BUNDLE, 4.75 GRAMS FAT, 45 PERCENT OF CALORIES FROM FAT.

Lentil Soup with Chinese Mushrooms and Oregano Pistou

Pistou is a traditional soup into which an herb paste is swirled at the last minute of cooking. Pistou originated in Genoa, Italy, but is also popular in France's Provence. Most often basil, garlic, and olive oil are used in the herb paste, but this version features fresh oregano to provide savory satisfaction with minimal fat and salt.

~~~~~~

1 cup dried lentils

1 tablespoon olive oil

2 medium onions, chopped

3 cloves garlic, mashed through a press

4 medium dried shiitake mushrooms, stems removed and minced

1 rounded tablespoon dried tree ear mushrooms, crumbled

2 medium tomatoes, chopped, about 1/2 pound

5 cups defatted chicken stock or vegetable stock

1/2 cup fresh oregano leaves

2 tablespoons freshly grated Parmesan cheese or soy Parmesan

1 tablespoon milk, light cream, or soy milk

SOAK the lentils overnight in 2 cups water.

HEAT a large stockpot, then pour in the oil. Add the onions and garlic and sauté over medium-high heat until fragrant and just wilted, about 3 minutes. Add the dried shiitakes and tree ears, along with the drained lentils, tomatoes, and stock. Bring to a boil, then reduce the heat to medium-low, cover tightly, and let simmer gently until the lentils are soft and the soup is rich and fragrant, about 2 hours.

WHEN you're ready to serve, combine the oregano, cheese, and milk in a processor or blender and whiz until pureed. Ladle the hot soup into bowls and swirl a teaspoon of the oregano mixture into each.

MAKES ABOUT 7 CUPS, OR 7 SERVINGS; 120 CALORIES PER SERVING, 3 GRAMS FAT, 22 PERCENT OF CALORIES FROM FAT.

Long-Cooked Vegetable Sauce

This sauce is terrific on pasta, polenta, and risotto. The slow-cooked base can be made up to five days ahead of time; refrigerate it until you're ready to use it, then heat and stir in the oregano and oil just before serving.

~~~~~

1 eggplant (about 1 1/4 pounds), peeled and diced

3 ripe tomatoes (about 1 1/2 pounds), peeled and diced

2 medium zucchini, diced

2 medium onions, finely chopped

1 red bell pepper, cored, seeded, and diced

2 cloves garlic, mashed through a press

3 sun-dried tomatoes, minced

1 cup diced button mushrooms

1 dried hot chili pepper (about 1 inch long), minced

1/4 cup minced fresh oregano

2 teaspoons olive oil

IN a large stockpot, combine the eggplant, fresh tomatoes, zucchini, onions, bell pepper, garlic, dried tomatoes, mushrooms, and hot pepper. Bring to a simmer over heat, then cover and let simmer gently for 6 hours, stirring occasionally.

ABOUT 5 minutes before you're ready to serve, stir in the oregano and olive oil. Then pour over polenta or toss with rice or pasta. A Chianti or Zinfandel makes a nice accompaniment.

MAKES 6 CUPS, OR 6 SERVINGS; 60 CALORIES PER SERVING, 1.5 GRAMS FAT, 22 PERCENT OF CALORIES FROM FAT.

Soft Polenta with Olives and Feta

Peppery oregano enhances the robust flavor of feta cheese.

~~~~~

2 cups cold vegetable stock or defatted chicken stock

1 cup yellow cornmeal

2 cups water

1 bay leaf

1/4 cup finely chopped pitted Greek olives

1 teaspoon olive oil

1/4 cup crumbled Greek feta cheese or soy Parmesan

2 tablespoons minced fresh oregano

1 clove garlic, mashed through a press

1 tablespoon fresh lemon juice

IN a bowl, whisk together the stock and cornmeal.

BRING the water to a boil in a large deep frying pan. Whisk in the cornmeal mixture and whisk well to combine. Toss in the bay leaf and bring to a boil over high heat. Continue to boil, whisking constantly, until the polenta is thick and porridge-like, about 10 minutes. Remove from the heat.

SWIRL the olives, oil, feta, oregano, garlic, and lemon juice into the hot polenta. Serve warm in shallow bowls, accompanied by a salad of a variety of greens. Sautéed dark greens, like kale and mustard greens, are also a tasty side dish for the polenta.

MAKES 4 SERVINGS; 210 CALORIES PER SERVING, 8 GRAMS FAT, 34 PERCENT OF CALORIES FROM FAT.

Penne with Green Chilies and Toasted Pine Nuts

In this simple, light pasta sauce, oregano marries the flavors of the tomatoes, green chilies, and garlic.

~~~~~

2 tablespoons pine nuts

1 teaspoon olive oil

2 cloves garlic, very finely minced

2 mild fresh green chilies, cored, seeded, and sliced

6 small Italian plum tomatoes (about 3/4 pound), chopped (canned whole are okay in a pinch)

3 cups hot cooked penne or other tubular pasta (from 1/3 pound dried)

1 tablespoon minced fresh oregano

Freshly grated Parmesan cheese or soy Parmesan

Dried hot chili peppers for garnish (optional)

HEAT a large sauté pan over medium-high heat. Add the nuts and stir constantly until they are toasty brown, about 2 minutes. Remove the nuts from the pan and keep them handy.

POUR the olive oil into the still-warm pan, and swirl it around to coat the bottom. Add the garlic, chilies, and tomatoes and sauté until the vegetables are just beginning to wilt, about 3 minutes.

IMMEDIATELY toss with the penne, pine nuts, and oregano. Sprinkle with the Parmesan and serve warm. If desired, serve dried hot peppers on the side, so if diners like, they can break a pepper open and sprinkle some of the seeds over the pasta.

MAKES 2 LARGE SERVINGS; 290 CALORIES PER SERVING, 7 GRAMS FAT, 24 PERCENT OF CALORIES FROM FAT.

parsley

~~~~~~~~~~~~~~~~~~~~~~~~~~~~~~~~~~~~~~~

multivitamin
in a leaf

*A*n Ayurvedic herbalist told me that my temporarily nervous stomach was due to "deranged vata," and that I should drink parsley juice after each meal until it subsided. He explained that in Ayurveda most people fall into one of three body-mind categories based on elements of nature: vata, in which air is the prominent element; pitta, which is associated with fire; and kapha, in which earth and water predominate. Those with vata in their constitution can become imbalanced (or too "airy") during times of extreme stress, which can result in stomach problems. The Ayurvedic answer is to introduce a pitta or kapha herb to balance the vata. In my case, pungent parsley increased my pitta element, stimulating digestion and eliminating the butterflies in my stomach.

~

TRY AN

HERBAL

DIURETIC

~

ENJOY A

BATH TIME

REFRESHER

~

RAISE AN

EASY-TO-

GROW

GREEN

~

Lore and Legend

Early Romans ate fresh parsley as an after-orgy refresher to mask the smells of alcohol and rich foods—a custom that may be the forerunner of today's parsley garnish. Both the Romans and the Greeks also fed parsley to their racehorses, to keep them strong and fast, but the Greeks themselves rarely ate the herb. The reason may be that the Greek hero Archemorus was devoured by evil serpents and parsley is said to have sprung from his spilled blood. Consequently, Greeks associate parsley with illness or death, and they use the herb to decorate graves. There's even a Greek expression meaning "in need of parsley" that refers to someone at death's door.

In the Middle Ages, parsley was credited with preventing hair loss. Herbalists would fry it with butter and flour and rub the resulting paste on people's heads three times throughout the year to preserve their tresses. Fresh parsley and parsley leaf tea were also recommended to cure plague, respiratory complaints, and angina.

Healing

Parsley is an herbal multivitamin. A cup of minced fresh parsley (about four ounces) contains more beta carotene than a large carrot, almost twice as much vitamin C as an orange, more calcium than a cup of milk, and twenty times as much iron as one serving of liver. And since parsley's taste is mild, eating a cup will not assault the taste buds.

One thing you'll notice after eating a lot of parsley is that it's a mild diuretic. That can be a plus for men with prostate problems and for women who retain water before menstruation. But since parsley can actually stimulate menstruation, women who are pregnant or who suspect that they might be pregnant should avoid eating parsley in large amounts.

Parsley tea is a popular diuretic in Germany and China, where herbalists recommend it to help control high blood pressure. For the Cherokee Indians, it is a traditional bladder tonic, to help prevent infections. To try parsley tea, steep two teaspoons of bruised fresh parsley leaves in one cup of boiling water, covered, for ten minutes. Strain and take three times a day for water retention.

Looking Your Best

If you're feeling tired and wilted, a parsley bath can help refresh you. Brew a strong parsley tea by steeping half a cup of bruised fresh parsley leaves in two cups of boiling water, covered, for twenty minutes, then strain and stir it into a drawn bath. For a quicker variation, pack a quarter cup of fresh parsley leaves into a large tea ball and hook it onto the bath faucet so that as the hot water comes out it runs through the parsley. For extra refreshment, after the bath rub Soothing Lavender Skin Oil (page 344) or an herbed body oil of your choice on still-moist skin.

Growing

Though parsley grows the world over, it is a native of the Mediterranean and likes at least six hours of full sun a day. To grow it, buy small organically cultivated plants. Prepare a rich version of the standard herb soil mix, combining two parts garden or potting soil, two parts peat, two parts compost or composted cow manure, and one part sand. Dig a hole for each plant that's twice the size of the root ball and set the plant in the hole. Fill in with the surrounding soil, and tamp it down. Water with warm water, and then water about once a week thereafter. Parsley looks good grown in bunches of five or seven plants together.

To grow parsley indoors, plant it in a tall pot, since the herb has a long taproot that needs space. Give parsley at least six hours of full sun a day, which can be augmented with ninety-watt halogen bulbs placed about three feet away. The halogen can be left on for up to twelve hours.

Cooking

Parsley has a warm, gentle flavor, green and piny, with a touch of camphor. Since it's so mild, you can use it just as you would use chopped fresh spinach—in salads, soufflés, timbales, frittatas, omelettes, soups, stir-fries, and savory Greek pies with feta cheese.

The best-tasting parsley is the type with flat leaves. It's gently piny and more aromatic than the curly kind, although the curly kind keeps longer once picked. Whichever variety you choose, keep it fresh by storing it in the refrigerator in a glass of water, with the stems submerged and the leaves dry. If you buy parsley, rather than grow your own, it may come with the roots attached, and they can go right in the water.

Persillade is the French name for fresh parsley minced with shallots or garlic, to be added to a sauté at the last minute of cooking. Try tossing a tablespoon of the raw mixture with sautéed broccoli or cauliflower to serve four. It's a healthier and more savory topping than butter. *Gremolata* is the Italian form of persillade, made by combining minced fresh parsley, garlic, and lemon zest. It's a nice addition to fish dishes, and the burst of flavor it offers is a good substitute for salt.

You might also want to try Hamburg parsley, a variety that's raised for its root. It looks like a parsnip but it tastes woodsy and piny, not sweet. Use it as you would parsnips—steamed and tossed with fresh dill, or sliced and added to vegetable soups.

Alu Chat
Roast Potatoes and Green Chilies

This dish is served in India as a vegetarian entrée or as a side dish with chicken or lamb.

~~~~~~

1½	pounds baking potatoes	¼	teaspoon cayenne, or to taste
2	teaspoons olive oil		
3	mild fresh green chilies (about 4 ounces), minced	2	tablespoons minced fresh parsley
		2	scallions, minced

PREHEAT the oven to 400°F.

CUT the potatoes into 1-inch cubes. Place them in a glass baking pan and toss them with the oil until well coated, then spread them in a single layer. Roast for 10 minutes, then add the chilies and stir well. Continue roasting until the potatoes are tender and lightly browned, about 10 minutes longer.

REMOVE the potatoes to a serving bowl and add the cayenne, parsley, and scallions. Serve warm or at room temperature.

MAKES 4 ENTRÉES OR 6 SIDE-DISH SERVINGS; 150 CALORIES PER SERVING, 2.2 GRAMS FAT, 14 PERCENT OF CALORIES FROM FAT.

Toasted Millet Tabbouleh

Millet is a tiny yellow grain that's popular in the cuisines of northern China, as well as parts of Africa. Since it is somewhat alkaline in nature, it can help soothe an acid stomach.

~~~~~

2 cups millet

3 cups defatted chicken stock or vegetable stock

Pinch of sea salt

1 bay leaf

6 scallions, minced

2 cups minced fresh parsley

1/4 cup minced fresh basil

Juice of 2 lemons (about 1/2 cup)

Juice of 1 small orange (about 1/4 cup)

3 tablespoons olive oil

2 tablespoons toasted slivered almonds (see Note)

TOAST the millet in a large stockpot (or a pressure cooker) over medium-high heat until golden brown, about 3 minutes. The millet will pop and crackle as it begins to toast, but that's okay. Add the stock, salt, and bay leaf and bring to a boil. Reduce the heat, cover, and let simmer until the millet is tender, about 20 to 25 minutes. (If you're using a pressure cooker, add the stock, salt, and bay leaf, cover and bring up to pressure. It will take about 15 minutes to cook the millet.)

MEANWHILE, in a large bowl, combine the scallions, parsley, basil, lemon and orange juices, and oil.

ADD the millet to the parsley mixture and toss well. Serve warm, at room temperature, or slightly chilled, sprinkled with the almonds.

MAKES 6 ENTREE SERVINGS; 405 CALORIES PER SERVING, 8 GRAMS FAT, 18 PERCENT OF CALORIES FROM FAT.

NOTE: Toast the almonds in a dry sauté pan over medium-high heat for about 2 minutes, or until they're golden. Stir constantly to avoid burning the nuts.

Spicy Couscous Cake with Avocado Relish

This recipe works equally well with white or whole wheat couscous, so use whichever you prefer. The whole wheat version tastes nuttier and, of course, offers a bit more dietary fiber.

~~~~~~

FOR THE CAKE:

1¹/₄ cups defatted chicken stock or vegetable stock

Juice of 1 lemon (about ¹/₄ cup)

1 teaspoon hot pepper sauce, or to taste

1 teaspoon olive oil

1 cup couscous

2 tablespoons minced fresh parsley

FOR THE RELISH:

1 avocado, peeled, seeded, and finely chopped

3 scallions, minced

1 orange, peeled, seeded, and finely chopped, with its juices

¹/₂ teaspoon chili powder

1 clove garlic, very finely minced

2 tablespoons minced fresh parsley

TO make the couscous cake, combine the stock, lemon juice, hot pepper sauce, olive oil, and couscous in a small saucepan. Bring to a boil, reduce the heat, and simmer, loosely covered, for about 5 minutes. Swirl in the parsley. Transfer the mixture to a 6-inch round casserole, pressing it firmly in with a spatula. (A 1-quart soufflé dish works well here.) Let cool. (If you're in a hurry, chill in the freezer for 10 minutes.)

TO make the relish, combine all the ingredients in a small bowl. Mash lightly with a large fork, leaving the avocado chunky.

TO serve, unmold the cake onto a plate. Slice into quarters and top with the relish. Or slice into smaller pieces, top with the relish, and serve as canapés.

MAKES 4 APPETIZER SERVINGS; 277 CALORIES PER SERVING, 8 GRAMS FAT, 26 PERCENT OF CALORIES FROM FAT.

Barley Dumplings with Parsley Sauce

This lemony parsley sauce is also good with flounder, haddock, and other mild whitefish.

~~~~~

1 cup pearled barley (about 6¹/₂ ounces)	2 cups defatted chicken stock or vegetable stock
3¹/₂ cups water	1 tablespoon olive oil
1 bay leaf	2 cloves garlic, finely minced
¹/₄ cup minced fresh chives	5 scallions, finely minced
1 tablespoon minced fresh oregano	2 cups minced fresh parsley
¹/₄ cup minced fresh basil	Juice of 1 lemon (about ¹/₄ cup)
About ¹/₄ cup whole wheat pastry flour	Freshly grated Romano cheese or soy Parmesan

RINSE the barley. Place it into a small saucepan along with the water and bay leaf, and bring to a boil. Reduce the heat to low, cover loosely, and simmer until the barley is tender, about 1 hour. Uncover and let cool.

SCOOP the barley into a processor and add the chives, oregano, basil, and ¹/₄ cup flour. Whiz until you have a ball of dough, about 10 seconds. If the dough feels sticky, add a bit more flour.

TO shape the dumplings, wet your hands and form the dough into about 20 walnut-sized balls.

POUR the stock into a large frying pan and bring it to a gentle bubble. Carefully set the dumplings in the bubbling stock, cover, and poach until cooked through, about 5 minutes. Don't let the stock boil, or the dumplings may fall apart.

TO make the sauce, heat a medium sauté pan over medium-high heat and add the oil. Add the garlic and scallions, reduce the heat to medium, and sauté until fragrant and slightly soft, about 1 minute, taking care not to let the garlic burn. Add the parsley and lemon juice and cook until the parsley is bright green and slightly wilted, about 2 minutes more. Pour the mixture into a processor or blender and whiz until pureed.

WHEN the dumplings are ready, remove them from the stock and arrange them in four shallow bowls. (If the sauce isn't ready, cover the bowls to keep the dumplings warm.) Spoon some parsley sauce into each bowl and swirl the dumplings around so they're completely coated. Sprinkle with cheese and serve warm, with a salad of mixed greens.

MAKES 4 ENTRÉE SERVINGS; 250 CALORIES PER SERVING, 4 GRAMS FAT, 18 PERCENT OF CALORIES FROM FAT.

Crisp Parsley Tortillas

4 whole wheat tortillas (8-inch diameter)

2 teaspoons Dijon mustard

1 cup finely minced fresh parsley

Freshly grated Parmesan cheese or soy Parmesan

HEAT a well-seasoned cast-iron skillet over medium-high heat. (If the pan's not well seasoned, paint on a little olive oil.)

MEANWHILE, spread the tortillas evenly with the mustard. Sprinkle on the parsley, and fold the tortillas in half.

REDUCE the heat under the skillet to medium and set two tortillas in the pan. Let them sizzle until lightly browned on the bottom and slightly puffed on top, about 2 1/2 minutes, then flip and brown the second side. Repeat with the remaining tortillas.

TO serve, slice into wedges with kitchen shears, sprinkle with Parmesan, and enjoy with the minestrone. They're also a nice snack on their own or as part of an assortment of appetizers.

MAKES 4 TORTILLAS; 80 CALORIES PER TORTILLA, 1 GRAM FAT, 12 PERCENT OF CALORIES FROM FAT.

Chick Pea Minestrone

In this recipe, parsley plays the role of a green vegetable instead of a flavoring herb. The minestrone goes well with Crisp Parsley Tortillas (see page 210).

~~~~~

1/2 cup chick peas
2 teaspoons olive oil
1 onion, finely chopped
2 carrots, finely chopped
1 leek, topped, tailed, rinsed, and chopped
3 1/2 cups defatted chicken stock or vegetable stock
1 cup finely chopped tomatoes
1 tablespoon minced fresh oregano or 1 1/2 teaspoons dried

1 tablespoon minced fresh thyme or 1 1/2 teaspoons dried
1/2 cup tiny shell pasta
Handful of chopped green beans (about 4 ounces)
1 cup finely minced fresh parsley
Freshly ground black pepper
Freshly grated Parmesan cheese or soy Parmesan

SOAK the chick peas overnight in about 1 1/2 cups of water; drain.

HEAT a large stockpot over medium-high heat, then add the olive oil. Sauté the onion, carrots, and leek until fragrant and soft, about 7 minutes. Add the stock, tomatoes, oregano, thyme, and the drained chick peas. Bring to a boil, then reduce the heat, cover loosely, and simmer until the chick peas are almost tender, about 1 hour and 15 minutes.

ADD the pasta and green beans and simmer until the pasta is tender, about 10 minutes more. Remove the soup from the heat and swirl in the parsley and black pepper to taste. Serve warm with Parmesan for sprinkling and with the tortillas.

MAKES 4 LARGE ENTRÉE SERVINGS; 200 CALORIES PER SERVING, 3 GRAMS FAT, 14 PERCENT OF CALORIES FROM FAT.

Black-Eyed Peas with Grilled Red Onion

In this salad, parsley's piny-camphor flavor brightens the taste of black-eyed peas.

~~~~~

1 cup black-eyed peas (cowpeas)	1/4 cup minced fresh parsley
2 tablespoons balsamic vinegar	2 scallions, minced
1 tablespoon olive oil	1 medium carrot, grated
3 red onions, thinly sliced and separated into rings	Pinch of sea salt
	Freshly ground black pepper

SOAK the peas overnight in water to cover; drain.

IN a medium saucepan, combine the peas and about 3½ cups of water and bring to a simmer. Simmer until just tender, about 1 hour. (Or use a pressure cooker, and cook for about 10 minutes.) Drain the peas and pat them dry.

MEANWHILE, prepare the grill or preheat the broiler.

IN a medium bowl, whisk together the vinegar and oil. Toss the onions with about 1 tablespoon of the dressing, to protect them from burning. Grill or broil them 4 to 5 inches from the heat until burnished, about 6 minutes. If using a grill, arrange the onions on a fine-mesh grilling screen, and use tongs for flipping.

ADD the onions to the dressing. Then add the peas, parsley, scallions, carrot, salt, and black pepper to taste, tossing well to combine. Serve at room temperature or slightly chilled as a main dish or side. This salad is great served warm with crusty bread, salsa, and guacamole for an entrée or as an appetizer with an accompaniment of briny olives.

MAKES 5 ENTRÉE SERVINGS; 200 CALORIES PER SERVING, 3 GRAMS FAT, 14 PERCENT OF CALORIES FROM FAT.

peppermint

~~~~~~~~~~~~~~~~~~~~~~~~~~~~~~~~~~~~~

brighter whites

Peppermint is ubiquitous in the Middle East. I thought about this while sipping peppermint tea on an airplane going from Cairo to Amman, Jordan. Before my flight I had enjoyed a spicy stew of potatoes, onions, tomato, and a spinach-like green called *molokai*. A little dish of chopped peppermint was served along with the stew, to contrast with the spicy taste.

Several days later, at the Gulf of Aqaba, my husband and I were strolling near the water and came too close to the Israeli border. A gruff soldier, armed with a machine gun, stopped us. But as we began to turn away, he smiled broadly and asked if we had any children. When we said "No," he gave us each a peppermint candy and told us to go home and get started.

~

SOOTHE

YOUR

STOMACH

~

REFRESH

ITCHY

SKIN

~

COOL

SPICY

FOODS

~

Lore and Legend

Peppermint is a native of the Middle East, especially common in Egypt, Jordan, and Israel. The Pharisees paid their tithes to the Pharaohs with the herb, and the Romans used mint as hair ornaments. Early Hebrews sprinkled mint leaves on the floors of their synagogues to freshen the air, a practice that was later used in churches in Rome.

In ancient Greece, mint was used to freshen baths, to treat hiccups, and to scrub feasting tables. Before battle, soldiers rubbed their weapons with mint for good luck.

Herbalists of the Middle Ages recommended mint tea to treat both digestive distress and the bites of mad dogs. After discovering that rats hated peppermint, merchants sprinkled it around stored grain and cheeses to keep the rodents away. Monks of the time, pining for a brighter smile, polished their teeth with fresh peppermint leaves—a practice that was clearly a predecessor of the peppermint-flavored toothpastes and mouthwashes of today.

Healing

In the Ebers Papyrus, the oldest known medical text, dating from about 1550 B.C., peppermint tea is the treatment of choice for indigestion. Current research validates this ancient prescription, revealing that peppermint tea helps soothe the stomach lining and fend off nausea and vomiting, and it encourages digestion by stimulating the gallbladder and liver, especially after a fatty meal. It also helps relieve flu symptoms and can stop hiccups. These healing properties are mainly due to the high proportion of menthol that peppermint contains.

Menthol is also responsible for the effectiveness of peppermint tea in clearing congestion from the head. One popular native American herb remedy for the common cold combines two teaspoons each of dried peppermint leaf and dried elder flower, steeped, covered, in one cup of hot water for ten minutes. East Indian Ayurvedic herbalists go one step farther and recommend peppermint tea to clear "emotional congestion." They say the herb is *sattvic*, or uplifting. Indeed, it is used as a stimulant by some bicycle racers in the Tour de France, who drink a combination tea of peppermint and rosemary prior to racing each day.

Whether you want to clear your head or digest your food, to make a cup of plain peppermint tea, steep one teaspoon of dried leaves in one cup of hot water, covered, for five minutes. Ayurvedic herbalists sometimes steep the leaves in a cup of hot milk, and Chinese herbalists often add a pinch of dried yellow chrysanthemum flower to the steeping brew, especially in hot weather.

After drinking a cup of hot peppermint tea you may notice that you feel slightly chilled. That's because peppermint stimulates the cold-perceiving nerves just below the surface of the skin, making it a boon in hot weather or for menopausal women suffering from hot flashes. But note that drinking large amounts of peppermint tea may inhibit iron absorption in severely anemic people.

Looking Your Best

Peppermint's cooling powers can also relieve itchy, chafed, or sunburned skin. Brew a strong tea by steeping two tablespoons of dried peppermint in one cup of boiling water, covered, until cool. Then strain and use the tea as a skin splash, after cleansing and before moisturizing, or add it to drawn bathwater. If you don't want to bother with brewing tea, you can get the same effect by using two drops of essential oil of peppermint in one cup of room-temperature water.

Growing

Peppermint likes a rich variation of the standard herb soil mix, combining two parts garden or potting soil, two parts peat, two parts compost or composted cow manure, and one part sand. Buy small organically grown mint plants and find a place for them in the garden that gets at least six hours of full sun a day. Dig a hole for each plant that's twice the size of the root ball and set the plant in. Peppermint spreads quickly, so if you want to keep it contained, sink a four-inch piece of edging around the plants. Fill the hole in with the surrounding soil and tamp it down. Soak with warm water, and water about once a week thereafter.

Cooking

Cool peppermint harmonizes well with hot-weather foods. The minced leaves are used in Egypt, Jordan, and Syria in chilled rice and cracked wheat salads. In certain parts of Africa, particularly Zimbabwe, Kenya, and Ethiopia, fresh mint leaves are served along with spicy foods to lend a balancing cool taste. The same goes in Thailand, Malaysia, and Indonesia, where fresh mint leaves become edible garnishes for fiery curries. Ayurvedics call the balancing of cool mint and hot food *anupana*, or harmonizing, meaning this combination not only tastes good, it may also help regulate your mood.

More Mints

Peppermint's cousins need the same growing conditions as peppermint. All can be used in recipes calling for peppermint.

CORSICAN MINT — Tiny, highly aromatic leaves containing lots of menthol. This is the favorite mint of many Italian cooks.

PINEAPPLE MINT — Aroma like peppermint with a touch of pineapple. The leaves are a pretty variegation of cream and green.

SPEARMINT — Smooth leaves with a milder flavor than peppermint.

APPLE MINT — Woolly leaves that smell like slightly fruity mint.

CURLY MINT — Heart-shaped curly leaves that taste like gentle peppermint.

ORANGE MINT — Pretty purple-edged heart-shaped leaves that have a slightly citrus edge.

Mint Syrup

Make this syrup ahead of time and store it in the refrigerator. When you're in the mood for an iced herb tea, swirl one or two tablespoons of the syrup into one cup of still or sparkling water, and enjoy.

~~~

1   cup dried peppermint leaf (about 1 ounce)

2   cups water

1   2-inch strip lemon peel

2   tablespoons honey or brown rice syrup

COMBINE all the ingredients in a small saucepan and bring to a boil. Boil until the liquid has been reduced by about half, about 4 to 5 minutes. Strain, bottle, and refrigerate.

MAKES ABOUT 1 CUP, OR 8 SERVINGS; 20 CALORIES PER SERVING, NO ADDED FAT.

Peppermint Blend Tea

Licorice root and peppermint give this tea sweetness without adding sugar or honey.

~~~~~~

1 tablespoon plus 1 teaspoon dried peppermint leaf	2 teaspoons dried raspberry leaf
3 slices Chinese licorice root (see Note)	1 teaspoon dried lemon grass
	1 quart boiling water

STEEP the herbs in the water, covered, for 4 minutes. Strain and discard the peppermint, raspberry leaf, and lemon grass. Return the licorice to the tea to give it extra sweetness. Enjoy the tea hot or chilled.

MAKES 4 CUPS, OR 4 SERVINGS; 5 CALORIES PER SERVING

NOTE: Chinese licorice is available at Chinese markets and herb shops. Don't substitute European or American licorice, both of which are strong laxatives.

Macedoine of Oranges and Plums

Macedoine (pronounced mass-ah-DWAHN) is the French name for fruit that has been soaked in an aromatic liquid.

~~~~~~

2 large navel oranges, peeled and sectioned	Juice of 1 lime (about ¹/₄ cup)
2 large red plums, pitted and sliced	Splash of pure vanilla extract
	About ¹/₄ cup (not packed) fresh mint sprigs

continued

COMBINE the oranges and plums in a large bowl. Add the lime juice, vanilla, and most of the mint, reserving a few sprigs for garnish. Mix well, cover, and refrigerate for at least 2 hours, or as long as overnight.

TO serve, discard the mint sprigs and scoop the fruit into chilled ice cream dishes. Garnish with the reserved mint sprigs.

MAKES 4 SERVINGS; 60 CALORIES PER SERVING, NO ADDED FAT.

 Zucchini with Mint and Lemon

Mint, chives, and turmeric perfume zucchini in this quick and simple dish.

~~~~~

1 pound zucchini, sliced into thick coins	5 thin lemon slices
Splash of olive oil	2 teaspoons minced fresh mint or 1 teaspoon dried
2 cloves garlic, very finely minced	1 tablespoon minced fresh garlic chives or regular chives
1/4 teaspoon ground turmeric	

BLANCH the zucchini in boiling water until almost tender, about 1 1/2 minutes. Drain and pat dry. The blanching helps tenderize the zucchini so it can be sautéed in very little oil.

HEAT a large sauté pan over high heat, then use a pastry brush to spread the olive oil around. Add the zucchini, garlic, turmeric, and lemon and sauté until the zucchini is soft and fragrant, about 5 minutes. Toss with the mint and garlic chives and serve warm or very slightly chilled—and be sure to eat the lemons too.

MAKES 4 SERVINGS; ABOUT 30 CALORIES PER SERVING,
TRACE OF FAT.

Banana-Cherry Tea Bread

This bread gets its sweetness from mint, cherries, and banana, with a touch of maple syrup.

~~~~~

1/3 cup pure maple syrup

2 small to medium very ripe bananas

1/4 cup canola oil

4 large egg whites or 1/2 cup Calendula Egg Substitute (page 47)

1/2 teaspoon pure vanilla extract

2/3 cup unbleached all-purpose flour

2/3 cup whole wheat pastry flour

2 teaspoons baking powder

1/4 teaspoon sea salt

1 tablespoon (packed) dried peppermint leaf

1/2 cup dried cherries or raisins

PREHEAT the oven to 375°F.

IN a medium bowl, combine the maple syrup, bananas, oil, egg whites, and vanilla. Beat well with an electric hand mixer until smooth.

IN another medium bowl, combine the flours, baking powder, salt, peppermint, and cherries. Fold the banana mixture into the flour mixture, using a large rubber spatula. Don't overmix; about 15 strokes should do it.

POUR the batter into a lightly oiled 8 1/2- by 4 1/2- by 2 1/2-inch loaf pan. Bake in the center of the oven until the edges are beginning to brown and a knife inserted in the middle comes out clean, about 50 to 55 minutes. Let cool in the pan for 10 minutes, then turn out onto a wire rack to cool before slicing.

MAKES 15 SLICES; 150 CALORIES PER SLICE, 4 GRAMS FAT, 24 PERCENT OF CALORIES FROM FAT.

Couscous with Saffron and Mint

Cinnamon, saffron, and mint give this tiny pasta a full, rich flavor with very little fat.

~~~~~

1 tablespoon olive oil	1/2 cup cooked chick peas
1 large onion, finely chopped	1/2 teaspoon ground cinnamon
1 clove garlic, very finely minced	1/2 teaspoon saffron threads, crushed
1 large tomato, cored, seeded, and finely chopped	2 cups cooked couscous
2 tablespoons raisins	1/3 cup chopped fresh peppermint

HEAT a sauté pan over medium heat and pour in the oil. Sauté the onion and garlic until golden brown, about 6 minutes. Add the tomato, raisins, chick peas, cinnamon, and saffron and cook until the tomato is wilted and the sauce is fragrant, about 5 minutes. Remove from the heat.

COMBINE the couscous, mint, and tomato mixture in a large bowl and toss well. Serve warm or at room temperature.

MAKES 4 SERVINGS; 190 CALORIES PER SERVING, 4 GRAMS FAT, 19 PERCENT OF CALORIES FROM FAT.

rosemary

~~~~~~~~~~~~~~~~~~~~~~~~~~~~~~~~~~~~~

head start
on healing

*I*n the Sonoran desert of Mexico, rosemary grows wild in huge bushes. But it's also planted in almost every garden, especially around cabbage plants, since it keeps cabbage beetles away. Sonoran women sometimes brew a tea of rosemary to soothe the headaches, nervousness, and depression associated with menstruation and menopause.

Lore and Legend

Rosemary has long been credited with having positive effects on the mind. Scholars in ancient Greece tucked fresh rosemary sprigs in their hair when studying, to help them remember what they learned. The Greeks also wore rosemary garlands to ward off the "evil eye." It was said that the herb refused to grow in the gardens of evil people, a belief that must have provided some gardeners with uncomfortable times. In the Middle Ages, rosemary was placed under pillows at night to prevent nightmares and, by day, tucked into pockets

~

DE-STRESS

THE

STOMACH

~

HELP

HEAL A

HEADACHE

~

HAVE

SHINY

HAIR

~

to ward off evil spirits. For centuries, it has also been a popular folk cure for stress, prescribed in tea form by Chinese, European, and Arab herbalists.

Healing

Modern science supports the use of rosemary tea as an antidote for stress. Rosemary contains a compound called rosmaricine that seems to relieve headaches the same way aspirin does, but without irritating the stomach. In fact, rosmaricine has what researchers call "smooth muscle activity," which means it can smooth and soothe the digestive system.

Some researchers also attribute the stress-subduing properties of rosemary tea to its abundance of calcium, a mineral that's known to calm the nerves. One tablespoon of dried rosemary contains about forty-two milligrams of calcium. According to Michael Tierra, an herbalist and teacher, rosemary's calcium is easily absorbed by the body.

To make rosemary tea, put two tablespoons of fresh rosemary or one tablespoon of dried into a sturdy mug. Pound the rosemary lightly with a spoon to release the aroma, then pour on one cup of boiling water. Steep, covered, for four minutes, then strain and drink warm. The taste is strong and piny, so you may want to add a twist of lemon, a pinch of ground cardamom, or a swirl of honey. While you're sipping the tea, be sure to take some deep breaths of its aromatic steam—a good balance of warm pine, camphor, and citrus—to boost the tea's calming effect.

Aromatherapists use rosemary to relieve digestive disorders and headache due to mental strain. Add about ten drops of essential oil of rosemary to about half a cup of good skin oil, such as grapeseed, for massage. Sometimes rosemary oil is combined half and half with lavender oil to help lift the spirits. Ten drops may sound scanty, but essential oils are very powerful and should be used only in tiny amounts.

Looking Your Best

Strong rosemary tea is a cleansing yet gentle hair rinse, especially good for people who use mousse, hair gel, hair spray, and other styling products. These products tend to leave a buildup on the hair, dulling its natural shine.

To prepare the rinse, combine one-third cup of fresh rosemary or three tablespoons dried and two cups of boiling water. Let steep, covered, until completely cool, then strain. Once a week wash your hair with a deep cleansing shampoo, rinse well, and then rinse with the tea, leaving it in your hair to keep it soft and stylable.

Growing

A native of the Mediterranean, rosemary looks like a small evergreen tree with pink, blue, or white flowers. Buy small organically grown plants and find a place for them in the garden that gets at least six hours of full sun a day. Rosemary likes the standard herb soil mix of two parts garden soil or potting soil, two parts peat, one part sand, and one part compost or composted cow manure. Dig a hole for each plant that's twice the size of the root ball, and set the plant in the hole. Sprinkle about a teaspoon of garden lime in the hole to help sweeten the soil, then fill in with the surrounding soil. Tamp down and soak with warm water. Rosemary should never dry out completely, so once or twice a week stick your finger in the soil—if it's almost dry, water.

In a mild climate, rosemary will grow forever into masses of tangled hedge. But if your winters are cold, even the hardy varieties bred to withstand the weather may not survive. One solution is to plant rosemary in pots that can be sunk right into the ground in your garden, then excavated and brought indoors when the temperature falls. While the rosemary is inside, give it at least four hours of full sun a day, which can be augmented by a ninety-watt halogen flood placed about three feet away from the herb. Check the soil for dryness every three days, and mist the rosemary every morning. Keep the area in which the rosemary is growing on the cool side—not over 65°F.

Another way to preserve rosemary through a cold winter is to leave the plants outdoors but shelter them with plastic water-filled teepees, available at garden centers and from garden catalogs. During the day, the teepees absorb sunlight, regulating the temperature inside. As the sun goes down, the water in the teepee cools, slowly giving off its stored heat so the rosemary stays warm. Normally used to extend the growing season of tomatoes, the teepees will save your rosemary from freezing and will let you harvest fresh rosemary all winter long.

Cooking

Rosemary's pine-camphor-citrus aroma comes from five main volatile oils and no fewer than eighteen minor ones. Such a complicated formula makes rosemary something of a loner, hard to pair with other herbs. Garlic and onion are exceptions, because they're robust but not combative. Lavender also works with rosemary since it contains some of the same volatile oils.

Traditionally, rosemary has been combined with fatty foods such as lamb and duck, since its piercing pine taste cuts right through their heaviness. But rosemary also enhances such lighter foods as winter squash, baby new potatoes, green beans, and dried beans, as well as balsamic vinegar–based marinades and vinaigrettes. Start out by using two teaspoons of minced fresh leaf in a recipe to serve four. If you have only dried rosemary, use a teaspoon for the same amount of food, but note that dried rosemary leaves are tough little spikes and must be very finely minced for comfortable eating.

Roasted Eggplant Spread

Gentle eggplant is especially receptive to the strong flavors of rosemary and garlic. In this recipe, tahini and sesame oil mellow out the raw garlic. Serve the puree with pita fans and cucumber batons for dipping, or use as a sandwich spread.

~~~~~

1 medium eggplant (about 1 pound)

2 cloves garlic, mashed through a press

Juice of 1 lemon (about ¼ cup)

2 tablespoons tahini

1 teaspoon minced fresh rosemary

1 teaspoon toasted (dark) sesame oil

PREPARE the grill or preheat the broiler.

PEEL and halve the eggplant. Grill or broil the eggplant, flipping frequently, until cooked through and fragrant, about 5 minutes.

IN a processor or blender, combine the eggplant, garlic, lemon juice, tahini, rosemary, and oil and whiz until smooth.

MAKES 1¼ CUPS; 15 CALORIES PER 1-TABLESPOON SERVING, 1 GRAM FAT, 58 PERCENT OF CALORIES FROM FAT.

Black Bean Hummus with Chipotles and Rosemary

In this bean dip, rosemary's lemon-piny notes lift the earthier vibrancy of the chilies.

~~~~~~

1 cup dried black beans
2 large dried chipotle chilies
2 cups vegetable stock or defatted chicken stock
6 cloves garlic, mashed through a press
1 medium carrot, chopped
1 tablespoon plus 1 teaspoon minced fresh rosemary

Juice of 2 lemons (about 1/2 cup)
1/4 cup tahini
1/3 teaspoon sambal (Vietnamese hot chili paste, or see page 114)

SOAK the beans overnight in 2 cups of water. Cover the chipotles with 1/2 cup of boiling water and let them stand overnight too.

IN a large stockpot, combine the beans and their liquid with the stock.

WHIZ the chipotles, with their liquid, and 4 of the garlic cloves in a processor or blender until minced. Add to the beans along with the carrot. Bring to a boil, then reduce the heat, and let simmer covered, until the beans are very soft, about 4 hours, adding more water if necessary. Let cool slightly.

SCOOP the beans into a processor or blender and add the remaining 2 cloves garlic, the rosemary, lemon juice, tahini, and sambal, and whiz until smooth. Serve with crusty French bread or pitas as an appetizer or snack.

MAKES ABOUT 2 1/2 CUPS, OR 10 SERVINGS; 120 CALORIES PER SERVING, 3 GRAMS FAT, 22 PERCENT OF CALORIES FROM FAT.

Whole Wheat Bread with Fresh Rosemary

Rosemary and garlic lend a savory robustness to whole wheat bread.

~~~~~~

About 1 cup warm water (about 115°F)

1 tablespoon active dry yeast

2 teaspoons brown rice syrup or barley malt

1 tablespoon olive oil

1¹/₃ cups (scant 6 ounces) whole wheat bread flour, plus extra for handling

1¹/₃ cups (scant 6 ounces) unbleached all-purpose flour

Pinch of sea salt

¹/₄ cup minced fresh rosemary

2 cloves garlic, minced

IN a large bowl, combine ¹/₂ cup of the water with the yeast. Stir in the brown rice syrup and 2 teaspoons of the oil.

SPRINKLE the flours, salt, rosemary, and garlic over the yeast mixture and mix well. Then add enough additional water to make a soft, pliable dough. Lightly flour a countertop and knead the dough until elastic and smooth, about 8 minutes. Shape the dough into a ball.

SET the dough in a lightly oiled bowl, turning it to coat the entire surface. Cover the bowl with plastic wrap and set in a warm place until the dough has doubled in size, about 40 minutes.

PUNCH down the dough with your fist, then let it rise again, covered, for about another 40 minutes, or until almost doubled in size. Punch down.

MEANWHILE, preheat the oven to 400°F.

LINE a large cookie sheet with parchment paper and place the dough in the center. Form the dough into a 14-inch disk, about ¹/₂ inch high. Rub the top and sides with the remaining 1 teaspoon oil. Bake in the center of the oven until cooked through and lightly browned on top, about 18 minutes. To determine if the bread is done, pick it up with an oven mitt and knock on the bottom of the loaf; if the bread sounds hollow, it's done. Set the bread on a wire rack to cool, then cut it into wedges with kitchen shears. Serve with saucers of olive oil laced with minced fresh sage for drizzling.

MAKES 4 HUGE SERVINGS; 170 CALORIES PER SERVING, 2 GRAMS FAT, 11 PERCENT OF CALORIES FROM FAT.

Lentil Soup with Red Miso and Rosemary

Though Japanese food purists may raise an eyebrow, rosemary and miso make a tasty combination. Miso is a Japanese bean paste that's available at Oriental markets and many supermarkets. It keeps for years in the refrigerator and is a handy condiment for swirling into soups and sauces.

1 cup green or brown lentils
3 large carrots, finely chopped
1 large onion, finely chopped
1 clove garlic, mashed through a press
6 cups vegetable stock or defatted chicken stock
2 tablespoons red miso
1 tablespoon minced fresh rosemary

SOAK the lentils overnight in 2 cups water; drain.

PUT the lentils into a large stockpot, and add the carrots, onion, garlic, and stock. Bring to a boil, then reduce the heat to low and simmer, loosely covered, for 2 hours.

JUST before serving, combine the miso and rosemary with about ¼ cup of the broth from the soup in a small bowl. Mash with the back of a spoon until you have a smooth paste. Remove the soup from the heat and swirl in the paste. Serve hot. (Try not to reheat again, because miso contains "friendly bacteria" that are good for your intestines but, unfortunately, are destroyed by boiling.)

MAKES 6 SERVINGS; 105 CALORIES PER SERVING, NO ADDED FAT.

Corn and Millet Bread with Rosemary

Unlike most herbs, which add light notes of flavor, rosemary is so fragrant that it can perfume even a hearty bread. Serve this one with soups or stews, use it for croutons, or slice it thin for toasting. It makes an especially tasty palette for grilled sweet peppers.

$1/3$ cup millet	$3/4$ cup unbleached all-purpose flour
1 cup boiling water	Pinch of sea salt
$1^2/3$ cups yellow cornmeal	$1^1/3$ cups buttermilk
2 teaspoons nonaluminum baking powder	2 tablespoons olive oil
$3/4$ cup whole wheat flour	1 tablespoon minced fresh rosemary

COMBINE the millet and boiling water in a small bowl and let soak until the water is absorbed, about 10 minutes.

MEANWHILE, preheat the oven to 400°F.

IN a large bowl, combine the cornmeal, baking powder, flours, and salt, stirring well.

IN a medium bowl whisk together the buttermilk, oil, and rosemary. Swirl in the millet, then fold the mixture into the dry ingredients. Don't overmix; about 15 strokes should do.

LIGHTLY oil a 9-inch glass pie dish with olive oil. Scoop in the batter and level off the top. Bake in the center of the oven until a thin knife comes out clean, about 25 minutes. Let the bread cool on a wire rack before slicing. Leftover bread will keep for up to 3 months, well wrapped and frozen.

MAKES 8 LARGE SERVINGS; 235 CALORIES PER SERVING, 5 GRAMS FAT, 19 PERCENT OF CALORIES FROM FAT.

Split Pea and Lentil Salad with Rosemary

The richness of dried tomatoes and rosemary's sharp pine gives a mellow fullness to lentils and dried peas.

~~~~~~

1/2	cup brown lentils	2	teaspoons olive oil
1/2	cup green split peas		Juice of 1 lemon (about 1/4 cup)
1/2	cup yellow split peas		
2	cloves garlic, chopped	1	large red onion, minced
2	quarts vegetable stock or defatted chicken stock	1	stalk celery with leaves, minced
5	sun-dried tomatoes, minced	1	large carrot, minced
1/2	cup orange lentils		Sea salt and freshly ground black pepper (optional)
1	tablespoon minced fresh rosemary or 1 teaspoon dried		

IN a large soup pot, combine the brown lentils, green and yellow split peas, garlic, and stock. Cover and bring to a boil, then reduce the heat, cover loosely, and simmer for 30 minutes.

ADD the tomatoes and orange lentils and continue to simmer until tender, about 15 minutes more. Drain and transfer to a large bowl.

IN a small bowl, combine the rosemary, olive oil, and lemon juice. Pour it over the lentil mixture, add the onion, celery, and carrot, and toss well. Add sea salt and black pepper to taste if you like. Serve the salad warm or at room temperature on a nest of lettuce or in radicchio cups.

MAKES 5 CUPS, OR 10 SERVINGS; 106 CALORIES PER SERVING, LESS THAN 1 GRAM FAT, ABOUT 7 PERCENT OF CALORIES FROM FAT.

Braised Leeks with Wine and Rosemary

Here the classic combination of rosemary and garlic offsets the tender oniony flavor of braised leeks.

~~~~~

4	large leeks, topped, tailed, and rinsed	1	clove garlic, mashed through a press
1/4	cup dry white wine	2	teaspoons olive oil
1	large ripe tomato, finely chopped, with its juices	1	teaspoon minced fresh rosemary or 1/2 teaspoon dried

SLICE the leeks lengthwise in half, keeping the leaves together. Set the leeks cut side down in a large sauté pan and add the wine, tomato and its juices, garlic, olive oil, and rosemary. Cover the pan and bring to a boil over high heat. Reduce the heat to medium and let the leeks bubble on until tender, about 4 to 5 minutes. Serve warm as a side dish with grilled fish.

MAKES 4 SERVINGS; 115 CALORIES PER SERVING, 3 GRAMS FAT, 24 PERCENT OF CALORIES FROM FAT.

Rotini and Mustard Greens with Lemon-Rosemary Vinaigrette

The simple trio of rosemary, garlic, and chives perfumes tangy mustard greens in this unusual but delicious sauce.

~~~~~

2 1/2 cups cooked rotini or other curly pasta (from about a scant 1/3 pound dried)

1 cup mustard greens or spinach leaves, sliced into ribbons

2 tablespoons minced fresh chives or garlic chives

2 tablespoons fresh lemon juice

1 tablespoon olive oil

3/4 teaspoon Dijon mustard

Splash of hot pepper sauce, or to taste

1 clove garlic, mashed through a press

1 tablespoon minced fresh rosemary or 1 teaspoon dried

COMBINE the rotini, mustard greens, and chives in a medium bowl.

IN a small bowl, whisk together the lemon juice, olive oil, mustard, hot pepper sauce, garlic, and rosemary. Pour the dressing over the rotini and toss well. Serve at room temperature or very slightly chilled.

MAKES 4 SERVINGS; 175 CALORIES PER SERVING, 4 GRAMS FAT, 21 PERCENT OF CALORIES FROM FAT.

sage

sore gum soother

~

SUBDUE

A SORE

THROAT

~

REFRESH

SKIN

AFTER

SHAVING

~

BOOST THE

FLAVOR OF

LOW-FAT

FOODS

~

On a recent trip to the Southwest, I had just checked into my room at an inn when an Indian woman knocked on the door. She was holding a shallow reed basket in her arms containing a bundle of smoking sage. As I looked at her, befuddled, she asked if I wanted my room "smudged." Having no idea what she meant, but nonetheless intrigued, I asked the Indian woman to explain smudging.

Lore and Legend

Sage has spiritual properties for the Papago and some other North American Indian tribes because of its clean aroma and silvery smoke. They use it for smudging ceremonies in which the sage (*S. apiana*) is tied into bundles and dried, then lighted to produce purifying sage smoke. The bundles, called "smudge sticks," can be small cigarette-sized wands or larger banana-sized torches, depending on the area to be smudged. To smudge my room at the inn, for example, the woman gently waved a large bundle around for about one minute. She carried the bundle from room to room for smudgings, then extinguished it to be reused as needed.

Sage bundles are waved around rooms, houses, cars, or people so that the trails of smoke can disperse and remove any gloomy or unfriendly feelings that are present. Although there is no scientific research on the spiritual or cleansing properties of sage smoke, smudging ceremonies do seem to be effective at making people feel better, happier, and lighter. In the Southwest and elsewhere, some psychologists I've spoken to smudge their offices after long days, because "people leave a lot of negativity behind."

Interestingly, a belief in sage's spiritual attributes is not limited to North America. The herb's Latin name, *salvia*, means "salvation," or "to save." Ancient Arabic and Chinese herbalists believed that drinking sage tea enhanced mental and spiritual clarity.

Healing

Modern herbalists report that sage's camphor and other volatile oils have antiseptic properties, which, when combined with the astringent action of sage's tannin, can help treat sore gums and mouth ulcers. Although you should check with a health professional about recurring sore gums, to make a mouthwash, steep one teaspoonful of fresh sage or one-half teaspoon dried in one cup of hot water, covered, for four minutes. Then swirl in a quarter teaspoon of salt and a teaspoon of cider vinegar. (Jamaican herbalists substitute lime juice for the vinegar.) Swish the mixture around in your mouth while it's still hot. To soothe a sore throat, you can gargle with the mixture, but spit it out when you're through.

Some herbalists prescribe drinking a cup of sage tea three times a day as a remedy to help slow down the production of breast milk at weaning time. But since drinking sage tea can cause uterine contractions, pregnant women should avoid it.

Looking Your Best

The same antiseptic and tannic qualities that help heal sore mouths make sage tea a soothing aftershave splash. For convenience, make a batch of the tea and keep it, covered and refrigerated, for up to a week. Splash it on cold, straight from the fridge, just after shaving. To soften your skin, mix the brewed sage tea with an equal amount of aloe juice.

Growing

Green sage is the easiest of all the varieties to grow, because it's less sensitive to severe winters than its purple, gold, or tricolored cousins. One secret of success with sage is to trim the plant into a mound in the fall, rather than in the spring, as many gardening experts advise. Test gardens in Pennsylvania, Missouri, and Oregon have shown that fall trimming prepares the plant for winter by leaving it clean and tidy, which helps protect it against possible rot and insect infestation. Additionally, in early spring, sage bursts into flower with beautiful purple spikes. Gardeners who trim sage in the spring may unknowingly clip away all the flower buds and miss out on a gorgeous flash of color.

For extra protection, check on your sage throughout the fall and winter, trimming away dead sprigs as they appear. If the leaves aren't covered with ice, you can even harvest and use sage in cooking through fall and very early winter. After that, sage begins to taste a bit goaty.

Sage can help protect other plants in your garden from disease and predator insects. When planted near rosemary, sage will help keep it from developing powdery mildew. Sage is also an insect repellent for members of the mustard-cabbage family, since it helps keep cabbage moths at bay. Although this effect is not scientifically documented, it seems to be the camphor aroma of sage that does the trick.

As for cultivation, buy organically grown sage plants for spring planting. Sage is happy with a typical herb soil of two parts garden or potting soil, two parts peat, one part sand, and one part compost or composted cow manure. Choose an area that gets at least six hours of full sun a day. Dig a hole twice the size of the plant's root ball, and set the herb in the hole. Heap the soil back up around the root ball and tamp it down firmly. Water newly planted sage plants, as well as mature ones, at the base of the herb so the leaves don't get wet. This trick will prevent spots from forming when sunlight hits water droplets on leaves. To know when to water sage, stick your finger right in the soil. If it feels dry, water. If not, check again the next day. Generally, established sage plants need watering about once a week.

Sage plants grown indoors in pots need to be near a window that offers at least six hours of sun a day. For the healthiest indoor sage, keep it trimmed to no more than twelve inches tall. If the sage starts to become "leggy," with long stems and thinly spaced, pale leaves, the plant needs more light. You can provide it with a ninety-watt halogen flood placed at least three feet from the sage. Check the soil for moisture twice a week by sticking your finger right in the pot. If the soil feels dry, water the sage; if not, check again the next day.

Cooking

Sage's robust taste of pine, camphor, and citrus comes from the combination of volatile oils it contains. Of all the varieties of sage, plain old green sage (*S. officinalis*) has the best balance of these oils, making it the best choice for cooking. Purple, tricolor, and golden sages are prettier and look great as garnishes on plates. But they contain too much camphor to use in cooking and can ruin a recipe.

I'll never forget the time I was judging a food and wine contest and tasted a breast of chicken stuffed with tricolored sage: It was as if the chicken was filled with Vicks VapoRub. On top of that, a mouthful of cabernet made the taste so metallic that it took an army of celery stalks to cleanse my palate. Green sage, by contrast, especially the young spring leaves and flowers, is subtle enough to be enjoyed fresh in green salads.

Sage is traditionally used in cooking to cut the fatty taste of such foods as sausages, duck, liver, cheese dishes, and meat pies. But its sharpness can also add strength to lighter vegetarian fare. Sprinkle a teaspoonful of minced fresh sage on a cup of sliced cooked butternut squash or sweet potatoes to make butter unnecessary. Or swirl a tablespoon of minced fresh sage (or one and a half teaspoons crumbled dried sage) into two cups of warm tomato-based vegetable soup. When creating your own recipes using sage, pair the herb with onion, garlic, shallot, or leeks, since its strong flavor steps on less assertive herbs.

Sage and Eggs

This recipe is incredibly simple, but it makes a perfect brunch for two, served with a side of grilled tomatoes. The sizzled sage gives eggs an irresistible, earthy, full aroma.

~~~~~

1 teaspoon olive oil	2 tablespoons freshly grated
1 teaspoon sweet (unsalted)	Romano cheese or soy
butter	Parmesan
7 large fresh sage leaves	Sage or chive flowers for
3 large eggs (see Note)	garnish (optional)
Splash of water	

continued

HEAT the oil and butter in a medium nonstick sauté pan over medium-high heat until the butter has melted. Then use a pastry brush to distribute the fats evenly in the pan. Arrange the sage leaves in the pan and let them sizzle for about 20 seconds, or until fragrant.

MEANWHILE, in a medium bowl, use a whisk to beat together the eggs and water.

POUR the eggs over the sage leaves and immediately sprinkle on the cheese. If necessary, rotate the pan so the egg mixture cooks evenly. The egg mixture will set in less than 2 minutes on a gas stove and take a bit longer on electric. When it's firm and no longer runny, slide the omelette onto a waiting plate, flipping half of the omelette over on itself. Serve at once, garnished with sage or chive flowers if you have them.

MAKES 2 SERVINGS; 180 CALORIES PER SERVING, 15 GRAMS FAT, 70 PERCENT OF CALORIES FROM FAT.

NOTE: If this is more fat than you're used to, bring it down a bit by substituting egg whites for one or both of the whole eggs. Two egg whites equal one whole egg.

Sweet Potato Salad with Sesame-Sage Dressing

Sage, combined with the nuttiness of sesame, improves the flavor of sweet potatoes.

~~~~~~

1 pound sweet potatoes, peeled and cut into 1-by 2-inch chunks	1 shallot, finely minced
	1 tablespoon toasted (dark) sesame oil
3 lemon slices	2 tablespoons toasted sesame seeds
1/2 teaspoon pure maple syrup	
2 tablespoons fresh lemon juice	1 tablespoon minced fresh sage or 1 teaspoon dried

STEAM the sweet potatoes over boiling water, to which you've added the lemon slices, until tender, about 11 to 12 minutes.

MEANWHILE, combine the maple syrup, lemon juice, shallot, sesame oil, sesame seeds, and sage in a medium bowl and stir well. Toss the sweet potato chunks with the dressing and serve warm or very slightly chilled.

MAKES 4 SERVINGS; 182 CALORIES PER SERVING, 6 GRAMS FAT, 28 PERCENT OF CALORIES FROM FAT.

Pintos with Sage and Garlic

Sage adds a hearty flavor to vegetarian beans without the usual fatty pork and bacon.

2 teaspoons olive oil

2 cloves garlic, mashed through a press

1 red bell pepper, cored, seeded, and minced

2 teaspoons minced fresh sage or 1 teaspoon dried

1/2 teaspoon hot pepper sauce, or to taste

1 1/2 cups cooked pinto beans (canned are okay, but rinse well before using)

HEAT a large sauté pan over medium-high heat and pour in the olive oil. When the oil is warm and fragrant, add the garlic and bell pepper and sauté for about 2 minutes. Rub the sage between your hands to release its aroma and add it to the pan, along with the hot pepper sauce. Sauté until the bell pepper has just begun to soften, about 2 minutes more. Add the beans and cook until heated through, about 3 minutes. Serve warm with crusty French bread, as a side dish or appetizer.

MAKES 4 SERVINGS; 95 CALORIES PER SERVING, 3 GRAMS FAT, 29 PERCENT OF CALORIES FROM FAT.

One-Hour Whole Wheat Sage Bread

Here's a great way to make a quick herbed bread. Enjoy it on its own or use it to make croutons, crostini, or sandwiches.

~~~~~~~

2	cups unbleached all-purpose flour	2	large egg whites, at room temperature, or $^1/_4$ cup Calendula Egg Substitute (page 47)
2	cups whole wheat bread flour	1	tablespoon olive oil
$^1/_2$	teaspoon sea salt	About $1^1/_2$ cups buttermilk, at room temperature or low-fat soy milk	
1	tablespoon baking powder		
$^1/_4$	teaspoon baking soda		
$1^1/_2$	tablespoons dried sage		

PREHEAT the oven to 425°F. Line a cookie sheet with parchment paper.

IN a large bowl, mix together the flours, salt, baking powder, and baking soda. Crush the sage between your hands and add it. Combine well, making sure the powder and soda aren't lumpy.

IN a medium bowl, whisk together the egg whites, oil, and $1^1/_4$ cups of the buttermilk. Slowly add the liquid ingredients to the dry ones, using a large wooden or rubber paddle to mix. Then stir in enough additional buttermilk to make a dough; the dough should be moist but not sticky. You may not need all the liquid. As the dough starts to get stiff, you may find it easier to scrap the paddle and use your hands.

WHEN the dough can be picked up without falling apart, set it on a floured board or counter and knead briefly for about 30 seconds. Shape the dough into a round loaf and set it on the parchment.

USE a sharp knife to slash an "X" about $^1/_2$ inch deep in the top of the loaf, to keep it from splitting during baking. Sprinkle on a bit of flour, for visual appeal. Bake in the center of the oven for about 40 minutes, misting the loaf with water from time to time to ensure a crisp crust. The bread is done when the bottom sounds hollow when tapped. Let cool before slicing and serving. This is great drizzled with herbed olive oil.

MAKES 1 LOAF, OR 8 SERVINGS; 256 CALORIES PER SERVING, LESS THAN 1 GRAM FAT.

Peasant Potatoes with Sage

Sage gives a favorable turn to sweet, nutty new potatoes (see Note).

~~~~~

1 1/2 pounds new potatoes
       (see Note)
4   cups dark, leafy greens,
       such as arugula,
       dandelion, or mustard,
       well rinsed, drained, and
       dried
1   tablespoon minced fresh
       sage

1   tablespoon minced fresh
       chives
3/4   teaspoon coarse mustard
1/4   cup light cream, skim
       milk, or low-fat soy milk
Splash of hot pepper sauce

IF the potatoes are large, cut them into bite-sized pieces (about 1 inch by 1/2 inch is a comfortable size). Steam the potatoes over boiling water, covered, until tender, about 12 minutes.

MEANWHILE, slice the greens into 1/4-inch ribbons. An easy way to do this is stack a bunch of leaves, roll them into a little cigar, and slice across the roll.

PAT the potatoes dry and toss them into a large mixing bowl along with the sage, chives, mustard, cream, and hot pepper sauce. Mix well to combine, but don't smash the potatoes. Serve the potatoes warm, on nests of the sliced greens.

MAKES 4 ENTRÉE SERVINGS OR 8 SIDE OR APPETIZER SERVINGS; 125 CALORIES PER ENTRÉE SERVING, 3 GRAMS FAT, 22 PERCENT OF CALORIES FROM FAT.

NOTE: The "new" in new potatoes refers to a stage of growth, not a variety of potato. New potatoes can be red, brown, yellow, blue, or red but no bigger than two inches in diameter. New potatoes are noted for their waxy texture, which is perfect in salads. By contrast, baking potatoes have a fluffy texture and can become mealy when steamed and used in salads. If you don't know what kind of potato you have, cut one in half and rub the two halves together. If the halves stick together, the potatoes are waxy and good for salads. If not, they're bakers and should be prepared accordingly.

Whole Wheat Spaghetti with Sage

Sage's sharpness lifts the flavor of whole wheat.

~~~~~

1	tablespoon olive oil	1/4	cup loosely packed fresh
3	cloves garlic, minced		sage leaves or
1/3	cup vegetable stock or	2	tablespoons dried sage
	water	4	cups hot cooked whole
10	sun-dried tomato halves		wheat spaghetti (from
	(no salt added)		about 8 ounces dried)

IN a small saucepan, combine the oil, garlic, stock, and tomatoes. Bring to a boil and boil until the liquid has been reduced to about 1/4 cup, about 2 minutes.

MEANWHILE, toss the sage leaves into a large serving bowl and add the hot spaghetti. The heat will release the aroma of the sage.

POUR the tomato mixture over the pasta, toss well, and serve warm.

MAKES 4 SERVINGS; 290 CALORIES PER SERVING, 3.5 GRAMS FAT, 11 PERCENT OF CALORIES FROM FAT.

Yellow Squash with Sage

Fresh sage and lemon juice team up to give a lively flavor to otherwise bland yellow summer squash.

~~~~~

1	pound yellow summer squash, sliced into thick coins		Splash of olive oil
		1	small onion, finely chopped
3	dried shiitake mushrooms, soaked in hot water until softened (reserve the soaking liquid)	1	clove garlic, peeled
		1	dried hot chili pepper
		2	teaspoons minced fresh sage
			Juice of 1/2 lemon

BLANCH the squash in boiling water until just barely soft, 1 to 2 minutes. (Blanching the squash makes it easier to sauté with minimal oil.) Drain the squash and pat it dry.

SLICE the mushrooms, discarding the stems, and pat them dry.

PREHEAT a cast-iron skillet over high heat, then use a pastry brush to paint on the oil; about 1/2 teaspoon will do the trick. When the oil is warm and fragrant, reduce the heat to medium-high and sauté the squash, mushrooms, onion, garlic, hot pepper, and sage until the squash is tender and lightly browned, about 5 minutes. If you need to add more liquid, use some of the reserved mushroom soaking water. Add the lemon juice and sauté for another 30 seconds. Remove and discard the garlic and hot pepper, and serve warm or at room temperature.

MAKES 4 SERVINGS; 50 CALORIES PER SERVING, TRACE OF FAT.

Roasted Tomatoes and Sage with Rigatoni

Sage perfumes ripe, red tomatoes as they roast.

~~~~~

1 tablespoon sweet (unsalted) butter	4 cups hot cooked rigatoni (from 8 ounces dried)
1 pound ripe plum tomatoes (about 8 medium-large)	Freshly ground black pepper
About 16 fresh sage leaves (twice as many leaves as tomatoes)	1/4 cup crumbled Greek feta cheese or soy Parmesan

PREHEAT the broiler or prepare the grill; if you're using charcoal it should be evenly white and hot.

PLACE the butter in a large bowl and set aside at room temperature.

SLICE the tops off the tomatoes, then core them. Squeeze out and discard the seeds. Tuck 2 sage leaves into each tomato, and set them on a broiler pan or grill rack. Broil or grill about 4 inches from the heat source until the tomato skins are burnished and bubbly, about 2 to 4 minutes on each side, depending on the size of the tomatoes.

continued

WHEN the tomatoes are done, slip off and discard their skins, using tongs if they are too hot to handle. Drop the tomatoes into the bowl with the butter. Mash the tomatoes and butter together with a fork, but keep the sage leaves whole. Tip in the rigatoni and toss well to combine. Serve warm in shallow bowls, sprinkled with pepper and the cheese.

MAKES 4 SERVINGS; 285 CALORIES PER SERVING, 5 GRAMS FAT, 16 PERCENT OF CALORIES FROM FAT.

Spring Vegetable Soup with Sage

Here's an example of how the vigorous flavor of sage adds life to a low-fat soup.

~~~~~

1/2	pound asparagus, trimmed and coarsely chopped	1	tablespoon minced fresh sage or 1 teaspoon dried
1 1/2	cups watercress leaves	2	teaspoons Dijon mustard
5	scallions, chopped	1 1/2	cups skim milk, whole milk, or low-fat soy milk
1	cup fresh peas	1 1/2	cups buttermilk or low-fat soy milk
1	carrot, minced		

STEAM the asparagus (minus some small, pretty tips reserved for garnish), watercress, scallions, peas, and carrot over boiling water, covered, until tender, about 7 to 8 minutes.

SCOOP the steamed vegetables, along with the sage and mustard, into a food processor or blender. Whiz until smooth and well blended, about 10 to 12 seconds.

IN a medium saucepan, bring the skim milk and buttermilk to a simmer. Stir in the vegetable mixture. Serve warm, garnished with the reserved asparagus tips. This is nice with a salad for lunch, or as a first course for dinner.

MAKES 4 SERVINGS; 115 CALORIES PER SERVING, TRACE OF FAT.

saint-john's-wort

smooth skin for tough customers

~

RELIEVE

ACHES AND

PAINS

~

FIND

HERBAL

HELP FOR

DEPRESSION

~

HAVE

SOFT,

SILKY

HAIR

~

I have a remote garden patch called "the frontier," where I purposely grow herbs the wrong way to find out what will happen. I plant them in the full heat of summer, which some experts say is sure to cause any herb to shrivel away. I water herbs in mid-day sun, a practice that can cause the leaves to have spots where the sun dries the water droplets. I stick herb sprigs right in the soil, to see if they'll root.

Indeed, "the frontier" does not often look picture-perfect. But one herb that's impervious to extreme heat, rude watering, and rootless planting is Saint-John's-wort. As a "roadside" weed with an adaptable root system, Saint-John's-wort springs up just about all over the world.

Lore and Legend

Saint-John's-wort got its name because the herb begins to bloom around the birthday of Saint John, which is June 24. *Wort* is a middle English word for "herb."

An old English tale holds that if you step on Saint-John's-wort at dusk on the Isle of Wight, you'll be whisked off on a magic horse and not return till dawn. In Wales, sprigs of Saint-John's-wort, named for each family member, were hung on a rafter overnight. In the morning, the most shriveled sprig indicated who would be the next to die.

Despite such dire predictions, herbalists through the ages have prescribed Saint-John's-wort tea to soothe frazzled nerves, depression, and insomnia and to cure bed-wetting. Crusaders used the flowers and leaves, mashed in lard, to heal their wounds.

Healing

Herbalists still recommend Saint-John's-wort, in oil form, for use topically on cuts, scratches, and minor burns. Many people also rub Saint-John's-wort oil onto stiff joints for temporary relief from the pain of arthritis, rheumatism, and sciatica. You can buy the oil in health food shops and herb stores, or make your own. Fill a widemouthed jar with loosely packed fresh Saint-John's-wort flowers and cover with olive oil. Seal the jar and leave it in a sunny window for three weeks, shaking the jar daily. Strain and discard the flowers, and you'll be left with a clear red oil that smells faintly floral.

The red color of Saint-John's-wort oil comes from a compound called hypericin. Research that shows that hypericin is useful in treating depression because it is a monoamine oxidase (MAO) inhibitor, which validates an old folk cure—a tea of Saint-John's-wort flowers and leaves for the blues and menopausal symptoms. It's made by steeping a tablespoon of the fresh leaves and flowers in a cup of hot water for four minutes; sometimes a tablespoon of lemon balm leaves is added. Before you try it, be sure to consult a health professional, for daily doses of hypericin can take up to three months to begin to work and may have side effects. Then, too, depression can be a serious illness that requires professional attention.

One possible side effect of ingesting Saint-John's-wort is increased photosensitivity. The U.S. Department of Agriculture (USDA) labeled the herb unsafe after reports that farm animals who ate a lot of Saint-John's-wort got badly sunburned. Although this effect has not been documented in human beings who take Saint-John's-wort in nonmedicinal amounts, one study has shown that in large doses, synthetic hypericin does cause photosensitivity in light-skinned males. So check in with a health professional before trying Saint-John's-wort internally.

Looking Your Best

Used externally, Saint-John's-wort tea is a great smoothing, soothing tonic for tired skin. It helps to restore the skin's natural balance and temporarily tightens facial pores. To make it, combine one ounce of fresh Saint-John's-wort leaves (one large handful) with four cups of water in a medium saucepan. Bring the mixture to a boil and simmer until it's a clear, light amber, about three minutes. Remove the pan from the heat and let it continue to steep for about five minutes more, then strain. The splash will have the healthy smell of spinach. Use it warm in cold weather and cool in hot weather, and follow with a moisturizer while your skin is still wet. You can also rub the tea on your neck, upper body, arms, legs, or anywhere else your skin is dry and itchy. For a whole-body benefit, pour the warm tea into your bathwater. Try this after airplane travel, which tends to dry out the skin, and at the change of seasons—especially summer to fall, when skin can become dull. The tea will keep, refrigerated, for up to five days.

The tea can also restore softness and pliancy to very dry hair. Try it if your hair has been exposed to too much midsummer sun or the heat of styling appliances. After shampooing, pour on one and one-half cups of Saint-John's-wort tea instead of a cream rinse. Rub it into your hair and scalp, then rinse. The Saint-John's-wort may diminish body in very fine hair, so it's best for coarser or overprocessed hair.

Growing

Native to Europe and North Africa, Saint-John's-wort will grow in any garden. With its woody stems, smooth oval bright green leaves, and big yellow flowers it's nice with bee balm, yarrow, and violets, a combination that has historical significance in the herb patch—they were all used medicinally by Cherokee Indians.

To raise Saint-John's-wort, buy small organically grown plants. The herb prefers six full hours of sun a day, but it will tolerate some shade. Prepare a standard herb mix of two parts garden or potting soil, two parts peat, one part sand, and one part compost or composted cow manure. Dig a hole for each plant that is twice the size of the root ball, and set a plant in each hole. Fill in with the surrounding soil, tamp down, then soak with warm water. After that, unless there is a drought, let nature do the watering.

Indoors, plant Saint-John's-wort in a wide shallow pot to give it room to spread. It needs about six hours of sun a day, which you can augment with a ninety-watt halogen bulb placed four feet away from the plant.

santolina

~~~~~~~~~~~~~~~~~~~~~~~~~~~~~~~~~~~~~~~

banish bugs

A summer fair in Lancaster County, Pennsylvania, featured a restored colonial tavern complete with barmaids in full dress, and food and drink of the times. Small bunches of a dried herb hung in the corners and one burnt-piny whiff told me it was santolina. A barmaid explained that the herb was hung in colonial pantries and kitchens to keep bugs away from the food. She also mentioned that even today among the Pennsylvania Dutch, santolina is used to keep provisions insect-free.

Lore and Legend

Native to the Mediterranean, santolina is especially common in North Africa. Ancient Middle Eastern herbalists used it in a strong tea to expel worms and as a wash for eyes irritated by too much desert sun and sand.

~

REFRESH

TIRED

FEET

~

PROTECT

CULINARY

HERBS

~

SET A

MOOD IN

A MOON

GARDEN

~

Sailors brought santolina to England in the 1700s, where it was used in sachets to repel moths. In English gardens, santolina was shaped and trained into graceful, decorative swirls. In Sicily, santolina was strewn in prisons to keep disease from spreading. While the effectiveness of this practice was not recorded, no doubt the prisons smelled better when santolina was used.

Healing

Try a santolina foot bath after a hike or a day of shopping, or whenever you need to relax. Pick four fresh ten-inch branches of santolina, and bruise them lightly with the back of a spoon to release their aroma. Add them to a basin filled with about two quarts of hot water and a splash of castor oil or olive oil. Put your feet in the basin and cover with a towel. Relax for about ten minutes, then dry your feet.

Growing

Since Elizabethan times, it has been the fashion to keep santolina clipped into tidy hedges, but this herb is even more beautiful when left to grow free-form. Its branches are shaped like thin-stemmed sea coral and fill in empty garden spaces with twining abstract shapes. The branches are topped with tight round yellow flowers that look like tiny shining moons and stars, especially at dusk.

Santolina comes in two colors: bright green and silvery gray. From a distance the gray variety looks like a slightly fuzzy lavender and so santolina is sometimes called "cotton lavender." The silver variety has slightly thicker stems and is currently the more popular of the two. It's used in moon gardens along with other silvery plants that glow in the moonlight. Aesthetics aside, you should make a place for santolina in your garden, since its robust fragrance tends to repel bugs.

To raise santolina, buy small organically grown plants. Find a place for them in the garden that gets at least six hours of full sun a day. Santolina likes a sandy variation of the standard herb mix, combining two parts garden or potting soil, two parts peat, two parts sand, and one part compost or composted cow manure. Dig a hole for each plant that's twice the size of the root ball. Set the plant in the hole and fill in with the surrounding soil. Tamp it down and soak with warm water, then let nature do the watering.

Silver santolina can be potted up, brought inside in the fall, and clipped into the shape of a Christmas tree. Its silvery color makes it look like a miniature snow-kissed evergreen. Set the santolina in a window that gets at least six hours of sun a day, which you can augment with a ninety-watt halogen bulb placed about four feet away.

savory

~~~~~~

historic love potion

Years ago I worked in a restaurant with a Greek chef, and we made a good team. He, being a meat eater, was especially careful to give a full flavor to vegetarian fare such as pilafs and polenta, using woodsy savory to make them more robust. I, being a vegetarian, used savory's aroma in my own way—to balance the fatty flavor of beef, duck, and pork. Using savory as one of our culinary secrets, we created tasty and memorable meals.

Lore and Legend

Savory has a fine reputation in the kitchen, but it got its start in the bedroom. To the ancient Egyptians, it was an aphrodisiac and a popular ingredient in love potions. The Romans were quick to pick up on the love connection and even renamed savory *satureia*, dedicating the herb to the satyr, the half-man, half-goat beast that lustfully roamed the woodlands of mythology.

~

HELP

DEFEAT

DIARRHEA

~

QUENCH

A THIRST

~

BOOST

THE FLAVOR

OF BEANS

~

The Romans brought savory with them to England, where the herb was mixed with beeswax and used as a back massage potion for unromantic women. Not without their own ideas, the French sipped savory mixed with wine as a love potion for either sex.

The romance stopped abruptly when colonists brought savory from England to America. They used the herb, of all things, in a tea to cure diarrhea. Since then, savory's only association with romance comes from the Cherokee Indians, who used the herb as a snuff to cure headaches.

Healing

Research shows that the colonists' instincts were correct: Savory contains tannins and other compounds that can help put an end to mild cases of diarrhea. Herbalists recommend one cup of tea a day, made from two teaspoons of fresh savory (or one teaspoon dried) steeped in one cup of boiling water, covered, for four minutes. Then strain and sip.

Some German herbalists prescribe one cup of savory tea a day for diabetics, since savory contains antidiuretic properties that can help keep diabetics from having a dry mouth, a common symptom. For this reason, people who tend to retain water may want to avoid drinking large amounts of savory tea.

Growing

In Southern Europe, where savory hails from, it is sometimes interplanted with onions to help repel potentially damaging onion root maggots. There are several varieties of savory to choose from: "Winter" savory stays green and edible all winter, while the "summer" variety dies away completely. Try a type called "creeping winter savory." The leaves are a bright, lively green and the plants make a fast-spreading edible border in the garden.

Savory needs at least six hours of full sun a day and likes the standard herb soil mix of two parts garden or potting soil, two parts peat, one part sand, and one part compost or composted cow manure. Buy organically grown savory and dig a hole for each plant that's twice the size of the root ball. Set the plant in the hole and fill in with the surrounding soil. Tamp the soil down and soak with warm water. After that, depending on the weather conditions, savory may need watering once a week.

Indoors, grow savory in a wide pot so it has room to creep. Give it at least six hours of sun a day, which can be augmented with a ninety-watt halogen flood placed about three feet from the herb.

The fact that savory reproduces vigorously leads us back to the herb's reputation as a love potion. Of course, there's never been a scrap of scientific support for this claim. Still, you can always snip off a handful of the numerous spring shoots and tuck them right into a pot of sandy soil, to make a new plant—a nice gift for someone you love.

Cooking

Savory has a slightly harsh woodsy taste reminiscent of thyme, and indeed one of its volatile oils is thymol, which gives thyme its characteristic flavor. For that reason, savory can be used like thyme in cooking. Both herbs are good "blenders," meaning they help to marry the various flavors in a dish. This property makes savory a natural addition to multi-ingredient recipes such as soups, stews, and sauces, for which a good proportion is one teaspoon of minced fresh savory (or half a teaspoon dried) for each serving.

Use the same amount of savory to make bean dishes and vegetables especially tasty. Try tossing it with pinto beans, hot broccoli, cauliflower, green beans, or cabbage just before serving. Savory lends a welcome depth to such vegetarian entrées as bean, tempeh, and tofu dishes. Start out with one teaspoon of minced fresh savory in a dish to serve four.

Couscous with Wild Mushrooms

Here's an example of how savory gives definition and strength to a vegetarian entrée.

~~~~~

2 cups vegetable stock or defatted chicken stock

1 cup whole wheat or white couscous

1 bay leaf

1 tablespoon olive oil

1 clove garlic, very finely minced

7 ounces mustard greens or kale, coarsely chopped

5 large fresh shiitake mushrooms, stems removed and sliced

3 ounces fresh oyster mushrooms, sliced

1 tablespoon minced fresh savory or 1 1/2 teaspoons dried

1 teaspoon balsamic vinegar

Freshly ground black pepper

Freshly grated Parmesan cheese or soy Parmesan

IN a medium saucepan, bring the stock to a boil. Stir in the couscous and bay leaf, cover, and remove from the heat. The couscous will absorb the stock while you prepare the rest of the dish.

HEAT a large sauté pan over high heat, then pour in the oil. Reduce the heat to medium, add the garlic, greens, and shiitake mushrooms, and sauté until the greens are not quite wilted, about 2 minutes. Add the oyster mushrooms and savory, and sauté until the greens have wilted and the mushrooms are cooked through, another minute or so. Add the vinegar and toss until fragrant, about 30 seconds.

COMBINE the greens mixture with the couscous, adding pepper and cheese to taste as you go. Serve as a light entrée, or as a side dish with fish.

MAKES 4 SERVINGS; 246 CALORIES PER SERVING, 5 GRAMS FAT, 22 PERCENT OF CALORIES FROM FAT.

Carrot and Potato Pancakes

A potato without salt can taste dull, but savory makes it come alive.

~~~~~

1   large baking potato (about ¹/₂ pound), peeled

3   medium carrots (about ¹/₄ pound)

¹/₄ cup whole wheat pastry flour

2   scallions, very finely minced

2   tablespoons minced fresh savory or 2 teaspoons dried savory

4   large egg whites, 2 whole eggs, lightly beaten, or ¹/₂ cup Calendula Egg Substitute (page 47)

1   tablespoon olive oil

Freshly grated Romano cheese or soy Parmesan

FINELY grate the potato and carrots and put them into a strainer that you've set in the sink, weighted down so the liquid drains out. Let drain for about 5 minutes. When well drained, transfer to a medium bowl and stir in the flour, scallions, savory, and eggs. Combine well.

HEAT a well-seasoned cast-iron skillet over medium-high heat for 3 minutes. (If you don't have a well-seasoned cast-iron skillet, use what you've got but don't preheat.) Reduce the heat to medium and pour in the oil. Using your hands, form the potato-carrot mixture into 4 firm cakes, and set them into the skillet. Sizzle until they're burnished and crisp, about 4 minutes on each side, pressing down frequently with a spatula. Sprinkle the cakes with Romano and serve hot. Or garnish with plain yogurt and fresh savory sprigs. The pancakes are a good side dish with lightly smoked shrimp or salmon.

MAKES 4 SIDE OR APPETIZER SERVINGS; 165 CALORIES PER SERVING, 4 GRAMS FAT, 21 PERCENT OF CALORIES FROM FAT.

Green Beans with Savory and Tomatoes

Savory embellishes the flavor of vegetables. Here, fresh green beans are featured, but be sure to try the recipe with zucchini and yellow summer squash. Slice them into coins and steam for three minutes before proceeding with the recipe.

~~~~~

1 pound green beans, topped and tailed

2 teaspoons olive oil

2 cloves garlic, mashed through a press

2 medium Italian plum tomatoes, chopped

1 tablespoon minced fresh savory

STEAM the beans over boiling water, covered, until bright green and just tender, about 7 minutes.

MEANWHILE, heat a large sauté pan over medium-high heat. Pour in the oil. Add the garlic and tomatoes and sauté until fragrant and saucy, about 5 minutes.

ADD the beans and savory to the tomatoes, tossing well. Serve as a side dish with polenta or an herb and cheese omelette. The beans are also tasty when slightly chilled and served as a side to risotto, with a glass of Chianti.

MAKES 4 SERVINGS; 60 CALORIES PER SERVING, 2 GRAMS FAT, 28 PERCENT OF CALORIES FROM FAT.

Tuna Steak with Green Olive Salsa and Roasted Peppers

Here savory bridges the strong flavors of olives, peppers, and sesame.

~~~~~

FOR THE SALSA:

1/2 cup pitted green olives
5   scallions, chopped
1   clove garlic, peeled
1   tablespoon balsamic
     vinegar
2   teaspoons olive oil
2   tablespoons tomato-based
     salsa

FOR THE TUNA:

1   pound fresh tuna, about
     1/2 inch thick
1   tablespoon fresh lemon juice
Splash of olive oil
1   tablespoon minced fresh
     savory or 1 teaspoon dried
1   teaspoon sesame seeds
2   roasted red bell peppers
     (see Note), thinly sliced

TO make the salsa, combine the olives, scallions, garlic, vinegar, olive oil, and tomato salsa in a processor or blender. Whiz until coarsely pureed; the salsa should be slightly chunky. Set aside.

PREHEAT the broiler or prepare the grill. Rub the tuna with the lemon juice and olive oil, then sprinkle on the savory and sesame seeds, pressing them into the flesh. Broil or grill the fish until cooked just through, about 3 to 4 minutes on each side. Serve warm, drizzled with the salsa and sprinkled with the sliced peppers.

MAKES 4 SERVINGS; 195 CALORIES PER SERVING, 5 GRAMS FAT, 25 PERCENT OF CALORIES FROM FAT.

NOTE: To roast peppers, halve, core, and seed them. Broil skin side up until the skins are black and charred. Transfer the charred peppers to a bowl and cover with a cloth napkin until they cool, at least 20 minutes. Then scrape off and discard the charred skin.

scented geranium

chase away the blues

~

SOOTHE

ANXIETY

~

TONE

THE

SKIN

~

ADD

FRAGRANCE

TO

FOODS

~

at a dinner in Harare, Zimbabwe, I received the gift of a rose geranium–scented handkerchief, which proved very refreshing over the next few days as I explored the steaming streets of the city. But it came in especially handy when I was riding in a taxi that was stopped and searched by armed soldiers. I clutched it to my nose as I stared down the barrel of the AK-47 Russian assault rifle that was inches away from my face. As the soldiers rummaged through the taxi, I barely dared to breathe. Finally, they were satisfied that we had no guns or bombs and sent us on our way. But I had learned a useful lesson about rose geranium—it is a potent antidote for anxiety.

Lore and Legend

Scented geraniums, rose and otherwise, are natives of South Africa. In the 1600s, sailors brought them to Europe, where herbalists used the fragrant dried leaves to scent bed pillows and wine, as well as to improve the smell of medicinal ointments. Colonists brought scented geraniums to the New World, and Thomas Jefferson had several varieties planted in the White House gardens.

But the great users of scented geraniums were perfumers in France and Victorian England. Natural rose fragrance, called attar of roses, is one of the most expensive aromas to extract. So when perfumers discovered the rose-scented geranium, many began to substitute its leaves for the flower petals of true rose when making essential oils for fragrances. The practice is still in full bloom, so to speak, for rose geranium remains a popular ingredient in perfumes today.

Healing

Aromatherapists use essential oil of rose geranium in massage, to soothe anxiety, lift depression, and balance the mood. Basil and lemon are sometimes blended in to give a slight snap to the rosy aroma. To make a rose geranium massage oil, add about four drops of essential oil (blended or straight) to two tablespoons of olive oil. Then massage your feet, arms, hands, and abdomen, or ask a friend to massage your back. For a similar relaxing effect, use the blend as a bath oil. Run a hot bath, then swirl in two teaspoons of the massage oil before you soak.

In Victorian England, fresh rose geranium leaves were strewn across bed sheets on hot summer nights. People would then lie naked on the leaves, and the warmth and weight of their bodies would release the herb's luscious rose aroma. Since the leaves are soft and velvety, this practice is well worth reviving.

Looking Your Best

Rose geranium makes a refreshing tonic for any type of skin. To try it, add three drops of the essential oil to half a cup of your favorite commercial cleanser, toner, or moisturizer. You can also combine three drops of essential oil of rose geranium with half a cup of spring water in a spray bottle. Use it to mist your face before applying moisturizer (or after shaving) and throughout the day, even over makeup.

Growing

Unlike the more familiar seed geraniums, scented geraniums are known for their fragrant leaves, not their flowers. There are about seventy-five different scented geranium varieties, including cinnamon, chocolate, ginger, lime, orange, nutmeg, and lemon, as well as rose. While lemon-scented geranium is usually very fragrant, other varieties can have stingy, barely recognizable scents that pale in comparison to the rose geranium. A light October frost may bring out the fragrance of some of these milder cousins, but why wait for fall when rose geranium generously offers a continual burst of aroma?

Scented geraniums like full sun and a sandy version of the standard herb soil mix, combining two parts garden or potting soil, two parts peat, two parts sand, and one part compost or composted cow manure. Buy small organically grown plants and dig a hole for each that's twice the size of the root ball. Set a plant in each hole, fill in with the surrounding soil, and tamp it down. Soak with warm water, then water about once a week thereafter.

Scented geraniums do well in pots, but may need more frequent watering. To intensify their fragrance, try working a scoop of composted cow manure into the soil once a month.

Indoors, scented geraniums need about three hours of full sun a day, which can be augmented with a ninety-watt halogen flood about four feet from the herbs. But keep the plants cool—they don't like it hotter than about 68°F.

Cooking

Scented geraniums, particularly rose, can uplift pallid foods such as custards and puddings, lending a surprising floral bouquet. Try heating about three tablespoons (not packed) dried rose geranium leaves in two cups of milk. Let the mixture cool, then strain away the leaves and use the milk to make your favorite vanilla pudding. (To dry rose geranium leaves, arrange them in a single layer on a dinner plate and store, uncovered, in a cool, dry place for about a week.)

The fresh leaves can also be a grace note in jellies, vinegars, honey, and dessert syrups—or even floated in finger bowls. Use five fresh leaves for each cup of liquid. Or try an old Shaker baking trick to lend sweetness and aroma to pie crusts by pressing about a dozen fresh leaves into the dough before filling and baking. Another lovely way to use the leaves is to tuck one into your sugar bowl to perfume the sugar for future uses, such as sweetening a cup of herbal tea.

Though scented geranium flowers are scant and small, they make a delicate addition to green and fruit salads. Add a couple of teaspoons of flowers for each serving.

Rose Crème Fraîche

Fragrant leaves add floral notes to this classic topping.

~~~~~

8 ounces heavy cream
1/4 cup loosely packed dried rose geranium leaves

1 tablespoon buttermilk

COMBINE the cream and leaves in a small saucepan. Heat until bubbles are just beginning to form around the edges of the pan and the cream reaches about 130°F. Remove the pan from the heat and let cool to room temperature.

STIR the buttermilk into the cream, then pour the mixture into a glass jar and cover it tightly. Shake for about 2 minutes. Then wrap the jar in a towel and keep it in a warm place for about 8 hours, until it is almost as thick as sour cream.

SET a coarse-mesh strainer over a bowl and pour the crème fraîche through it. With the back of a spoon, press the leaves against the strainer as hard as you can to create pale green swirls of aromatic oil from the leaves in the white of the crème. Keep pressing until the leaves are totally macerated and the crème is fragrant. Serve with fresh fruit salad or drizzled on a fruit tart.

MAKES ABOUT 1 CUP; 50 CALORIES PER 1-TABLESPOON SERVING, 6 GRAMS FAT, ALMOST 100 PERCENT OF CALORIES FROM FAT.

NOTE: If this recipe is too high in fat for you, cut the fat in half by mixing the crème fraîche with an equal amount of nonfat vanilla yogurt before serving.

sorrel

~

FIND A

SPRING

SOURCE OF

VITAMIN C

~

HELP

PREVENT

FLU

~

GIVE

SPRING

FOODS A

LEMONY

TANG

~

lemonade in a leaf

One hot July in Cairo, just before I thought I'd completely wilt away, I was given a cool tea made from sorrel leaves, colored fuchsia with hibiscus flowers. After one glass I felt cooler, and by the end of the second glass, although the weather was still scorching, I once again felt comfortable enough to carry on with my day. An Egyptian herbalist offered an explanation—sorrel's lemony taste has "cooling" properties that help "refrigerate" the body from the inside out.

Lore and Legend

Some Irish historians say that sorrel, not clover, may have been the original shamrock, and that it may have been the arrow-shaped, three-cornered sorrel leaf that St. Patrick used as a model for the Trinity.

But throughout the rest of the world, sorrel's uses were more corporeal than spiritual. Early Egyptians and Romans nibbled on fresh sorrel leaves after overeating, both for their soothing effect on the digestive system and for their diuretic properties, relieving bloating. In North America, two hundred years ago, sorrel was eaten as "lemonade in a leaf." When a farmer became thirsty during spring planting, he would just reach down, pluck up some wild sorrel, and eat it. That sour-citrusy taste was prized throughout the world as a wake-up call for taste buds dulled by winter foods. In the days before refrigeration, sorrel was often the first fresh food that people ate each spring. In Europe it was a popular ingredient in spring tonics, taken to help prevent scurvy. It's now well known that scurvy is caused by a vitamin C deficiency, and though vitamins weren't identified until 1907, our ancestors' instincts were correct. Fresh sorrel leaves are a good source of vitamin C.

Healing

The vitamin C in sorrel probably explains its popularity as a cure for respiratory ailments. Eskimos eat fresh spring sorrel, which they call sour dock, to ease the digestive problems that come with spring flu. Navajo herbalists use chopped fresh sorrel leaves topically to treat sores in the mouth. (Pack it on the area, then press on your face to release the juice. Keep it in for up to thirty minutes, then repeat with fresh sorrel.) Some health experts, including Nobel Prize laureate Linus Pauling, believe that a diet high in vitamin C can boost the body's natural defenses enough to help prevent and lessen symptoms of flu and other ailments, such as mouth ulcers and colds.

The USDA says that sorrel contains up to thirty-eight milligrams of vitamin C per half cup of raw (not packed) leaves, about as much as half an orange. But some herbalists say the same amount of sorrel contains up to eighty milligrams per half cup and add that it's easily assimilated by the body. The discrepancy may come from the different growing conditions of the samples tested.

Still, it may not be wise to make sorrel your only source of vitamin C. Like many other common foods, including spinach, sorrel contains oxalic acid, a compound that can prevent your body from absorbing calcium. Used as an herb, in amounts of up to half a cup (not packed) a day, sorrel is not considered harmful. In fact, sorrel's lemony tang can brighten your food and your mood.

Growing

Sorrel grows and reproduces so frantically that you're better off seeking a machete than gardening advice, but here goes: The herb likes a dry version of the standard herb mix, combining two parts garden or potting soil, two parts peat, two parts sand, and one part compost or composted cow manure. Buy small organically grown plants and dig a hole for each that's twice the size of the root ball. Set each plant in a hole, fill in with the surrounding soil, tamp the soil down, and soak with warm water. Then, unless there is a drought, let nature do the watering.

For indoor growing, give sorrel a wide pot so it can spread out. Clay pots are better for sorrel than plastic, because clay is more porous and will keep the soil drier. Give sorrel four hours of full sun a day, which can be augmented with a ninety-watt halogen flood placed about three feet from the plants.

Cooking

Sorrel has been a favorite spring culinary herb for centuries, especially in Europe. As the weather gets warmer, sorrel leaves toughen up a bit, and with cool weather they lose their lemony taste. So stick to spring sorrel. It blends perfectly with other spring herbs such as dill, chives, and watercress, and complements such spring foods as new potatoes, salmon, soft-shelled crab, peas, strawberries, and spinach. Use one tablespoon of minced fresh sorrel for two servings of these foods. Or steam equal parts of sorrel and spinach together, tossing with toasted sesame seeds and lemon juice before serving.

There are several varieties of sorrel, and the most fresh- and lemony-tasting is French sorrel (*Rumex scutatus*). When you see sorrel in the supermarket produce section, it's most likely French sorrel, but ask to be sure.

Wild sorrel varieties are less refined. Common sorrel (*R. acetosa*) has darker leaves with a slightly more green and musty taste. Wood sorrel (*Oxalis acetosella*) is the lively little clover-like herb that pops up frequently in the unsterilized soil of potted plants. It contains too much oxalic acid to taste good, but its juice is still recommended by herbalists, particularly in Germany, for various stomach ailments. Just to avoid confusion, note that there's a Bajan (from Barbados) beverage called sorrel that's made from a red fruit (also called sorrel), with a spicy, citrusy taste, but is no relation to the herb.

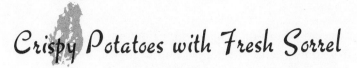

Crispy Potatoes with Fresh Sorrel

Blanching the potatoes beforehand helps them brown and get crisp in very little oil.

~~~~~

1 pound small new potatoes	2 tablespoons minced fresh sorrel
1 tablespoon olive oil	

SLICE the potatoes thin. Steam over boiling water, covered, until barely tender, about 5 minutes.

HEAT a well-seasoned cast-iron skillet over medium-high heat. Swirl in the oil so that the bottom of the pan is well coated. (If you don't have cast-iron, use a nonstick pan but don't preheat.)

PAT the potatoes dry and layer them evenly in the skillet. Reduce the heat to medium and let the potatoes sizzle, without stirring, until browned, about 4 minutes on each side. Just before you remove the potatoes from the heat, sprinkle on the sorrel. Serve warm.

MAKES 4 SERVINGS; 125 CALORIES PER SERVING, 1 GRAM FAT, 8 PERCENT OF CALORIES FROM FAT.

Penne with Mushrooms and Fresh Sorrel

This easy-to-make dish is great for spring picnics.

~~~~~

1 tablespoon olive oil	1 cup chopped tomatoes (canned are okay)
12 ounces mushrooms, sliced	
2 cloves garlic, mashed through a press	6 cups hot cooked penne or other tubular pasta (from about 3/4 pound dried)
1 medium onion, sliced	
1 dried hot chili pepper (about 2 inches long)	1/3 cup minced fresh sorrel leaves

continued

HEAT a large sauté pan over medium-high heat, then pour in the oil. Add the mushrooms, garlic, onion, and hot pepper and sauté for about 5 minutes. Stir in the tomatoes and cook until saucy and fragrant, about 7 minutes more.

IN a large bowl, toss the penne with the sauce and sorrel. Serve warm.

MAKES 6 SERVINGS; 240 CALORIES PER SERVING, 2 GRAMS FAT, 8 PERCENT OF CALORIES FROM FAT.

Soft-Shelled Crabs with Fresh Sorrel

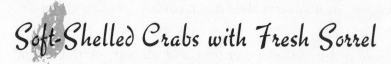

In this perfect blending of spring flavors, sorrel adds a lemony tang to soft-shelled crabs.

2	teaspoons olive oil	1/3	cup dry white vermouth
1/2	cup cornmeal	1	teaspoon Dijon mustard
8	small to medium soft-shelled crabs, cleaned	2	tablespoons minced fresh sorrel

HEAT a large well-seasoned cast-iron skillet over medium-high heat, then add the oil. (If you don't have a cast-iron skillet, use a large nonstick sauté pan, but don't preheat.)

MEANWHILE, sprinkle the cornmeal on a counter and press the crabs into it so that it sticks to their moist surfaces.

ARRANGE the crabs in the skillet and sizzle them for about 2 to 3 minutes on each side, until they've turned red and are cooked through. Remove the crabs from the skillet and keep them warm. Add the vermouth and mustard to the skillet and turn the heat up to high. Let the mixture boil, stirring constantly, until slightly thickened. Swirl in the sorrel, then drizzle over the crabs. Serve warm.

MAKES 4 SERVINGS; 185 CALORIES PER SERVING, 3.7 GRAMS FAT, 18 PERCENT OF CALORIES FROM FAT.

southernwood

~~~~~~

preserve your roots

*I*f the smell of mothballs disagrees with you, you can safely turn the protective care of your woolens over to the herb southernwood. An old-fashioned French name for southernwood is *garderobe* ("closet"), as in guarding clothes. French people hang tufts of southernwood in closets to keep moths away, as do the Pennsylvania Dutch. I've adopted the practice myself, but for extra protection I pack each woolen item with its own branch of southernwood.

Lore and Legend

As repellent as moths may find it, to the human nose, southernwood smells good. Its clean, fresh aroma is piny with a touch of citrus. That could be why, in the 1800s, during the days of the long Sunday sermon, people in Mediterranean countries often stashed sprigs of southernwood in their pockets before going to church. The crisp fragrance may have helped them stay alert.

~

MOTH-

PROOF

WOOLENS

~

TREAT

BLEMISHED

SKIN

~

GROW A

POLLUTION-

RESISTANT

HERB

~

On other days of the week, young men rubbed fresh sprigs of southernwood on their faces, since the herb was rumored to stimulate beard growth.

Looking Your Best

Southernwood won't give you facial hair, but a soothing rinse can help banish blemishes. To try it, combine two tablespoons of chopped fresh southernwood and one tablespoon of raw rolled oats in a mug. Pour on one cup of boiling water, cover, and let steep for five minutes. Strain and splash on your face three times a day, after cleansing and before moisturizing. You can store the brew in the fridge, covered, for up to five days.

Growing

Southernwood's silvery-green feathery leaves make it a wonderful backdrop for more colorful herbs. Plant it at the back of a border, with calendula, purple sage, golden sage, tricolor sage, purple basil, or golden thyme in front. Southernwood can grow tall enough to collapse onto shorter herbs, so keep it upright with regular pruning.

As well as visually complementing other herbs, southernwood will help protect them. It repels burrowing creatures that chew on the roots of other plants. Use branches of southernwood as a mulch around susceptible herbs such as echinacea. As an extra deterrent to lurking enemies, stomp on the southernwood mulch to release its aroma.

Southernwood likes the standard herb soil mix of two parts garden or potting soil, two parts peat, one part sand, and one part compost or composted cow manure. Buy small organically grown plants and dig a hole for each that's twice the size of the root ball. Set each plant in a hole, fill in with the surrounding soil, and tamp down. Soak with warm water; then, unless there is a drought, let nature do the watering.

Southernwood grows too lanky indoors, but it works well in pots on a terrace. It is especially suited to city gardens, since it is impervious to even the fiercest smog. In fact, though this attribute has not been scientifically documented, it seems to absorb certain pollutants. Nonsmoking drivers may want to try stuffing their car ashtrays with fresh southernwood to mitigate the unpleasant odors of city driving.

speedwell

~~~~~~

low-stress gardening

*F*or me, both cooking and gardening can summon confusing emotions. There are times when I spend hours preparing a meal and no one blinks an eye. Or I spend all day pruning and weeding the garden and it looks as if I haven't made a dent. The other side of the coin is the meal I whip up in no time that's an instant sensation. The garden parallel is speedwell, the maintenance-free herb that makes my garden look as if I've spent hours on it. Come drought, hailstorms, or cold snaps, speedwell flourishes and rarely displays a disagreeable yellow leaf.

Lore and Legend

In the 1600s, European herbalists advised their arthritic patients to fry speedwell leaves in lard, mix in some flour, and then apply the hot dough to their sore joints. The warm compress often provided quick relief from pain, and that may be why speedwell got its name. But

~

CALM A

COUGH

~

SOFTEN

TOUGH

CALLUSES

~

CREATE A

NATIVE

AMERICAN

GARDEN

~

speedwell was also prescribed for long-term cures. Women drank speedwell leaf tea as a dieting aid, and also after a miscarriage, to help cleanse the body.

Though speedwell is a native of temperate Europe and New Zealand, it's common throughout North America. One traditional Cherokee Indian cure for coughs is a tea made by boiling speedwell leaves.

Healing

Modern science confirms speedwell's efficacy as a cough remedy, for it contains a compound, leptandrine, that acts as an expectorant. Herbalists today don't prescribe it very often since it tastes extremely bitter. But if you want to try speedwell tea for respiratory congestion, you can make it more palatable by mixing it with Chinese licorice, using one tablespoon of bruised fresh speedwell leaves and two slices of dried Chinese licorice root. Steep the herbs in one cup of boiling water, covered, for four minutes, then strain and sip.

Looking Your Best

Speedwell is great for softening hardened skin on your elbows and your feet. To try it, pick a large, fresh speedwell leaf, fold it up, and bruise it with your fingernail. Then rub it vigorously on the area. The juice of the leaf will soften very dry skin or calluses and make your pumice stone or cream more effective.

Growing

If you want the kind of speedwell that's nearly carefree, be sure you buy the purple-flowered variety. Pink- and white-flowered varieties are commonly sold commercially, but they can be quite finicky. The white-flowered variety can't take hot sun or drought, and the pink is stingy with its blossoms. By contrast, purple speedwell flowers with gorgeous spikes bloom continuously from May through September. Snip off the blossoms as they die to give the plant extra flower power.

Speedwell can grow taller than three feet, but it will flower just as happily if you keep it clipped to about four inches as a ground cover. In fact, in the wild, speedwell is normally a low-growing perennial.

Speedwell likes a rich version of the standard herb mix, combining two parts garden or potting soil, two parts peat, two parts compost or composted cow manure, and one part sand. Buy small organically grown plants and find a place for them in the garden that gets at least four hours of full sun a day. Dig a hole for each plant that's twice the size of the root ball, and set a plant in each hole. Fill in with the surrounding soil and tamp it down. Soak with warm water; then, unless there is a drought, let nature do the watering. Speedwell can become spindly indoors, so keep it outside.

When choosing herbs to complement speedwell, you might consider planting a North American Indian garden. Use speedwell with echinacea, peppermint, yarrow, tansy, catnip, mustard, and thistle—all herbs cultivated or harvested in the wild by Indian tribes for traditional medicine.

Cooking

Can you eat speedwell? Yes and no. Speedwell leaves are tastiest in very early spring, when they're small, young, and tender. At this time they taste like peas and can enhance a salad of other spring greens such as cress, spinach, and dandelion leaf. Like most greens, they offer the benefits of citric acid, an organic form of vitamin C. Unfortunately, as the plant grows, the leaves become larger and their texture gets too tough to be enjoyable. And as summer wears on and the temperature rises above 70°F, speedwell leaves become too gaggingly bitter.

tansy

~

SOOTHE

TIRED

FEET

~

KEEP

APHIDS

OUT OF

THE

GARDEN

~

MAKE

YOUR OWN

INSECT

REPELLENT

~

automatic insect repellent

*F*or two summers straight, the beautiful pink clematis in my garden was plagued by aphids. Just when it was ready to bloom, the leaves turned a sick yellow, then the entire plant shriveled down to its roots. The third year, determined to have blooms, I laid a one-inch-thick mulch of bruised fresh tansy leaves at the base of the clematis, then soaked the mulch with hot water. To my delight, the aphids stayed away and the clematis bloomed more beautifully than ever.

Lore and Legend

In the days before people bathed frequently, social gatherings could be unpleasant without strewing herbs. Aromatic herbs were strewn on a floor or street, and as people walked on them, the herbal fragrance was released to sweeten the air. Tansy was a favorite strewing herb, especially in England. When James II was crowned king in 1685, tansy was strewn over his entire half-mile march to the throne.

Tansy's strong smell—peppery camphor with a touch of citrus—is so potent that it was even strewn in coffins or used in embalming from pre-Christian times through the American Revolution. In the days before refrigeration, chefs used it to mask the smell of rancid meat, as well as in place of pepper in soups and stews. They also baked tansy cakes for Easter, combining the herb with eggs, cream, sugar, wine, and nutmeg.

Early European herbalists recommended drinking tansy tea to expel worms from the body or infusing the leaves in hot buttermilk as a wash to promote clear skin. Highland Scots, however, were not so fond of tansy, naming it "Stinking Willie," after a reviled Lowlands warrior.

Healing

After a long day, you can refresh your spirits, and your feet, with a tansy foot bath. Steep a quarter cup of bruised fresh tansy leaves in one cup of boiling milk, covered, for ten minutes. Strain the leaves away and pour the scented milk into a basin of hot water. Dip your feet in, cover with a towel, and let them soak for ten minutes.

Growing

To raise tansy, buy small organically grown plants. Find a place for it in the garden that gets at least four hours of full sun a day. Prepare the standard herb soil mix of two parts garden or potting soil, two parts peat, one part sand, and one part compost or composted cow manure. Dig a hole for each plant that's twice the size of the root ball, and set the plant in the hole. Fill in with the surrounding soil and tamp it down. Soak with warm water; then, unless there is a drought, let nature do the watering.

Tansy spreads freely. To keep it from taking over the garden, you should start watching it in early March. As soon as you see tiny tansy runners peeking up out of the soil, grab each one and zip it straight back to the mother plant, then right out of the soil. In the spring, tansy's roots are shallow, so if you remove the runners then, the tansy will stay fairly well contained throughout the year.

Tansy's ferny leaves make a nice backdrop for thyme. Better yet, unlike true ferns, it will gladly grow in scorching sun and requires almost no work. It will also help protect your garden by attracting ladybugs, who prey on insects that like to eat herbs, and by repelling ants, who attract damaging aphids. One of its volatile oils, tanacetin, is actually marketed in Russia as an insect repellent.

Try making an insect-repelling tansy spray by soaking one cup of bruised fresh leaves in a quart of hot water for about an hour. Strain the leaves away, saving them for mulch, and spray the liquid on your plants. The aroma is quite refreshing, like that of a daisy with touches of camphor, citrus, and pine added.

To enjoy tansy in the house, plant it in a wide pot. If you like, you can plant the spring runners that you've zipped out of the ground right into the soil. Indoors, tansy likes to be near a window that gets at least four hours of sun a day. Augment the light, if you need to, with a ninety-watt halogen bulb placed about three feet from the plant.

tarragon

give high blood pressure the boot

At a multi-course banquet in Hong Kong, most of the dishes contained garlic. Scallops with garlic and hot peppers, Chinese greens with black beans and garlic, lobster with ginger and garlic—they were all delicious, but by the end of the meal (even for a garlic lover), the taste was overpowering. Fortunately, the host was clever, and before dessert each diner received a tiny dish of fresh tarragon to eat as a breath freshener. It was far more effective than any other breath freshener I've had before or since, including commercial and herbal types, and I now make tarragon the happy ending to every pungent meal I serve.

Lore and Legend

Tarragon has been used in the Middle East since at least the thirteenth century. Arab physicians of the time had people chew on tarragon before administering un-

~

DISCOVER A

POSSIBLE

LINK IN

CANCER

~

PREVENTION

~

ENJOY AN

HERBAL

SOURCE OF

POTASSIUM

~

ADD

SOPHISTICATED

FLAVOR TO

YOUR COOKING

~

pleasant-tasting medicines. To see why, try chewing a teaspoon of fresh tarragon leaves or half a teaspoon of dried. At first you'll notice tarragon's anise-camphor taste, but soon you'll realize that your tongue has become slightly numb—the perfect state to taste, or shall we say not taste, a bitter medicine.

Healing

Contemporary physicians and researchers have gone farther with tarragon, discovering that it contains a compound called rutin, which is being investigated for its ability to help prevent cancer. Although this connection is not yet established, it is known that rutin can help regulate blood pressure levels. Tarragon is also a good source of potassium, a mineral that can help prevent high blood pressure and strokes. One tablespoon of dried tarragon contains 145 milligrams of potassium. For comparison, three ounces of chicken, considered a rich source of potassium, contains 195 milligrams.

The best way to get the benefits of tarragon is simply to eat it. Don't make a tea of it, because boiling water may deplete tarragon's potassium. Try a tablespoon or two fresh, or a teaspoon or so dried, in a heart-healthy green salad; dress the salad with fresh lemon juice and olive oil, and the tarragon will taste sweet and licorice-like. The essential oils in the lemon tone down tarragon's camphor and keep it from making your tongue feel numb.

Herbal Sources of Potassium

HERB	MG./TBS.
Anise seed	97
Basil	154
Caraway seed	91
Celery seed	91
Chili powder	144
Cumin seed	107
Dillweed	108
Fennel seed	98
Tarragon	145
Turmeric (ground)	172

Sources for these figures are from the U.S. Department of Agriculture, *Agriculture Handbook* No. 8–2, January 1977. Figures are for dried herbs.

Growing

There are two main varieties of tarragon, but French is the tastiest. The different types look almost identical, so before you purchase a plant, rub its leaves between your fingers. If their smell is an anise-camphor combination, you've got the tasty French tarragon. If they smell faintly sour, the plant is Russian tarragon, the type you don't want to buy.

Choose small organically grown plants. One tip for raising tarragon is to plant it in not-quite-full sun. Tarragon's root system is shallow and a bit of shade will keep it from fainting on very hot days. Mulch also helps, protecting the roots from both extreme heat and cold.

Prepare a rich version of the standard herb mixture, combining two parts garden or potting soil, two parts peat, two parts compost or composted cow manure, and one part sand. Dig a hole for each tarragon plant that's twice the size of the root ball, and set the plant in. Fill in with the surrounding soil and tamp it down. Soak with warm water. Then, to determine when to water again, stick your finger in the soil. Water only when the soil is completely dry. Tarragon hates soggy soil and will eventually tell you so by contracting root rot and flopping over dead.

Tarragon will also grow happily indoors near a sunny window that gets about four hours of full sun a day. Augment the light, if you need to, with a ninety-watt halogen flood, placed about four feet from the plant. Give tarragon a wide pot to accommodate its shallow roots, and don't water it until the soil has completely dried out.

Cooking

Apart from lemon, not many flavors mingle well with tarragon, so it's often used on its own in recipes. An exception to the rule is one of the most famous classic French blends, "fines herbes," which includes chervil, parsley, chives, and tarragon. The chervil, parsley, and chives in the blend aren't assertive enough to challenge tarragon: They serve merely to enhance its distinctive taste.

But don't be intimidated by tarragon's strength of character. Several classic recipes depend on tarragon for their very identity. Béarnaise sauce is not Béarnaise without tarragon, and the same is true of veal Marengo, tartar sauce, and tarragon vinegar–based hollandaise. It can also enhance any creamy soup, as well as many sauces and mayonnaise. Start with a teaspoon of minced fresh tarragon (or half a teaspoon of dried) in a recipe to serve four. Just remember to add tarragon to the food right before serving. Boiling tarragon for too long can make it bitter.

Fresh Mushroom Spread with Tarragon

Tarragon gives dimension to the earthy flavor of mushrooms.

~~~~~

1 teaspoon olive oil	4 sun-dried tomatoes, minced
12 ounces fresh button mushrooms, very finely minced	1 tablespoon balsamic vinegar
1 clove garlic, mashed through a press	1/2 teaspoon minced fresh tarragon or 1/4 teaspoon dried
1/4 cup minced onion	

PREHEAT a large sauté pan over medium-high heat, then pour in the oil. When it's hot, add the mushrooms, garlic, onion, tomatoes, and vinegar and sauté until all the liquid has evaporated, about 5 minutes. Quickly swirl in the tarragon and remove the pan from the heat. Serve warm or slightly chilled on crusty bread as an appetizer or snack, or make a sandwich on a baguette with melted mozzarella.

MAKES 1 1/2 CUPS, OR 6 SERVINGS; 22 CALORIES PER SERVING, LESS THAN 1 GRAM FAT, 33 PERCENT OF CALORIES FROM FAT.

Spinach with Fresh Tarragon

All three of the fresh ingredients in this dish—spinach, tarragon, and scallions—are abundantly available and at their best in the spring.

~~~~~~

2½ cups loosely packed, cleaned and stemmed fresh spinach

1 teaspoon olive oil

Splash of hot pepper sauce, or to taste

1 teaspoon minced fresh tarragon

2 scallions, very finely minced

STEAM the spinach over boiling water, covered, until it has wilted slightly and become vibrant green, about 4 to 5 minutes for average-sized leaves. Drain well and pat dry.

IMMEDIATELY toss the spinach with the olive oil, hot pepper sauce, tarragon, and scallions and combine well. Serve warm with grilled fish, or toss with 2 cups of cooked pasta for a more robust side dish.

MAKES 4 SERVINGS; 35 CALORIES PER SERVING, LESS THAN 1 GRAM OF FAT.

Variation: Substitute kale or mustard greens for the spinach.

Seitan Stew with Tomatoes and Tarragon

Seitan is a wheat-based substitute for beef that is available at health food stores and many supermarkets. When combined with tarragon, bay leaf, wine, and tomatoes, it makes a satisfying "meaty" stew.

~~~~~

2 teaspoons olive oil	1 bay leaf
1 medium onion, sliced	1 tablespoon minced fresh
2 cloves garlic, minced	tarragon or 1 teaspoon
9 ounces seitan, sliced	dried
(about 1½ cups)	1 teaspoon dried zatar
3 Italian plum tomatoes,	(available at Middle
chopped (canned are okay)	Eastern groceries) or dried
¾ cup vegetable stock or	thyme (see Note)
liquid from the seitan	Pinch of sea salt
¼ cup dry white wine	

HEAT a large frying pan over medium-high heat, then add the oil, swirling it around to cover the bottom. Sauté the onion and garlic until fragrant and lightly browned, about 3 to 4 minutes. Add the seitan and sauté for a couple of minutes more, until it just begins to brown.

ADD the tomatoes, stock, wine, bay leaf, tarragon, zatar, and salt and bring to a boil. Reduce the heat, cover loosely, and simmer until the cooking liquid is slightly thickened and saucy, about 20 minutes. Serve warm with rice and a salad.

MAKES 2 LARGE ENTRÉE SERVINGS; 200 CALORIES PER SERVING, 4.5 GRAMS FAT, 20 PERCENT OF CALORIES FROM FAT.

NOTE: Zatar is a thyme-like herb, popular in Middle Eastern cooking.

Grilled Vegetables with Tarragon

Zucchini, summer squash, eggplant, and bell peppers all benefit from tarragon's anise zing.

~~~~~

4 small to medium zucchini (about 1 pound), cut into 1/3-inch slices

4 small to medium yellow summer squash (about 1 pound), cut into 1/3-inch slices

1 large eggplant, cut crosswise into 1/3-inch slices

2 red bell peppers, cored, seeded, and quartered

4 scallions, cleaned but roots left on

1/4 cup olive oil

2 tablespoons balsamic vinegar

1 teaspoon Dijon mustard

1/4 cup fresh tarragon leaves

Pinch of sea salt

COMBINE the zucchini, squash, eggplant, peppers, and scallions in a large bowl.

IN a small bowl, whisk together the oil, vinegar, mustard, tarragon, and salt. Pour the dressing over the vegetables and toss well. Let the vegetables marinate for at least an hour, or as long as overnight.

PREPARE the grill or preheat the broiler.

USING tongs, lift the vegetables out of the marinade, knocking off the tarragon leaves so they won't burn. Grill the vegetables 4 inches from the heat, turning once, until cooked through, about 10 to 15 minutes. Remove the individual vegetables as they finish cooking and set them back in the marinade. Serve warm as a light entrée, along with chilled soup, or as an appetizer or side dish.

MAKES 4 LARGE SERVINGS; 235 CALORIES PER SERVING, 14 GRAMS FAT, 53 PERCENT OF CALORIES FROM FAT.

NOTE: The proportion of fat looks high here, but be aware that it comes from heart-healthy olive oil. Nonetheless, if you like, you can cut it in half by replacing 2 tablespoons of the olive oil with 2 tablespoons of defatted chicken stock or vegetable stock. The catch is that then you must watch the vegetables like a hawk while they're grilling, because the decreased amount of oil will encourage them to burn faster.

thyme

give a cough the cold shoulder

~

KEEP

MOUTH

AND GUMS

HEALTHY

~

CUT BACK

ON SALT

IN COOKING

~

PREVENT

WHITEFLY

IN HOUSE

AND GARDEN

~

While visiting Amman, Jordan, I delighted in a dozen kinds of fragrantly cured olives, savory spinach pies, grilled vegetable sandwiches on fresh pitas with cucumber sauce, and herbed breads in every shape. What many of the foods had in common was an herb called zatar, which grew only in the wild, in rocky places. A few days later, I found zatar on a side trip to Jerash, an ancient Roman city about an hour outside of Amman. It had sprung up between the centuries-old stones of the city's amphitheater, and it smelled and looked like a small, slightly grayish English thyme with leaves about twice as long. I was in fact informed that the botanical name for zatar is *Thymbra spicata*—an herb that, for culinary purposes, is interchangeable with common thyme.

Lore and Legend

In Biblical times, people sacrificed animals, particularly lambs, to invoke the influence of the gods. To make the lambs more enticing to the celestial powers, they were often sprinkled with thyme. The idea may have derived from ancient Egypt, where embalmers used thyme to ready mummies for their heavenly journeys. Or it may simply have reflected the human fondness for the combination of lamb and thyme. In Greece, lambs were even encouraged to graze in fields of wild thyme to make them tastier for eating.

Healing

Whatever the herb's divine appeal may be, modern medicine is discovering new uses for thyme right here on earth. It contains a volatile oil, thymol, which has antiseptic and antibacterial properties that are particularly effective in keeping mouths and gums healthy. Thymol is often used in commercial mouthwashes, and some researchers claim it can kill bacteria in forty seconds.

The same properties make thyme a popular ingredient in commercial cough syrups for both adults and children. If you object to taking cough syrup that contains sugar, artificial flavor, or artificial color, and can't find a commercial brand without these additives, try a cup of thyme tea for a cough. Steep two tablespoons of fresh thyme (or one tablespoon dried) in a cup of hot water, covered, for four minutes. Some herbalists recommend using half thyme and half plantain (the herb *Plantago*, not the fruit), especially when a stuffy nose accompanies the cough.

Aromatherapists have known about thyme's respiratory-healing properties for at least two centuries. They have been using massages with essential oil of thyme to help rid people of coughs, sore throats, colds, and even cranky digestion. To try it, add five drops of essential oil of thyme to one-quarter cup of olive oil. Then massage a small amount into your neck, upper body, and feet, or have a friend massage your back.

Another old-fashioned practice that's popping up again is using thyme to preserve foods. Ancient chefs packed meats and other foods in thyme to keep them from spoiling. Now the USDA reports that thyme, as well as peppermint and cinnamon, seems to be effective at keeping potatoes from sprouting—a natural alternative to irradiation and chemical spraying.

Another benefit of thyme is its high iron content—over five milligrams per tablespoon of the dried herb, or more than a quarter of the Recommended Daily Allowance of eighteen milligrams. To see how thyme stacks up, half a cup of lima beans, considered an excellent source of iron, contains under three milligrams of iron.

The problem in getting iron from a vegetable source, such as thyme, is that the body has some difficulty absorbing it unless it's accompanied by some vitamin C. In fact, vitamin C may increase absorption of thyme's iron by three times. So if you're brewing up a cup of high-iron thyme tea, squeeze in a wedge of lemon.

High-Iron Herbs

HERB	MG./TBS.
Anise seed	2
Basil	2
Black pepper	2
Celery seed	3
Cinnamon	2
Cumin seed	4
Fenugreek seed	4
Oregano	2
Thyme	5
Turmeric (ground)	3

Figures in this chart come from the U.S. Department of Agriculture, *Agriculture Handbook* No. 8–2, January 1977. Figures are for dried herbs and spices and are rounded to the nearest milligram. The suggested RDA for iron is 18 milligrams.

Growing

Thyme is low and shrubby, so plant taller herbs, such as yarrow and tansy, behind it. There are hundreds of varieties of thyme, and not all are suitable for eating. So before you buy a thyme plant, rub the leaves between your fingers and smell them. If the leaves aren't fragrant—peppery with a touch of clove—the thyme is probably an ornamental, rather than the culinary type.

Try at least a couple of the unusual culinary varieties, since they're just as easy to grow as common thyme. Lemon thyme is outstanding for cooking; try adding some to scallops during the last second of sautéing. Caraway thyme is excellent in curries, or in salads dressed with curry vinaigrette.

Thyme likes a dry version of the standard herb mix, combining two parts garden or potting soil, two parts peat, two parts sand, and one part compost or composted cow manure. Find a place in the garden that gets at least six hours of sun a day. Dig a hole for each plant that's twice the size of the root ball. Sprinkle a tablespoon of sand into each hole, then set a plant in each and fill in with the surrounding soil. Tamp down the soil and soak with warm water. Then, unless there is a drought, let nature do the watering. Thyme plants like to be sprayed with a fish-emulsion fertilizer once a week during warm weather. But wait for a rain to wash away the fish emulsion before you cook with the thyme again.

Thyme is tastiest in the spring, summer, and fall. To help keep thyme plants from dying back during the winter, prune them hard, to about six inches, in midsummer. After pruning, run your hands through the branches to untangle and stimulate them.

To encourage growth, follow the same procedures for thyme planted in pots inside. (Because of the smell, you will want to move the thyme outside temporarily when fertilizing with fish emulsion.) As for light indoors, thyme needs six hours of sun a day, which can be augmented with a ninety-watt halogen flood placed about four feet from the plants. Clay pots, because they are porous and keep the soil drier than plastic ones, are best for thyme.

Thyme is a natural whitefly repellent, so keep it in the house if you grow bay. Outside, dig it in around bay and lemon verbena and it will help keep them whitefly-free. Thyme will attract bees to your garden, so plant it around fruit trees and roses, which need pollination. Beekeepers also put thyme to work, planting it around hives to attract bees to the area. It's a practice that's been around for centuries, since thyme-flavored honey was considered to be the "nectar of the gods."

Cooking

Thyme tastes green and slightly peppery, with a touch of clove. Though it lends foods a little pizzazz on its own—try sprinkling it on fish before grilling—most cooks prize it for its effectiveness at marrying other flavors. If you think of herbs in the language of music, thyme is neither a shrill soprano nor a booming baritone: It's a harmonious tenor, adding balance to a wide range of notes.

If the stew needs some snap, thyme can help by encouraging the ingredients to cooperate. Similarly, when the vinaigrette needs "just a little something," many cooks reach for thyme. If you are trying to cut back on salt, add some thyme instead—it has the ability to give a flat taste sparkle. Swirl it into soups during the last five minutes of cooking, and add it to such vegetarian entrées as polenta and risotto. To use thyme in cooking, add one tablespoon of fresh leaves (or one and a half teaspoons dried) to a recipe to serve four. Use only the leaves, as the stems can be tough. To remove thyme leaves from the stems easily, hold a stem at the very top in one hand. Run the thumb and first finger of your other hand down the stem, zipping the leaves off as you go.

Whole Roasted Shallots with Fresh Thyme

Unlike some herbs, thyme retains its fragrance when exposed to high heat.

~~~~

1½ pounds shallots, unpeeled
Handful of fresh thyme sprigs
    (about ¼ cup), plus
    extra leaves for sprinkling

1 tablespoon olive oil
2 tablespoons balsamic vinegar
Freshly ground black pepper

PREHEAT the oven to 400°F.

IN an 8-inch-square baking pan, combine the shallots, thyme, olive oil, and vinegar. Roast in the center of the oven until the shallots are just tender, about 45 to 55 minutes, stirring occasionally. Let the shallots sit just until they're cool enough to handle, then peel them. (Save the peels to make stock; see Note.)

TOSS the shallots with black pepper to taste and the extra thyme, and serve warm as an accompaniment to grilled or poached fish.

MAKES 6 SERVINGS; 86 CALORIES PER SERVING, 2 GRAMS FAT, 21 PERCENT OF CALORIES FROM FAT.

NOTE: You can use the shallot peelings to make a rich stock to use as a base for soups and sauces. Put the skins in a medium saucepan along with 4 cups of water and a handful of fresh thyme. Bring to a boil, then reduce the heat, cover loosely, and let the stock simmer gently for about 25 minutes. Strain and use to make such soups as French onion or vegetable, or use instead of water for cooking whole grains.

Mushroom-Zinfandel Sauce with Fresh Thyme

Thyme's clove scent refines the earthiness of mushrooms.

~~~~~

5   dried shiitake mushrooms
    (about 1½ inches in
    diameter)
4   sun-dried tomato halves
    (no salt added)

1   cup vegetable stock
1   teaspoon soy sauce
¼   cup red Zinfandel
1   teaspoon minced fresh
    thyme or ½ teaspoon dried

IN a small saucepan, combine the mushrooms and tomatoes. Pour in the stock and let soak for 1 hour. Then fish the mushrooms out of the stock, discard the stems, and thinly slice. Remove the tomatoes from the stock and thinly slice, and return both to the stock.

STIR the soy sauce and wine into the stock. If you're using dried thyme, add it now. Bring the mixture to a boil, and boil until the sauce is rich, dark, aromatic, and reduced in volume by about one third. Remove from the heat. If you're using fresh thyme, stir it in, and serve the sauce warm, drizzled over grilled fish or tofu.

MAKES 4 SERVINGS; 21 CALORIES PER SERVING, TRACE OF FAT.

Easy Olives

Thyme, olives, and vinegar are a classic and delicious combination.

~~~~~

1   cup Sicilian olives (big
    fleshy green ones with pits)
2   teaspoons olive oil

2   teaspoons balsamic vinegar
5   sprigs fresh thyme

continued

PLACE the olives in a large glass jar and cover with the oil and vinegar. Rub the thyme between your hands to release its aroma, then add it. Cover the jar and refrigerate overnight or for as long as two weeks. Serve the olives at room temperature on an antipasto tray, with focaccia, or with an assortment of cheeses and breads.

MAKES ABOUT 20 OLIVES, OR 10 SERVINGS; 15 CALORIES PER SERVING, 2 GRAMS FAT, ALMOST 100 PERCENT OF CALORIES FROM FAT.

Thyme-Grilled Swordfish

Thyme and garlic-scented olive oil is great on eggplant, bell peppers, or tofu, as well as fish. It lets you perfume grilled or broiled foods without worrying about delicate herbs burning and spoiling the taste.

~~~~~~

Small handful of fresh thyme sprigs
2 cloves garlic, peeled

2 tablespoons olive oil
1 pound swordfish (with no dark parts), about 1/2 inch thick

PUT the thyme into a small sauté pan and gently pound it with a pestle to release its fragrant oils. Add the garlic and olive oil, and heat over medium-low heat until warm and fragrant, about 2 to 3 minutes. Remove the pan from the heat, discard the garlic, and let the oil cool, covered, before using (see Note).

PREPARE the grill or preheat the broiler. Brush both sides of the swordfish with about 2 teaspoons of the thyme oil. (Brushing the fish, instead of the grill, will help keep the fish from sticking.) Grill or broil the fish about 5 inches from the heat source until cooked through, about 4 minutes on the first side and 2 minutes on the second side.

MAKES 4 SERVINGS; 130 CALORIES PER SERVING, 4 GRAMS FAT, 30 PERCENT OF CALORIES FROM FAT.

NOTE: To store thyme oil, discard the wilted thyme and replace it with about 3 fresh sprigs. Pour the oil into a covered glass jar, and refrigerate. Use 2 to 3 teaspoons per pound to season foods before grilling, broiling, or baking.

Sautéed Sea Scallops with Thyme and Sherry Glaze

Mustard and sherry usually require a bit of cream to blend their flavors, but thyme can bring them into harmony without adding fat.

~~~~~~

2 tablespoons minced fresh thyme, plus a few sprigs for garnish

2 cloves garlic, mashed through a press

Juice of 1 lemon (about ¼ cup)

1 pound sea scallops

1 tablespoon olive oil

1 tablespoon dry sherry

½ teaspoon Dijon mustard

IN a medium bowl, whisk together the minced thyme, garlic, and lemon juice. Add the scallops, turning them gently until well coated. Let marinate for about 20 minutes.

HEAT a large sauté pan over medium-high heat, then pour in the oil. Lift the scallops out of the marinade with a slotted spoon and add them to the pan; reserve the marinade. Sauté the scallops until just cooked through, about 3 to 4 minutes for average-sized scallops. Remove them from the pan and keep warm.

POUR the reserved marinade into the pan, along with the sherry and mustard. Using a spatula to stir constantly, let the sauce bubble until reduced to a glaze, about 1½ minutes. Drizzle the glaze over the scallops, garnish with thyme sprigs, and serve warm.

MAKES 4 SERVINGS; 155 CALORIES PER SERVING, 5 GRAMS FAT, 29 PERCENT OF CALORIES FROM FAT.

Brown Rice with Corn and Greens

Thyme, bay, and garlic can bring a satisfying savor to salt-free whole-grain dishes.

~~~~~~~

1	cup short-grain brown rice	1	bunch mustard greens, kale, or broccoli rabe (about 7 ounces), stems removed
1/4	cup dried cracked corn		
2 1/2	cups hot vegetable stock or defatted chicken stock	1/4	cup freshly grated Parmesan cheese or soy Parmesan
1	bay leaf		
2	teaspoons olive oil		
2	cloves garlic, minced	1	tablespoon minced fresh thyme or 1 teaspoon dried

COMBINE the rice, corn, stock, and bay leaf in a medium saucepan and bring to a boil. Reduce the heat and simmer, stirring frequently, until the rice is tender and all the liquid has been absorbed, 30 to 45 minutes.

MEANWHILE, heat the olive oil in a large sauté pan over medium-high heat. Add the garlic and greens and sauté until the greens are just wilted, about 2 minutes. Remove from the heat.

WHEN the rice is done, swirl in the greens, along with the cheese and thyme. Let sit for about 5 minutes, then serve warm or at room temperature as a first course, side dish, or entrée.

MAKES 4 ENTRÉE SERVINGS; 245 CALORIES PER SERVING, 5.5 GRAMS FAT, 21 PERCENT OF CALORIES FROM FAT.

Apple-Cranberry Pancakes with Lemon Thyme

Vanilla and lemon thyme work together to give low-fat pancakes a flavor boost.

~~~~

3/4 cup whole wheat pastry flour

3/4 cup unbleached all-purpose flour

1 1/2 teaspoons baking powder

Pinch of sea salt

2 tablespoons dried cranberries or raisins

2 tablespoons toasted oats (see Note)

1 tablespoon minced fresh lemon thyme or regular thyme or 1 1/2 teaspoons dried

2 tablespoons all-fruit apple butter

1/2 teaspoon pure vanilla extract

2 large egg whites or 1/4 cup Calendula Egg Substitute (page 47)

1 cup buttermilk or soy milk

1 medium apple, grated (about 1/2 cup)

IN a medium bowl, combine the flours, baking powder, salt, cranberries, oats, and thyme.

IN another medium bowl, combine the apple butter, vanilla, egg whites, buttermilk, and apple. Beat well with an electric hand mixer. Fold into the dry ingredients, using a large rubber spatula to combine well. Don't overmix; about 15 strokes should do it.

HEAT a well-seasoned cast-iron skillet over medium-high heat. (If you don't have one, use a nonstick sauté pan but don't preheat.) Ladle 3-tablespoon-sized scoops of batter into the heated skillet. Let the pancakes sizzle until medium-brown and cooked through, about 3 minutes on each side. Serve warm.

MAKES 12 PANCAKES, OR 4 SERVINGS; 255 CALORIES PER SERVING, TRACE OF FAT.

NOTE: To toast oats, toss them into a hot dry skillet over medium-high heat and swirl around until golden, about 2 minutes.

Raspberry Squares with Lemon Thyme

Lemon thyme adds snap to the almonds in a health-conscious version of a classic dessert.

~~~~~

1 cup unblanched almonds	2 tablespoons minced lemon thyme
1 cup rolled oats	
1/2 cup unbleached all-purpose flour	1/2 cup pure barley malt
	1 teaspoon ground cinnamon
1/2 cup whole wheat pastry flour	Pinch of sea salt
1/3 cup canola oil	1 1/4 cups (10 ounces) all-fruit raspberry jam
2 tablespoons fresh lemon juice	

PREHEAT the oven to 350°F.

TO roast the almonds, heat them in a large dry sauté pan over high heat for about 5 minutes, stirring constantly and watching carefully so they don't burn. Let cool, then put the roasted almonds into a processor or blender and whiz until finely ground. Transfer to a medium bowl.

TOAST the oats the same way; they will take about 4 minutes. Add them to the almonds along with the flours.

COMBINE the oil, juice, thyme, barley malt, cinnamon, and salt in a medium bowl, beating well with an electric hand mixer. Fold into the flour mixture, using a large rubber spatula, until a loose dough forms.

SCOOP half the dough into an 8- by 11 1/2-inch glass baking dish, pressing it evenly over the bottom and about 3/4 inch up the sides with your hands. If it seems very sticky, press through a sheet of waxed paper. Spread the jam evenly over the dough.

SHAPE the remaining dough into golf ball–sized pieces and flatten them between your hands. Place them on the jam; they won't cover the jam completely. Bake in the center of the oven for about 20 minutes, or until the dough has cooked through and comes slightly away from the sides of the baking dish. Let cool completely, then slice into 24 squares.

MAKES 24 SERVINGS; 130 CALORIES PER SERVING, 6 GRAMS FAT, 43 PERCENT OF CALORIES FROM FAT.

yarrow

~~~~~~~~~~~~~~~~~~~~~~~~~~~~~

famous fever fighter

~

HELP

HEAL

CUTS AND

SCRATCHES

~

SMOOTH

STRESSED

SKIN

~

STIMULATE

THE

COMPOST

HEAP

~

One August afternoon, when I was visiting a friend and her daughter, Allie, a young neighbor on roller blades dropped by. Suddenly, she slipped and slid into my friend, whose chair collapsed onto Allie, badly bumping her right leg. As Allie turned pale and whimpered, I ran for the yarrow.

I picked about two loose cups of fresh yarrow leaves and a handful of comfrey leaves, then threw them into the food processor to make a paste. I packed the paste onto Allie's leg, covered it with a napkin, and held it there while we talked and she calmed down. Twenty minutes later, I repeated the process with fresh herbs, then rinsed the area and left it unbandaged.

The next day, Allie came to my house on her own roller blades. Her leg was bruise-free, thanks to the yarrow poultice.

Lore and Legend

Before the invention of antiseptics and bandages, people often used poultices of fresh herbs to stop bleeding and infection. Yarrow was so prized for this purpose that the French called it the *herbe aux charpentiers,* because carpenters used it on their banged-up thumbs and fingers. In China, where yarrow is called *shicao,* the herb was brewed into a tea and prescribed as a topical antibiotic.

Also in China, the dried stems of yarrow were used to tell the future. The traditional *I Ching (Book of Changes)* suggested tossing fifty yarrow sticks into the air. The pattern in which they landed was matched to a corresponding pattern in the book, which had an accompanying fortune. This was called the Yarrow Stick Oracle; in the modern version, three coins are tossed instead of the yarrow.

Healing

Western scientific studies vary widely in their conclusions about yarrow's effectiveness in treating wounds. The problem may come from the herb itself, which seems to have a wildly different chemical composition depending on its variety, where it is grown, the season, the soil, and the weather. To solve the problem, commercial herbalists have begun working to "standardize" yarrow—to offer a variety guaranteed to have been tested for, and to contain, certain healing properties. In years to come, standardization may banish variations in the chemical composition of yarrow, as well as other herbs.

There is one healing property of yarrow on which researchers do agree—its fever-breaking activity. Taken as a hot tea, yarrow can help reduce a fever by inducing sweat. Yarrow tea may also help to lower blood pressure levels, since it dilates the blood vessels near the skin's surface.

Using yarrow tea to fight fevers may have the seal of approval from modern research, but it's not a new remedy. Yarrow was long used to bring down body temperature by the Fox, Ojibwa, Paiute, Cheyenne, Yuki, and Aleut Indian tribes. It's also been a popular fever buster for years in India, where it's called *gandana.*

To make yarrow tea, steep a tablespoon of fresh leaves and flowers (or a teaspoon of dried) in a cup of boiling water, covered, for four minutes. For a fever caused by cold or flu, herbalists recommend adding a tablespoon each of fresh elder flower and peppermint to the brew (or a teaspoon and a half each of dried). Drink a cup three times a day. The tea tastes a bit medic-

inal, so you may want to add some honey. Don't overdo it; some health professionals find that excessive use of yarrow tea may prevent your body from
absorbing iron.

Looking Your Best

Yarrow tea can also be used externally as a great astringent cleanser or splash,
and it's especially helpful for those who live in polluted cities. Thanks to the
tannins it contains, the herb temporarily tightens pores and firms the skin.
Men who have just shaved off mustaches and beards find yarrow tea useful
for restoring their long-hidden skin. For convenience, make a batch of yarrow
tea and keep it, covered and refrigerated, for up to five days.

Growing

Yarrow likes the standard herb mix of two parts garden or potting soil, two
parts peat, one part sand, and one part compost or composted cow manure.
Grown in partial shade, its leaves are long, feathery, and a light, delicate green.
For more robust yarrow with shorter, stouter leaves of a livelier green, plant
it in full sun.

Buy small organically grown yarrow plants. Varieties with yellow flowers are often said to be the most medicinally beneficial, but the leaves that
prevented Allie's leg from bruising came from a pink-flowering plant. Red-
and white-flowering yarrow are also available.

Dig a hole for each plant that's twice the size of the root ball. Set a
plant in each hole and fill in with the surrounding soil. Tamp it down and
soak with warm water. Then, unless there is a drought, let nature do the
watering.

Be sure to add a handful of yarrow leaves and flowers to the compost
bin each week, since they contain compounds that help turn compost into
perfect herb garden soil.

Calming Herbs

Chamomile

Lavender

Lemon balm

Lemon verbena

Catnip

Energizing Herbs

Ginger

Hot pepper

Peppermint

Rosemary

Good-Morning Herbs

Basil

Lavender

Lemon grass

Scented geranium

Vitamin- and Mineral-Packed Herbs

Dill

Parsley

Tarragon

Thyme

Herbs to Tame a Headache

Feverfew

Rosemary

Decongesting Herbs

Anise hyssop

Bee balm

Garlic

Ginger

Hot pepper

Hyssop

Mustard

Nasturtium

Herbs for Good Digestion

Coriander

Fennel

Ginger

Lemon verbena

Oregano

Peppermint

Herbs for Aching Muscles

Ginger

Hot pepper

Peppermint

Herbs for Cuts and Scratches

Calendula

Echinacea

Lavender

Yarrow

Herbal Insect Repellents

Feverfew

Garlic

Sage

Santolina

Southernwood

Tansy

Herbs for Smooth Skin

Calendula

Chamomile

Evening primrose

Lavender

Saint-John's-wort

Herbs for a Brighter Smile

Peppermint

Sage

Thyme

Herbs with a Past

Bay leaf

Garlic

Ginger

Savory

Easy-Cooking Herbs

Bay leaf

Chervil

Chives

Oregano

Parsley

Savory

Sorrel

Thyme

Easy-Growing Herbs

Borage

Burnet

Chives

Germander

Dill

Evening primrose

Lovage

Speedwell

An Every-day Herbal

using herbs to rejuvenate, heal, and beautify

~~~~~

cooking with herbs

smart seasonings

Seasoning is the soul of great cooking. The cook who seasons with herbs respects the flavors of foods and insightfully and creatively enhances them. Fennel seed and garlic will uplift fresh salmon, for example, when a heavy cream sauce would only be an oppressive mask. Learning to use herbs skillfully not only will make your cooking healthier, but will enlighten the sensual pleasure of preparing food.

To cook with herbs, you must be involved with the food. If you're making black bean soup and think rosemary might work in it, taste the soup. Then smell the rosemary. Will they go together? You decide. If you're uncertain about your instincts, begin by briefly studying the classic herb combinations (page 301). Knowing that dill is a classic with fish, basil is a winner with tomatoes, and coriander leaf is commonly used in spicy Thai food can be a guide. These combinations withstand the test of time because the herbs enhance the foods, rather then mask or overpower them.

Using Fresh Herbs

Fresh herbs are alive, so using them automatically brings a fresh energy to the foods with which you pair them. For bold results in a salad, soup, stew, or sauté, use a teaspoon of minced fresh herb for each person you're serving. For example, if you're whipping up a shrimp and scallop salad, dressed with fresh lime juice and olive oil, you'd add a tablespoon plus a teaspoon of minced fresh oregano to enough salad to feed four people. If you're shy about herbing, start with half that amount, toss it in, and let the flavors develop for about twenty minutes. Then taste the salad. Adjust the oregano to suit your taste. The only way to learn is by doing.

Since fresh herbs are generally minced before being added to foods, it's good to know some tips on easy mincing. To remove fresh herb leaves from their tough stems, hold a sprig at the top with one hand. With your other hand, pinch the stem gently but firmly and run your thumb and finger down it, zipping off the leaves as you go. This is a great technique for fresh thyme, oregano, marjoram, rosemary, and small-leafed basil. As for the mincing, use a very sharp knife. For mincing large amounts of herbs, you can use an electric spice grinder or food processor.

Exactly when to add fresh herbs depends on what you're cooking. In long-simmering soups and stews, for example, add fresh herbs about fifteen minutes before the dish is done. That way the delicate fresh herb flavors won't simmer away. For uncooked foods, such as salsas and salad dressings, let the herbs marinate with the other ingredients for about twenty minutes, to give the flavors time to bloom.

To keep fresh herbs fresh, set a bouquet right into a glass filled with water, cover with a plastic bag, and refrigerate. Keep the leaves dry to avoid yellowing and soft spots, and the herbs will keep for up to two weeks.

Using Dried Herbs

When fresh herbs are unavailable, dried can sometimes stand in. Their flavors are more stable than fresh herbs, so they can be added to soups and stews at the beginning of cooking. Since dried herbs are more concentrated, less is needed than with fresh. A good rule of thumb is to use about one and a half teaspoons of dried herb in a dish to serve four people, about half of the amount of fresh herb you would use. Before adding dried herbs to a dish, rub them between your hands until they are fragrant. The warmth of your hands will help release the flavor. Another flavor-enhancing trick is to steep dried herbs in a warm liquid before adding to a dish. For example, sprinkle dried tarragon into a little cup of warm stock before adding to a simmering soup.

These tricks won't help herbs that have been stored too long. Be sure to do a flavor check before using dried herbs. Rub a pinch of herb between your fingers, and if it doesn't yield an aroma, discard it. To help herbs retain their flavors, store them in tightly covered glass bottles, preferably opaque brown or blue, in a cool dry place away from the heat of the stove. Whole-leaf dried herbs will remain aromatic for six to eight months. Never buy or store ground herbs, because the aromas dissipate too soon. Grind what you need as you use it.

The best dried herbs are those you dry yourself, in, of all places, the microwave. The flavors remain livelier than if you simply hang them to dry and there is less risk of molding and rotting. To dry herbs, arrange about a cup of fresh leaves on a paper towel. Set the towel right on the microwave floor and zap the herbs, uncovered, until dry to the touch, about one and a half to two minutes, stopping at thirty-second intervals to stir. Let the dried herbs cool, then place in a jar and store them in a cool dry place, where they'll last for about eight months. If the dried herbs pick up a bit of moisture, set the jar (if microwave-safe), minus the cover, right in the microwave and zap for about twenty seconds. Let the herbs cool before re-covering. Herbs that dry

Making Herbed Condiments

To make an herb-based vinegar, oil, or honey, choose the herbs you particularly like, or try one of these combinations.

Making an Herbed Vinegar

Pack about 3 tablespoons of fresh herbs into a one-and-a-half-cup glass jar, then pound them lightly with a spoon to bruise them and release their aromas. Heat about a cup of vinegar (but don't boil), and pour it over the herbs. Let the vinegar cool, then cover and stash it in a cool place for a couple of weeks before using in vinaigrettes, to deglaze pans, to snap up soups and well in the microwave include basil, mint, lemongrass (which should be minced), oregano, rosemary, tarragon, and thyme.

If you don't want to fuss with the microwave, there's an easy alternative. Just stash a bouquet of fresh herbs in the back of the refrigerator, spread out on a piece of waxed paper, and it will dry in a couple of weeks. Don't put the herbs in the produce drawer, which would keep them too moist. Basil, mint, tarragon, rosemary, and dill can be dried using this method. After drying, they should be stored whole-leafed in tightly covered glass jars in a cool, dry place.

Freezing Herbs

Another quick way to preserve fresh herbs is to freeze them. First remove the leaves from their tough stems. Use a pastry brush to whisk away any dirt that might be on the leaves, and be sure the leaves are completely dry. Then pack the leaves into a freezer bag or container and freeze. You can use frozen herbs as you would fresh, about a tablespoon plus a teaspoon in a recipe to serve four. You don't even have to defrost them. Simply reach into the bag or container, snap off as much as you need, and mince. Their flavor will be good, but their color can darken, so frozen herbs are best added to such hot foods as soups, stews, sauces, and sautés, at the last moment of cooking. Herbs that freeze well are basil, lovage, sage, thyme, and dill. They'll keep for about a year in the freezer.

sauces without having to use salt, and in marinades. Herbed vinegars will keep for about a year.

Flavor Combinations for Herbed Vinegars

Basil, bay leaf, and garlic with cider vinegar: Use in a marinade for fresh tuna before grilling.

Coriander leaf, dried hot chili pepper, and garlic with white wine vinegar: Combine with soy sauce and use as a dipping sauce for egg rolls.

continued

Sage and chive blossoms with red wine vinegar: Toss with just-steamed sweet potato chunks.

Mint and lemon peel with cider vinegar: Use in a marinade or sauce for mild white fish, like flounder, or drizzle on ripe tomatoes.

Making an Herbed Oil

Since fat carries flavor throughout a dish, an herbed oil is a more intense flavoring than a vinegar. This intensity means that you can use less in recipes and still maintain a high flavor level. A salad to serve four, for example, can get by with a tablespoon of herbed oil, or even less. To make your own herbed oil, pack about three tablespoons of fresh herbs into a one-cup glass jar. Pound the herbs lightly with a spoon to bruise them and release their aromas. Heat about half a cup of olive oil until it's warm, then pour it on the herbs. Let the oil cool, then cover and refrigerate for a couple of weeks before using. It will last for about nine months, covered and refrigerated. Use the oil to paint on fish or vegetables before grilling, in vinaigrettes, in marinades for vegetables, and in dressings for whole-grain salads.

Flavor Combinations for Herbed Oils

Ginger, garlic, and lemon grass with olive oil: Paint on fish before grilling or use in a sauce for Asian noodles like soba. (Store the oil in the refrigerator.)

Thyme, tarragon, parsley, and chives with olive oil: Add garlic and use in a marinade for mussels.

Cinnamon stick, ginger, black peppercorns, and bay with olive oil: Toss with just-steamed winter squash or turnips.

Dried hot chili peppers, thyme, and garlic: Toss with cooked couscous, rice, or barley.

Making an Herbed Honey

For drizzling on warm muffins or swirling into a cup of steaming herbal tea, nothing beats pure honey that's been infused with herbs. To try it, heat one cup of honey in a small saucepan until warm and liquid. Meanwhile, in a one-and-a-half-cup jar, combine about a quarter cup of different fresh herbs. Pound them lightly with a spoon to release the aroma. Pour the warm honey over the herbs and let it cool. Strain before serving. The honey will keep, refrigerated, for about six months.

Flavor Combinations for Herbed Honeys

Orange peel, saffron, and cardamom with a dark honey: Use in a marinade for curried chicken.

Lavender and rosemary with a wildflower honey: Swirl into chamomile tea for a relaxing beverage.

Hyssop and thyme with a light honey: Swirl into tea to temporarily banish sinus or other nasal congestion.

Classic Herb Combos

Use this list as a primer when you begin to cook with herbs, then advance to your own combinations. For four servings, start with about a tablespoon plus a teaspoon of fresh or frozen herbs or one and a half teaspoons of dried. In blends that combine both fresh and dried herbs, combine to suit your taste.

To make a fresh chili "powder," combine minced fresh hot chilies, minced fresh garlic, minced oregano, and cumin seed. Use to flavor soups, stews, and beans and rice.

Combine and grind at least four of these spices to make an East Indian curry powder: fennel seed, coriander seed, cumin seed, ginger, black pepper, mustard seed, fenugreek seed, garlic, minced fresh hot peppers, cayenne, and turmeric. (Turmeric gives classic curry powder its yellow color.) Use in marinades or sauces for tofu, chicken, or such vegetables as cauliflower and eggplant.

Quatre épices, or "four spices," is used in classic French cooking to flavor roast meats. It includes ground black pepper, nutmeg, ginger, and cinnamon. Remove the pepper and the blend becomes all-American pumpkin pie spice.

continued

Chinese five-spice powder can be used to season the cooking oil when sautéing eggplant, green beans, chicken, or pork. To make it, combine and grind cinnamon, fennel seed, whole cloves, star anise, and Szechuan peppercorns. Fresh minced garlic is always added before sautéing to balance the flavor.

To make a pickling spice, combine dill seed, mustard seed, bay leaves, and minced fresh garlic. Use it to pickle tiny cucumbers, beets, or carrots.

The Word on Wine and Herbs

Dorothy and Alton Long of the American Wine Society evaluate wines based on how they taste with different foods. Here are some classic examples:

- At one sampling it was discovered that fresh basil and red cabernet are a pleasant and aromatic combination. In fact, the basil cuts some of the sharp astringency and tannin taste of the wine.

- Tarragon also is an excellent match with cabernet, especially Australian cabernets.

- Cabernet and similar red wines are also a good match with garlic and other earthy flavors. But they bring out the peppery taste in

A bundle of aromatic herbs, called a "bouquet garni," is used in French cooking to flavor stocks, soups, and stews. Combine parsley, thyme and bay in a tea ball, and add to a simmering soup; remove before serving.

"Fines herbes" is a French favorite, combining chervil, parsley, tarragon, and thyme. Add the combo to sauces or soups at the last minute of cooking.

thyme and oregano, and in fact, the more peppery the herb, the less the cabernet holds up.

- French white Beaujolais goes well with dill—especially if the dill is flavoring a tasty salmon fillet. Dill and salmon also pair well with a white seyval blanc, which gives the dish a delicate lemony taste.

- A sweeter white wine, like German Riesling, is a good match for spicy Mexican and Thai foods that feature hot peppers. The combination isn't so surprising if you consider that spicy Ethiopian food is traditionally served with a sweet honey wine. Alone, the honey wine is too sweet, but it's simply great when paired with the hot peppers in the food.

growing herbs

digging in

*E*ven if your gardening experience amounts to growing bean sprouts in a jar, you can raise beautiful and delicious herbs without a single chemical. Anyone can, since herbs are among the easiest plants to grow. But while the techniques offered here will be a huge help, the best learning comes from doing, by getting your hands dirty. Only then will you understand the soil and discover the personality of each herb. Soon you'll instinctively know what each herb needs—when the rosemary needs water, when to cut back the thyme, and how the chervil tells you when it's getting too much sun and needs to be moved.

Specific instructions for cultivation are given in the chapters on individual herbs, but here are some general guidelines.

Zoned Out

If you're growing herbs outside, either in pots or the ground, the first thing to know is when to plant. Planting too early may cause herbs to freeze in some climates, and planting too late may result in poor growth from too much heat. Gardening experts have devised elaborate zoning maps, on which you can locate your area, find what zone you're in, and plant according to it. But a much easier approach is to follow the Mother's Day rule: Plant herbs as close to Mother's Day as possible. It's as simple as that.

Most herbs need light, at least six hours of full sun a day, but a few actually prefer the shade. If you have a shady area, these herbs are for you: angelica, chervil, ginseng, sweet cicely, sweet woodruff, and violet.

For Herbs, It's a Dirty World

If you cook, you know that the better your stock, the better your soups and sauces will be. The same goes for growing herbs, since good chemical-free soil helps grow the best specimens. If you're already growing flowers or vegetables, you can interplant herbs among them, because the soil conditions required are about the same.

If you're just starting out with an herb garden, find a space that gets at least six hours of sun a day. Then go out and dig in the soil. Imagine tiny rootlets pushing their way through the soil, and prepare a mixture that will ease their journey. If the soil contains a lot of clay, it will feel hard, so work in some peat to soften it. If the soil feels muddy, work in some sand for better drainage. The process is like mixing bread dough; the addition of various ingredients in different proportions is needed to produce the best texture, and you can feel if it's right by working it with your hands. Your goal is soil that is rich in color and sifts easily through your fingers.

To enrich the soil, swirl in some composted cow manure (available in garden centers, it's virtually odorless). Some hold that manure can make the soil too rich, causing herbs to lose their essential oils and thus lack aroma. But recent tests show that it's high-nitrogen chemical fertilizers, not composted manure, that can diminish an herb's essential oils. If you wish, in place of cow manure, you can use one of the "designer doos" currently on the market. These are fancy manures, coming from such diverse creatures as llamas and crickets.

Your next consideration should be the pH of the soil, that is, its acidity or alkalinity. Herbs absorb nutrients better at the proper pH level, and most experts say that herbs need a reading of 6.5 to 7.0, slightly acidic to neutral. To check out the pH of your soil, pick up a soil test kit or pH paper from a garden center. Or phone the local branch of the Department of Agriculture and ask if they have a soil test service and how it works. Soils in humid areas tend to be slightly on the acidic side, and soils in dry areas tend to be slightly alkaline. If your pH registers below 6.5, your soil is acidic and can be balanced with ground limestone. If the test indicates excessive alkalinity, the pH level can be corrected with sulfur powder. Note that, unlike most herbs, lavender, rosemary, and thyme like soil that's slightly more acidic than 6.5.

To create ideal soil conditions, plant herbs in raised beds. A raised bed setup holds water and nutrients longer than normal garden soil, because they stay within the frame. An extra plus is that you can plant herbs closer together, because the ideal growing conditions eliminate competition between plants. Also called French beds, these use bottomless wooden frames that sit atop the existing soil. Many herb gardeners have good luck with two-by-eights nailed together. Your frames can be any shape that fits your landscape, square, triangular, or rectangular, but make them no wider than an arm's length so you can work easily with your plants. Don't overbuild—remember that the bigger they are, the more soil it will take to fill them, and that most herbs don't take up too much room. Sink each frame slightly into the soil. Then add a soil mixture of two parts garden or potting soil, two parts peat, one part sand, and one part compost or composted cow manure.

You can also plant herbs in pots, using the same soil-peat-sand-manure mixture. Potted herbs will dry out a bit faster than those in beds, but they make interesting accents throughout the garden and around the yard. And if you don't have a yard, potted herbs can be grown on a balcony, terrace, steps, roof garden, or even inside on a sunny windowsill. Choose pots shaped to match the herb you want to grow. For instance, a creeping rosemary is best in a wide shallow pot. A tall lemon verbena needs a deep pot.

Which Herbs to Grow?

Consider your needs. To choose herbs for use in cooking, take a look at your spice rack. If you're big on thyme, tarragon, and rosemary, those are herbs you should plant. If you've had the same bottle of marjoram for years, don't plant it, because you probably won't use it. If you love herb teas, plant lots of mint, plus lemon balm, anise hyssop, cinnamon basil, and lemon thyme.

Your culinary needs are just the beginning. Carry on to let your imagination run free, creating a garden that's as useful or fanciful as you like. You can plant medicinal herbs, such as echinacea and feverfew, or herbs to attract butterflies, such as anise hyssop, lavender, the mints, bee balm, rosemary, sage, thyme, and speedwell. You might also want to plan an herb garden around the color of flowers, using all purple-flowering ones, for instance. Or you can make a moon garden, with silvery herbs, such as clary sage and silver santolina, that glow in the moonlight. And how about one featuring herbs from plays, such as mugwort from *A Midsummer Night's Dream* and rosemary from *Hamlet?* Let your imagination be your guide.

Healthy Herbs for Growing

Buying small herb plants instead of seeds can eliminate some moments of anxiety. Tucking happy, healthy basil plants into the ground is easy. Waiting for little faces to peek through the ground and distinguishing them from weeds is harder. Be sure to insist on herbs that have been started and raised without chemicals. (They are not uncommon.)

As for size, the herb plants that come in nursery six-packs are about right. Some herbs, like basil, have long taproots and don't like to be transplanted after a certain point. Choose herb plants the way you choose greens for a salad. Bright color, lush leaves, and no brown spots are indications of health. If you're working with rootless cuttings, for the fastest rooting, slip the shoots into a solution of one part honey to three parts water. Be sure that just the stem—no leaves—is in the solution. When roots begin to pop out, plant the new herb in a sandy soil.

Pest Prevention and Remedies

Your herb garden is an ecosystem, and so by matching plants carefully you can help protect against pests and diseases. For example, if you're planting basil, pair it with protectors such as rosemary and sage, which will repel unfriendly insects. Two rosemary plants and two sage plants are enough to protect about a dozen basil plants.

It's also a good precaution to surround your herb patch with chives, which are handy for repelling aphids. Add marigolds to the group to fend off maggots and rabbits; be sure to buy the bright orange, smelly kind. If marigolds don't appeal to you, plant them in pots and move them in and out of trouble areas as needed. Santolina, southernwood, and tansy are also potent pest fighters (see pages 247, 265, and 270).

Other organic remedies for pests include eucalyptus tea, which is used in Australia and Mexico as a spray to get rid of aphids. Steep two teaspoons of dried eucalyptus leaf in one quart of hot water, covered, for one hour, then strain and spray. Similarly, in Europe, a spray of dried elder tree leaves is used. Gardeners who use it got the idea straight from the elder leaves themselves, which are immune to aphid infestation.

Whitefly is an herb pest that's so tiny it's hard to see. But if you flick a plant and if it looks as if dust is flying off, it's whitefly, which sucks the sap from plants. To prevent and to get rid of it, interplant feverfew among such vulnerable herbs as lemon verbena and bay, or make a spray (see tansy, page 270; feverfew spray is made the same way). Feverfew spray is also effective against spider mites, which weave tiny webs among your herbs, sucking out the sap as they go.

Another way to send aphids, mealybugs, whitefly, and spider mites packing is to burn cedarwood incense. You can do this indoors or out. Inside, light one wand of incense per room. Outside, burn one wand every fifteen feet or so in the garden. The wands can be stuck right in the soil.

Basil and echinacea are particularly susceptible to Japanese beetles, those rapacious little bugs that can strip an entire plant of leaves overnight. To keep them from destroying your crop, buy Japanese beetle traps and hang or stake them about twenty feet away from the herbs. Be sure to buy the kind of traps that have both a sex lure and a floral lure. The sex lure attracts the male Japanese beetles and they zip right over, straight into the trap. That leaves the females, who are attracted to the floral scent and sashay over—and you know the rest of the story. Some traps come equipped only with the sex lure, which leaves the female to decimate your herbs, so read labels before you buy. It also helps to coordinate with your neighbors and encourage them to adopt the same pest-control methods. If you hang beetle traps and they spray chemicals, more beetles will end up at your place.

Slugs like to munch on all herbs, but they're easy to trap. Beer was the favorite bait for years, but now researchers at the University of Colorado have reported an even more effective liquid. Sink an aluminum pie plate in the soil so it's even with the ground and slugs can slither in. Then fill the plate with a mixture of one cup of water, half a teaspoon of sugar, and a quarter teaspoon of baking yeast. The slugs are attracted, slide into the mixture, and, since they don't swim, then they don't make it out.

Putting the Birds to Work

Herb garden allies also include birds. After Labor Day, encourage them with a simple plastic tube feeder, hung about five feet off the ground, filled with the black oil variety (not striped or hulled) of sunflower seeds. Set an aluminum pie plate under the feeder and sprinkle some seeds in it so the birds will see the food while flying by and stop in for a bite. Hopefully, they will stay and nest. Cardinals, finches, chickadees, nuthatches, and others should find the feeder attractive. Around Memorial Day, stop filling the feeder and the birds will stick around, feasting on garden pests before the pests eat your herbs.

The Bunny Garden

Also on the prowl for your herbs are rabbits. The best solution is to plant a small bunny garden so they'll stay out of the rest of yours. Try to find out where they come from and position the bunny garden between their nest and your herbs, then plant petunias, which bunnies love. A two-foot square filled with petunias, with some extras standing guard around the herbs, should do the trick.

As an extra safeguard, many herb gardeners leave tufts of pet hair around the herb garden, the idea being that the bunnies smell the cats or dogs and stay away. You can get the pet hair from the brush after grooming your pet, or borrow some cat hair from a friend. In the spring you'll need a regular supply, since birds will pick up the pet hair to use in their nests.

Techniques for Planting

Recommendations for individual herbs appear in each herb section; here are the general guidelines. The first step is to dig a hole slightly deeper and wider than the pot the herb comes in. Gently remove the herb from its pot, taking the soil around the roots with it as you go. Set the herb in the prepared hole, and fill in with the surrounding soil, tamping it down with your hands. Leave an inch or two of the bare stem under the leaves and above the soil, to make room for mulch. Mulching protects herbs from temperature extremes and helps keep the soil evenly moist. It also almost eliminates the need to weed. Lay on about an inch or so of mulch, then water in a gentle drizzle to avoid traumatizing the young herbs. Many herb gardeners like cocoa shell mulch because it keeps its rich brown color, unlike many bark-type mulches that fade in the sun. Besides, it smells like chocolate when it's wet, which seems a fitting topping for an aromatic herb garden.

Another trick to help herbs avoid shock during transplanting is to spray with chamomile tea (see page 55). The best time to do this is in the early morning, so the herbs dry off nicely before the hot sun hits.

Finally, you can help herbs adapt to their new environment with as little stress as possible by watering with a compound called Rescue Remedy. Available at herb shops, health food stores, and some pharmacies, it's a blend of herbs and flowers that's meant to relax people, but it works on herbs too. Add four drops to a quart of water, then water the herbs.

Maintaining Herbs

If you've planted in good soil, you won't need to feed your herbs. But a weekly spray of fish emulsion will prevent them from looking sluggish. Buy fish emulsion at a nursery, or through a catalog, and mix with water according to the manufacturer's directions. As you will discover when every cat in the neighborhood becomes your best friend, fish emulsion smells like fish. But the smell goes away after a rain, leaving happy, healthy herbs. (Indoor herbs should be moved outside for spraying.) Or you can concoct your own herb tonic.

Herb Tonic for Healthy Herb Plants

½ teaspoon dried plantain herb

½ teaspoon dried horsetail herb

½ teaspoon dried nettle

½ teaspoon dried yarrow

1 clove garlic

1 kelp tablet (about 150 micrograms), crushed

6 cups boiling water

COMBINE all of the ingredients, pour on the water, and let steep, covered, for five minutes. Then strain and use to water herbs. Or make a sun tea, letting the herbs steep all day. The tonic provides nutrients that herbs need, and it helps keep pests away. (In case you're wondering, the garlic doesn't influence the flavor of the herb that's being watered.)

YOU can also use this tonic on newly planted herbs, to give them a good start in life. In one seedling trial, the tonic was tested on a group of red Indian mustard plants. Half were watered with plain water, and half were watered with the tonic. After two weeks, the mustard plants watered with the tonic were twice as tall as the ones watered with plain water, and their leaves were a livelier shade of green.

As for daily maintenance, you can spread out coffee grounds or used tea leaves at the base of herbs, both in the garden and inside in pots. Grounds and tea leaves give herbs an instant shot of nitrogen, which they need to help their leaves grow. While you're at it, be sure to remove and discard any torn, yellow, or dead leaves from the herb plants. Keeping herbs tidy makes them less vulnerable to enemy bugs.

Compost is another excellent nutrient source for herbs, and, after all, why should you waste valuable garbage? No matter where you live, you can have a compost bin. Some high-rise apartment buildings even put them outside on the roof. Most garden centers have plans for building a bin, and some actually sell ready-to-assemble kits. The secret to successful composting—that is, to avoid attracting rodents and other critters—is to use only vegetable and fruit scraps and clippings from the garden. Don't use meat, bones, or any dairy or animal products at all.

Chamomile and yarrow leaves will help the compost break down, but don't expect immediate results. Let the compost cook at its own rate, adding to it frequently and stirring occasionally. It can take up to two years, but as the compost in the bin breaks down, the volume shrinks. The material at the bottom of the bin will be the first that you can dig into the herb garden or use to top-dress potted herbs.

Harvesting Herbs

The best way to pick herbs is to keep in mind their dignity. Don't just hack off careless handfuls, roots and all, or you'll traumatize the plants. Use scissors, shears, or sharp fingernails to snip two- to three-inch sprigs from herbs such as thyme, oregano, marjoram, and rosemary.

While you're snipping, also consider future growth. For example, sweet basil grows in rosettes of leaves. Snip off the top rosette, leaving the pair of smaller rosettes underneath to grow, and then move on to other plants. In this way you can increase your basil yield almost five times. The worst sin in harvesting herbs is to strip away the leaves, leaving a naked stem. Doing so can reduce the herb's growth, if not kill it—and the poor thing will look ridiculous.

As for your own well-being when harvesting herbs, bend your knees and hips instead of bending straight-legged from the waist. Your neighbors may think you look pretty silly, but you will avoid the dreaded "basil back," which can linger on long after your herbs have frosted over.

Tucking Herbs in for the Winter

The official name for putting the herb garden to bed for the season is "wintering over." Cleaning up herbs and making them cozy for the cold months will encourage them to be healthy and tasty when they reappear in the spring.

First make sure that all the annuals, those herbs that need replanting in the spring, are removed, roots and all. These include basil, borage, scented geranium, parsley, lemon verbena, and coriander.

Next take a good look at each perennial (those herbs that reappear each spring) with an eye for trimming it back to a tidy winter length. For years, the conventional wisdom was to cut back spring-blooming herbs in the fall, and summer-blooming herbs in the spring. But trimming back all herbs in the fall has genuine advantages. It not only gives herbs a fresh start in the spring, but it also eliminates dead growth that can cause herbs to rot and attract harmful insects.

Be sure to remove any damaged or dead branches, but don't trim healthy growth any shorter than six inches. Always use sharp pruners for trimming herbs to their winter lengths, because clean cuts are less traumatic. If you don't have pruners, use sharp kitchen shears or the sharpest scissors you have in the house.

Always trim herbs to their natural shape. For example, trim sage into bushy mounds. The same goes for thyme, tarragon, oregano, marjoram, the mints, lemon balm, hyssop, germander, santolina, and southernwood. Hearty growers, like the mints, chives, and bee balm, can be thinned out by using a trowel or shovel to dig out clumps of the plant, roots and all. Replant the clumps elsewhere in your garden, or share them with a friend.

Silver-leafed herbs such as lavender, silver santolina, rosemary, and silver thyme can be more delicate than their greener cousins. One way to give them extra winter protection is to cover them gently with evergreen boughs. This is especially helpful if the silver herbs are exposed to north winds.

Advice from the Farm

Another secret to bedding down the herb garden for the winter comes from organic farmers. They add nitrogen to their soil by planting a legume-type cover crop, which automatically sends out extra nutrients. No herb garden, or even pot of herbs for that matter, is too small to benefit from this technique. Just get some alfalfa, rye, or buckwheat seed at a garden supply center, toss it on the soil around the herbs, and then cover with a bit more soil. The cover crop will die before spring, so you won't have to fuss over or harvest it.

If you're wondering what your neighbors might think of you growing alfalfa, just wait until they see you out watering your herb garden in the middle of winter. That's what you'll need to do if the ground becomes too dry. You'll also need to check each herb from time to time, trimming away dead branches and rearranging pine needle mulch and evergreen covers. When the first tiny leaves of the mints and balms peek out in spring, you'll be glad you tucked them in properly.

aromatherapy

~~~~~~~~~~~~~~~~~~~~~~~~~~~~~~~~~~~~~~

come to
your senses

*T*wo thousand years ago, among the Australian aborigines, when someone was depressed, the tribe knew just what to do. They dug a pit and lined it with hot coals, then added a thick layer of herbs and flowers and a sprinkling of water on top. The person lay over the steaming herbs and was covered with kangaroo skins to create a penetrating, healing sauna that relieved the depression. Not so different were the ancient Egyptians, who bathed in herbs and flowers for mind and body tune-ups. Rose petals, for instance, were a popular addition to the bath to soothe and soften the skin, as well as the disposition. It was simple aromatherapy—easing the mind and body with herbs and flower essences.

Inhaled or absorbed essences make their way into the brain, where they can help mend psychological and physiological ills. A new science called "fragrance psychology" has sprung up to help determine the effects of various scents.

Aromatherapists use essences that are distilled from herbs and flowers. Since no heat is applied directly to the herbs, their essence stays active. The essence is often called an "essential oil," even though it's not oily. An essential oil is intensely concentrated, often referred to as "the soul of the herb," so it's used reverently, drop by drop.

For most common ailments, an aromatherapist decides what essential oil, or combination, is appropriate and advises you on how it's to be administered—through inhalation or through absorption into the skin. For instance, if you have a cough, an aromatherapist might suggest steam inhalation with essential oils of eucalyptus and hyssop. That means you should add about three drops each of the essential oils to a basin of hot water, then drape a towel over your head and breathe in the aroma for about ten minutes. To relieve anxiety, an aromatherapist might suggest a full body massage with essential oil of lavender. About fifteen drops of essential oil to a quarter cup of massage oil, such as grapeseed or olive, is all that's needed. Aromatherapy advocates also recommend a peppermint essential oil massage to help prevent colds and flu. As a bonus, it helps keep the skin looking good despite pollution, stress, sun, and dry office air.

Another popular form of aromatherapy is the aromatic bath, wonderful for refreshing the body and mind. Draw a hot bath and swirl in about five drops of essential oils, then soak in the tub for about ten minutes. Essential oil of rosemary will invigorate you, while essential oil of marjoram is extremely relaxing. If you don't have essential oils on hand, use a quarter cup of dried herbs tucked into a cheesecloth bag. Tie the bag to the bathtub faucet so the aroma of the herbs is released while the water runs, then let the bag float in the water. Hop in and enjoy, using the cheesecloth herb bag to scrub and stimulate your skin.

Essential oils can also be administered through an aromatic diffuser, which emits cool puffs of fragrance into the air. One English airline disperses a relaxing lavender aroma during delays on overseas flights. Just before arrival the same airline disperses a citrus combination to refresh passengers and crew. Similar scents waft through the air-conditioning systems in more than one Japanese corporation, encouraging employees to sail through the day.

Home Aroma

After checking with an aromatherapist or health professional about what essences are right for you, you can set up an aroma first aid kit to keep at home. An aromatherapist may recommend essential oil of lemongrass for colitis and cranky digestion; essential oil of thyme for colds, coughs, and sore throats; and essential oil of eucalyptus for sinus problems and asthma. Use the oils in baths or in steam inhalation, or simply dot a couple of drops on a tissue and inhale.

Essential Buying

To buy the best-quality herbal essence, first make sure the label reads "essential oil." If it says "fragrance oil," the aroma may be synthetic and won't have the healing effect you're looking for. Another way to tell if an essential oil is pure or not is the price. If you run across a group of different essential oils that are all the same price, they're probably not pure, because essential oils vary in price according to their ease of distillation and availability. Oils like peppermint and basil, for instance, are much less expensive than rose and jasmine.

Look for essential oils that come in amber, cobalt, or other opaque bottles. That ensures the essences have not been exposed to and weakened by the sun. Store them in a cool place, such as the refrigerator. Most essential oils will last for about two years, though citrus oils last for only one year.

You'll find essential oils at herb shops or health food stores, or consult the resource section at the end of the book (pages 389–392).

Commonsense Caution

In phytotherapy, a cousin to aromatherapy, essential oils are taken internally, via a few drops of essential oil either mixed with small amounts of water or placed on a sugar cube for easy ingestion. Since some essential oils can be highly toxic if taken internally, never attempt this kind of treatment on your own. Always follow the advice of a health professional.

Essences and Acupuncture

Dr. Kadmbii Barnad of Western Australia has developed a new mode of therapy that combines herb and flower essences with acupuncture. Choosing an essence thought to be effective in treating a patient's complaint, she drops a small amount on the skin at the appropriate acupuncture point on the body, before inserting the acupuncture needle. For example, one of the essences Dr. Barnad uses to treat stress is the flower of purple flag, an herb that European herbalists prize for a tea of its root, which soothes stress-induced skin eruptions. Barnad reports that the combination of essences and acupuncture has been quite effective in treating the ailments of the three hundred families that come to her medical clinic, evidence that her method deserves further study.

Aromatherapy at a Glance

Though you should always consult with an aromatherapist or health professional before attempting any sort of treatment, this chart will give you some foundational knowledge of the aromatherapy recommendations for minor health complaints. A typical prescription might be to splash two drops of the essential oil of choice on a tissue and inhale.

IF YOU FEEL	AND WANT TO FEEL	ESSENTIAL OIL
Groggy	Alert	Rosemary
Stuffy in the head	Decongested	Eucalyptus, Thyme, Pine, Camphor, or Tea Tree
Motion sick	Balanced	Peppermint or Ginger
Irritable or frazzled	Calm and refreshed	Chamomile, Basil, Lavender, Jasmine, or Patchouli
Depressed	Happier	Lemon Balm, Clary Sage, or Rose Geranium
Anxious and can't sleep	Relaxed and sleepy	Marjoram, Lavender, or Chamomile
Hung over	Clear-headed	Peppermint, Lavender, or Fennel
Jet-lagged	Human	Lemongrass or Rosemary
Chilly	Warm	Juniper
Too warm	Cool	Peppermint

cancer

herbs for prevention

*T*he evidence that what you eat can help prevent cancer is overwhelming. Research is particularly encouraging about the tissue type of cancers, called carcinomas, which include cancers of the breast, colon, prostate, and other organs. Experts suggest cutting down on fats, eating more high-fiber foods, eating foods high in vitamins A and C, eating garlic, and eating cruciferous vegetables, which are those in the cabbage family. Here are the particulars, and how herbs help in prevention.

Slash the Fat

Two kinds of fats have been implicated in cancer development. One type is polyunsaturated fat, found in sunflower oil, safflower oil, and corn oil. Polyunsaturated fats can change their structure once inside the human body. The process involved is called oxidation and it creates free radical cells that have been linked to colon and other types of cancer.

The second type of fat to avoid is saturated fat, the kind found in butter, cheese, and meat. These fats can encourage hormone production, raising the odds of contracting cancer of such organs as the breast, uterus, and ovaries.

The bottom line is that passing up foods high in fat in favor of those low in fat can help prevent cancer. But when you cut the fat from food, you also cut the flavor. Herbs can come to the rescue by punching up the taste of low-fat foods and making them robust enough to quell your feelings of deprivation. A simple pasta with broccoli, for example, will benefit from fresh minced thyme and garlic. If your taste buds still need some fat, toss in a small amount of olive oil, a monounsaturated fat that will neither oxidize in the body nor encourage hormone production.

Eat Foods High in Vitamins A and C

These nutrients, called *antioxidants,* destroy the cancer-causing free radical cells in the body, such as the ones created by polyunsaturated oils. Most fresh herbs contain vitamin C and beta carotene, the plant form of vitamin A. Beta carotene is linked with helping to prevent cancers of the lung, esophagus, and bladder, and vitamin C shows promise in helping to prevent colon cancer. The larger-leafed herbs, like mustard, dandelion, and sorrel, contain more of these nutrients, simply because of their size. Adding them, and any other fresh herbs, to your recipes automatically adds a bodyguard factor to your diet. Remember that vitamin C is weakened by heat, so for maximum benefits, use fresh herb leaves in salads, sandwiches, dips, and as garnishes for cooked foods.

Another herbal source of vitamin C is an ancient Ayurvedic East Indian potion called *chavanprash.* The main ingredient is the Indian gooseberry, also called *amla,* each of which is said by some herbalists to contain 3,000 milligrams of vitamin C. The amlas are cooked down with sesame oil or clarified butter, then various powdered herbs are added to form a sweet, thick paste. Luckily, the amla contains beneficial tannins that prevent its vitamin C from being destroyed by heat or processing. You can buy chavanprash at herb shops, health food stores, or Indian markets, but be sure amla (also called *Emblica officinalis,* or *E. ribes*) is the first ingredient, not sugar. Dosage is generally one-half teaspoon to one teaspoon two to three times a day, right off the spoon and chased with hot liquid, or swirled into hot tea and sipped.

Adopt the Cabbage Family

Cabbage and its kin, the cruciferous vegetables, contain cancer-fighting compounds called indoles. Many people dislike the members of this family, but with herbal helpers the cruciferous vegetables can be made more·palatable—even delectable.

CRUCIFEROUS VEGETABLE	COOKING METHOD AND HERB
Turnip	Steam quartered roots, then toss with minced tarragon and parsley
Rutabaga	Steam sliced roots, then toss with prepared mustard and minced chives
Cauliflower	Steam florets, then toss with minced dill, toasted sesame seeds, and fresh lemon juice
Broccoli	Steam spears, then toss with olive oil and minced savory
Brussels sprouts	Quarter sprouts, then sauté with leeks, sliced apples, and minced ginger
Cabbage	Slice and add to simmering soup stock along with garlic, lovage, and parsley
Kale and mustard greens	Sauté with olive oil and garlic, then pile on a crusty whole wheat roll
Kohlrabi	Quarter and steam, then toss with sesame seeds, ginger, and garlic

Note that some cruciferous vegetables, like broccoli and kale, contain calcium, which can help prevent colon cancer.

Embrace the Herbal Cancer Fighters

The sulfur compounds that give garlic, onions, and chives their characteristic flavor also help to prevent cancer. To be most effective, these plants should be eaten raw, so try mincing and adding to vinaigrettes and dips or swirling into sauces after cooking.

On a sweeter note, the oil extracted from caraway seeds contains compounds called monoterpenes that help prevent cancer. Add caraway seeds to bread dough, curry blends, marinades for vegetables, and salad dressings.

In your kitchen you probably already have an herb that may help prevent cancer of the digestive tract, lung, liver, and skin. It's plain old green tea, a popular folk cure for centuries in Japan and Vietnam. (Green tea is from the same plant as black tea, but differs in processing.) Recently, medical research pinpointed a compound in green tea, epigallocatechin gallate (EGCG), that acts as an antioxidant to protect the body from potentially damaging free radical cells. The Japanese drink an average of two to three cups a day. The Vietnamese drink about two cups a day, always after a meal and often infused with the flowers of the herb jasmine. Any way you drink it, note that green tea contains caffeine, so if you're not used to it, expect a mild buzz. To make a cup of green tea, steep one teaspoon of the tea in one cup of boiling water, covered, for two to three minutes. A pinch of dried peppermint tea makes a flavorful addition.

Tune Up Your Immunity

Medical experts agree that a good hedge against disease is to keep your immune system running in top form. Certain herbs contain compounds called polysaccharides that can boost your immune system to help it fight cancer. Echinacea is one. Sea herbs such as nori, kelp, and arame (pronounced ARE-uh-may) also can help strengthen your immune system. If these sea herbs sound unfamiliar, you may know nori as the edible green sheet in which sushi is wrapped. You can also slice it into strips and use it as a garnish for soups and salads. Kelp can be ground into a powder and sprinkled on popcorn or rice salads. Arame is usually simmered with other vegetables until tender. It's especially tasty with shiitake mushrooms, which also offer cancer-fighting polysaccharides.

Chemotherapy, Radiation, and Herbs

If you are undergoing chemotherapy treatments right now, here are four herbs that may help relieve nausea and make you feel more balanced and positive. Note that the essential oils should not be taken internally without professional supervision.

- Basil: Make a tea by steeping one teaspoon of the dried herb in one cup of boiling water, covered, for four minutes. Sip it slowly and enjoy its uplifting aroma. For a stronger dose of basil, put two drops of essential oil of basil on a tissue and inhale every few minutes, or as needed.

- Rose geranium: To lighten your mood, place two drops of the essential oil on a tissue and inhale every few minutes as needed.

- Ginger: To help deter nausea, eat a slice or two of candied ginger. Or put a couple of drops of essential oil of ginger on a tissue and inhale every few minutes as needed.

- Peppermint: To help relieve dizziness, make peppermint tea by steeping one teaspoon of the dried herb in one cup of boiling water, covered, for four minutes. Or place a couple of drops of essential oil of peppermint on a tissue and inhale every few minutes, or as needed.

If you are undergoing radiation treatments, essential oil of lavender can help soothe your skin.

After a radiation treatment, run a hot bath. Swirl in about seven drops of essential oil of lavender, then soak in the tub, submerging the part of you that has been exposed to radiation. Soak for about fifteen minutes. For extra comfort, you can add about four drops of essential oil of lavender to half a cup of your favorite after-bath moisture lotion, shake, and apply.

colds, coughs, and flu

~~~~~~~~~~~~~~~~~~~~~~~~~~~~~~~~~~~~

respiratory rescue

*T*he best way to get through the cold and flu season, many herb experts say, is to prevent sickness by keeping your immune system tuned up. In addition to regular exercise and stress management, they recommend taking echinacea tincture and eating garlic to boost your immunity. Some herbalists also recommend eliminating all dairy products from the diet to aid prevention. But if you do get a cold or the flu, you may already have one or two remedies in your kitchen cabinet and not even know it.

Herbs to Clear Congestion Caused by Colds

Thyme does a great job of temporarily clearing head and nasal congestion. Make a tea of the dried herb by steeping one teaspoon in one cup of boiling water, covered, for four minutes. Strain. Then drink it hot. If you have it on hand, add one teaspoon of dried plantain herb to the thyme.

Thyme is a favored Jamu (Indonesian) herb for colds. For congestion relief Jamu-style, boil a pot of water, then remove it from the stove and swirl in a tablespoon of dried thyme. Position your head comfortably over the pot and make a tent over all with a towel. Breathe deeply and relax for about ten minutes.

Ginger tea will also help clear head and nasal congestion. Grate a handful of fresh ginger and squeeze about two teaspoons of the juice right into a cup. Cover with boiling water and sip; no need to steep. In Japan, a slice of ginger is combined with a slice of dried lotus root and about a cup and a half of water. It's simmered for twenty minutes, strained, and downed hot.

Natives of the Caribbean, particularly Antiguans, drink a tea made of dried peppermint and basil, which they call *nuna bush*. Toss a teaspoon of each herb into a cup and pour on one cup of boiling water. Cover and let steep for four minutes, then sip. Sometimes a twist of lemon or lime is added.

From Australia comes eucalyptus, which you may know as a popular ingredient in many cough/cold lozenges. For clearing a stuffed head and nose, boil a pot of water, then remove it from the stove and swirl in a handful of dried eucalyptus leaves or three drops of essential oil of eucalyptus. Position your head comfortably over the pot and make a tent over all with a towel. Breathe in deeply and relax for about ten minutes.

Extract of goldenseal is a popular herbal decongestant, often paired with extract of echinacea. Goldenseal works by soothing and drying out the mucus membranes (which can cause problems for women who are experiencing the vaginal dryness that comes with menopause). Check with a health professional before taking goldenseal.

Chinese herbalists use ephedra tea for decongestion, hay fever, allergy-induced asthma, and bronchitis. They call it *ma huang*—which is important to know, since there are several similar American species that are not as effective for decongestion. (You may know a synthetic form of ephedra as pseudoephedrine, the decongestant ingredient in the drug Sudafed.) The Chinese boil one teaspoon of the herb in one cup of water, covered, for ten minutes, then strain and drink. Two cups a day is the maximum, since ephedra is a stimulant and can give you more of a buzz than a cup of coffee. For that reason, people with high blood pressure should avoid ephedra. And since ephedra can cause uterine contractions, pregnant women also must avoid it.

The Chinese also use a ready-made aromatic called white flower oil available at herb shops, health food stores, and Chinese pharmacies. It's a clear liquid, sold in small glass bottles, that contains essences of mint with some camphor. The idea is to sprinkle a few drops of white flower oil on a tissue and inhale to clear the nasal passages temporarily. White flower oil is good for travelers, since it doesn't need to be brewed into a tea before using.

A similar bottled brew, *jao san*, comes from Vietnam. It's a clear green liquid in a small bottle, used exactly the same way as white flower oil.

Herbs for Colds and Flu

At the very onset of a cold or flu, you might try an old Italian folk remedy that is not medically validated, but might make you feel better. Combine one carnation (an organically grown dianthus like Sweet William or Clove Pink), a two-inch cinnamon stick, and a two-inch ribbon of orange peel in a cup of red wine, and bring to a boil. Simmer, covered, for ten minutes, then strain and drink. Relax for about ten minutes after drinking, then take a nap or go to bed. To have a ready supply of the right carnations when you need it, grow them, then dry them and store in a tightly closed glass jar for up to a year.

Jamu (Indonesian) herbalists recommend boneset herb to relieve fever, congestion, and other symptoms that come with the flu. Indonesians call boneset *kumis kucing,* which means "the cat's mustache," because the leaves of the herb droop like a cat's whiskers. To make a tea, combine two teaspoons of dried boneset herb in one cup of boiling water and steep, covered, for about ten minutes, then strain. Drink immediately, since the tea is most effective against fever when it's hot. Coincidentally, European herbalists also use boneset for fever from colds and flu.

Substances that make you sweat out a fever are known as diaphoretics. One of the best is plain old lemon, and it's even better if you add thyme. Chop a whole lemon and combine it with a cup of water and a teaspoon of dried thyme in a small saucepan. Bring to a boil and simmer, covered, for about five minutes, then strain and drink.

Herbs for Coughs

The herb mullein soothes and relaxes the lungs and bronchial tubes, which helps ease a cough. Mullein grows wild all over the eastern United States, but it is most commonly used in tincture form. (You can buy mullein at herb shops and health food stores.) A normal dosage is about twenty-five to thirty drops of tincture in a small amount of water, taken three times a day. But since everyone's needs are different, check with a health professional, especially if coughing persists.

Thyme, especially in hot tea form, relaxes the lungs enough to encourage the flow of mucus and cure coughing. To make a tea, steep one teaspoon of dried thyme in one cup of boiling water, covered, for four minutes, strain, then drink hot.

Hyssop contains a volatile oil that has antispasmodic properties, so it's helpful with the kind of cough that flares up from time to time throughout the day. To make hyssop tea, steep two teaspoons of dried herb in one cup of boiling water, covered, for ten minutes, then strain. European herbalists often throw in a teaspoon of the dried herb horehound, but the taste is so bad a lot of people avoid it.

To soothe a scratchy cough, Jamu (Indonesian) herbalists mix the juice of the aloe vera herb, which they call "aloe jelly," with an equal part of honey, and swallow. (Ingestible aloe is available at herb shops and health food stores.) Aloe is a demulcent, which is a substance that has soothing properties, and some smokers swallow it to ease the discomfort of smokers' cough.

Herbs for a Sore Throat

In the Caribbean, the herb balm of Gilead is used to soothe and help cure a sore throat. To make a tea, steep two teaspoons of the dried buds in one cup of water, covered, for ten minutes, then strain. Drink hot.

American herbalists recommend the dried root of osha, a relative of lovage, to soothe a sore throat. Try chewing a small, pea-sized piece; the juices should ease the discomfort.

diabetes

~~~~~~

the sugar story

*T*hough there are a number of conditions that fall under the diabetes umbrella, one kind, Type II diabetes mellitus (Type II DM), is particularly common in the United States. In Type II diabetes, the pancreas either stops producing insulin entirely or fails to produce enough. Insulin is necessary for proper absorption of glucose, which provides energy, among other functions.

The incidence of the disease has increased six times since the late 1930s, coinciding with the era when Americans began to eat more fatty and processed foods. In contrast, cases of Type II DM remain relatively rare in most African countries, where the diet consists primarily of low-fat whole grains and fresh vegetables. When these Africans move to the United States and adopt a more fatty, processed diet, their rates of Type II DM increase.

The clues as to the causes of Type II DM are adding up. Many researchers and medical experts are beginning to establish a correlation between diet and Type II DM. Among the current recommendations to help prevent and to manage Type II DM is a low-fat, high-soluble-fiber diet that is heavy in whole grains and vegetables, combined with daily exercise. The roles of certain herbs and specific foods are also coming into the picture.

Fenugreek and Fiber

Scientists have known for some time that adding soluble fiber (the kind found in oat bran and apples, for example) to the diet can help regulate blood sugar levels in Type II DM. Now a study in India reports that the seeds of the herb fenugreek, which contain over 50 percent soluble fiber, can help do the same. In the study, patients added ground fenugreek to their diet at the rate of about one hundred grams, or a quarter pound (about two-thirds cup of ground fenugreek seed) a day. Sugar excretion was reduced by an average of over 50 percent.

Fenugreek is a common culinary herb in India. The seed is ground and used in curry blends to flavor chick peas, beans, and vegetables. Ground fenugreek seed is also stirred into milk and taken as a digestive tonic, and it stands in for some of the wheat flour in bread recipes. (Since it is a uterine stimulant, fenugreek should not be taken by pregnant women.)

Garlic Is Good

Studies also show that garlic and onion seem to have a slight ability to help regulate blood sugar levels. On an average, digesting concentrations of garlic and onion can improve glucose tolerance in Type II diabetics by about 10 percent.

Minerals May Be Better

Researchers at Rutgers University in New Jersey have discovered that a deficiency of the mineral manganese can adversely affect the release of glucose in Type II DM. It's possible, therefore, that introducing manganese into the diet can help regulate blood sugar levels. Until research proves it to be true, adding manganese to the diet in the form of herbs is a tasty move and possibly one way to help prevent Type II DM.

High-Manganese Herbs and Spices

HERB	MG./per 100 g
Ground cardamom	28
Ground cinnamon	17
Ground cloves	30
Ground ginger	26
Saffron	28

The figures in this chart are from the U.S. Department of Agriculture, *Agricultural Handbook* No. 8–2, January 1977. Note that the figures are for 100 grams (about 4 ounces); the average adult needs only about 2.5 to 5 milligrams a day of manganese. Also note that the combination of the herbs and spices listed would, with the addition of turmeric and garlic, make a tasty curry blend.

Interestingly, the USDA reports that cinnamon and cloves, along with bay leaf and ground turmeric, may help regulate blood sugar levels by helping the body better manage its insulin. Though the theory is still in the test tube stage, it can't hurt to spice up a muffin recipe with some cinnamon and cloves.

Consult an Expert

While diet, exercise, and herbs may improve a diabetic's condition, Type II DM is a complex and serious condition that requires the help of a health professional. It must be diagnosed with lab tests and managed with the help of experts.

fighting fatigue

~~~~~~

mend the mind/ body burnout

Simply put, fatigue is lack of mental and physical energy. There's no single magic herb to cure fatigue, but some suggestions from around the world may help. However, medical researchers agree that the best remedy is to eat foods that give you energy, to avoid foods that zap energy, to exercise, and to take herbs that help increase the stamina of both mind and body.

Note that these are strategies to combat simple fatigue, occasional spells of feeling run-down, burned out, and worn out. Be sure to check in with a health professional if fatigue persists. Chronic fatigue is a disease in itself, but it may also indicate anemia, low blood sugar, low thyroid function, mononucleosis, or heart disease, among other problems. In addition, certain medications, such as antibiotics, high blood pressure medication, and birth control pills, can cause fatigue.

Slash the Fat

A diet high in fat is one of the most common causes of fatigue. Bite for bite, fat contains twice as many calories as carbohydrates and protein. Fat takes longer to digest, and your body uses up a lot of vitality digesting it.

To make foods satisfying without fat, season them with herbs. Instead of a fatty cream sauce on the flounder, enhance it with lemon and tarragon. In place of a heavy cheese sauce on the cauliflower, toss it with rosemary and a splash of olive oil. You may discover new tastes—and be alert enough to enjoy them.

Add Exercise

Walking, playing tennis, bicycling, and jogging all energize the body by helping it to use oxygen more efficiently. Experts recommend exercising for about twenty minutes three to five times a week. If you're a beginner, start slowly, and check with a health professional about what activities would be best for you. Herb gardening appeals to many people. Or you may enjoy dancing, using a treadmill, or exercising with friends at a health club. If you'd rather exercise alone, use a home video or tune into a television exercise show. Regardless of what you pick, focus on making exercise part of your life from now on. No excuses.

Cut Caffeine

The caffeine rush you get from coffee, black tea, some sodas, and chocolate can deplete the B vitamins in your body. One of their jobs is to help produce adrenaline, so without your normal stock of B vitamins, you can become fatigued more easily. The caffeine rush also causes a rise in blood sugar levels, and what goes up will come down. When blood sugar levels fall, fatigue sets in.

On top of that, caffeine can keep you awake at night, sapping your energy the next day. For a good night's sleep, it's best to avoid caffeine entirely or at least not to drink it after noon. If you need a pick-me-up, try thyme tea with lemon and cayenne: Steep one teaspoon of dried thyme in a cup of hot water, covered, for four minutes, strain. Then add the juice of half a lemon and, if it suits your taste, a pinch of cayenne. This brew comes in especially handy at around four in the afternoon, when people's blood sugar levels are generally low. It's also good in the morning.

Shun the Sugar

Like caffeine, refined sugars such as white sugar, brown sugar, and honey make your blood sugar levels rise and fall, which can eventually cause fatigue. One solution is to use sweet-tasting herbs, to replace sugars. Instead of sprinkling a fruit salad with sugar, toss in anise hyssop leaves. Sprinkle half a grapefruit with ground cinnamon, in place of brown sugar. And be sure to avoid sugary snacks like candy bars. If you're feeling fatigued and in need of a snack, eat a piece of fresh fruit, or drink a cup of peppermint tea.

Herbs to Fight Fatigue

A variety of single herbs and herb blends is used to treat fatigue throughout the world. A health professional can help you decide which best fits into your personal antifatigue program, in addition to recommending the correct dosage.

Chinese Ginseng

This is the most famous, and most expensive, of all the herbal fatigue fighters. The root of the plant is used both to improve physical and mental stamina and as a general stimulant.

Ginseng contains saponin compounds that act on the nervous system to fight fatigue and improve overall mind/body performance. In one Japanese study, Chinese ginseng was compared to methamphetamine and caffeine. While the ginseng boosted both the mental and physical abilities of study participants, the methamphetamine and caffeine increased only the physical abilities and actually slowed the mental ones.

Ginseng connoisseurs prefer roots that are at least six years old. Small portions of the roots may be chewed, or a half teaspoon of powdered root can be simmered, covered, in a saucepan with a cup of water for ten minutes and taken as a tea. The brew is normally drunk three times a day for four to six weeks. Some herbalists hold that taking vitamin E along with ginseng boosts the herb's powers.

The other varieties of ginseng are the American, which is less of a stimulant than its Chinese cousin, and the Siberian, which Chinese herbalists recommend using as a vitality tonic and Russians to boost mental abilities. American ginseng is prepared in the same way as the Chinese. Siberian ginseng is commonly available in extract or capsule form.

Energy Tonic Soup

Tonic herb soups like this one are popular in China, though usually chicken or pork is added. Traditionally, this soup is served in the fall and winter, to provide extra energy and warmth during the chilly seasons.

~~~~~

8   dried shiitake mushrooms
2   small Chinese or American
    ginseng roots
1   slice dried Chinese licorice
    root
1   slice fresh ginger
2   cloves garlic, minced
1   onion, chopped
1   carrot, chopped

1   dried hot chili pepper
3/4 cup pearled barley
6   cups vegetable stock
1   tablespoon minced fresh
    thyme or 1 teaspoon dried
1   teaspoon olive oil
2   teaspoons red barley miso
Minced fresh chives or minced
    scallions for garnish

SOAK the mushrooms in hot water to cover until soft, about ten minutes. Then discard the stems and slice thin (reserve the soaking liquid).

IN a large soup pot, combine the mushrooms, with their soaking water, the ginseng, licorice, ginger, garlic, onion, carrot, hot pepper, barley, and vegetable stock. If you're using dried thyme, add it now. Bring the soup to a boil, then reduce the heat and simmer, loosely covered, until the vegetables and barley are tender, about 1 hour.

REMOVE the soup from the heat and swirl in the fresh thyme, if using, and the olive oil. Scoop the miso into a small strainer and set the strainer into the soup, using a spoon to press the miso through the strainer and into the soup. Serve hot, sprinkled with the chives.

MAKES 4 HUGE SERVINGS; 225 CALORIES PER SERVING, 1 GRAM FAT, 4 PERCENT OF CALORIES FROM FAT.

Guarana

The seeds of the Brazilian herb guarana contain guaranine, a compound that can restore and revitalize the body and mind. Guarana is available ground in capsules, and herbalists recommend 1200 milligrams per day as a short-term remedy to fight fatigue and promote mental clarity. English herbalists recommend guarana more frequently than those in the United States, especially to people who are fatigued from overwork. Those who take guarana say the herb seems to be particularly restorative when taken with a light, low-fat meal.

Gotu Kola

The leaves and root of this East Indian herb are used to relieve mental fatigue and promote clarity of the mind. Gotu kola is available at herb shops, health food stores, and Indian markets. Ayurvedic herbalists recommend it for use during meditation and yoga, saying it promotes a higher consciousness. In fact, in Sanskrit, gotu kola is called *brahmi,* which means "cosmic consciousness." In India, a teaspoon of dried gotu kola leaves is steeped in a cup of hot water, covered, for four minutes, strained, then taken as a tea. In Vietnam, the herb is made into a thick green tea and served chilled as a revitalizing tonic in hot weather.

Mu Tea

This popular Japanese blend combines a number of herbs and spices, including ginger, cinnamon, ginseng, parsley root, and Chinese licorice. The exact ingredients vary according to the blender, but it's brewed by steeping one teaspoon (or one bag) in one cup of water, covered, for four minutes. It's served hot in winter and chilled in the summer, and it can be mixed half-and-half with apple juice. Mu tea gently energizes the body.

Chinese licorice root is an excellent fatigue fighter. In fact, in China, slices of the dried root are chewed to manage fatigue. The taste is pleasant and sweet, and Chinese herbalists also combine the root with peppermint and honeysuckle for a restorative tea. Chinese licorice root, however, can elevate blood pressure levels, so people with high blood pressure should avoid it.

Beat the Heat

People who live in extremely hot climates have their own brand of fatigue and the folk cures to go with it. When ancient Egyptians felt wilted, they bathed in calendula flowers and milk for rejuvenation. These days, Egyptians rejuvenate with a chilled tea of red hibiscus flower. The same goes for the Sudanese, who drink a chilled hibiscus tea with lemon, called *kharda.* In the steamy sections of China, residents perk up with a tea made of dried yellow chrysanthemum.

hay fever and asthma

keep breathing

*H*ay fever isn't caused by hay, nor is it a fever. It is an allergic reaction to plant pollen and mold spores that can last for up to seven months—from April to November. Asthma is similar in some ways, but it affects the bronchial tubes and lungs, rather than the nasal passages. It's a serious condition that requires professional treatment. For the latest information on asthma, you can call the National Lung Line Service at 800–222–LUNG (Monday through Friday, 8 A.M. to 5 P.M. Mountain Time); in Denver, call 303–355–LUNG. You can speak to a Lung Line nurse about lung disease or immune system diseases, or you can order literature on respiratory diseases or immune system diseases.

The strategies that follow are not a substitute for medical treatment, but they may bring some relief.

Avoiding Pollen and Mold

It can be difficult to predict when a hay fever or asthma attack will occur. But there are steps you can take to help prevent pollen and mold from taking over. Most experts agree that it's a good idea to keep your house cool, filtered, and dry. The air in a house with central air-conditioning has less pollen than the outside air, especially if the air-conditioning unit has a filter to block pollen from entering. The same goes for air in a car; keep the air-conditioning on and the windows up. As for mold, keep your house dry, using a dehumidifier if you need it. It's also smart to avoid cigarette smoke, which can contribute to nasal and lung irritation.

Some hay fever and asthma sufferers find water-canister vacuum cleaners helpful for breathing easy at home. As pollen, dust, and other allergens are vacuumed up, they become trapped in water. That means there's no chance of allergens blowing back out into the air, which is what can happen with many cloth and paper vacuum bags. For extra-easy breathing, three drops of essential oil of peppermint, lemon, or eucalyptus can be added to the water before vacuuming.

But realistically, you can't keep yourself locked in a sealed environment forever to avoid hay fever or asthma. Sooner or later you're going to venture out into the pollen-filled world. Luckily, there are a number of herbs that can help reduce and sometimes eliminate the symptoms of hay fever and asthma.

Breathe Easy with Nutrients

Vitamin C seems to contribute to easy breathing. In one fourteen-week-long asthma study, half the people took 1000 milligrams of vitamin C a day, and the other half took a placebo. The placebo group reported having an average of twenty-four medium to heavy asthma attacks, while the vitamin C group reported only three attacks. When the C-takers stopped taking the vitamin, the asthma returned within eight weeks. Clearly, it makes sense to add vitamin C–rich fresh herbs to your meals to help keep your immunity strong. While most fresh herbs contain some vitamin C, sorrel offers the most, and it's available fresh in spring, just when the pollen is gearing up. You can also try the vitamin C-packed Ayurvedic herb blend, chavanprash.

Fresh herbs also offer beta carotene, the plant form of vitamin A. Adding beta carotene to the diet in the form of such large, leafy herbs as mustard and dandelion can help keep your mucus membranes, including those in the nose and lungs, from overproducing.

Calcium is another nutrient that can help improve lung function, according to the *Journal of the International Academy of Preventive Medicine*.

A good herbal source of calcium is dill seed, which contains about one hundred milligrams per tablespoon—more than found in a third of a cup of skim milk. Or try half a cup of chopped raw dandelion greens for almost two hundred milligrams of calcium. Herb-based calcium may be doubly helpful to allergy sufferers, since some herbalists recommend eliminating dairy products from the diet entirely to help cure allergies.

Take It Easy

Herbalists also recommend soothing air passages by relaxing the rest of the body, using meditation and a cup of hot herbal tea. One good herb to help you calm down is skullcap, which got its name from the shape of its flowers. The Chinese call it *scute,* from its first botanical name, *Scutellaria.* It's often combined with such other nerve-tonic herbs as passionflower, wild oat, hop flower, and chamomile, and blends can be purchased dried or in liquid form, to make a relaxing hot tea.

Aromas for Easy Breathing

To quickly open stuffed nasal passages due to hay fever, fill a basin with hot water and drop in about three drops of essential oil of eucalyptus. Make a tent with a towel draped over your head, and breathe the eucalyptus steam slowly for about five minutes. For more head-clearing ideas from aromas, see the chapter on Aromatherapy (page 313).

Specific Herbs and Blends to Try

Most allergy-fighting herbs are recommended in blends. Some are in a homeopathic form, which refers to a system of curing ailments using minute doses of what may be ailing you in the first place. Proponents of homeopathy say it assists the body's natural means of healing itself. A typical homeopathic herbal remedy for hay fever might include a combination of red onion, the herb eyebright, a variety of the herb artemesia, and goldenrod. These blends, available at herb shops and health food stores, often come in pill form. Some herbalists recommend similar blends for allergies caused by pet hair.

Other blends, in the form of bulk teas, tea bags, capsules, or extracts, may include the herb ginkgo, which contains ginkgolides, compounds that smooth and soothe lung tissue and relax constricted bronchial tubes. Chinese herbalists have recommended ginkgo for treating asthma for centuries, and it's currently being investigated by Western researchers as well.

Nettle is another herbal folk cure recently studied for treating hay fever. In one study, 57 percent of the participants claimed nettle to be moderately to highly effective in relieving hay fever symptoms, particularly watery eyes and runny noses. Health professionals recommend nettle in tablets or tea blends, along with such other herbs as eyebright and goldenseal to dry up mucus membranes. Since it can elevate blood pressure levels, nettle should be avoided by those with hypertension.

Ephedra, which the Chinese call *ma huang,* is another potent antiallergic herb. It contains alkaloids that help soothe bronchial spasms, making it effective against asthma as well. Though ephedra shows up in antiallergy herb blends, health professionals sometimes recommend it alone. It should never, however, be used by people with high blood pressure, since ephedra has strong hypertensive properties.

Astragalus root is another Chinese herb that is recommended for hay fever, for sinus disorders, and as a lung tonic for asthmatics. It is the main ingredient in the famous Chinese herbal allergy potion called "jade screen tablets." Apart from the tablets, astragalus is often recommended in combination with ginseng root.

Research on astragalus shows that it can help strengthen the body's immune system and that it has some antibacterial effects. On the folklore side, the Chinese name for astragalus is *huang chi, chi* being translated as "essential energy." Astragalus, claim Chinese herbalists, can strengthen an allergic person's essential energy, since *chi* is generated from the lungs.

headaches

soothe a ruffled brow

*D*ozens of daily events can cause a common headache. But most of the throbbing and aching is actually food- or tension-related. What you eat and how you eat it can make the blood vessels in the brain dilate, causing a throbbing headache. And when you're stressed, the muscles in your shoulders, back of the neck, and scalp contract, which can cause a tension headache.

Headaches may be common, but sometimes they are a symptom of another, possibly serious, condition. Be sure to see a health professional if you have headaches every day, if your headaches come with dizziness and nausea, or if you become nonfunctional when you have a headache. If you're a migraine sufferer, you may get relief from the herb feverfew (see page 108).

When Food Is to Blame

If your headache is accompanied by a stomachache, its cause may be something you ate or drank, especially if the headache is at the front of your head. Such headaches follow overindulgence, particularly in more alcohol and sugar than you're used to. In Japan, the remedy is umeboshi plum with perilla. Not actually a plum, but a tiny apricot, umeboshi are pickled in salt along with strips of purple perilla, which is a minty-tasting herb. The combination is available in jars at Oriental markets and health food stores; ask for *ume plum* (pronounced OO-me). The taste is very salty, and Japanese herbalists say the saltiness helps put the body back into balance by contracting the tissues that have become overexpanded from excessive alcohol and sugar.

Buy the whole plums, not plum paste. For a normal headache, bite off about a quarter of a plum (they're soft) along with a strip of perilla, and keep both in your mouth until they dissolve. For a whopper headache, herbalists recommend popping a whole plum, plus perilla, in your mouth and continuing to suck on the pit for about an hour after the plum and perilla have dissolved. The ume plum and perilla remedy has not been scientifically documented, but its advocates claim it is so effective that they keep it on hand at all times and insist on taking it along when traveling.

In Mexico the remedy for food- and alcohol-related headaches is a tea made of a teaspoon of alfalfa seed and a teaspoon of dried orange leaf, steeped in one cup of boiling water, covered, for five minutes. The brew is then strained and sipped, and devotees of the remedy claim it is great for a hangover. Though there have been no formal studies on the alfalfa-orange combo, health professionals do recommend drinking nonalcoholic liquids for a hangover to replenish body fluids lost in the dehydration caused by alcohol.

Less exotic, but nonetheless exalted by its fans, is rosemary tea. Since rosemary contains compounds that tone and soothe circulation and digestion, it may calm a food-related headache. To make rosemary tea, steep one teaspoon of dried herb or two teaspoons of fresh in one cup of boiling water, covered, for four minutes. Then strain and drink hot. For a lighter approach, rub a two-inch sprig of fresh rosemary to release its aroma, then toss the rosemary in your glass of drinking water.

The same goes for peppermint tea, which is what herbalists call a carminative, or an herb that promotes digestion. This property helps to explain why peppermint tea can help a food-related headache. If digestion is normalized, the head may normalize also. To make peppermint tea, steep one teaspoon of dried herb (don't use fresh, it's not strong enough) in one cup of boiling water, covered, for four minutes. Then strain and drink hot.

Herbs for a Tension Headache

This type of headache pain often comes from the back of the neck and travels up. To relieve it, Japanese herbalists recommend steeping one teaspoon of dried chamomile flowers in one cup of boiling apple juice, covered, for four minutes. Then strain and sip.

Chinese herbalists favor the root of the herb *dong quai,* which is a Chinese variety of angelica. Dong quai has antispasmodic properties, which means it may soothe the spasms in your head. It's also a mild sedative. Dong quai root is most commonly available dried and ground in capsule form, but in a Chinese market you can find sliced dried root. To make a tea, boil one large slice of dong quai root in two cups of water, uncovered, until the water has reduced to one cup, about ten minutes. Then remove the root and sip the tea. (The root, by the way, may be used one more time.) In India, where dong quai is called *choraka,* the roots are simmered in milk.

Another Indian remedy for tension headaches is powdered dried yellow chrysanthemum. Half a teaspoon of the dried herb is mixed with one cup of water and sipped, hot or cold. Ayurvedic East Indian herbalists claim chrysanthemum has a calming effect on a tense head, neck, and shoulders, especially in hot weather. Chinese herbalists also recommend yellow chrysanthemum tea to ease a tension headache when the weather gets steamy.

Herbal Aspirin Substitutes

The bark of the white willow was the original source of aspirin, before the drug was produced synthetically. Its key headache-busting ingredient is salicylic acid. The problem with white willow is that it tastes awful, so don't even try to drink it in tea form. Instead, take it in capsules, which can be purchased from an herb shop or health food store.

A better-tasting herb is meadowsweet. The leaves, which smell like almonds, contain methyl salicylate, a compound that turns into salicylic acid when the leaves are dried. To make meadowsweet tea, combine two teaspoons of dried herb with one cup of hot (not boiling) water. Cover and steep for five minutes, then strain and sip. It's very important to cover the brew, as the steam will cause the salicylic acid to dissipate.

The Direct Approach

Headaches can often be relieved by rubbing an aromatic herbed oil directly into the area that hurts. You can buy a ready-made herbed oil, such as Chinese white flower oil, which contains menthol and camphor. Dot a bit of the oil on your fingers and rub into the back of the neck, the temples, or anywhere there is pain. Rub, pressing firmly, for fifteen seconds. Relax for fifteen seconds, then rub for fifteen seconds again. Keep rubbing and relaxing until the area is warm. You can repeat this every fifteen minutes until you feel better.

To make your own headache oil, combine ten drops of essential oil of marjoram in a quarter cup of olive oil, and mix well. Use the same method as for white flower oil. Store the oil in a cool dry place until you need it.

healthy skin and hair

tonics, lotions, and potions

*F*or healthy hair and skin, what goes in the body comes before what goes on it. Eating lots of vegetables and fruits to enhance the skin with nutrients like beta carotene and vitamin C is a must. So is cutting out caffeine, alcohol, cigarettes, and refined sugar, substances that many herbalists believe can cause dull hair and skin, as well as cause early signs of aging. That said, herbs can be used both internally and externally to condition and revitalize hair and skin.

Internal Tonics for Healthy Skin and Hair

As one Pennsylvania Mennonite herbalist put it, the skin acts as a third kidney. When the kidneys are overloaded, the skin picks up the slack by helping to flush out toxins. The result may be dull or blemished skin. To keep the kidneys toned, Pennsylvania Mennonites drink a tea of parsley and red clover made by combining half a teaspoon of each dried herb in one cup of boiling water. The tea is steeped, covered, for four minutes, then strained, sipped warm or chilled. Often, the red clover is combined with dried burdock root, echinacea, and yellow dock, a group of herbs that helps the body flush out waste. The resultant brew is particularly recommended for dull or blemished skin. In the spring, dandelion is added.

Some German herbalists recommend nettle tea to keep the kidneys toned. One teaspoon of dried nettle is steeped in one cup of boiling water, covered, for four minutes. The taste is rather dull, so if you prefer, you can add a couple of teaspoons of dried nettle to a vegetable soup to serve two and get the job done. Note that nettle is hypertensive, so if you have high blood pressure, avoid it.

A livelier tonic is a hot lemon and cayenne tea used in parts of Africa and the Caribbean as a mild cleansing brew for the liver and intestines. It's made by using a lemon reamer to remove all the juice and pulp from half a lemon. A sprinkle of cayenne is added, and a cup of boiling water is poured over all. Occasionally, for extra cleansing, a pinch of ground turmeric is added. The tea is sipped hot. Since the acidic lemon juice can erode tooth enamel over a period of time, be sure to brush your teeth after a lemon-cayenne tonic. Some U.S. and European spas have adopted the tea as the only way to start the day.

As for the hair, many herbalists recommend a tea of the herb horsetail—a good source of silica, a mineral that can help your body absorb the calcium it needs to produce healthy hair, nails, and skin. Be sure to buy dried spring horsetail, since older plants can be internally irritating if taken over a period of time. Make a tea by steeping two teaspoons of dried horsetail in one cup of boiling water, covered, for fifteen minutes, strain, then sip. Herbalists recommend a regimen of one cup three times a day for fourteen days, followed three or four times a year.

Herbs for the Skin

When purchasing a skin cream, especially for your face, be aware that just because a cream has herbs in it doesn't mean it's good. Avoid products that contain mineral oils or other petroleum products. After longtime use, they can clog pores and eventually dry out the skin. Instead, look for products that contain nut or seed oils such as almond or sesame. Also avoid products that contain alcohol, which is a cheap emulsifier and preservative that will dry out the skin. Vitamin E and wheat germ oils are natural preservatives and emulsifiers that are good for your skin.

Lavender is a natural soother for the skin. Use this aromatic oil on damp skin to subdue sunburn (but not as a sunscreen). Or use it as a bath oil, rub it on the temples for a refreshing mini-massage, or even dot it on insect stings for relief from itching. This is an infused (steeped) oil, not an essential oil, so it can be used like the bath and body oils with which you're familiar. (Do not take lavender oil, infused or essential, internally without professional supervision.)

Soothing Lavender Skin Oil

2 cups fresh lavender flowers
7 2-inch sprigs fresh rosemary
1 2-inch ribbon dried orange peel

1 1/4 cups olive oil, grapeseed oil, or peanut oil, or a combination (see Note)

POUND the lavender and rosemary lightly in a mortar to release the aromas. If you don't have a mortar, spread the herbs on a sheet of waxed paper and pound lightly with a rolling pin.

PACK the herbs into a 2-cup jar, along with the orange peel, and pour on the oil. Cover the jar and shake well. Leave the jar in a sunny window for two weeks, shaking the jar daily. Then strain and enjoy. Tightly covered and refrigerated, the oil keeps for up to a year.

MAKES ABOUT 2 CUPS.

Variation: If you don't grow lavender, buy 1 cup of organically grown dried flowers and carry on with the recipe. As for the rosemary, you can substitute 2 teaspoons dried for the fresh.

NOTE: Olive is the heaviest, grapeseed is the lightest, and you may use only one or any combination of the three you like.

Herbs for Oily Skin

Rose geranium, lemon, and lavender all can help normalize an oily complexion. To begin with, use a cleanser containing rose geranium. If you can't find one, mix three drops of essential oil of rose geranium with a quarter cup of the cleanser you're using now.

For extra care, add three or four drops of essential oil of rose geranium to half a cup of distilled or mineral water. Pour the mixture into a small spray bottle, and spritz your face after washing it, before applying moisturizer, and throughout the day. The spray won't disturb makeup. Even if you don't normally have oily skin, the spray is welcome in the summer when you're feeling wilted.

Another refreshing trick is to add several fresh or dried lavender flowers (or three or four drops of essential oil per half cup) to your facial toner. The lavender will help normalize the excess oil in your skin. To make your own toner, mix half a cup of liquid witch hazel (an herb from a tree bark) with a tablespoon of cider vinegar, and add the lavender to that.

Herbs for Blemishes

Herbalists generally don't like to treat skin eruptions externally—they prefer to treat the whole person from the inside out. But for a quick fix, try essential oil of lemon grass, peppermint, tea tree oil, extract of myrrh, or Chinese white flower oil. (This is the only case in which you should ever use essential oils of lemongrass and peppermint directly on your skin.) Drip a few drops of oil on a cotton swab and dot it right on the blemish.

Ayurvedic East Indian herbalists recommend a ready-made cream of turmeric and sandalwood that can be dotted on blemishes to make them disappear. The cream also can be rubbed into a particular area to prevent an outbreak. Ask for turmeric cream at an Indian market.

A similar combination, used by Jamu Indonesian herbalists, is available at Asian markets. It's called *sekar sari* and combines two varieties of turmeric powder plus powdered sandalwood. It's intended to be mixed with water and spread over a clean face, neck, and/or upper body—and down from there if you're in the mood. (It's very messy.) The sekar sari is allowed to dry, then rinsed off, leaving your skin in a wonderfully glowing condition. It's good for all skin types, broken out or not. For very dry skin, a couple of drops of rosewater should be added.

Herbs for Dry Skin

The all-time tropical favorite for normalizing dry skin is the natural jelly of the aloe vera plant. Start with fresh leaves and slit them open with a paring knife or fingernail, then press out the jelly. Rub it on in the shower when your skin is warm, moist, and receptive, then rinse it off.

Another dry skin soother comes from Vietnam. Put an egg white into a bowl and add one drop of essential oil of sandalwood or lemon. (If you don't have the essential oils on hand, just add two drops of fresh lemon juice.) Mix lightly, then spread it on your just-cleaned face and neck (under the eyes, too). Relax until it's dry, about fifteen minutes. When you rinse off the mask your skin will look and feel smooth and soft.

You can also make a moisturizing mask from honey. Honey is a natural humectant, which means it attracts moisture to the skin. Mix about a quarter cup of pure honey with a drop of essential oil of sandalwood, clary sage, or rose. Apply the mixture to a dry, clean face, rubbing it into your skin vigorously for about thirty seconds. Relax for about fifteen minutes. Rinse the honey off with warm water to which you've added a splash of vinegar, herbed or otherwise.

For extra moistening after a facial or just after washing, add rose water to your toner, using one teaspoon to each half cup. Or splash warm water on your face and neck, then rub your skin with rose water. For touch-ups throughout the day, you can add about a teaspoon of rose water to a half-cup spray bottle filled with distilled water or mineral water. The spray won't disturb makeup, and its softening properties are a must during airplane travel.

Another spray to make for dry skin is one of neroli (orange blossom) and sandalwood. Add about three drops of essential oil of each herb to half a cup of water. Spray your face with the mixture after cleansing and before moisturizing, and then throughout the day. To quickly buff dead skin cells away, spray your face well with neroli-sandalwood spray, then pour about a tablespoon of refined white sugar into your hand. Pat the sugar over your face and rub very gently in circles; don't apply pressure. Rub for about thirty seconds, then let the sugar sit for a minute before rinsing with cool water. The sugar treatment is best done at night, to give the skin a chance to relax.

Herbs for Tired, Stressed Skin

If your life-style has taken away your healthful glow, there are a number of herbal potions that can provide temporary relief. One is an ancient remedy called "Virgin's Milk." To make it, combine seven drops of tincture of benzoin (an herbal resin, available at pharmacies) and two drops of rose water with one cup of water. After washing your face, and before moisturizing, rub your skin with the mixture, and you will see it begin to glow. Keep the Virgin's Milk in the fridge, where it will last for about five days.

Jamu Indonesian herbalists use leftover black tea in the same manner, rubbing it into the skin after washing and before moisturizing. Yarrow tea works equally well. These remedies don't provide the same glow as Virgin's Milk, but the tannin temporarily tightens up the skin.

Another facial revitalizer is a mask made of powdered clay and brewed peppermint tea. To try it, buy bentonite and kaolin clays at your health food store. Combine a handful of each in a bowl and pour on enough brewed mint tea to make a paste. Press the mask on clean skin and relax until it's dry, about seven minutes. Rinse the mask away with warm water, then apply a toner and moisturizer. Even better, rinse the mask away with a tea made of the herb Saint-John's-wort. To make it, boil a handful of fresh leaves and flowers in four cups of water for three minutes. Steep, covered, for five minutes more, then let cool. Strain and rinse your face. For convenience, you can make the rinse ahead and stash it in the fridge for up to five days.

You might want to treat your face to an oatmeal and chamomile mask, to tighten pores and refresh your complexion. To try it, grind half a cup of rolled oats in a blender or processor until very finely ground. Don't skimp on the grinding or the mask will be a mess to apply. Mix the oats with enough brewed chamomile tea to make a paste that will spread easily over the skin. Cleanse your face and neck, then splash on warm water to open your pores. Press on the mask, then lie back and relax until it's dry, about ten minutes. Rinse off the mask, splash your skin with a toner, and apply a moisturizer while your skin is still damp. For a dry skin variation, add a tablespoon of organically grown dried rose petals to the chamomile tea when you're brewing it. If you don't have rose petals, stir half a teaspoon of rose water into the brewed tea. For oily skin, add a tablespoon of cider vinegar to the tea before mixing it with the oats. Or add a tablespoon of fresh or dried lemongrass to the tea when you're brewing it.

Herbs for Irritated Skin

For hot, itchy skin conditions, such as sunburn, mix equal proportions of fresh aloe jelly and your regular moisturizer, then apply to damp skin. (To get the jelly out of the aloe leaf, slit it with a fingernail or paring knife and squeeze the jelly out into the palm of your hand.) The aloe jelly will help to make your skin feel cool and soft. To avoid getting dried out from the sun in the first place, some herbalists advise that you begin to prepare two weeks in advance before a vacation by omitting caffeine, alcohol, and refined sugar from your diet. Sunscreens and aftersun creams that contain essential oil of lavender will also help to keep your skin soft.

As for skin that's irritated from shaving, splash on cool peppermint or chamomile tea. Make the tea extra-strong by using two teaspoons of dried herb to one cup of boiling water, and steep, covered, for five minutes. Chill before using. The splash will keep in the refrigerator for up to five days. Or you can freeze it in ice cube trays. When your skin needs to cool off, just melt a cube.

Herbs for Puffy, Irritated Eyes

Dip two cotton pads in chamomile tea and set the pads right on your closed eyes. Then lie back and relax for about ten minutes.

Herbs for Hair

Herbs are potent tonics for the hair, and it's easy to make your own herbal hair treatments. But since beautiful, healthy hair begins with proper cleansing, the first thing to do is to purchase a good shampoo.

These days almost every shampoo contains at least an herb or two; rosemary, nettle, and kelp are popular. But a shampoo needs more than herbs to help your hair behave beautifully. The experts recommend you look for a shampoo that's pH-balanced. If it's too acidic, your hair will become dried out. Additionally, if you color or perm your hair, an acid shampoo will cause the color to fade faster and the perm to go limp more quickly. On the other hand, if a shampoo's too alkaline, it won't get your hair clean. Stay away from shampoos that contain waxes. They're added to formulas to help condition the hair, but they wind up leaving the hair coated and not really clean. And if your scalp is sensitive, avoid shampoos that contain lauryl sulfate, opting for the more gentle cleansing alternative of laureth sulfate.

Herbal Hair Conditioners

BASIL FOR HEALTHY HAIR To add shine to hair, rinse with a basil vinegar. To make it, heat one cup of cider vinegar until hot, not boiling, then toss in three tablespoons of fresh basil. Steep, covered, for twenty minutes, then strain. Rub a tablespoon or two into your scalp and hair and leave on for about two minutes before rinsing out.

CHAMOMILE FOR DRY HAIR Use this conditioner once a week on dry or overprocessed hair. The olive oil works best with coarse, curly hair, and the grapeseed oil is better for fine, straight hair. If your household members vary in hair textures, go for the grapeseed; if you can't find grapeseed oil, use canola oil.

> $^1/_3$ cup dried chamomile flowers
>
> $^1/_3$ cup olive oil or grapeseed oil

Combine the flowers and oil in a glass jar and cover. Set the jar in a sunny window for two weeks, shaking the jar daily. At the end of two weeks, strain away the flowers.

To use, brush your hair. Moisten your hands with water and drop a bit of the oil onto each palm. One teaspoon on each palm is enough for shortish hair. Then rub the oil into the ends of your hair, keeping it away from the scalp. For extra conditioning, oil your hair, then wrap your head in a hot wet towel. Leave the oil on for ten to fifteen minutes, depending on how dry your hair is. Then shampoo and style as usual. Keep the oil in the fridge and bring it back to room temperature before using. The recipe makes enough for nine short-hair treatments.

Herbs by Hair Color

To try one of the following conditioning treatments, combine all of the ingredients for your hair color in a processor or blender and whiz until smooth. Rub the mixture into clean, wet hair, then cover with plastic wrap or a shower cap and relax for ten minutes (now's a good time for an herbal facial, too). Rinse your hair very well and style as usual.

FOR BLONDE HAIR: Use a peeled banana, two tablespoons of brewed chamomile or calendula tea, and a raw egg yolk.

FOR AUBURN HAIR: Use half a cup of ripe strawberries, two tablespoons of brewed basil tea, and a raw egg yolk.

FOR BLACK AND BROWN HAIR: Use two tablespoons of instant espresso, two tablespoons of hot brewed rosemary tea, and half a ripe avocado.

The Calendula Connection

The bright yellow blossoms of calendula are prized for their skin-soothing properties. Creams and lotions, made from the herb, are available at herb shops and health food stores, but you can easily make your own.

Calendula Skin Oil

Calendula skin oil is gentle enough for babies and elderly people, and it's great for massage. Rub this oil into dry cuticles, heels and feet, elbows, even chapped lips. For an under-eye cream, lightly pat it on while your skin is damp. To smooth your hands after gardening, wash them, rinse, and rub with the oil while still wet.

The recipe gives you a choice of base oils. Grapeseed is the lightest of the three and is absorbed most quickly by the skin. Avocado is also light. Olive, on the other hand, is heavier and more protective. Olive is a good choice for skin that's exposed to the elements, say, when skiing, gardening, sailing, or working outside in all weather.

1 cup packed fresh calendula petals (about 1 ounce)

2 cups olive oil, grapeseed oil, or avocado oil

1/2 cup wheat germ oil

COMBINE all of the ingredients in a large glass bottle, cover, and set in a sunny window for two weeks, shaking every day. Strain and store refrigerated.

MAKES 2 1/2 CUPS.

Variation for Extra-Dry and Mature Skin: Add 1/3 cup fresh clary sage leaves and flowers and 1/4 cup fresh Saint-John's-wort leaves to the ingredients, then carry on with the recipe.

Calendula Skin Toner

This bracing splash is soothing and toning. It's especially helpful for balancing skin that faces pollution daily.

~~~~~

3½ cups liquid witch hazel
½ cup packed dried calendula petals (about ½ ounce)

5 2-inch sprigs fresh rosemary

COMBINE all of the ingredients in a large glass bottle, cover, and set in a sunny spot for seven days, shaking once a day. Strain. Keep a small bottle in the bathroom for daily use and store the rest in the refrigerator. Splash on your face after cleansing skin and before moisturizing, or dot on insect bites to stop itching.

MAKES ABOUT 3½ CUPS.

Variation for Oily Skin: Substitute fresh mint for the rosemary, and toss in a 2-inch ribbon of lemon rind. Then carry on with the recipe.
Variation for Aftershave: Mix one part calendula skin toner (regular or oily) with one part aloe vera jelly.

Calendula-Milk Facial

Try this mild exfoliation treatment once or twice a week in the winter, when your skin needs a lift. It's also rejuvenating at the change of seasons, and after airplane travel.

~~~~~

Petals from 2 fresh or dried calendula flowers (about 2 tablespoons)

⅓ cup boiling water
2 tablespoons instant nonfat dry milk

continued

STEEP the calendula petals in the water until cool, about 20 minutes. Be sure to cover the brew, to keep the aroma from escaping. Meanwhile, cleanse your face and neck, then rinse with warm water to open your pores.

SCOOP the milk into a little bowl and add enough calendula tea, minus petals, to make a loose paste. Press the paste onto your warm skin and relax until the paste is almost dry, about five minutes. Leaning over the sink, gently rub the almost-dried paste off your skin, using gentle circular motions. Then rinse with cool water, splash on a toner, and moisturize while your skin is still damp.

MAKES ENOUGH FOR 1 FACIAL.

Calendula-Rosemary Styling Spray

Use this as you would any hair gel or mousse. It's got medium holding power and is good for women, men, and children. The spray will not create a buildup on your hair, nor will it weight down natural waves. The aroma disappears when the spray dries.

~~~~~

1/3 cup beer
Petals from 1 fresh or dried
    calendula flower (about 1
    tablespoon)

2 2-inch sprigs fresh rosemary
    or 2 teaspoons dried

COMBINE all of the ingredients in a small saucepan and heat for 1 minute; don't boil. Then let stand, uncovered, overnight.

STRAIN and discard the herbs. Pour the liquid into a small spray bottle. Squirt on your hair after shampooing and style as usual, or squirt on dry hair for extra body. Store refrigerated.

MAKES ABOUT 1/3 CUP.

Calendula-Grapefruit Styling Lotion

This liquid gel has medium-strong holding power.

~~~~~~

Petals from 2 fresh or dried
calendula flowers (about 2
tablespoons)
1/2 cup boiling water

Juice of 1/2 pink grapefruit,
strained

STEEP the calendula petals in the water until the brew is cool, about 20 minutes. Then stir in the grapefruit juice.

TO use, pour some of the lotion into the palms of your hands and work it through your hair while it's damp, just after shampooing; then style as usual. For extra waves, work the lotion into dry hair, then scrunch. Store refrigerated.

MAKES ABOUT 1 CUP.

Aloe jelly also makes a good styling lotion. Slit a leaf with a fingernail or paring knife and squeeze out the jelly. Rub it between your hands, then apply to wet hair.

high blood pressure

the silent stalker

*T*he higher your blood pressure, the higher your chances of heart disease, heart failure, stroke, severe nerve damage, kidney failure, and hardening of the arteries. Since high blood pressure (hypertension) can cause so many serious health problems, you should never treat it by yourself. But along with following a health professional's advice, experts say there are four steps to normalizing and preventing high blood pressure. They're easy to remember because they spell out REDS, and red is the color of the blood in the vessels that will thank you for treating them more gently. REDS means:

Relax

Exercise

Diet

Salt

Relax

Stress is not going to go away, but herbs can help you cope with it. Certain herbs are what herbalists call "nervines," and drinking a cup of tea made from one or a blend may help soothe your nerves. A blend of chamomile and valerian is a popular calming combo. To make it, combine half a teaspoon of each herb in one cup of boiling water and steep, covered, for four minutes. Then strain and drink instead of caffeine-rich beverages like coffee, black tea, and colas.

Exercise

Light aerobic activity, such as walking or bicycling, may help keep blood pressure normal by keeping blood vessels more elastic. Researchers also suspect that exercise helps your body to normalize fluids at the cellular level, reducing the volume of blood in the vessels, which in turn lowers blood pressure.

Diet

Keeping your weight at a normal level can help regulate your blood pressure. When you put on the pounds, your body releases more adrenaline-type hormones that can result in high blood pressure. Additionally, when your body has more fat cells, it releases more insulin. The extra insulin can cause sodium retention, which can cause blood pressure to rise.

Salt

Some of the most convincing evidence that salt can elevate blood pressure levels is the fact that people who live in areas where a low-sodium diet is the norm rarely have high blood pressure. This is evident in parts of Africa, but when these native Africans move to the United States and adopt a high-sodium diet, their blood pressure levels go way up. To further prove the salt–blood pressure connection, research reveals that people who have high blood pressure have more sodium in the walls of their blood vessels than people with normal blood pressure levels.

So what do you do about salt? Get it out of your life by replacing the salt in cooking with herb blends. With the liveliness that herbs can bring to foods, your taste buds won't cry out for salt.

Try combining equal parts of dried basil and oregano and dried ground lemon zest in a saltshaker. Mix well and add a teaspoon or two of raw rice to keep the mixture from caking. Sprinkle on green beans or broccoli, or use in place of salt in marinades and salad dressings. Another good combination is ground celery seed, ground cumin seed, dried sage, and dried marjoram. Or fill a pepper mill with whole allspice, coriander seed, and white and black peppercorns. Keep it handy and grind it over food whenever you have a salt craving. The mixture is especially tasty on plain popcorn.

Amazing Minerals

Besides following the REDS rule, you can protect yourself against high blood pressure by adding three high-mineral herbs to your diet: tarragon, dill, and mustard. Researchers say potassium seems to counteract sodium's negative effect on blood pressure levels. Tarragon is a good herbal source of potassium, at 145 milligrams per tablespoon. For comparison, three ounces of chicken, which is considered a top source of potassium, contains 195 milligrams. Since potassium is sensitive to water, be sure not to cook it in liquid. Instead, sprinkle tarragon on food just before serving.

Second in line is calcium. Researchers at Oregon Health Sciences University in Portland say that making sure to get 1000 milligrams of calcium a day can lower the odds of developing high blood pressure from 20 to 1. Dill seed is a good herbal source of calcium, with about 100 milligrams per tablespoon—as much calcium as three quarters of a cup of cottage cheese.

Swedish researchers believe that a third mineral, magnesium, works with potassium and calcium to normalize blood pressure levels. Ground mustard seed contains about thirty-three milligrams per tablespoon, or about one tenth of the daily recommendation.

A European Formula

European herbalists, particularly in England and Germany, recommend two herbs for normalizing high blood pressure: hawthorn berry and mistletoe twigs. (*Never* eat mistletoe berries, they're poisonous.) Hawthorn berries help normalize the heartbeat, while the mistletoe helps to strengthen the walls of blood vessels. To make a tea, combine two teaspoons of dried hawthorn berries with one teaspoon of dried mistletoe twig in one cup of boiling water. Cover and let the brew steep for fifteen to twenty minutes. Then strain and sip. Herbalists recommend drinking one cup of the tea three times a day, but check with a health professional to find out what's right for you.

Mushroom and Herb Condiment for High Blood Pressure

This savory side dish contains magnesium from mustard, calcium from dillseed, and potassium from tarragon—all minerals believed by researchers to help lower blood pressure levels. And Japanese herbalists believe that shiitake mushrooms help lower blood pressure. They recommend eating three to five shiitakes per day for one week, then three to five shiitakes one or two times a week thereafter. Though this treatment is not scientifically documented, some who have tried the shiitake plan (along with REDS) report normal blood pressure levels in as little as two weeks.

~~~~~

5 dried shiitake mushrooms
1/2 cup water
Splash of Worcestershire sauce, or to taste
1 clove garlic, minced

1/2 teaspoon dry mustard
1/2 teaspoon dillseed
1 teaspoon minced fresh tarragon or 1/2 teaspoon dried

SOAK the mushrooms in the water until just soft, about 20 minutes. Reserve the soaking liquid. Slice away and discard the stems, then slice the mushrooms.

IN a small saucepan, combine the mushrooms, and the soaking liquid, the Worcestershire sauce, garlic, mustard, and dillseed. Bring to a boil and boil until the liquid has been reduced to about a tablespoon. Stir in the tarragon, and serve atop grilled fish or cooked rice as a condiment.

MAKES 1 SERVING; ABOUT 20 CALORIES PER SERVING, NO ADDED FAT.

Daily Garlic

A more familiar herb for bringing down high blood pressure is garlic. Two of the compounds it contains, allicin and ajoene, help reduce both high blood pressure and high blood cholesterol levels. Most experts agree that garlic works best if taken daily (one clove or the equivalent), over a period of time. Getting garlic into your life as a heart tonic can reduce your risk for cardio-vascular disease.

Getting Flushed

Such mild diuretic herbs as fresh parsley can help reduce blood pressure by flushing water and sodium out of the body, thus lightening the load on the heart and blood vessels. You might also want to try a Japanese herbal remedy, corn silk tea. To make it, combine a half cup of fresh corn silk with four cups of boiling water and let the mixture steep, covered, for five minutes. Strain, then sip. The tea, which is extremely thirst-quenching, smells like sharp, fresh, green corn. The color is opal-green to clear and the brew is slightly viscous. You can use it as a soup stock or to cook rice or other grains. This cure is also favored by the Papago Indians, who toast the corn silk before brewing (use a dry cast-iron pan over medium to medium-high heat and toast, stirring, for about five minutes).

minor cuts and scratches

heal the hurts

When you scrape a leg while gardening or cut a finger in the kitchen, it seems especially appropriate to reach for an herbal first aid kit for the remedy.

The Green Healers

Comfrey is what herbalists call a vulnerary, an herb that encourages the healing of external wounds. To try it, make a poultice by mashing the leaves in a food processor or mortar, then pack the paste on the cleaned cut, scrape, or bruise. Cover the poultice with a cloth and leave to treat for twenty to thirty minutes. Repeat until healing begins, up to eight times a day.

Some herbalists mix comfrey half-and-half with fresh yarrow leaves, which have astringent properties that help shrink swollen tissue and help stop bleeding. The comfrey-yarrow combination is also helpful in preventing bruises, especially if applied right after the injury. If you don't grow these herbs, you can find ready-made creams that contain them at herb shops and health food stores.

You can also make your own healing potion by combining equal parts of finely chopped fresh comfrey and yarrow leaf in a saucepan with olive oil just to cover. Heat gently, loosely covered, for about 20 minutes; don't allow to boil. Strain away the leaves and measure the oil. For each three quarters of a cup, add half an ounce of grated pure beeswax, and heat gently until the wax has melted. Pour the mixture into jars and allow it to harden. Rub the cream on washed cuts, bruises, and scratches. It will keep, refrigerated, for up to a year.

The Cool Healer

Unlike the green healers, aloe requires no preparation before use. Just slit open a leaf with a paring knife or fingernail and rub the jelly on a cleaned cut or scratch. You can cover the area with gauze, or use the skin of the aloe itself as an herbal bandage. Take care to place the aloe skin with the jelly side toward the wound, since the outer skin can have small thorns that could irritate the wound. The same treatment will work for minor skin burns.

Mellow with Yellow

The yellowy-orange flower of calendula heals burns as well as skin inflammations. To try it, steep the petals from one blossom in a cup of boiling water, covered, for five minutes. Let the tea cool to room temperature, then strain and pour it over the inflamed skin. If you prefer, you can purchase calendula creams and gels at herb shops and health food stores.

Relief on the Spot

An herbal cure for bruises is arnica, available in gel and spray forms in health food stores. Arnica is a mountain herb that looks like a little daisy and is especially great for bruises because of its antiinflammatory properties. It's poisonous if taken internally, so don't use it on broken skin.

Swedish bitters, a liquid herbal preparation designed to soothe a sour stomach, also takes the itching out of bug bites. Available in bottles in health food stores and herb shops, it can be dabbed directly on a bite. Take a small bottle along on picnics and other outdoor adventures.

pollution solutions

the delicate balance

Without the technology and conveniences of the twentieth century, our lives would probably be less rich. But there is a price attached to progress: pollution that's eroding our health. Some of the pollutants in our atmosphere are lethal, such as the radioactive substances released during the accident at Chernobyl, which can build up in the body and promote leukemia and bone cancer. One of these pollutants, strontium 90, has been in the atmosphere since World War II, when nuclear bombs were tested in the United States and released in Japan. The natural world may offer some promising palliatives for such man-made ills.

Herbs That Heal

Both Japanese and U.S. studies show that sea herbs may help prevent the absorption of strontium 90.

These herbs include kelp, kombu, nori, hijiki, and arame. The alginate compounds these sea herbs contain can help keep the intestines from absorbing new doses of radiation and may possibly flush out previously absorbed radiation.

You'll find sea herbs at Oriental markets, herb shops, and health food stores, sold dried in packages. The easiest to get to know is nori, toasted green sheets that taste like slightly briny spinach. Use it as a wrapping for a ball of rice, or slice and toss with skinny Chinese noodles. Most experts advise eating two to three servings a week of sea herbs for maximum protection against radioactive substances. If you find the taste of sea herbs unpleasant, kelp is available in capsules and tablets. Check with a health professional about the dosage that's right for you.

Herbs for Immunity

The immune system is the body's line of defense against pollutants as well as disease. Strengthening it can make the body more resistant to such pollution-induced respiratory illnesses as asthma and allergies. Echinacea, an herb that has antimicrobial activity, helps to keep the lymph system tuned up, which can keep your nose, eyes, ears, throat, bronchial tubes, and lungs operating in top form even if you live in a polluted or smog-filled area. Herbalists say that the best way to take echinacea is in the fresh tincture form. A health professional can help you decide how much to take.

Herbalists also recommend the herb marshmallow to help keep the immune system running properly. The root of the herb becomes smooth and soft in liquid and was, in fact, originally used to make marshmallow confections. These days the root is used to make a tea, by steeping one teaspoon of dried minced root in one cup of boiling water, covered, for ten minutes. As you may discover, marshmallow is a very gentle laxative. It speeds bowel transit time, thereby reducing the absorption of toxins in the digestive tract.

Protective Nutrients

Antioxidants are bodyguard molecules that prevent damage from the destructive molecules known as free radicals, which can develop because of air pollution, cigarette smoking, and drinking alcohol. The damage can result in premature aging and cell mutation, or even cancer. To keep free radicals in check, add beta carotene and vitamin C to your diet. Fresh herbs are good sources of both. Sorrel and dandelion leaves contain the most vitamin C and should be eaten uncooked, since vitamin C is heat-sensitive. For beta carotene, look to the darker leaves—nasturtium and mustard as well as dandelion and sorrel. The greener the leaf, the more beta carotene it contains.

Go for the Green

Another antioxidant is green tea, which contains free radical–fighting polyphenol compounds. Brew a cup by steeping one teaspoon of dried green tea in one cup of boiling water, covered, for two to three minutes. Japanese herbalists recommend drinking it straight, while Vietnamese herbalists toss in a petal or two of dried jasmine during steeping.

Love Your Liver

When it comes to air pollution, radiation, cigarette smoke, and alcohol abuse, the liver is the organ that takes it on the chin. Among the liver's many jobs is flushing the body of unwanted toxins. For this reason, many herbalists recommend toning up the liver with herbs from time to time. European herbalists often prescribe milk thistle, which contains a compound called silybin that helps improve liver function. Burdock root and dandelion root are also popular liver tonics. In fact, these blends are beginning to be known as "the party herbs," since some folks take them in tablet form the day after drinking a few too many.

Chinese herbalists recommend the herb bupleurum to cleanse the liver. It's often prescribed with the herb cyperus to women for irritability during PMS. Chinese herbalists believe that irritability reflects liver problems. Ayurvedic (East Indian) herbalists agree, and treat liver problems with ground turmeric, the spice that makes curry powder yellow.

The liver controls so many important functions of the body that it can be dangerous to attempt to diagnose or treat yourself. Always consult with a health professional to find out what's right for you.

Antipollution Tonic

Arame (pronounced AR-uh-may) is a sea herb with a gentle taste, especially when it's soaked before cooking. It's popular in Japanese cooking, where it is often sautéed with onions and carrots. It comes dried in packages in tiny purple-black shreds, available at herb shops and health food stores.

~~~~~

1 ounce dried arame
Splash of olive oil
1 clove garlic, minced
1 medium onion, thinly sliced
1 cup corn kernels (from 2 ears)

Splash of soy sauce (low sodium is okay)
Splash of toasted (dark) sesame oil
2 tablespoons minced fresh chives

WASH the arame in several changes of water, then drain and rinse a final time. Let it drain in a colander for a robust flavor, or soak it in cool water for 10 minutes for a more delicate taste.

HEAT a cast-iron skillet over high heat, then add the olive oil and use a pastry brush to spread it around. Reduce the heat to medium-high, add the garlic and onion, and sauté until wilted and fragrant, about 2 to 3 minutes.

ADD the arame to the skillet, along with about 1/2 cup of its soaking water; if you haven't soaked it, use fresh water. Cover and bring to a boil, then reduce the heat and simmer for about 20 minutes. Add the corn and soy sauce and simmer, uncovered, until all the liquid has evaporated, about 5 minutes. Sprinkle on the sesame oil and chives, toss, and serve warm.

MAKES 4 SERVINGS; 85 CALORIES PER SERVING, TRACE OF FAT.

Variation: Hijiki, a sea herb with a stronger taste, can be cooked in the same way.

Free Radical-Fighting Tonic

This beverage can be helpful if you live in a polluted or smog-filled area, or if you smoke cigarettes or drink too much alcohol. The carrot juice contains the antioxidant beta carotene; the lemon offers vitamin C, for a double dose of antioxidants; and the echinacea helps enhance the immune system.

~~~~~

1 cup fresh carrot juice

1 eyedropperful of echinacea tincture (about 28 drops)

1 tablespoon fresh lemon juice

COMBINE all the ingredients in a glass and mix well to combine. Then enjoy.

MAKES 1 SERVING; 90 CALORIES PER SERVING, NO ADDED FAT.

sparkling teeth and gums

keep smiling

S ince smiling may be the most important facial gesture we have, it's smart to protect your teeth and gums from decay and disease. Daily brushing and flossing are the key preventive elements, but if you add a few herbs to the routine, you may be able to keep a beautiful smile forever.

Dental Care with a Difference

For a change of pace, you might try a traditional Ayurvedic East Indian toothpaste, a homemade paste made of mustard oil (from mustard seeds) and salt. Mix a teaspoon of mustard oil with a quarter teaspoon of sea salt, spread the mixture on a toothbrush, and use it to polish your teeth. Then dab it on a finger for a gum massage. Indians also rub their teeth and gums with fresh herb leaves, such as basil, mango leaf, neem leaf, and curry leaf. In a more Western version, a fresh sage leaf rubbed on teeth and gums after a meal is exceptionally refreshing. Take some leaves along on a picnic.

Several excellent prepared Ayurvedic toothpastes are available at herb shops, Indian markets, and health food stores. They usually contain such herbs as myrrh, to help prevent infection; chamomile, to soothe the gums; peelu, to remove plaque; and peppermint for a clean feeling. The best of these toothpastes are the ones from India. Try one: Your teeth will feel very clean and silky, and your gums will tingle. (If you dot a bit of one of these Indian toothpastes on a facial blemish, it will clear up quickly.)

Try as you may, sometimes it's just impossible to brush your teeth after a meal. If that's the case, drinking a cup of green tea may help dissolve plaque.

The Goods on Gums

Though infected gums need the attention of a health professional, there are a number of herb-based rinses that can help prevent and cure the soreness. One North American folk cure that is still popular is a tea of the root goldenseal. The herb is an astringent, which means it helps shrink sore and swollen tissues, and it contains berberine, which is antibacterial. To make goldenseal tea, swirl one teaspoon of powdered root into one cup of boiling water, then cover and steep for ten minutes. The taste is very bitter, so add some honey if you like. Swish the tea around in your mouth, holding it for as long as you can, then spit it out.

Other herbal aids are as close as your spice rack: sage and thyme. Sage contains tannins, which help heal sore gums, and thyme contains thymol, an essential oil that is a strong antiseptic. (In fact, many commercial mouthwashes contain thymol.) To make a mouthwash, steep a teaspoon or two of either dried sage or thyme, covered, in one cup of boiling water for five minutes. Then strain and rinse your mouth with the tea. For prevention, dip your dental floss in the tea prior to flossing. (Dip just the part that touches your teeth, keeping your fingers dry to avoid slipping.)

Instant Breath Refresher

Chronic bad breath can come from digestive problems and should be discussed with a health professional. But for a casual refresher with no added sugar, do what's done in Egypt and Jordan—chew on a whole clove.

stomach and digestive distress

~~~~~~

when food is rude

"Chew your food well." "Don't eat fatty foods." "Eat more fiber." "Don't gulp water while you eat." "Don't eat too much." "Don't eat too fast." "Sit up straight while you're eating."

These instructions are all good advice for preventing stomach and digestive problems. And while you're at it, add "Don't eat when you're upset" to the list, since stress is also a heavy hitter when it comes to digestion. Yet even if we follow these dicta, we inevitably suffer the occasional bout of digestive distress. Of course, severe stomach pain or chronic flatulence, diarrhea, or constipation can be signs of serious conditions and should be checked with a health professional. But for the occasional spell of trouble, herbs can help.

Fighting Flatulence

Beans, cabbage, Brussels sprouts, broccoli, and other high-fiber foods, such as wheat bran, can cause intestinal gas. But since they're important sources of fiber and other nutrients, it's a good idea to eat them regularly. By pairing herbs with these foods, you can calm your intestines while keeping these important nutrients in your diet.

For beans, the Mexicans swear by the herb epazote, which is available dried at herb shops and health food stores. It has light to medium green leaves and a very strong citrus/parsley/camphor taste. To use it, add one teaspoon of dried leaves to every two cups of simmering beans or lentils. Garlic, bay, cumin, and hot peppers go well with epazote.

In Egypt and Jordan, zatar is the antidote for beans. A wild herb that tastes like peppery, intense thyme, it is available dried in herb shops and Middle Eastern markets; sometimes it is mixed with sesame seeds. Try about half a teaspoon of zatar per serving in bean dishes and stews. It's also sprinkled on flat pizza-like breads and in marinades for grilled chicken.

When it comes to gas-forming broccoli, cabbage, and other members of the cruciferous family, Ayurvedic East Indian herbalists recommend cooking them with mustard seed. Try a half teaspoon of crushed seed to two cups of vegetables in a stir-fry or sauté. Lemon and yogurt are also commonly added to the mustard to help keep gas at bay.

Both Indian and Middle Eastern cooks use fennel seed and cumin seed, cooked in food or chewed raw after a meal, to get rid of gas. Japanese herbalists recommend fennel, sometimes combining it in a tea with Chinese licorice, cinnamon, and mint. (Use half a teaspoon of each herb, steeped in one cup of boiling water, covered, for ten minutes.) This combination is so popular in Japan that it's available as commercial after-dinner lozenges.

For gas from simple overeating, European herbalists recommend two prepared brews. One is called *eau de Melisse,* a liquid herb extract containing lemon balm (melissa), clove, coriander, nutmeg, lemon, cinnamon, angelica, and watercress. One teaspoon in a half cup of water is the usual dose. The other, Swedish bitters, contains aloe, thistle, angelica, senna, myrrh, saffron, peppermint, and several other herbs; one teaspoon is consumed in one cup of water with the meal.

Both of these are available in health food stores and herb shops, but in a pinch you can try drinking a cup of plain peppermint tea—or just head for your spice rack and grab the bottle of dried oregano. Herb blends called "Italian seasoning" will work, too. Add two teaspoons of either to a cup of boiling water, cover, and steep for four minutes. Then strain and sip. Oregano is particularly effective in cases of indigestion and overeating.

Sometimes gas is caused by food allergies, particularly to dairy products and wheat. Check with a health professional if you think you have food allergies, and you may be given an herb or two to alleviate your discomfort. For a wheat allergy, herbalists often recommend windflower, white bryony, and club moss. For dairy allergies, it's windflower and club moss. These herbs are generally given in minute, homeopathic doses.

Black Bean Burritos with Epazote

Epazote helps make beans easier to digest.

~~~~~

1 tablespoon olive oil

1 leek, topped, tailed, rinsed, and minced

2 cloves garlic, mashed through a press

2 tablespoons fresh epazote or 2 teaspoons dried

1 teaspoon minced fresh oregano or 1/2 teaspoon dried

1 teaspoon chili powder, or to taste

1 teaspoon hot pepper sauce, or to taste

Pinch of ground cinnamon

2 cups cooked black beans (canned are okay if rinsed before using)

4 soft flour tortillas (made without lard)

2 tablespoons grated low-fat Jack-type cheese or soy mozzarella

2 tablespoons fresh lemon juice

1 cup canned Italian plum tomatoes

HEAT a nonstick sauté pan over medium-high heat and add the oil. Toss in the leek, garlic, epazote, oregano, chili powder, hot pepper sauce, and cinnamon, and sauté until the leek is tender and the mixture is fragrant, about 5 minutes. Stir in the beans. Remove from the heat.

DIVIDE the bean mixture among the tortillas, positioning it along one edge. Sprinkle with the cheese and roll up neatly. Set the burritos seam side down in the sauté pan, and heat over medium-high heat until lightly browned, about 2 minutes.

MEANWHILE, combine the lemon juice and tomatoes in a processor or blender and whiz until the tomatoes are coarsely chopped.

FLIP the burritos over in the pan and pour on the tomato mixture. Cover loosely and simmer until heated through, about 5 minutes. Serve warm.

MAKES 4 SERVINGS; 304 CALORIES PER SERVING, 8 GRAMS FAT, 23 PERCENT OF CALORIES FROM FAT.

Whole Roasted Cauliflower with Mustard Marinade

Here, healthful cauliflower is made more digestible with the aid of mustard, cumin, and yogurt.

~~~~~~

1 cup plain nonfat yogurt or plain soy yogurt	1/2 teaspoon freshly ground cumin seed
2 tablespoons prepared mustard	1/2 teaspoon paprika
2 cloves garlic, minced	1 head cauliflower with tight buds

IN a small bowl, combine the yogurt, mustard, garlic, cumin, and paprika.

SET the stem of the cauliflower in the hole of a ring or tube pan, then set the ring pan in a larger pan to catch any drips. (This setup allows the cauliflower to roast more evenly.) Spoon the yogurt mixture evenly over the cauliflower, covering the entire head. Let marinate for about 15 minutes.

MEANWHILE , preheat the oven to 500°F.

BAKE the cauliflower, still in the ring pan, in the center of the oven until cooked through and richly burnished on the outside, about 20 to 25 minutes for a small head. Cut the cauliflower into serving pieces right from the ring pan and serve hot as a side dish.

MAKES 4 SERVINGS; 60 CALORIES PER SERVING, TRACE OF FAT.

That Burning Sensation

Heartburn (which, by the way, has nothing to do with the heart) can be caused by fatty foods, coffee, and cigarette smoking. The herb remedy of choice is kelp, which contains soothing alginic acid. Kelp is available at Oriental markets in sheets or as a powder, and can be added to soups and stews to taste. If you don't like the taste, you may want to try it in tablet or capsule form instead.

Prescription for Hemorrhoids

Hemorrhoids are swollen blood vessels in the anal area. Lack of exercise, too much sitting, and pregnancy can all contribute to the development of hemorrhoids, as can fatty foods, coffee, and cigarette smoking. But the biggest culprit is lack of fiber in the diet. If you have hemorrhoids, be sure to eat more vegetables and whole grains, but also keep a calendula preparation on hand. You can make your own oil (page 350) or buy a tube of calendula cream or gel at an herb shop or health food store. Apply to the cleaned area and the calendula will help it heal. You can also add calendula flowers to your bath. Add the petals from about four flowers plus two tablespoons of Epsom salts to a hot bath, and soak for about fifteen minutes.

Controlling Constipation

Herbalists generally don't like to treat constipation, since it is usually a symptom of another problem that should be addressed, such as poor diet, lack of exercise, or failing to drink enough water (eight full glasses a day are recommended). But certain circumstances, such as travel, jet lag, and stress can cause temporary constipation in even the healthiest of people. Here are some herbal strategies for those occasional bouts.

Ayurvedic (East Indian) herbalists have created a blend called *triphala,* meaning "three fruits," which is available ground or in tablet form at herb shops, health food stores, and Indian markets. Elderly people in India take triphala at least once a week to stay regular. Check with a health professional about what dose is right for you.

Jamu (Indonesian) herbalists recommend a blend of black pepper and cayenne called *cabe jawa.* To try it, mix a pinch each of ground black pepper and cayenne with the juice of half a lemon into one cup of boiling water, then sip. In the African savannah, the Diola tribe sips a similar brew for constipation.

A sweeter remedy from Egypt is anise seed tea. Lightly crush two tablespoons of anise seed, and steep them in boiling water, covered, for ten minutes. For the same results, the whole seeds can be chewed and swallowed. Egyptians also make an anise liqueur, called *arak,* which they believe is a digestive and whole-body tonic.

Do Away with Diarrhea

Diarrhea is a message from your body that it wants to get rid of something— food that was past its prime when you ate it, a bug that's going around, or a food to which you are allergic. Herbalists feel that the best approach to diarrhea is to let the body expel the irritant. But if treatment is necessary, they recommend herbs that are demulcents, which soothe mucus membranes, including those in the intestines.

One of the most popular demulcents is slippery elm, from the inner bark of a tree. To try it, mix a tablespoon of the dried powdered bark (available in herb shops and health food stores) in two tablespoons of water until it forms a smooth paste. Add the paste to half a cup of water and bring to a boil. Reduce the heat to a simmer, cover loosely, and simmer for about ten minutes. Then sip.

Slippery elm tea is a bit gluey, which is one way to identify a demulcent. The same goes for other digestive demulcents, such as kudzu, available at health food stores, herb shops, and many supermarkets. Japanese herbalists recommend this relative of arrowroot as a tea. Mix a tablespoon of ground kudzu with two tablespoons of water until smooth, then add to a cup of water and bring to a boil. Boil until the tea is clear, about two minutes. Then sip. Sometimes a drop or two of tamari is added, as the salt it contains helps calm the out-of-whack intestines.

Tannins, which are compounds found in such herbs as hyssop and green tea, will also help calm intestines that have been wrestling with diarrhea. To make a soothing tea, steep one teaspoon of ground hyssop or green tea in one cup of boiling water, covered, for two minutes; strain, then sip. European herbalists, especially German ones, recommend chewing on a teaspoon of dried bilberry or blueberry to get the intestines back into shape.

stress

~~~~~~

just relax

*C*hinese herbalists refer to stress as the "disturbed spirit," and we all suffer from it at times. Regular exercise, massage, and meditation can all serve to "calm the spirit," but herbs can also help.

Chinese Secret

One popular Chinese herb for stress is dong quai, which is the root of Chinese angelica. Though dong quai has not been scientifically investigated in the West, Chinese studies show that the herb contains vitamin B_{12}, a relaxant. Dong quai is available in root form, for tea making, at Chinese markets, or in tablet form from herb shops and health food stores. It can be taken in two ways—small daily doses or a large dose when stress hits. A health professional can tell you which way is best for your particular condition and may mix it with other herbs, such as asparagus root and scute.

Scute, known as skullcap by Western herbalists, contains flavanoid compounds that relieve tension and help tonify the nerve system. It's generally taken in tea form by steeping two teaspoons of the dried herb in one cup of boiling water, covered, for ten minutes. Some herbalists recommend taking scute tea three times a day for stress.

The European Approach

German and English herbalists also prescribe skullcap, usually in tea blends with other calming herbs such as passionflower, chamomile, valerian root, catnip, tila (linden flower), and hops. (Hops, by the way, should not be taken during bouts of emotional depression, since it can make the condition worse.)

Lavender is another popular calming herb. To try it, steep one or two teaspoons of the dried flowers, covered, for four minutes in one cup of boiling water. Add a teaspoon of dried rosemary leaves if a headache accompanies the stress.

Another slant on stress comes from Wales, in the form of a line of products known as the Bach flower and herb remedies, available at herb shops and health food stores. The remedies were created to "lift negative states of mind," and there are almost forty different single remedies, including chicory, honeysuckle, and mustard. Rescue Remedy is recommended by herbalists for acute stress. It combines five different herbs and flowers, and fans keep it on hand at all times. Check with an herbalist or health professional as to dosage.

Global Nostrums

Mexican herbalists recommend orange leaf tea to relieve stress. You can buy the leaves dried in Mexican groceries or at herb shops. To make a tea, steep one teaspoon of dried orange leaf in one cup of boiling water, covered, for four minutes. The taste is light, fruity, and pleasant and the tea itself has a slight orange tinge. Orange leaf's relaxing properties have not been scientifically documented, but proponents claim it is extremely relaxing.

Caribbean herbalists favor bamboo leaf tea to promote relaxation. They steep about two teaspoons of dried leaf (available in herb shops and health food stores) in one cup of boiling water, covered, for four minutes. Sometimes a bay leaf is added. For stressed babies, Caribbean herbalists recommend a teaspoon of the fresh juice of the soursop fruit, taken orally, to ease the little ones to sleep.

Japan's cure for stress is a tea made from the sea herb kombu, available in Asian markets, herb shops, and health food stores. To try it, rinse a two-inch strip of dried kombu in water to remove the salt, then boil it in two cups of water, uncovered, for ten minutes. The taste is slightly briny and fresh. If you like, you can use it as a base for vegetable soup.

Another popular Japanese remedy is mu tea, a blend of Chinese lico-rice, cinnamon, ginger, cloves, peony root, Japanese ginseng, Chinese parsley root, and other herbs. Light and slightly sweet, it is available at herb shops and Oriental markets. Japanese herbalists say mu tea gives the body and mind balance, making stress easier to handle.

Relaxing Rose Tonic

Ayurvedic East Indian herbalists often recommend rose as a relaxing beverage, especially in hot weather. This brew combines rose in the form of rose water, with relaxing chamomile. It adds banana and yogurt, both of which contain tryptophan, which can help alleviate stress.

~~~~~~~

1 mango
1 banana, peeled
2 teaspoons rose water

1 cup plain nonfat yogurt or plain soy yogurt
3 ice cubes made from chamomile tea

USING a sharp knife, peel the mango and slice it right into the blender, to catch the juice as you work. Add the banana, rose water, yogurt, and chamomile cubes and whiz until very smooth. Enjoy immediately.

MAKES 2 CUPS, OR 2 SERVINGS; 192 CALORIES PER SERVING, NO ADDED FAT.

tight muscles, aches, and pains

～～～～～～～～～～～～～～～

rub away
the pain

*F*rom a stiff neck and tight shoulders to a
cranky lower back, most minor aches and pains can be
soothed with herbs. At the simple end of the scale are
the mint-based or hot pepper–based preparations you
can pick up at any pharmacy. These products are rubefacients, which, when rubbed on an achy area, increase
circulation. An exotic version is jao san, a clear mint-
based liquid recommended by Vietnamese herbalists
and available at herb shops and Oriental markets. To
use it, put a few drops right on the achy area, say the
back of the neck. Use a penny to rub the jao san in,
and keep rubbing until the area is red. Then relax for a
few minutes.

Chinese white flower oil, also available at herb
shops and Oriental markets, is equally effective. It's
made of two mints plus camphor. Rub it into the achy

area until it feels warm. Wash your hands afterwards, since you don't want to get white flower oil in your eyes or other sensitive parts.

Jamu (Indonesian) herbalists favor a waxier rub, sometimes known as tiger balm, found at herb shops, health food stores, and Oriental markets. Like white flower oil, it's made of camphor and mint, but also includes cajeput oil and clove oil. There are two kinds of balm, white and red; the red is stronger. Use either as you would white flower oil, rubbing it into the achy area until it feels warm. Then wash your hands well.

Making Your Own

In less than five minutes you can make your own ginger oil, which some Japanese herbalists recommend for tight and achy muscles. The formula is one part ginger juice to one part olive oil. To make ginger juice, just grate fresh ginger root, then squeeze the gratings in your hand to release the juices. Two tablespoons of grated ginger will make about a half teaspoon of juice. For the best results, make ginger oil fresh each time you use it. Rub it into your neck and shoulders, lower back, knees, or sore hands and feet.

German and English herbalists use Saint-John's-wort oil for temporary relief of minor aches and pains. You can make your own (see page 244) or pick up a bottle at herb shops or health food stores. To use the oil, rub it into the sore area until it feels warm.

The Water Method

Hot baths are soothing for sore leg and back muscles, especially if herbs are added. Pack about a quarter cup of dried rosemary or peppermint in a large tea ball or muslin herb bag and hang it on the faucet so the water runs through. Then add about a tablespoon of cider vinegar to the drawn bath, hop in, and relax for about fifteen minutes. For extra-achy muscles, add a tablespoon or two of Epsom salts or ginger juice. To promote relaxation, add about a tablespoon of dried chamomile to the tea ball. To help keep skin smooth add the same amount of lavender. Be sure to use the tea ball or muslin bag, or the herbs will stick to your skin and could clog your drain. Herbalists say that hot herb baths are great for relieving arthritis pain, since floating in the water takes the body weight off the sore joints.

for men only

prostate fate

The prostate gland is actually a little group of glands, located just beneath the male bladder. When men approach the age of forty, testosterone production gradually begins to decrease, and in many cases the prostate responds by swelling—a condition known as benign prostate hypertrophy (BPH). As the prostate swells, it can cramp the urethra, making urination slow, difficult, and sometimes painful. In extreme cases, the prostate can swell up to the size of an orange, causing urine to back up into the bladder, where it can promote infections. By the age of sixty, 50 percent of all American men experience BPH. The symptoms of prostate trouble can include frequent night urination, painful ejaculation, bowel trouble, and lower back pain. Any one who has them should seek prompt attention from a health professional.

Healthy living habits may help prevent BPH, for many researchers feel that a high-fat diet, alcohol consumption, and cigarette smoking can contribute to the condition. Herbs may aid in prevention and treatment too.

When it comes to preventing and curing BPH, the most widely recommended herb is saw palmetto berry. Scientific evidence concerning the effectiveness of saw palmetto is mixed, but anecdotal evidence is supportive. Some men claim the herb helped reduce the size of their prostates, actually saving them from surgery.

Herbalists often pair saw palmetto with damiana, which contains antiseptic as well as alkaloid compounds that may act on the body in a similar way to testosterone. You'll find these two herbs in health food stores, usually blended in tea or tablet form, along with lesser amounts of such diuretic herbs as corn silk, kelp, parsley, buchu, and bearberry (*uva ursi*). German herbalists often add the small-flowered willow herb (not the tree) to the brew. For a tea, steep one teaspoon of a saw palmetto blend in one cup of boiling water, covered, for fifteen minutes.

Chinese herbalists recommend the root of Chinese ginseng to tune up the male reproductive system. Though this treatment has not been scientifically documented in the West, the Chinese claim that the saponin compounds in ginseng have a hormone-like structure that may help strengthen the male reproductive system. To try ginseng, chew a pea-sized piece of the root or simmer a quarter teaspoon of powdered root in one cup of boiling water, covered, for ten minutes. Since ginseng can raise blood pressure levels, if yours is high, avoid this herb.

Minerals may also play a role in preventing prostate problems. According to several studies, zinc is especially important because it can reduce levels of prolactin, the hormone that encourages the prostate to swell. A great source of zinc is pumpkin seeds. Buy the unsalted green ones that are sometimes labeled *pepitas*. Munch on a handful (about 2 tablespoons) a day.

Or, as Japanese herbalists recommend, you can make a pumpkin seed and purple perilla condiment. Perilla is a purple-leafed, minty-tasting herb that is popular in Japanese cooking, where it adds flavor and color to pickled ginger, cooked beans, and fish dishes. It is available dried in packages at herb shops and health food stores. First toast the pumpkin seeds in a dry cast-iron or nonstick pan over medium-high heat, for about two minutes, stirring constantly so they don't burn. Remove the seeds from the pan and let them cool. Crumble the dried perilla into a jar, using half as much perilla as pumpkin seeds. When the seeds are cool, chop them fine in a mortar or spice grinder; don't puree. Mix the chopped seeds with the perilla and serve sprinkled on salads, rice, bean dishes, or soups. The condiment will keep in the refrigerator for months.

for women only

~~~~~~~~~~~~~~~~~~~~~~~~

havoc-free hormones

*T*o make a point, a masseuse grabbed my ankle and firmly pressed her thumb against the inside ridge about an inch below my ankle bone, toward my heel. "It feels sensitive, doesn't it?" she asked. Admitting that it did, I wondered how she knew. She said that a nerve that runs through the area goes to and from the uterus. Since women are almost always either premenstrual, menstruating, postmenstrual, pregnant, or going through menopause, the area is almost always sensitive.

There's only one way to look at this constant hormonal ebb and flow, and that's with a positive attitude. If you dread getting your menstrual period, it's likely to be worse than it could be. If the idea of menopause gives you anxiety just thinking about it, all you're doing is setting yourself up for a hard time. But if you prepare your body and mind for these changes, going through them can be a lot easier than if you remain in the dark about your own body. Even better, some herbalists say that since women's bodies are constantly changing, women become accustomed to change in general and adapt more easily to the ebb and flow of life.

Herbalists also say that women can help ease hormonal changes, whether menstrual, menopausal, or otherwise, with diet and exercise, as well as activities that promote relaxation such as yoga, meditation, and massage. A health professional can help you discover what herbs or combinations are best for you, as well as what your personal dosage should be.

Premenstrual Syndrome

Though PMS is a condition that's more common than the common cold, the symptoms vary from woman to woman. Some women become easily agitated and extremely irritable, in which case it helps to give up caffeine. Many women also find that a combination of two herbs, evening primrose and dong quai (the root of Chinese angelica), will put them back on an even keel. The oil of the seeds of evening primrose contains a compound called gamma-linolenic acid (GLA), which the body needs but can't make itself. Taken in capsule or liquid form, evening primrose helps to regulate hormone levels and has a mildly calming effect. Dong quai is also calming and, since it has mild muscle-relaxing abilities, helps alleviate menstrual cramps.

Dong quai is part of a famous Chinese tea for women called "four things soup," available at Oriental markets. In addition to dong quai it contains peony root, rehmannia (a cooked root that looks like tar), and ligusticum (Chinese lovage root). Though its effects have not been scientifically documented in the West, four things soup is recommended for regulating the menstrual cycle and as a general tonic for the female reproductive system. Women, both Chinese and Western, who take it say it banishes bloat, keeps the skin healthy and clear, lessens cramps, and helps prevent anxiety and irritability.

Many herbalists recommend black cohosh for treating menstrual cramps. Most women take it in tincture form, available at herb shops or health food stores. The root of black cohosh contains salicylic acid, the painkilling ingredient in aspirin.

A remedy for bloating is parsley tea. Steep one teaspoon of dried herb in one cup of boiling water, covered, for four minutes. The taste isn't great, so add some lemon to give it a lift. You can also try adding fresh dandelion greens to your salads to help relieve water retention. Or make corn silk tea (see page 358).

PMS often brings a craving for chocolate that some herbalists believe is a sign of magnesium deficiency. To combat it, spread a tablespoon of prepared mustard on a chunk of crusty whole grain bread, for about one tenth of your daily requirement of magnesium.

Another mineral that's important in treating PMS is calcium. About a week and a half before menstruation, calcium levels in the body drop. And when calcium levels are low, you have more menstrual cramps. For low-fat calcium, add broccoli and kale to your diet, plus dill seed—a tablespoon provides as much calcium as three quarters of a cup of cottage cheese.

Along with PMS irritability, bloating, and cramping, some women become depressed. Though its effects are not scientifically documented, aromatherapists recommend clary sage as an antidepressant and to lift the spirits. To use it, add about three drops of essential oil of clary sage (available at herb shops and health food stores) to four ounces of your hand or body cream, and apply as usual. Or dot a drop on a tissue and inhale. Essential oil of rose geranium is sometimes added to clary sage, using equal parts of each essence.

Menopause

Evening primrose and dong quai, both mildly sedative and balancing, are as effective for anxiety and irritability in menopause as they are for PMS. The pair is also useful in treating hot flashes, and some women report fewer and less intense flashes within a week of beginning to take evening primrose and dong quai on a daily basis. Note that evening primrose should not be taken by women who have breast cancer.

Another remedy for hot flashes is drinking peppermint tea. Since peppermint contains compounds that cool the skin, keeping a jug of the tea handy can be helpful for flashes.

An herb that helps the endocrine system balance hormone production, and helps prevent fatigue, is chaste berry. It's available in tea blends, usually accompanied by passionflower. The berries were used by ancient Greek and Roman herbalists to lessen sexual desire in women, and that's where the herb got its name. Scientific evidence to confirm or deny the effects on sexuality is scant, but be aware of the possibilities. Women also report that Siberian ginseng (alone or in blends) is as effective as chaste berry in eliminating fatigue.

As a general tonic tea for balancing emotions during menopause, many herbalists recommend passionflower and catnip. Passionflower is a nervine, that is, an herb that helps relieve nervous tension and anxiety. In combination with catnip, which is a very mild sedative, it makes a tea that can help level emotions. Combine a teaspoon of both dried herbs in one cup of boiling water and steep, covered, for four minutes. Strain, then sip.

Another symptom of menopause is vaginal dryness, which can cause discomfort during sexual intercourse. To relieve it, Calendula Skin Oil (page 350) can be rubbed lightly into the walls of the vagina, or use straight wheat germ oil or the oil from a crushed capsule of vitamin E. Also note that certain herbs, like goldenseal, can dry out the mucus membranes and should be avoided by women who suffer from vaginal dryness.

After menopause the bones can become porous, a condition known as osteoporosis. To make sure your bones stay strong, avoid caffeine, which can rob your bones of calcium. Add calcium to your diet with kale and other dark leafy greens, sea herbs such as hijiki, arame, and nori, and nettle tea and dill seed.

Pregnancy

While most herbs and drugs are to be avoided during pregnancy, raspberry leaf tea is actually recommended. Especially in England, herbalists prescribe it to combat morning sickness, to help prevent miscarriage, and as a uterine tonic. To make a tea, steep one teaspoon of dried raspberry leaf in one cup of boiling water, covered, for five minutes. Drink the tea three times a day.

Other herbs can be helpful after delivery, particularly in stimulating the production of breast milk. These herbs, known as galactagogues, include fennel seed, anise seed, and fenugreek seed. A tea can be made by boiling one teaspoon of seed in one cup of water for five minutes. Choose one seed or a tasty blend.

Yeast Infection

This is a condition you should not diagnose yourself. But once a health professional has made a diagnosis, you certainly can treat it yourself. Herbalists recommend using tea tree oil, an herbal essence that comes from the Australian melaleuca tree and is available at health food stores and herb shops. Tea tree oil is antiseptic, antifungal, and anti-infectious. To try it, add three to five drops of tea tree oil to a small travel-size douche bag and fill it with one cup of warm water. Some authorities recommend using one teaspoon of tea tree oil to one cup of warm water, a dosage that most women find much too strong.

Herbs and Pregnancy

These herbs may cause early uterine contractions or birth defects if taken internally during pregnancy:

Lovage

Cascara sagrada (an ingredient in many herbal laxative blends)

Senna leaf (an ingredient in many herbal laxative blends)

Pennyroyal

Ephedra (an ingredient in many herbal cold, allergy, and asthma blends)

Ginseng

Goldenseal

Note: Pennyroyal is also used as a flea repellent, so remember to keep it away from pregnant dogs and cats as well as pregnant humans.

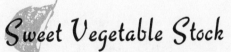

Sweet Vegetable Stock

During PMS it's not uncommon to get a craving for sweets. Instead of grabbing a doughnut, keep this stock on hand and sip a cup, warm. It will help regulate your blood sugar levels, thanks to the Chinese licorice. If you have high blood pressure, you must omit the licorice, but the soup will still be soothing. For a heartier soup, add some sautéed mushrooms and scallions and skinny Chinese noodles.

continued

1	carrot, grated	1	slice dried Chinese licorice
1	leek, topped, tailed, rinsed, and minced		root (omit if you have high blood pressure)
1	parsnip, grated	6	cups water
1/2	cup grated white cabbage		

COMBINE all the ingredients in a medium saucepan and bring to a boil. Reduce the heat and simmer, loosely covered, for 20 minutes. Strain and sip warm. This will keep for about 5 days, covered and refrigerated.

MAKES 6 CUPS, OR 6 SERVINGS; ABOUT 10 CALORIES PER SERVING, NO ADDED FAT.

 Winter Tonic Soup for Women

This tasty broth combines a number of Chinese herbs that can help tone the female reproductive system. You'll find the herbs at Chinese pharmacies, herb shops, and health food stores.

1 1/4	cups roasted barley tea (see Note)	1	slice dried Chinese licorice root (omit if you have high blood pressure)
1	tablespoon dried lycii berries		
1	slice fresh ginger	1	large dried shiitake mushroom

COMBINE all the ingredients in a small saucepan and bring to a boil. Reduce the heat, cover loosely, and simmer until the berries are soft and the soup is fragrant, about 20 minutes. Slice the shiitake, discarding the stem, and put it back in the soup to enjoy.

MAKES 1 SERVING; ABOUT 20 CALORIES PER SERVING, NO ADDED FAT.

NOTE: Roasted barley is available at herb shops, Chinese pharmacies, and health food stores. To make a cup of tea, add two tablespoons of roasted barley to one cup of water and boil until a rich dark brown, about 5 minutes. Then strain. Korean and Chinese herbalists say that barley tea is a good liver tonic.

glossary of common and botanical herb names

Some of these names may seem a bit odd and off-putting, but they're good to know. For instance, if you're at an herb nursery and looking for a particular herb, knowing the botanical name will help make sure you don't come home with the wrong thing. The same goes for buying herbs at shops for culinary and medicinal uses. If you just ask for "ginseng," without the botanical name, you could be sold any one of several varieties. So before you shop for a new herb, check this list and jot down the botanical name to bring along.

Aloe   *Aloe vera & spp.*
Angelica   *Angelica archangelica*
Anise hyssop   *Agastache foeniculum*
Arnica   *Arnica montana*
Astragalus (root)   *Astragalus membranaceus radix*
Balm of Gilead   *Populus gileadensis*
Bamboo leaf   *Phyllostachys & spp.*
Basil   *Ocimum basilicum*
Bay leaf (sweet bay)   *Laurus nobilis*
Bearberry   *Arctostaphylos uva-ursi*
Bee balm   *Monarda didyma*
Benzoin   *Styrax benzoin*
Boneset   *Eupatorium perfoliatum*
Borage   *Borago officinalis*
Buchu   *Agathosma betulina*
Burnet   *Poterium sanguisorba*
Calendula   *Calendula officinalis*
Catnip   *Nepeta cataria*
Chamomile (camomile)   *Matricaria recutita*
Chaste berry (tree)   *Vitex agnus-castus*
Chervil   *Anthriscus cerefolium*

Chinese licorice root   *Glycyrrhizae uralensis*
Chives   *Allium schoenoprasum*
Clary sage   *Salvia sclarea*
Club moss   *Lycopodium*
Coriander   *Coriandrum sativum*
Corn silk   *Zea mays*
Damiana   *Turnera aphrodisiaca*
Dill   *Anethum graveolens*
Dong quai   *Angelica sinensis*
Echinacea   *Echinacea purpurea*
Elder flower   *Sambucus nigra*
Epazote   *Chenopodium ambrosioides*
Ephedra   *Ephedra sinica*
Eucalyptus   *Eucalyptus globulus*
Evening primrose   *Oenothera biennis*
Fennel   *Foeniculum vulgare*
Fenugreek   *Trigonella foenum-graecum*
Feverfew   *Tanacetum parthenium*
Galangal   *Alpinia officinarum*
Garlic   *Allium sativum*
Germander   *Teucrium chamaedrys*
Ginger   *Zingiber officinale*

Ginkgo *Ginkgo biloba*

Ginseng, American *Panax quinquefolius*

Ginseng, Chinese *Panax ginseng*

Ginseng, Siberian *Eleutherococcus senticosus*

Goldenseal *Hydrastis canadensis*

Gotu kola *Centella asiatica*

Green tea *Camellia sinensis*

Guarana *Paullinia cupana*

Hawthorn berry *Crataegus laevigata*

Hop flower *Humulus lupulus*

Horehound *Marrubium vulgare*

Horsetail *Equisetum arvense*

Hot pepper *Capsicum & spp.*

Hyssop *Hyssopus officinalis*

Kava kava *Piper methysticum*

Kelp *Fucus versiculosus*

Lavender *Lavandula angustifolia*

Lemon balm *Melissa officinalis*

Lemon grass *Cymbopogon citratus*

Lemon verbena *Aloysia triphylla*

Lovage *Levisticum officinale*

Marshmallow *Althaea officinalis*

Meadowsweet *Filipendula ulmaria*

Milk thistle *Silybum marianum*

Mistletoe (twig) *Viscum album*

Mugwort *Artemisia vulgaris*

Mullein *Verbascum thapsus*

Mustard *Brassica & spp.*

Myrrh *Commiphora myrrha*

Nasturtium *Tropaeolum majus*

Neroli *Citrus vulgaris*

Nettle *Urtica dioica*

Oregano *Origanum vulgare (heracleoticum)*

Parsley *Petroselinum crispum*

Passionflower *Passiflora incarnata*

Peelu *Salvadora persica*

Peppermint *Mentha piperita*

Perilla *Perilla frutescens*

Plantain *Plantago lanceolata & spp.*

Red clover *Trifolium pratense*

Rose *Rosa centifolia*

Rosemary *Rosmarinus officinalis*

Sage *Salvia officinalis*

Saint-John's-wort *Hypericum perforatum*

Sandalwood *Santalum album*

Santolina (lavender cotton) *Santolina chamaecyparissus*

Savory *Satureja*

Saw palmetto *Serenoa repens*

Scented geranium *Pelargonium & spp.*

Scute (skullcap) *Scutellaria lateriflora*

Small-flowered willow herb *Epilobium parviflorum*

Sorrel *Rumex scutatus*

Southernwood *Artemisia abrotanum*

Speedwell *Veronica officinalis*

Sweet cicely *Myrrhis odorata*

Sweet woodruff *Galium odoratum*

Tansy *Tanacetum vulgare*

Tarragon *Artemisia dracunculus*

Tea tree *Melaleuca alternifolia*

Thyme *Thymus vulgaris*

Turmeric *Curcuma longa*

Violet *Viola odorata*

White bryony *Bryonia alba*

White willow *Salix alba*

Wild oat *Avena fatua*

Windflower *Pulsatilla*

Witch hazel *Hamamelis virginiana*

Yarrow *Achillea millefolium*

Yellow dock *Rumex crispus*

herbal resources

Herb Plants, Seeds, and Fertilizers

If you can't locate a local grower who has what you need, check out these sources.

The Flowery Branch
P.O. Box 1330
Flowery Branch, GA 30542

Offers hundreds of herb seeds and plants. Keep the catalog, since only supplements are sent thereafter.

~

Shepherd's Garden Seeds
30 Irene Street
Torrington, CT 06790
203–482–3638

Carries unusual herbs like Asian mustard and bronze fennel (seeds only). Catalog includes interesting recipes.

~

Sandy Mush Herb Nursery
Route 2
Surrett Cove Road
Leicester, NC 28748
704–683–2014

The catalog contains almost sixty pages devoted to herb plants, plus some seeds. It also includes tips on choosing herbs, and a common and botanical name cross-reference.

~

Caprilands Herb Farm
534 Silver Street
Coventry, CT 06238
203–742–7244

Large variety of scented geranium plants, herb books, and information on workshops and tours that the farm offers.

~

Ohio Earth Food
5488 Swamp Street, N.E.
Hartville, OH 44632
216–877–9356

Great source for organic fertilizers, including fish emulsions.

~

Gardens Alive!
Highway 48
P.O. Box 149
Summan, IN 47041
812–623–4201

Huge selection of organic products, including fish emulsion.

Ready-to-Use Dried Herbs, Extracts, and Essential Oils

Herbalist and Alchemist
P.O. Box 458
Bloomsbury, NJ 08804–0458
201–479–6679

Great selection of herb extracts (Western and Chinese); herb oils, ointments, ceremonial herbs, tea blends, dried Chinese herbs and tonics, and books.

~

Simplers Botanical Company
P.O. Box 39
Forestville, CA 95436
707–887–2012

Offers nonalcohol herb extracts, oils, essential oils, skin care products, and books.

~

Angelica's
147 First Avenue
New York, NY 10003
212–677–1549

One of the world's great herb stores, offering dried herbs, extracts, books, and skin care products. No catalog, but if you know what you want, they will send it to you. (There's a $50 minimum for mail orders, so you may want to order with a friend.)

~

The Lhasa Karnak Herb Company
2513 Telegraph Avenue
Berkeley, CA 94704
510–548–0380

Over five hundred herbs and herbal products, plus friendly service.

~

Tatra Herb Company
P.O. Box 60
222 Grove Street
Morrisville, PA 19067
215–295–5476

Catalog offers very fine quality single herbs, blends, homeopathic formulas, essential oils, extracts, lotions, and hair and skin products.

~

Herb Pharm
P.O. Box 116
Williams, OR 97544
503–846–7178

Catalog offers herbal extracts (called "herbal drops"), fresh herb juice extracts, Chinese herbs, culinary herbs, books, pamphlets, and information on how to calculate herb doses for kids.

~

Herbs for Kids
P.O. Box 837
Bozeman, MT 59711
406–587–0180

Herb blends formulated by herbalist and mother Sunny Maver, host of the radio show *Natural Solutions*. Write or phone for a brochure or phone (Monday through Friday, 9 A.M. to 5 P.M. Mountain Time) with questions or comments on herbs for kids.

~

Nature's Apothecary
997 Dixon Road
Boulder, CO 80302
800–999–7422
(in Colorado, 303–440–7722)
Fax: 303–440–0440

Offers dozens of fresh herb extracts, oils, salves, cough syrups, and aromatherapy essences. The company is owned by Debra Nuzzi, a knowledgeable herbalist.

~

East West Products, Ltd.
P.O. Box 1210
New York, NY 10025
212–864–1342

Huge selection of Chinese tonic herbs, Western herb formulas, Ayurvedic herb formulas, and herbal skin care products, plus hundreds of single herbs. If these people don't have what you're looking for, they'll try to find it.

~

Gaia Herbs
62 Old Littleton Road
Harvard, MA 01451
508–456–3049

Excellent-quality, fresh herb extracts, formulated by Ric Scalzo, a talented herbalist.

~

Original Swiss Aromatics
Pacific Institute of Aromatherapy
P.O. Box 606
San Rafael, CA 94915
415–459–3998

Top-quality aromatherapy essential oils and skin care blends.

~

Bazaar of India Imports
1810 University Avenue
Berkeley, CA 94703
510–548–4110
Fax: 415–548–1115

Huge selection of Ayurvedic herbs, blends, oils, and skin care products.

~

Neal's Yard Remedies
15 Neal's Yard
Covent Garden
London SW3 6NR
England
71–351–6380

Herb oils, capsules, skin care products, aromatherapy essential oils, toothpaste, soaps, and bulk herbs.

~

Shirley Price/Wesley House
Stockwell Head, Hinckley,
Leicestershire LE10 1RD
England 0455–615466
(in New York, 718–492–9514)

Offers aromatherapy essential oils, including one of the world's finest essential oils of lavender.

~

3000 B.C.
7946 Germantown Avenue
Philadelphia, PA 19118
800-AROMATIC (in Pennsylvania or Philadelphia, 215–247–6020)

Huge selection of herb- and plant-based skin and bath products, essential oils, and aromatherapy products, including hard-to-find lines like Oja and Nature's Symphony.

Herbal Skin Care

Dr. Hauschka Skin Care Center
435 West 44th Street
New York, NY 10036
800–243–1117 (in New York,
315-4168)

A line of pure herb-based skin products, including a famous rose cream for dry skin.

~

Shivani
Devi, Inc.
P.O. Box 377
Lancaster, MA 01523
800–BEST–211

Ayurvedic herb-based beauty items including an excellent moisturizer, facial cleanser, skin

oil, bath soap, and shampoos safe for permed and colored hair.

~

Kiehl's
109 Third Avenue
New York, NY 10003
212–677–3171
Fax: 212–674–3544

Established in 1851, Kiehl's has a huge selection of herb- and plant-based products for skin and hair. The staff is friendly and knowledgeable.

~

Essence to Essence
47 Newtown Lane
East Hampton, NY 11937
516–324–0254

Luxurious creams and lotions for the face and body, made from fine plant and herb essences. Custom aromatherapy blends, for jet lag, for example, can also be ordered.

Herb Publications

Herbalgram
P.O. Box 201660
Austin, TX 78720–1660
512–331–8868

A quarterly journal packed with information. Editor Mark Blumenthal is level-headed and intelligent, and it shows in the magazine.

~

The American Herb Association Quarterly Newsletter
P.O. Box 1673
Nevada City, CA 95959

Edited by herbalist and author Kathi Keville, this publication contains international herb news and information on the latest herb research.

~

The Herb Companion
201 East 4th Street
Loveland, CO 80537
303–669–7672

Published six times a year, this is a good magazine for herb beginners and those interested in using herbs in crafts. Contains interesting culinary recipes.

~

Newsletter of the American Herbalists Guild
California School of Herbal Studies
P.O. Box 39
Forestville, CA 95436

A must for practicing herbalists. Many of the articles are written by David Hoffman, director of the California School of Herbal Studies.

~

Medical Herbalism
P.O. Box 33080
Portland, OR 97233

A clinical publication for practicing herbalists, featuring case studies and science reviews.

Herb Education

California School of Herbal Studies
9309 Highway 116
Forestville, CA 95436
707–887–2012

Classes taught by founder David Hoffman, plus Mindi and Jim Green, owners of Simplers Botanical Company. Correspondence courses available.

~

Pacific Institute of Aromatherapy
P.O. Box 606
San Rafael, CA 94915
415–459–3998

Lectures and correspondence courses that include the science behind aromatherapy.

~

Yo San University
12304 Santa Monica Boulevard
Suite 104
West Los Angeles, CA 90025
213–826–1383

A four-year school for Chinese medicine, including Chinese herbs.

~

The Ayurvedic Institute
P.O. Box 23445
Albuquerque, NM 87192
505–291–9686

Directed by Dr. Vasant Lad, offering a full-time study program on Ayurveda and Ayurvedic herbs.

~

National Institute of Medical Herbalists
9 Palace Gate
Exeter EX1 1JA
England
0392–426022

Associated with the University of Exeter, Centre for Complementary Health Studies.

~

The American Botanical Council's Herb Line
1–900–226–4545

Choose from five or six subjects, such as a book review, the history and use of a particular herb, recent herbal studies, and information on medicinal herb regulation. The cost is ninety-five cents per minute. Parental consent required for callers under eighteen.

~

The Herb Research Foundation
1007 Pearl Street, Suite 200
Boulder, CO 80302
303–449–2265
Fax: 303–449–7849

Not a school, the foundation does herb literature searches among its thirty-thousand-plus pages of technical information. Founded by Rob McCaleb, founder of Celestial Seasonings Teas.

bibliography

Books and Publications

Arano, Luisa Cogliati. *The Medieval Health Handbook*. New York: George Braziller, 1976.

Balch, James, and Balch, Phyllis. *Prescription for Nutritional Healing*. Garden City Park, NY: Avery Publishing Group, Inc., 1990.

Boericke, William. *Homeopathic Materia Medica with Repertory and Indian Drugs*. New Delhi: B. Jain Publishers, Pvt., Ltd., 1927.

Bremness, Lesley. *Herbs*. Pleasantville, NY: Reader's Digest Association, Inc., 1990.

Carse, Mary. *Herbs of the Earth*. Hinesburg, VT: Upper Access Publishers, 1989.

Castleman, Michael. *The Healing Herbs*. Emmaus, PA: Rodale Press, 1991.

Dash, Dr. Bhagwan. *Ayurvedic Cures for Common Diseases*. Delhi: Hind Pocket Books, 1989.

Dharmananda, Subhuti. *Pearls from the Golden Cabinet*. Long Beach, CA: Oriental Healing Arts Institute, 1988.

Duke, James A. *CRC Handbook of Medicinal Herbs*. Boca Raton, FL: CRC Press, Inc., 1985.

Duke, James, and Foster, Steven. *Eastern/Central Medicinal Plants*. Boston: Houghton Mifflin Company, 1990.

Editors of *Prevention* Magazine. *Fighting Disease*. Emmaus, PA: Rodale Press, 1984.

———. *Everyday Health Tips*. Emmaus, PA: Rodale Press, 1988.

Foster, Steven. *Botanical Series 301–314*. Austin, TX: American Botanical Council, 1991.

Guernsey, Dr. Egbert. *Homeopathic Domestic Practice*. New York: Boericke and Tafel, 1882.

Herbalgram. Austin, TX: American Botanical Council.

Hoffman, David. *The Holistic Herbal*. Shaftesbury, England: Element Books, Ltd., 1986.

Hylton, William. *The Rodale Herb Book*. Emmaus, PA: Rodale Press, 1974.

Kloss, Jethro. *Back to Eden*. Loma Linda, CA: Back to Eden Books Publishing Co., 1971.

Kowalchik, Claire, and Hylton, William. *Rodale's Illustrated Encyclopedia of Herbs*. Emmaus, PA: Rodale Press, 1987.

Lad, Dr. Vasant. *Ayurveda, the Science of Self-Healing*. Wilmot, WI: Lotus Press, 1984.

Lavabre, Marcel. *Aromatherapy Workbook*. Rochester, VT: Healing Arts Press, 1990.

Lust, John. *The Herb Book*. New York: Bantam Books, 1987.

Mabey, Richard. *The New Age Herbalist*. New York: Collier Books, 1988.

McNair, James K. *The World of Herbs and Spices*. San Ramon, CA: Ortho Books, 1978.

Mansfield, Louise. *Gardening with Herbs for Flavor and Fragrance*. New York: Dover Publications, 1933.

Meyer, Clarence. *Old Ways Rediscovered*. Glenwood, IL: Meyerbooks, 1988.

Meyer, Joseph E. *The Herbalist*. Hammond, IN: Hammond Book Company, 1934.

Millspaugh, Charles F. *American Medicinal Plants*. New York: Dover Publications, 1974.

Mindell, Earl. *Earl Mindell's Herb Bible*. New York: Simon & Schuster, 1992.

Moore, Michael. *Medicinal Plants of the Desert and Canyon West*. Santa Fe: Museum of New Mexico Press, 1989.

Mooreman, Daniel E. *Medicinal Plants of Native America*. Ann Arbor: University of Michigan Museum of Anthropology, 1986.

Mowrey, Daniel B. *The Scientific Validation of Herbal Medicine*. New Canaan, CT: Keats Publishing, 1986.

Niethammer, Carolyn. *American Indian Food and Lore*. New York: Collier Books, 1974.

Phillips, Roger, and Foy, Nicky. *Herbs*. New York: Random House, 1990.

Potterton, David. *Culpeper's Color Herbal*. New York: Sterling Publishing Co., Inc., 1983.

Price, Shirley. *Practical Aromatherapy*. Wellingborough, England: Thorsons Publishing Group, 1987.

Shook, Dr. Edward E. *Elementary Treatise in Herbology*. Beaumont, CA: Trinity Center Press, 1974.

Staff of the L. H. Bailey Hortorium, Cornell University. *Hortus Third*. New York: Macmillan Publishing Company, 1976.

Tantaquidgeon, Gladys. *Folk Medicine of the Delaware*. Harrisburg: Pennsylvania Historical and Museum Commission, 1972.

Teeguarden, Ron. *Chinese Tonic Herbs*. Tokyo and New York: Japan Publications, Inc., 1984.

Theiss, Barbara and Peter. *The Family Herbal*. Rochester, VT: Healing Arts Press, 1989.

Tierra, Michael. *Planetary Herbology*. Santa Fe: Lotus Press, 1988.

———. *The Way of Herbs*. New York: Washington Square Press, 1990.

Tisserand, Maggie. *Aromatherapy for Women*. Rochester, VT: Healing Arts Press, 1988.

Tisserand, Robert B. *The Art of Aromatherapy*. Rochester, VT: Destiny Books, 1977.

Treben, Maria. *Health Through God's Pharmacy*. Steyr, Austria: Wilhelm Ennsthaler, 1989.

———. *Health from God's Garden*. Rochester, VT: Healing Arts Press, 1988.

Tyler, Varro E. *The New Honest Herbal*. Philadelphia: George F. Stickley Company, 1982.

U.S. Congress. *Unconventional Cancer Treatments*. Washington, DC: Office of Technology Assessment, 1990.

Weiner, Michael A. *Earth Medicine–Earth Food*. London: Collier-Macmillan Limited, 1972.

Weiss, Gaea, and Weiss, Shandor. *Growing and Using the Healing Herbs*. Emmaus, PA: Rodale Press, 1985.

Weiss, Rudolf Fritz. *Herbal Medicine*. Beaconsfield, England: Beaconsfield Publishers Ltd., 1988.

Willard, Terry. *The Wild Rose Scientific Herbal*. Calgary, Canada: Wild Rose College of Natural Healing Ltd., 1991.

Special thanks to Miss Elsie Fugett for her gracious gift of an ancient herbal manuscript, and to Miss Lynn Gillette and Mrs. Elizabeth Gillette for the use of the medical manuscripts of Edgar Worthington, M.D., and Lavina Matilda Shellenberger Worthington.

recipe index

subject index